The Price of a Vote in the Middle East

Clientelism and ethnic favoritism appear to go hand-in-hand in many diverse societies in the developing world. But, while some ethnic communities receive generous material rewards for their political support, others receive very modest payoffs. *The Price of a Vote in the Middle East* examines this key – and often overlooked – component of clientelism. The author draws on elite interviews and original survey data collected during his years of field research in Lebanon and Yemen: two Arab countries in which political constituencies follow sectarian, regional, and tribal divisions. He demonstrates that voters in internally competitive communal groups receive more, and better, payoffs for their political support than voters trapped in uncompetitive groups dominated by a single, hegemonic leader. Ultimately, politicians provide services when compelled by competitive pressures to do so, whereas leaders sheltered from competition can, and do, take their supporters for granted.

DANIEL CORSTANGE is an assistant professor at Columbia University, a faculty fellow in the Association for Analytic Learning about Islam and Muslim Societies (AALIMS), and a member of Evidence in Governance and Politics (EGAP). His research has won awards in international relations, political methodology, and fieldwork. He has conducted field research in a number of Arab countries, including Egypt, Jordan, Lebanon, Morocco, and Yemen.

Cambridge Studies in Comparative Politics

General Editors
Kathleen Thelen   *Massachusetts Institute of Technology*
Erik Wibbels   *Duke University*

Associate Editors
Robert H. Bates   *Harvard University*
Gary Cox   *Stanford University*
Thad Dunning   *University of California, Berkeley*
Anna Grzymala-Busse   *University of Michigan, Ann Arbor*
Stephen Hanson   *The College of William and Mary*
Torben Iversen   *Harvard University*
Stathis Kalyvas   *Yale University*
Margaret Levi   *Stanford University*
Peter Lange   *Duke University*
Helen Milner   *Princeton University*
Frances Rosenbluth   *Yale University*
Susan Stokes   *Yale University*

Other Books in the Series
Michael Albertus, *Autocracy and Redistribution: The Politics of Land Reform*
Ben W. Ansell, *From the Ballot to the Blackboard: The Redistributive Political Economy of Education*
Leonardo R. Arriola, *Multi-Ethnic Coalitions in Africa, Business Financing of Opposition Election Campaigns*
David Austen-Smith, Jeffry A. Frieden, Miriam A. Golden, Karl Ove Moene, and Adam Przeworski, eds., *Selected Works of Michael Wallerstein: The Political Economy of Inequality, Unions, and Social Democracy*
Andy Baker, *The Market and the Masses in Latin America: Policy Reform and Consumption in Liberalizing Economies*
Lisa Baldez, *Why Women Protest? Women's Movements in Chile*
Kate Baldwin, *The Paradox of Traditional Chiefs in Democratic Africa*
Stefano Bartolini, *The Political Mobilization of the European Left, 1860-1980: The Class Cleavage*
Robert Bates, *When Things Fell Apart: State Failure in Late-Century Africa*
Mark Beissinger, *Nationalist Mobilization and the Collapse of the Soviet State*
Nancy Bermeo, ed., *Unemployment in the New Europe*

Continued after the Index

The Price of a Vote makes an array of innovative and well-supported contributions to debates about clientelism and shows through meticulous analyses and a wealth of data the ways in which different forms of representation affect the dynamics of clientelism in societies with politicized ethnic and religious groups. The theory of the "ethnic monopsony," which is contrasted to competitive and monopolistic forms of ethnic political dynamics, introduces a new way of thinking about the material payoffs of clientelism in the Middle East and beyond. Corstange's book is a model of rigorous social science and empirical creativity.

Melani Cammett, *Harvard University*

Daniel Corstange's book is a rich synthesis of intrepid field work and insight into the web of connections between patronage and ethnic politics. Combining fine-grained analysis with a surefooted mastery of theory, The Price of a Vote is an incisive portrait of the motives and mechanisms of politics in the Middle East and beyond. It will be read widely and profitably.

Donald L. Horowitz,
James B. Duke Professor of Law and Political Science
Emeritus Duke University

The study of clientelism takes a huge step forward with Daniel Corstange's The Price of a Vote in the Middle East. Through incisive polling and extensive fieldwork, Corstange demonstrates that political patrons will offer meager inducements to their co-ethnics unless they are forced to compete for votes against rival providers of goods and services. His "ethnic monopsony" theory delivers scholars a powerful tool for explaining variations in clientelism, not only in the Middle East but wherever ethnicity shapes politics.

Jason M. Brownlee, *The University of Texas*, Austin

Corstange has written an extremely impressive book on patterns of clientelistic payoffs. Relying on extensive fieldwork and data collection in Lebanon and Yemen, Corstange builds a solid and insightful theory illustrating the influence of electoral competition on clientelism more generally. This first-rate work is admirable for its theoretical breadth, solid research, empirical richness, and methodological rigor.

Amaney A. Jamal,
Edwards S. Sanford Professor of Politics, Princeton University

Why don't all voters gain equally from supporting ethnic patrons? In this well-written book, Dan Corstange turns our attention to the importance of clientelist structures. Where intra-ethnic competition is absent – that is, in ethnic monopsonies – voters gain less from their support of co-ethnic candidates. The theory is clearly explicated, and the empirical evidence drawn from Lebanon and Yemen is rich, diverse, and compelling. This is an excellent contribution to the literature on clientelism, ethnic politics, and election in non-democratic regimes, with lessons that extend well beyond the Arab world.

Ellen Lust, *University of Gothenburg*

The Price of a Vote in the Middle East

*Clientelism and Communal Politics
in Lebanon and Yemen*

DANIEL CORSTANGE
Columbia University, New York

CAMBRIDGE
UNIVERSITY PRESS

University Printing House, Cambridge CB2 8BS, United Kingdom

One Liberty Plaza, 20th Floor, New York, NY 10006, USA

477 Williamstown Road, Port Melbourne, VIC 3207, Australia

4843/24, 2nd Floor, Ansari Road, Daryaganj, Delhi - 110002, India

79 Anson Road, #06-04/06, Singapore 079906

Cambridge University Press is part of the University of Cambridge.

It furthers the University's mission by disseminating knowledge in the pursuit of education, learning and research at the highest international levels of excellence.

www.cambridge.org
Information on this title: www.cambridge.org/9781107514409

© Daniel Corstange 2016

This publication is in copyright. Subject to statutory exception and to the provisions of relevant collective licensing agreements, no reproduction of any part may take place without the written permission of Cambridge University Press.

First published 2016
First paperback edition 2017

A catalogue record for this publication is available from the British Library

Library of Congress Cataloging in Publication data
Names: Corstange, Daniel, author.
Title: The price of a vote in the Middle East : Clientelism and Communal Politics in Lebanon and Yemen / Daniel Corstange.
Description: New York, NY : Cambridge University Press, 2016. |
Series: Cambridge studies in comparative politics | Includes bibliographical references and index.
Identifiers: LCCN 2015040725 | ISBN 9781107106673 (Hardback)
Subjects: LCSH: Voting–Middle East. | Patronage, Political–Middle East. |
Patron and client–Middle East. | Ethnicity–Middle East. |
BISAC: POLITICAL SCIENCE / Government / International.
Classification: LCC JQ1758.A95 C67 2016 | DDC 324.956–dc23 LC record available at http://lccn.loc.gov/2015040725

ISBN 978-1-107-10667-3 Hardback
ISBN 978-1-107-51440-9 Paperback

Cambridge University Press has no responsibility for the persistence or accuracy of URLs for external or third-party internet websites referred to in this publication, and does not guarantee that any content on such websites is, or will remain, accurate or appropriate.

Contents

List of figures			page xi
List of tables			xiii
1	Introduction		1
	1.1	An Empirical Puzzle	2
	1.2	Ethnicity, Clientelism, and Development	4
		1.2.1 Clarifying Terms	4
		1.2.2 Diversity and Development	5
		1.2.3 Clientelistic Constituencies	7
		1.2.4 Ethnicity and Clientelism	9
	1.3	The Argument	10
		1.3.1 Uncertainty in Clientelistic Exchange	10
		1.3.2 Monitoring and Delivering	11
		1.3.3 Clientelism and Ethnic Networks	12
		1.3.4 Ethnic Monopsonies	13
		1.3.5 Observable Implications	15
	1.4	The Evidence	17
		1.4.1 Why Lebanon and Yemen?	17
		1.4.2 Data and Methods	19
		1.4.3 Findings	21
	1.5	Plan of the Book	23
2	Ethnic Constituencies in the Market for Votes		25
	2.1	Introduction	25
	2.2	Transactions in the Market for Votes	26
		2.2.1 Patron–Client Linkages	27
		2.2.2 Barriers to Clientelistic Exchange	29
		2.2.3 Tools to Reduce Transaction Costs	32

	2.3	*Ethnicity and Transaction Costs*	35
	2.3.1	Demand-Based Mechanisms	36
	2.3.2	Transactions-Based Mechanisms	38
	2.3.3	Transacting in Ethnic Networks	39
	2.4	*Ethnicity and Protected Vote Markets*	43
	2.4.1	Origins of Monopsony	43
	2.4.2	Monopsony Maintenance	45
	2.5	*Implications*	47
	2.5.1	Market Power	47
	2.5.2	Which Voters?	48
	2.5.3	Elite Strategies	49
	2.6	*Conclusion*	50
3	**Communal Politics in Lebanon**	52
	3.1	*Introduction: An Electoral Puzzle*	52
	3.2	*Institutions and Communalism*	54
	3.3	*Christian Competition*	57
	3.3.1	Competing Factions in the Independence Era	57
	3.3.2	Rivalries and Splits in the Independence Intifada	60
	3.3.3	Intensifying Factional Rivalries	61
	3.3.4	Real if Uninspiring Choice	63
	3.3.5	Christians in Demand	66
	3.4	*Shia Cartel*	67
	3.4.1	Emerging Competition in the Independence Era	67
	3.4.2	Constrained Rivalry in the Post-War Era	71
	3.4.3	Closing Ranks After the Independence Intifada	72
	3.4.4	Uneasy Alliance	75
	3.5	*Sunni Monopsony*	77
	3.5.1	Pre-War Competition	78
	3.5.2	Wartime Vacuum	79
	3.5.3	The Post-War "Money Militia"	80
	3.5.4	Maintaining Dominance	83
	3.5.5	Sunni Dominance in Comparative Perspective	86
	3.6	*Conclusion*	89
4	**Communal Politics in Yemen**	90
	4.1	*Introduction*	90
	4.2	*Institutions and the Politics of Unification*	91
	4.2.1	Two Yemens	91
	4.2.2	United Yemen	93
	4.3	*Communal Politics in United Yemen*	95
	4.4	*Competition for Sunni Support*	99
	4.4.1	Conservative and Progressive Voters	100
	4.4.2	Retribalizing Voters	101
	4.4.3	Southern Voters	102

Contents ix

    4.5 *Stagnant Competition for Zaydi Support*   105
        4.5.1 *Early Unity-Era Competition*   106
        4.5.2 *The "Wahhabi" Push*   107
        4.5.3 *Eliminating Zaydi Alternatives*   109
        4.5.4 *The Patronage Pull*   113
        4.5.5 *Zaydi Stagnation and Sunni Competitiveness*   116
    4.6 *Conclusion*   117

5 Contemporary Clientelism   119
    5.1 *Introduction*   119
    5.2 *Parties and Programs*   120
    5.3 *Personalized Politics*   125
    5.4 *Partisanship in Comparative Perspective*   128
    5.5 *Patrons and Clients*   131
    5.6 *Communal Clienteles*   137
    5.7 *Machines in Motion*   143
        5.7.1 *Observing and Inferring Voting Behavior*   144
        5.7.2 *Rural Clientelism*   150
    5.8 *Conclusion*   154

6 Captive Audiences and Public Services   156
    6.1 *Introduction*   156
    6.2 *Cheap Votes and Poor Services*   157
    6.3 *Hypotheses*   159
    6.4 *Data and Methods*   160
        6.4.1 *Outcomes: Electricity and Water Access*   161
        6.4.2 *Model Setup*   162
    6.5 *Findings*   164
        6.5.1 *Electricity*   167
        6.5.2 *Water*   169
        6.5.3 *Obverse Dynamics in the Yemeni South*   170
    6.6 *Conclusion*   173

7 Intermingled Vote Markets   175
    7.1 *Introduction*   175
    7.2 *Diversity and Patronage Targeting*   176
    7.3 *Hypotheses*   178
    7.4 *Data and Methods*   179
        7.4.1 *Outcomes: Infrastructure and Public Sector Jobs*   179
        7.4.2 *Model Setup*   181
    7.5 *Findings*   183
        7.5.1 *Services and Infrastructure*   183
        7.5.2 *Public Sector Employment*   187
    7.6 *Conclusion*   192

8	Perverse Competition and Personalized Patronage		194
	8.1	Introduction: Who Competes for Whom?	194
	8.2	The Politics of Sycophancy	195
		8.2.1 Political Dominance and Surplus Clients	196
		8.2.2 Surplus Clients and Perverse Competition	197
		8.2.3 Signaling with Sycophancy	198
		8.2.4 Signaling Costs and Sycophancy	200
	8.3	Hypotheses	202
	8.4	Data and Methods	203
		8.4.1 Outcomes: Public Display of Political Iconography	203
		8.4.2 Explanatory Variables	208
		8.4.3 Model Setup	211
	8.5	Findings	211
		8.5.1 Public Displays of Iconography	212
		8.5.2 Connections and Iconography	213
		8.5.3 Emphasizing Political Connections	216
	8.6	Conclusion	218
9	Conclusion		220
	9.1	Introduction	220
	9.2	Reviewing the Scope of the Argument	221
	9.3	Ramifications	223
		9.3.1 Ethnic Politics	223
		9.3.2 Clientelism	225
		9.3.3 Democracy	227
		9.3.4 Durability	229
	9.4	Future Research	234
Bibliography			235
Index			253

Figures

2.1	Patron–Client Exchange as a One-Shot Prisoner's Dilemma	*page* 30
3.1	2007 By-Election Results: Sunni Landslide, Christian Cliffhanger	53
3.2	Lebanese Forces Campaign Billboard, 2009: (Left) Second Independence, (Right) Third Republic	63
3.3	Amal–Hizballah mural: "We all resist" (Beirut, Summer 2008)	74
3.4	Omar Karami Billboard: "Dignity (*karama*) is more precious than money" (Tripoli, summer 2008)	85
3.5	Omar Karami Billboard: "The Karamis: A family with roots" (Tripoli, summer 2008)	86
3.6	Parties' Popular Support by Sect, 2005 and 2009–2010	87
4.1	Yemeni Self-Identification	97
4.2	Cloning in Yemen: Mastheads of the UPF's *al-Shoura* Newspaper	110
4.3	Popular Vote Share in Parliamentary Elections, 1993–2003	116
5.1	Trust in Parties (Arab Barometer, First Wave)	129
5.2	Importance of Connections (Arab Barometer, First Wave)	130
5.3	Party-Distributed Ballots, Beirut (2009)	148
6.1	Effect of Political Domination on Access to Electricity	165
6.2	Effect of Political Domination on Access to Water	166
6.3	Southern Effect on Access to Services in Yemen	172
7.1	Distribution of Respondents at Different Levels of District Diversity	182
7.2	Political Dominance Decreases Electricity, Water, and Infrastructure Quality in Homogeneous Areas	186

7.3	Political Dominance, Mixed Neighborhoods, and Public Sector Jobs	189
7.4	Political Dominance, Mixed Neighborhoods, and Perceptions of Merit in Government Hiring	191
8.1	Lebanon: Hariri Political Imagery	204
8.2	Yemen: Salih Political Imagery	206
8.3	Public and Private Sector Jobs and Political Iconography	210
8.4	Dominated Constituents Display More Iconography	212
8.5	Effect of Connections on Iconography Display	215
8.6	Effect of Importance of Government Connections on the Increase in Iconographic Postings by Community Type	218

Tables

6.1	Summary Statistics for Electricity and Water Access: Means and Medians (Standard Deviations, Interquartile Ranges)	page 162
6.2	Electricity Outages (Ordinary Least Squares on $\sqrt{hours/day}$)	167
6.3	Water Outages (Ordinary Least Squares on $\sqrt{hours/day}$)	169
7.1	Diversity, Services, and Infrastructure	184
7.2	Political Dominance and Public Sector Jobs	188
7.3	Mixed Neighborhoods and Government Employment	188
7.4	Political Dominance and Perceptions of Merit in Government Hiring	191
8.1	Political Domination and the Display of Political Imagery	207
8.2	Explaining Political Iconography Display (Probit Regression)	214

I

Introduction

Clientelism and ethnic favoritism, in combination, riddle the diverse societies of the developing world. Politicians dole out patronage rewards to coethnics by building schools in their villages, paving roads in their neighborhoods, packing the civil service with community members, handing out medicine to supporters, and "fixing" their parking tickets. In exchange, citizens offer up their political support to elites not because of programs or ideology, but rather because of payoffs facilitated by shared ethnicity. To most people, then, the "who gets what" questions of day-to-day politics appear to have ethnic answers.

As familiar as this stylized account of ethnically-based clientelism may be, it misses a crucial part of the story. To wit: the purported beneficiaries of ethnic favoritism, the mass constituents whose support puts their coethnics in power, often receive meager rewards in exchange. They may get jobs in the civil service but are paid a pittance to do them, a school for their village without desks or even roofs, or a dirt-floor building for a health clinic without staff or electricity. Ethnic favoritism can help us explain why desirable resources flow along ethnic lines, but it cannot explain why, for many people, the flow is closer to a trickle than a deluge. How, then, can ethnic favoritism coexist with ethnic neglect? Why would citizens tolerate poor services instead of shopping their political support around? Under what conditions can politicians get away with taking their coethnic constituents for granted?

The answer I propose in this book is the ethnic monopsony: a political constituency defined along communal lines that is dominated by a single, vote-buying patron or party. Clientelistic relationships are susceptible to uncertainty and opportunism, but ethnic networks facilitate patron–client exchange between coethnics by reducing their transaction costs. These transactions-based advantages, however, segment the vote market into ethnic constituencies with high barriers to entry and exit. When coethnic elites vie against each other for support within their community, they compete to provide benefits to community members to win their backing. When, in contrast, a single, hegemonic leader dominates an ethnic group, the absence of credible coethnic rivals shelters that leader from internal contestation for community support. Protected from competitive pressures, monopsonists enjoy the luxury to pick and choose which coethnics to patronize, and offer more modest rewards than a competitive market would fetch. The end result is fewer and cheaper payoffs for constituents in dominated communities.

This introductory chapter lays out the book's broad themes, sketches its theoretical arguments, and summarizes its core findings. I begin with a motivating empirical puzzle: why would constituents in politically pivotal ethnic communities tolerate meager rewards for their political support? Next, I synthesize what we think we know about ethnicity and clientelism, and then develop the book's main theoretical claim about ethnic monopsonies. After introducing the book's main research venues – Lebanon and Yemen, two diverse societies in the Arab world – I summarize some of the book's main empirical findings.

1.1 AN EMPIRICAL PUZZLE

Communal politics animates much of the day-to-day distributional competition over "who gets what" in Lebanon and Yemen. Although political parties in both countries solemnly commit themselves to pursue "development," "state-building," and "the rule of law," few people pay much attention to these claims. Instead, politicians spend most of their time jockeying on behalf of constituencies based on sect, tribe, extended family, and region over who gets hired into the civil service, where the roads get paved, and who keeps their electricity longest. Some constituencies, of course, appear to enjoy privileged access to state resources by dint of the political influence of their representatives. But while ethnic favoritism may be rampant, just below the surface, so is neglect.

Consider, for example, the dynamic among Lebanese Sunnis, whose hegemonic leader can tap both state resources as well as his own multibillion-dollar fortune to dispense as patronage. Some Sunnis have benefited handsomely from their political connections, of course, yet many mass constituents see little of this largesse. A traditional notable from the city of Tripoli – alternately Lebanon's "second city" and its "capital of the Sunnis" – has repeatedly emphasized this grievance, such as in this speech to his fast-dwindling supporters:

Where in Tripoli is the state, which had showered promises upon it just before the last elections? Where is the state's electricity and water? Where are the health and educational services, and relief for the poor? ... Are you not the inhabitants of the largest Sunni city in Lebanon? Do you not live in the poorest city in Lebanon?[1]

---

[1] The speaker is Omar Karami, scion of Tripoli's most prominent notable family and a former prime minister who has been eclipsed by the Saida- and Beirut-based Hariri family. See "Karami launches harsh attack on Geagea: we are the Sunni Unionist Arabs," *al-Nahar*, 21 April 2007.

1.1 An Empirical Puzzle

Notwithstanding the historical rivalry between Sunni elites from Lebanon's major cities, it is difficult to reconcile the high degree of support for a single leader within the Sunni community with the apparent neglect suffered by his coreligionists in a city they dominate demographically and politically. At a minimum, it might encourage us to revisit what we think we know about clientelism and communal politics.

In Yemen, meanwhile, Zaydi Shia tribesmen can ask themselves many of the same questions that Lebanese Sunnis ask.[2] Despite the widely-held perception that the ruling regime is dominated by tribal figures, the Zaydi regions are among the poorest, least developed, and most lawless in the entire country. The paramount shaykh of the country's most powerful tribal confederation – also the speaker of parliament – frequently highlighted the material deprivation of the tribes and urged the state to provide them with basic services and infrastructure:

Transforming a tribesman from a warrior to a farmer is very easy to achieve, especially if agricultural and irrigation projects are established, wells are dug, and roads are run to his lands.[3]

Yet, as another eminent shaykh with a senior post in the ruling party observed:

No doubt about it: right now, no services or infrastructure are going out to the tribal areas ... [even though] everyone wants to put down his gun, go to school, take his kid to a clean clinic, and drink clean water.[4]

Hence, the tribes, ostensibly key constituencies for the ruling party, have seen only meager rewards for their political support, although some of the shaykhs have been well-compensated for delivering their tribes' loyalty. Again, we might wonder why the tribesmen would put up with this state of affairs – or if they even have a realistic choice.

As with any two societies, Lebanon and Yemen have their share of idiosyncrasies and differ in non-trivial ways. Nonetheless, they also share crucial similarities, and we see variations on the same basic story playing out in both

---

The "capital of the Sunnis" moniker comes most recently from Tripoli MP Muhammad Kabbara (a member of Hariri's parliamentary bloc), although various versions of the same descriptive trope have been in circulation for decades. See "Kabbara to Khazen: Tripoli is the capital of the Lebanese Sunnis" and "Tripoli to remain patriots' capital, Karami says," *NOW Lebanon*, 13 and 17 December 2010, respectively.

[2] Zaydis (sometimes known as "Fivers") form a branch of Shia Islam that concentrates in Yemen and differs doctrinally from the largest branch of Shiism ("Twelvers") that prevails elsewhere in the Muslim world, particularly in Iran, Iraq, and Lebanon. For overviews of doctrinal details, see the early chapters in Coulson (1964) and Momen (1985).

[3] Shaykh Abdallah bin Hussein al-Ahmar was, until his death in late-2007, the paramount shaykh of the Hashid tribal confederation and long-running speaker of parliament. The quote comes from Yahya's (2004, 23) hagiography.

[4] Interview, senior shaykh, Bakil tribal confederation, Sanaa, February 2006.

places: constituents who should be well-compensated as members of pivotal communities instead face neglect from their leaders. The core dynamics that make these two countries worth comparing form a mix of communal politics, clientelism, and starkly divergent competitive environments within their different constituencies.[5]

1.2 ETHNICITY, CLIENTELISM, AND DEVELOPMENT

Although scholars across the social sciences had long studied ethnic and communal politics in the developing world, cross-national work in the late-1990s that linked Africa's economic underdevelopment to its ethnic diversity inspired a massive body of research on the connections between social diversity and development. Meanwhile, a revival of scholarship on clientelism and machine politics in the developing world emerged in the 1990s and 2000s, revisiting and extending an older body of work on patron–client relationships that had stagnated after the 1970s. I briefly review some of the core ideas in these literatures, and then synthesize them to form the backdrop against which I develop my main argument about ethnic monopsonies.

1.2.1 Clarifying Terms

In everyday language, people use terms such as "race," "ethnicity," "tribe," and "sect" to refer to social categories that appear to be loosely similar to one another, but sometimes imply that a particular cleavage is qualitatively distinct from other types. Scholarly use of the terms, however, focus on the ascriptive, descent-based attributes – real or putative – of these social categories. Consequently, here, and throughout the rest of the book, I follow Horowitz's (1985, 41) inclusive conception of ethnicity "that embraces differences identified by color, language, religion, or some other attribute of common origin." Notwithstanding ongoing debates over conceptualization and operationalization, this definition has become the de facto standard in academic studies of ethnicity, at least among political scientists.[6] Ascription is, of course, a simplifying assumption, and societies employ numerous ways to bend their own classification rules; the key characteristic, as I develop later in the book, is that ethnic groups have high, rather than insurmountable, barriers to entry and exit. This expansive

---

[5] To varying degrees, each component of this mix features the distributive politics found throughout both the Middle East and the developing world more generally. Binder (1999); Blaydes (2011); Collins (2006); Daghir (1995); Davis (2008); Jabar and Dawod (2003); Joseph (2008); Khoury and Kostiner (1990); Lindholm (1986); Makdisi (2008); Peteet (2008); Richards and Waterbury (1996); Rida (1992).

[6] Precursors to Horowitz's (1985) definition can be found in, for example, Kasfir (1976, chs. 2–3) and Melson and Wolpe (1970). Compare Posner (2005) and Chandra (2006) for some of the contemporary debate, as synthesized in Varshney (2003, 2007).

definition enables us to make meaningful comparisons across similar cleavage structures regardless of the nominal differences that distinguish groups. Hence, I use the terms "ethnic" and "communal" interchangeably, and introduce variations on the main theme for sectarian and tribal groups as needed.

Informally, people use the term "clientelism" to refer to a wide range of normatively undesirable transactions between politicians and their supporters, ranging from explicit vote buying to more ambiguous exchanges such as pork-barrel politics and constituency service. More precisely, however, scholars define clientelism as contingent, direct exchange of material rewards for political support.[7] As states democratize or otherwise make use of electoral mechanisms to allocate resources, votes have become the most common resource that the average client can offer, although politicians may also value other forms of support such as participation in rallies or riots, especially when playing a "dual game" to influence institutional rules as well as win electoral support.[8] In return, patrons offer money, a breathtakingly wide range of consumer goods, subsidized school fees, medical care, utilities, access to government permits and licenses, exemptions from the rule of law, and public employment.[9] The distinguishing characteristic of clientelistic exchange is not the targeting per se, but rather the quid pro quo: only compliant voters receive rewards, at least in principle. Such transactions are not so simple in practice, of course, and many of the phenomena we associate with clientelism and machine politics are, in fact, efforts to monitor and enforce the quid pro quo – points to which I return in detail later in the book.

1.2.2 Diversity and Development

Ethnic competition has long been suspected of impeding development, and cross-national empirical research appears to bear out this suspicion. Beginning

---

[7] Compare Kitschelt (2000); Kitschelt and Wilkinson (2007b); Stokes (2007); Wantchekon (2003); Weitz-Shapiro (2014). Early studies of clientelism by political scientists drew heavily on work from anthropology and sociology, the two disciplines in which the concept of clientelism originated. Perhaps as a result, early generations of theorizing emphasized the affective and face-to-face nature of the patron–client relationship (Lemarchand, 1972; Lemarchand and Legg, 1972; Powell, 1970; Scott, 1969, 1972; Weingrod, 1968). Later generations, however, have downplayed these elements as non-central to "modern" or "mass" clientelism, in which the number of personal relationships a patron would need to maintain would be far beyond any individual's capacity. Hence, subsequent work has focused heavily on the role of brokers as intermediaries between politicians and clients (Auyero, 1999, 2001; Johnson, 1986; Kasara, 2007; Stokes et al., 2013).

[8] See Cammett (2011, 2014); Huntington and Nelson (1976); Mainwaring (2003); Schedler (2002).

[9] For examples, see Auyero (1999, 2001); Bates (1981); Blaydes (2011); Cammett (2011, 2014); Cammett and Issar (2010); Chubb (1982); Corstange (2012b); Jamal (2007); Robinson and Verdier (2013); Schaffer (2007b); van de Walle (2007).

with Easterly and Levine's (1997) seminal but controversial article that connects Africa's slow rate of economic growth to its high degree of ethnic diversity, many studies have linked diversity to underdevelopment via the underprovision of productive public goods, poor macroeconomic policy choice, excessive government consumption, corruption, insecure property rights, and political instability.[10]

Although this line of inquiry has identified several intriguing empirical regularities, the microfoundations of these aggregate outcomes are unclear. Most explanations invoke some form of ethnic favoritism in the political allocation of scare resources, but at least three broad families of mechanisms could account for such behavior. One set rests on shared tastes, another on technology, and a third on strategic selection – put another way, "what people want," "ease of use," and "self-fulfilling prophecies," respectively.[11]

The first family of mechanisms rests on individual tastes and preferences. Simplistic versions claim that people have a natural affinity for coethnics and prefer to cooperate with them, but such explanations have largely been discredited in recent work and find little empirical support.[12] A more compelling version of the argument holds that people cooperate with coethnics not simply because they are coethnics, but rather because they share similar tastes in outcomes. Nonetheless, it is not immediately apparent how to apply this claim to competition over material resources – for example, why people should have diverging preferences over infrastructure such as schools on the basis of ethnicity rather than income or residential location.[13]

An alternate set of mechanisms posits an ethnic information advantage: social networks are much denser within groups than across them. People consequently enjoy better information, direct and indirect, about in-group members than out-group members, so they are better able to monitor each other's

---

[10] Among an ever-growing list of studies, compare Alesina et al. (1999, 2000); Alesina and La Ferrara (2005); Annett (2001); Arcand et al. (2000); Baldwin and Huber (2010); Collier (1999); Collier and Hoeffler (1998); Easterly and Levine (1997); Fearon and Laitin (2003); Keefer and Knack (2002); Knack and Keefer (1995); Mauro (1995, 1998); Montalvo and Reynal-Querol (2005).

[11] Habyarimana et al. (2009) offer the three families synthesis; compare also Alesina et al. (1999); Miguel and Gugerty (2005).

[12] For an overview of the theoretical debates, see Varshney (2003, 2007). For empirics, see Habyarimana et al. (2009). A slightly more developed version of the natural affinity argument is that people hold other-regarding preferences for their coethnics, although why altruism should be directed specifically at coethnics is usually left unspecified beyond occasional invocations of evolutionary biology (Hammond and Axelrod, 2006; van den Berghe, 1978). While we might be able to imagine such a mechanism functioning within small-scale kin groups, it is difficult to imagine how it could apply – directly, at least – to large-scale ethnic groups in which two randomly-selected members are, for all practical purposes, unrelated.

[13] Compare, for example, Alesina et al. (1999, 2000), and counterpoints in Habyarimana et al. (2009).

activities and sanction misbehavior.[14] These explanations commonly side-step questions about choice of network, its maintenance, and opportunistic switching between them, however. The last family of mechanisms posits that people select coethnic partners strategically because they expect coethnics to cooperate and non-coethnics not to do so, although the origins of this self-reinforcing equilibrium are usually unspecified.[15] Such an equilibrium is, however, a valuable club good, the provision of which should suffer from free-rider problems and opportunistic deviations.

These various explanations all purport to account for what we observe as ethnic favoritism, although some claims are more compelling and empirically better supported than others.[16] In isolation and in the abstract, each attempts to account for greater within-group cooperation, but many observers have argued that ethnicity becomes especially salient in the context of competition over material resources.[17] Consequently, we need to understand how greater cooperation in the abstract translates into political constituencies and the political allocation of scarce resources among them. In jumping from social links to political ones, it helps to examine the phenomenon of clientelism as one prominent form of political linkage.

1.2.3 Clientelistic Constituencies

What links politicians to their constituents? In the idealized responsible partisan model, we imagine that politicians offer policy programs that spell out what they intend to offer constituents in exchange for the latter's political support. Ideologies and party labels, in turn, summarize the contents of the programs and translate them into convenient information shortcuts. Whichever party wins the election then implements its program; the electorate rewards competent parties with reelection, and punishes incompetence or broken promises by voting them out of office in the next election.[18]

As normatively attractive as this idealized story may be, programmatic linkages are *not* the primary mechanisms connecting most of the world's population

---

[14] See Bowles and Gintis (2004); Fearon and Laitin (1996); Greif (1994, 2006); Habyarimana et al. (2009); Miguel (2004); Miguel and Gugerty (2005).
[15] Compare Bowles and Gintis (2004); Chandra (2004); Greif (1994, 2006); Habyarimana et al. (2009); Horowitz (1985). Note that the strategic selection mechanism shares with tastes-based explanations the risk of being tautological: coethnics interact with coethnics because coethnics interact with coethnics.
[16] Habyarimana et al. (2007b, 2009) find significant empirical support at the individual level for the technology and strategic selection mechanisms, but no evidence that the simple tastes mechanism operates. Also see Miguel (2004) and Miguel and Gugerty (2005) for evidence consistent with technology and strategic selection.
[17] See, for example, Bates (1974, 1983b); Chandra (2004); Collier (1999); Eifert et al. (2010); Fearon (1999); Horowitz (1985, 1999); Posner (2005).
[18] See Kitschelt (2000, 2010) for a discussion of the responsible partisan model.

to most of the world's politicians. In many developing-world societies – whether governed by democracies or electoral autocracies – clientelism, rather than programs, links politicians to their constituents. In such environments, party programs are frequently non-credible, uninformative, or non-existent, hence sharply curtailing the effectiveness of programmatic linkages. Although parties may trumpet their ideologies in the relevant venues, relatively few "true believers" expect them to pursue, much less fulfill, their programs when in office. The vast bulk of voters, in contrast, discount programmatic promises.[19]

As described previously, clientelistic transactions are contingent, direct exchanges of political support for material rewards, which can take a wide variety of forms in practice – seemingly limited only by the imaginations of voters and the parties that cultivate them. Although patrons may engage in distributive targeting of excludable goods, a lively debate surrounds the question of which voters they actually target. One set of arguments holds that core supporters – loosely and variably defined as ideological voters, those "on the network" for patronage distribution, or even simply coethnics – are easier to reach and can be rewarded more efficiently. Core supporter arguments face two broad challenges, however: why parties would pay for votes they already expect to receive, and why unaffiliated voters would not just declare themselves as core supporters and dilute the patronage resources available. Hence, dissenting views argue that "near-median" voters are decisive in elections, so parties target inducements to swing voters rather than their core supporters. Yet these claims face the critique that there should be few core ideologues to neglect in clientelistic systems, while enforcing the quid pro quo is likely to be harder among swing voters. Consequently, a third batch of arguments suggests that parties diversify their targets under different conditions, sometimes focusing on core or swing, and sometimes pursuing both.[20]

Targeted rewards and quids pro quo are central features of clientelism. Connecting these components to ethnic politics means understanding how ethnicity facilitates precision targeting and enforceable exchanges of rewards for support. In the context of doing so, we can also conceptualize how ethnicity delimits the otherwise ambiguous sets of core and swing voters, and whether or not there can be a swing within the core.

---

[19] For reviews on clientelistic linkages in the abstract, see Hicken (2011); Kitschelt and Wilkinson (2007a); Stokes (2007). On ineffective programmatic linkages, see Blaydes (2011); Keefer (2005, 2007); Keefer and Vlaicu (2008); Magaloni (2006); Stokes et al. (2013).

[20] A formal literature continues to investigate the conditions under which a party would favor one strategy over the other (Cox, 2010; Cox and McCubbins, 1986; Dal Bó, 2007; Dekel et al., 2008; Dixit and Londregan, 1996; Gans-Morse et al., 2014; Lindbeck and Weibull, 1987). A burgeoning empirical literature finds support for both predictions (Blaydes, 2011; Calvo and Murillo, 2004, 2013; Cammett, 2011, 2014; Fleck, 1999, 2001; Magaloni, 2006; Nichter, 2008; Stokes, 2005; Stokes et al., 2013; Weitz-Shapiro, 2014).

1.2.4 Ethnicity and Clientelism

How can we connect what we know about ethnicity with what we know about clientelism? Even though they are distinct concepts, a voluminous body of evidence documents ethnic favoritism in the allocation of material resources – which appears to confirm that there is an empirical affinity between ethnicity and clientelism. Ethnicity seems to be about how politicians define their constituencies, and clientelism is about how they service and maintain those constituencies. Why, though, would a patron prefer an ethnic clientele over some other kind?

All ballots are equal at the counting stage regardless of who casts them, so politicians must have auxiliary reasons for cultivating coethnic support. Meanwhile, a job is a job and a bag of rice is a bag of rice regardless of who supplies it, so constituents, too, must have reasons for supporting coethnic politicians beyond the mere coincidence of shared ethnicity. If the commodities being traded – votes and material rewards – are valuable independently of who supplies them, *ethnicity's contribution must come from facilitating trades, not in determining what gets traded.*

What do existing theories suggest about how ethnicity could facilitate clientelistic exchange? Although shared-tastes stories offer little direct help, information technology mechanisms make coethnic transactions cheaper, and strategic selection mechanisms make such exchanges more credible. Additionally, given the stylized facts about ethnic favoritism and ascriptive social categories, ethnic constituencies seem to follow the core model: politicians reward their coethnic supporters and do not bother to expend resources on non-coethnics. Taking these dynamics to their logical conclusion, there should be no swing voters at all when all constituencies are ethnically based because people cannot "swing" between ascriptively defined ethnic groups.[21] Yet, rather than assume ethnic groups to be undifferentiated monoliths, it is important to recognize within-group diversity and contestation – that is, the degree to which there may be within-group swing voters with an outside option or alternate bidder for their votes.

Observing ethnically-based clientelism, and explaining the mechanisms that support it, does not yet tell us much about how the benefits of coethnicity are shared out between patrons and clients. Rewards may indeed flow along ethnic lines, but we cannot yet explain when the flow is a deluge and when it is a mere trickle. It is much easier to understand why constituents support their coethnic politicians when the rewards for doing so are lucrative than miserly.

---

[21] Compare the "election as census, census as election" observations in Chandra (2004); Ferree (2006); Horowitz (1985); Kertzer and Arel (2002); Maktabi (1999). The commonly made simplifying assumption of perfect ascription implies infinite entry and exit costs. In practice, of course, fixed boundaries are rarely fixed in an absolute sense, and people may shift the boundaries and group definitions for strategic purposes (cf. Bowles and Gintis, 2004; Fearon, 1999; Ichino and Nathan, 2013; Posner, 2005).

Yet pittances are frequently what constituents get – why do they tolerate it? And how can politicians get away with it? This book's answer is ethnic vote monopsonies, the theory of which I sketch in the next section.

1.3 THE ARGUMENT

Under what conditions must elites promote the welfare of their coethnic mass constituents, and when can they take those same constituents for granted by offering minimal rewards for political support? This book argues that competition within ethnic groups, or the lack thereof, explains who elites can neglect and who they cannot. Defining constituencies with ascriptive membership rules cuts off constituents' exit options and makes them captive audiences for communal elites. Enforcing in-group unity, in turn, cuts out the electoral competition that would otherwise bid up the value of their votes. When hegemonic elites can form ethnic monopsonies, they become the sole credible buyers of their communities' votes. Favoritism and neglect are, therefore, joint outcomes of this constituency-building process. Elites favor their coethnics *because* their votes are cheap relative to others. Constituents, in turn, tolerate meager rewards in the absence of within-group competition because they have little choice in the matter.

1.3.1 Uncertainty in Clientelistic Exchange

As sketched earlier, clientelism is a prominent mechanism linking politicians to their constituents in the developing world where programmatic linkages are non-credible and ineffective. It is a form of distributive politics that revolves around the contingent exchange of material resources and political support. Clientelism heavily emphasizes the quid pro quo of the exchange. Enforced reciprocity means that patrons employ what Magaloni (2006) has called a "punishment regime" in which they funnel benefits to compliant supporters and withdraw them from deviants. They emphasize this regime because clientelistic exchange occurs against a backdrop of opportunism that, if unchecked, would undermine the possibility of exchange.

Both patrons and clients face temptations to cheat each other in every transaction, the patron by taking the client's vote and withholding the payoff, and the client by taking the patron's reward and staying home – or, worse still, voting for the patron's opponents. They transact in a strategic environment akin to a prisoner's dilemma: exchange makes both better off, but both also face incentives to renege on their partners. Both, consequently, have incentives to develop mechanisms to make their promises of exchange credible. Nonetheless, several important asymmetries in the relationship compel patrons to invest in tools to operate the punishment regime in an efficient manner.

1.3 The Argument

The first asymmetry is market power. There are many clients and only a few patrons, and the latter have incentives to economize on tracking their many patron–client relationships. Second, the secret ballot, however nominal, yields asymmetric observability. Clients can confirm when they have received tangible rewards such as a bag of rice more easily than patrons can confirm their clients' vote choices. Third, social norms against vote trafficking favor the client. Those who "take the money and run" receive social plaudits, while patrons who offer to buy, much less try to enforce the agreement, are villified for desecrating the sanctity of the ballot. Consequently, patrons face strong incentives to internalize the cost of building the machinery to operate the punishment regime.

1.3.2 Monitoring and Delivering

One prominent resolution to the prisoner's dilemma in theory, and opportunism in clientelistic exchange in practice, has been to embed individual, episodic exchanges in ongoing relationships with repeated interactions.[22] Under the right conditions, the shadow of the future deters defection in the present as the fear of foregone future rewards outweigh one-shot, opportunistic gains. Maintaining such relationships is not costless, however, and both parties to the exchange benefit from keeping maintenance costs as low as possible. Patrons, who must keep track of large numbers of dyadic relationships, face particularly strong incentives to build machines in order to leverage economies of scale and minimize unit maintenance costs.

The patron's organizational machinery serves double duty as both a monitoring mechanism and a tool to distribute rewards. In its former capacity, the machine keeps track of clients' behavior and keeps the patron informed about their reliability and expected compliance with the clientelistic contract. In doing so, it reduces the patron's uncertainty about the exchange. By making the patron more willing to transact exchanges, better monitoring also encourages clients to comply because their actions are less likely to be misconstrued – either as defection when clients are trying to comply, or compliance when they are trying to defect.

Machines also have a more benign face that complements the implicit threat communicated by their monitoring functions. In particular, they serve as the delivery mechanisms through which patrons distribute rewards on a day-to-day basis.[23] Machines consequently help lower the transaction costs associated with distribution. In the process, they embed clients in ongoing relationships that provide desirable benefits alongside implicit threats to withdraw those

---

[22] Auyero (1999, 2001); Axelrod (1984); Kitschelt and Wilkinson (2007a); Kreps et al. (1982); Scott (1969, 1972); Stokes (2007).
[23] See Auyero (1999, 2001); Despres (2005); McCaffery (1993); Riordon (1905); Stokes (2005); Weitz-Shapiro (2014); Werner (1928).

benefits from wayward clients. Machines consequently differ in an important way from domestic spy services such as the East German Stasi or the infamous Arab *mukhabarat* in that they are simultaneously the instruments of rewards as well as threats. Hence, such organizations maintain patron–client relationships and give clients positive inducements to comply rather than solely cultivate fear of the consequences of defection.

Patrons embed their machines deeply into clients' social networks, which is usually seen as a means for the machines to monitor clients. Doing so, however, serves a complementary function: it helps clients monitor their patrons. More specifically, it enables clients to confirm the patron's largesse because information about rewards spreads throughout clients' social networks. This information helps other, in-network clients verify that the patron is providing rewards as promised. It also serves as a publicity tool to recruit other voters on the social network by providing trustworthy evidence of the benefits of supporting the patron. Consequently, embedding machines in social networks helps patrons maintain their links with core supporters as well as attract swing voters with credible promises of rewards.

1.3.3 Clientelism and Ethnic Networks

Machines reduce uncertainty and transaction costs by embedding themselves deeply in clients' social networks. Left in the abstract, this dynamic could, in principle, apply to *any* such network, whether based on ethnicity, occupation, school, hobby, or whatever else. Nonetheless, ethnicity emerges repeatedly in different societies as the network of choice over its alternatives. Structurally, ethnic links make clientelism more efficient by facilitating in-network information transmission even as they limit information flows across networks. Lower transaction costs within ethnic groups compared to across them, in turn, makes clientelistic linkages relatively more efficient within groups.

Ethnic communities, at high levels of aggregation, are far too large to coincide with members' personal, day-to-day networks. They are, instead, what Anderson (1991) has called imagined communities: most members will never meet each other, so cannot directly be part of a dense network. Yet we need not conceive of ethnic communities as unified, all-encompassing social networks, with everyone capable of learning about everyone else with minimal cost. Instead, they are amalgamations of smaller networks, internally dense and more loosely connected to each other.[24]

Ethnic groups at high levels of aggregation are descent-based identity categories, but shared descent in communities that number in the millions is metaphorical rather than literal. Such groups, however, pyramid down to lower levels of aggregation in which "descent" becomes progressively less putative or

---

[24] Compare Hardin (1982); Olson (1965) on federations of small, dense groups.

imaginary. These lower-level units are often kin groups and extended families, which tend to concentrate residentially and are highly connected socially.[25] Consequently, networks at lower levels of aggregation are better suited to serve as monitoring and distributive channels when compared to broader identity categories that encompass more people than could reasonably be connected. Employing ethnic networks, then, really means employing the smaller units within the ethnic group, even if observationally, the smaller units aggregate into the appearance of ethnic networks.[26]

To the degree that people's social networks are densest at low-level units, and those units are embedded within a broader ethnic community, information flows are much stronger and cheaper within ethnic groups than across them. For patrons, it is costlier to monitor clients and distribute rewards to them if they are not on the network. For clients, it is harder to verify that out-of-network patrons are fulfilling promises, so they too find it easier to monitor a coethnic rather than a non-coethnic patron. Consequently, the information technology mechanism gives rise to the strategic selection mechanism – people select their partners based on better information.

Hence, we can locate the microfoundations for the strategic selection mechanism in the technology mechanism: ethnic favoritism arises from structural conditions that reduce transaction costs. Ethnic networks are internally dense and enable patrons and clients to monitor each other more cheaply when both are on the same network. Patrons rarely bother to cultivate non-coethnics because the transaction costs of doing so are higher. Clients, in turn, are proven right in their expectations that they cannot get rewards from non-coethnic patrons because they almost never witness such exchanges. Hence, in equilibrium, we observe ethnic favoritism because the structure of ethnic networks reduces the transaction costs of clientelistic exchange within networks to the degree that transactions outside of the networks are too inefficient in comparison to be worthwhile.

1.3.4 Ethnic Monopsonies

Ethnic networks facilitate clientelistic exchange by reducing transaction costs. Because those costs are lower between coethnics than between members of

---

[25] See Horowitz (1985, 59), as well as Dixit (2004); Fafchamps (1992). Readers may notice some parallels to anthropology's old segmentary lineage models that have subsequently been subject to criticism (Caton, 1987; Dresch, 1988, 1986; Gellner and Munson, Jr., 1995). My point is not to revive that debate, but rather to draw on the insight that "common descent" can be an inclusive concept but made more exclusive by successively narrowing the criteria that make it common to members.

[26] Note that this contention is consistent with the often-remarked factionalism that exists within ethnic groups, and the propensity of patrons to exclude lower-level units that are nominally part of the latter's ethnic groups.

different ethnicities, they buttress the strategic selection mechanism that we observe as ethnic favoritism. The label "favoritism" can, however, be misleading because, when used loosely, it implies favorable terms to the exchange for clients. So far, however, nothing in the dynamics of the exchange relationship speaks of how the benefits of the exchange are divided up between the patron and the client. Yet ethnic vote markets suffer from imperfect competition – a potential boon for buyers and a disadvantage for sellers.[27]

Recall that one of the key features of ethnic constituencies is that an ascriptive, descent-like membership rule defines who is and is not a constituent. Ascription, in turn, implies that there is little boundary permeability between groups; unlike voluntary organizations, people cannot join or leave at will. Consequently, ascription limits the alternatives available to defectors – hence facilitating exchange. It also, however, cuts off constituents' entry and exit options and restricts them to transacting with coethnics. Consequently, clients cannot make credible threats to shop for alternate patrons outside their ethnic community.

Hence, emphasis on ethnic clienteles cuts off interethnic competition for votes, and politicians cater to their core, coethnic supporters. In the absence of *interethnic* competition between buyers, however, the degree of market power that patrons enjoy – the ability to set prices and quantities – depends crucially on the degree of *intraethnic* competition for clients. Returning to the language of the core versus swing voter debate, we can pose a fundamental question: has a single party captured the core, or are there swing voters within that constituency?

When intraethnic competition between patrons exists – that is, when there are multiple vote buyers within the community – competing patrons bid up the value of their coethnics' votes. Buyers have less discretion in picking and choosing clients because they need support from as many as they can get to win office. In contrast, when competition is absent, there is little incentive for hegemonic patrons to dispense lucrative rewards to constituents. This latter environment constitutes an ethnic vote monopsony. The lack of electoral rivals means that dominant politicians can patronize supporters from a position of market power. Ethnic monopsonies consequently approximate what has been called the "single machine assumption" – the simplifying proposition that there is just one vote buyer in a given election – while competitive communities approximate the dueling machines dynamic.[28]

This theory of ethnic vote monopsonies helps to resolve the puzzle with which I opened the book: how can ethnic favoritism and neglect coexist? Politicians reward their coethnic clients not out of some deep-seated affinity for

---

[27] Compare Bates (2008, ch. 3) and Kasfir (1976, chs. 2–3) on the incumbent's dilemma and the shrinking political arena in Africa.
[28] Gans-Morse et al. (2014); Kitschelt (2010); Lust (2009); Nichter (2008); Stokes (2005, 2007, 2009).

strangers, but because ethnic social networks reduce transaction costs and make it more efficient to cultivate coethnics than members of other communities. In other words, they patronize coethnics because they can do so more efficiently, which makes their votes cheaper relative to the cost of buying votes from other communities. Moreover, when they can eliminate intraethnic competition – by pushing the importance of "unity," for example – they can get away with modest payouts to clients in the absence of an electoral impetus to pay more. Mass constituents tolerate such a dynamic not because they derive pleasure from watching their "betters" consume the surplus, but because they have little choice in the matter. Lacking viable alternatives, they support their coethnic patrons because even small rewards are better than no rewards.

1.3.5 Observable Implications

The aforementioned theory sketch lays out my main arguments about ethnic vote monopsonies. Subsequent chapters in the book will develop these claims in more detail, but here I pause for a moment to lay out some of the observational implications of the theory. As I work through the applied component of the book, I will be matching up these core claims to a series of empirical expectations that translate their mid-level abstractions into more specific claims that can be tested explicitly against the data I have collected.

The first observable implication, and the core prediction of the theory, can be stated succinctly as follows:

Observable Implication 1 *Constituents in dominated communities receive more modest material payoffs than do constituents in competitive communities.*

Mass constituents in monopsonized communities – those dominated by a single patron – should receive less lucrative payoffs for their political support than constituents in communities that are internally competitive. This core claim follows from the qualitatively different competitive environments that characterize the different communities. Constituents with choices among patrons enjoy a dynamic of politicians competing for, and consequently bidding up the value of, their votes. Monopsonists, in contrast, need not fear being outbid by rival patrons and can offer lower, "take it or leave it" payoffs for votes. These payoffs should translate to lower purchase prices for votes: poorer public services, cheaper individual handouts, and fewer or lower-paying public employment opportunities.

A second observable implication complements the first:

Observable Implication 2 *Constituents in dominated communities vary more in the magnitude of their material payoffs than do constituents in competitive communities.*

There should be considerably more variability in the magnitude of rewards enjoyed in monopsonized constituencies compared to their internally competitive counterparts. This claim follows from the lack of credible electoral competition in the former, which grants monopsonists greater discretion over which clients to target for rewards than politicians in more competitive communities enjoy. Politicians typically distribute a diversified portfolio of patronage rewards, which includes both club goods, such as localized public works projects, and private goods, such as jobs or scholarships. Because they do not face electoral pressures to court every voter, hegemonic leaders can be choosier when targeting payoffs, and, with more market power, can select beneficiaries from a pool of nominal clients on the basis of efficiency considerations. Consequently, monopsonists enjoy more leeway to leverage economies of scale in the distribution of club goods to localities where their constituents concentrate, as with rural villages, and discretionary power to target individuals for private rewards, as in demographically mixed areas where their clients intermingle with non-supporters. Dominated constituencies should, therefore, experience more variation in who gets what compared to competitive communities, with subsets of "haves" and "have-nots."

A third observable implication reinforces the second's emphasis on dominant politicians' discretion over who to target for rewards:

Observable Implication 3 *Constituents in dominated communities compete with each other for patronage resources.*

We should observe more competition for scarce patronage resources in dominated communities than in their electorally competitive counterparts. This claim follows from the qualitatively different electoral environments in which patrons and their clients operate. Because monopsonists do not face a credible electoral threat, they do not need active support from the entire community. Consequently, they can reward some clients and neglect others because the latter lack alternate buyers for their votes. Monopsonists ration the supply of benefits, which requires clients to compete with each other to obtain a share. This dynamic implies that monopsonized constituents should turn up in droves for rallies and demonstrations and express slavish, sycophantic admiration for their patrons – not out of sincere devotion, but rather with an eye to the material payoff. Hence, monopsonies should be characterized by perverse competition: voters vying for patronage rather than politicians competing for votes.

Therefore, the theory of ethnic monopsonies makes at least three broad predictions that can be tested empirically. First, monopsonized constituents should receive fewer benefits than do constituents in other communities. Second, hegemonic politicians should be able to price discriminate more than their counterparts in competitive communities, so can target rewards much more precisely. Finally, given the discretion enjoyed by monopsonists, their nominal clients should find themselves forced to compete with one another to claim the patronage that the monopsonist rations out. Let us turn now to a sketch of the book's empirics to find out how these predictions fare in the field.

1.4 THE EVIDENCE

The study of ethnic politics in the developing world has long concentrated in Africa, along with a few non-African cases such as India, Indonesia, or Malaysia.[29] Ethnic politics is hardly region-specific, however. We observe it, for example, in the indigenous politics of Latin America, clan politics in the Central Asian states, and the racial and linguistic divisions found in some of the advanced democracies such as the United States, Canada, or Belgium.[30] Empirical studies of clientelism, in turn, have long been dominated by Latin America, where the phenomenon holds special salience in the region's politics.[31] Nonetheless, clientelism is simply a linkage mechanism rather than a Latin American perversity, and has been studied extensively in patronage democracies like India, wealthier states like Japan and Italy, and in electoral autocracies like Egypt and Jordan.[32]

This book examines communal politics and clientelism jointly in the Middle East. In particular, I focus on two key empirical venues in the Arab world: Lebanon and Yemen. The former was, itself, one of the "usual suspects" in the study of both ethnic politics and clientelism until a lengthy and devastating civil war took Lebanon off of most scholars' agendas.[33] Yemen, meanwhile, is less well known outside of anthropology, although western language work in the social sciences is appearing more frequently.[34] Clientelism and communal politics are central in both countries, and the varying competitive environments that prevail in their different communities provide an empirical treasure trove with which to make within- and cross-venue comparisons.

1.4.1 Why Lebanon and Yemen?

Lebanon and Yemen are fragile countries in the Arab world whose geopolitical importance – the former, Hizballah's home base, the latter, a haven for al-Qaida and other militant organizations – has overshadowed their more prosaic domestic politics. Formally, Lebanon uses a mix of consociational institutions

---

[29] For developing world illustrations outside Africa, see, for example, Horowitz (1985); Lijphart (1977). For India-specific work, compare Chandra (2004); Varshney (2002); Wilkinson (2006).
[30] Birnir (2007); Collins (2006); Lijphart (1977); Van Cott (2007 a,b).
[31] Auyero (1999, 2001); Calvo and Murillo (2004, 2013); Greene (2007); Magaloni (2006); Stokes (2005); Weitz-Shapiro (2014).
[32] Blaydes (2011); Chandra (2004); Chubb (1982); Lust (2009); Putnam (1993); Scheiner (2007); Stokes et al. (2013).
[33] Pre-war Lebanon featured, for example, in Lijphart's (1977) work on consociational democracy and Geertz's (1963) work on what he called "the integrative revolution." Post-war Lebanon is reemerging as an attractive venue for studying clientelism (Cammett, 2011, 2014; Cammett and Issar, 2010; Corstange, 2012b; Salti and Chaaban, 2010).
[34] In addition to earlier scholarship by Burrowes (1987) and Carapico (1998), relatively recent work by political scientists and economists include Browers (2007); Carapico (1998); Colton (2010); Day (2012); Egel (2013); Phillips (2008, 2011); Schwedler (2006); Wedeen (2008); Yadav (2013).

and power-sharing arrangements to manage cleavages between its sectarian communities. Incentives build into its electoral system stimulate cross-community alliances and preclude direct competition between communities over parliamentary seats and key executive posts. Yemen began its unification era as a fledgling democracy after its northern and southern halves merged in 1990, but deteriorated over time into an electoral autocracy in the aftermath of the 1994 civil war. Its straightforward electoral system, based on single-member districts with plurality rules, introduced disproportionality between the popular vote and seats in parliament, and contributed to the growing dominance of the ruling party.

Despite the parties' rhetorical flourishes and omnipresent sloganeering, programs and ideologies are secondary concerns for most people. Instead, elections of varying degrees of competitiveness and cleanliness revolve around patronage politics. Clientelism is therefore a central element of politics in both countries, and communal links of one form or another connect patrons to clients. Consistent with Horowitz's (1985) inclusive conception of ethnicity that focuses on ascriptive social categories, we can compare political dynamics based on Lebanon's sectarian and family divisions with those invoking Yemen's tribal, sectarian, and regional distinctions.

Lebanon and Yemen are both diverse countries with weak governments, but they differ in their formal governing institutions, degree of socioeconomic development, and exposure to regional conflicts. As such, comparing the two approximates a most different systems design. Our interest here is not in similiarities or differences between Lebanon and Yemen as countries, however, but rather between the communities within them. Importantly, both countries offer variation in the degree of internal competition within their different communal groups. In particular, each has at least one community within which lively electoral contestation takes place – albeit not always on a level playing field. Each also has at least one constituency that has more or less "unified" behind a single, hegemonic leader. We can, therefore, look for differences between monopsonized and competitive communities within each country, and then assess the degree to which these between-community distinctions replicate in both Lebanon and Yemen.

In Lebanon, a Sunni monopsony emerged from the vacuum of the civil war in the early-1990s and peaked in its dominance after the 2005 "Independence Intifada" and the withdrawal of Syrian forces from the country. Shia voters, in contrast, enjoyed clientelistic alternatives between the two main Shia parties, even after the traditional rivals closed ranks to form a collusive alliance after 2005. Christians, meanwhile, witnessed fierce competition between rival parties for Christian popular support. These claims are, of course, simplifications, but the key point for now is that we observe points along a continuum of internal competition across Lebanon's sectarian communities.

In Yemen, meanwhile, the ruling party progressively developed a monopsony among the tribes in the Zaydi Shia community by systematically buying up the loyalties of tribal leaders and freezing out alternatives for Zaydi votes. In contrast, it has continued to vie with the opposition for the loyalty of the country's Sunni communities – put together, the demographic majority. Although Yemeni elections are inequitable and resemble those held in other electoral autocracies, the various opposition parties offer legitimate alternatives for Sunni voters, even as they failed to sustain, over time, an attractive electoral alternative for Zaydi tribesmen. Once again, these claims are simplifications; the key point for now is that, like Lebanon, Yemen has both a monopsony and competitive communities to compare.

Empirically, the presence of both monopsonies and electorally competitive communities in each country venue provides substantial inferential advantages. First, it enables us to compare and contrast the dynamics in the communities within each country in a broadly controlled environment. Doing so allows us to hold a variety of institutional, developmental, and cultural influences constant. This degree of control, although imperfect, increases our confidence that the differences we observe between the constituencies actually are products of their differing competitive environments rather than some other confounding factor.

Second, we can also compare and contrast the differences in dynamics across the two country venues. Doing so helps us probe the generalizability of the findings. Should the basic dynamics replicate in two different societies, we can be more confident that the findings reflect systematic political processes rather than a country-specific luck of the draw. Variations on the basic themes I am proposing, in turn, can suggest additional factors worth examining in future research and other venues.

Although Lebanon and Yemen are both Arab countries, the theory developed in this book is not bound by region; nothing about ethnic monopsonies rests on specifics from the Arab or Muslim worlds. Instead, the argument applies, in principle, to societies with salient ethnic divisions and clientelistic politics. In practice, we should expect this theory to apply best in the diverse societies of the developing world where parties use patronage to service electoral constituencies defined along communal lines.

1.4.2 Data and Methods

The empirical evidence I use in this book comes from a variety of primary and secondary source data. I gathered the former during approximately two years of field research spread over several trips to both countries. These included site visits to Lebanon in the spring of 2005, along with trips in the summer of 2008 and spring of 2009, and analogous trips to Yemen in the winter of 2004–2005, from the summer of 2005 to the summer of 2006, and the spring of 2010. I gathered secondary sources, considerably more sparse for Yemen than Lebanon, in between field visits. Moreover, I made use of the countries' newspapers and online news agencies – even Yemen's are sporadically web-accessible – to keep abreast of domestic events.

By necessity, I have employed mixed methods in collecting and analyzing the data used in this book. The "necessity" reflects a nod to practical data limitations. What information is available in and about these two countries is scattered, fragmented, and sometimes of questionable reliability. I have, consequently, mixed quantitative and qualitative evidence in the hopes that each will tell enough of the story to advance the argument when called upon. The qualitative data have been most helpful in illuminating the elite side of the story: what the patrons and parties are doing. The quantitative, survey-based evidence, in turn, has been indispensible in piecing together the client's side of the story: who gets what, and how much.

The qualitative data come in a variety of forms, including elite interviews, newspaper coverage, party literature, government publications, and classic soak-and-poke immersion. The last of these more than compensated with comprehension for what it lacks in a dignified label and, in particular, helped me understand which questions were worth asking and how to ask them – advantages that extended, in turn, to the surveys. The most important sources for understanding dynamics among elites were, unsurprisingly, the elites themselves. I gathered these data via over 100 interviews of political party leaders and operatives, tribal shaykhs, religious figures, civil society activists, journalists, parliamentarians, ministers, and various other government officials. I restrict attribution for all interviewées to studiously vague occupation and seniority even when their statements appear unremarkable – the intent is to provide cover for those statements that are sensitive.[35]

The quantitative data for this book, which I use extensively in later chapters to examine the client's side of the story, come from original mass attitude surveys I conducted in both field sites. Both surveys were nationally representative and utilized face-to-face interviews and comparable questionnaires. The Lebanon survey comprises 1000 respondents, with the sample drawn and interviews administered by Beirut-based MADMA Co. in the fall of 2005. The Yemen survey, in turn, includes 1440 respondents, with the sample drawn and interviews conducted by the Sanaa-based Yemen Polling Center in the spring of 2007.[36] These data provide systematic and comparable

---

[35] Politics is a gentleman's sport in neither Lebanon nor Yemen. A number of interviewées had previously been exiled, and a non-trivial number of them have either been threatened with or subjected to violence or legal trouble for their politics. Moreover, some interviewées keep their livelihoods only by remaining in the good graces of their superiors, not all of whom would be enthusiastic about what their subordinates have to say behind closed doors. I hope, at any rate, that I have provided all of my interviewées with that most valuable of resources under such circumstances: plausible deniability.

[36] Given its relatively small and compact size, I sampled from all provinces in Lebanon. Yemen is much larger and more spread out, and for practicality, I drew the sample from a random draw of approximately half the provinces whose chances of inclusion in the sample were directly proportional to their population sizes. I imposed two auxiliary constrains on the province sampling, however. First, at least one province needed to come from those that constituted the former southern republic. Second, safety concerns required that we not include

1.4.3 Findings

evidence of what mass constituents experience in their relations to their political patrons.

Given the competitive dynamics in these two field venues, what should we expect to observe in the data? Vote monopsonies should reduce the welfare of regular people in both societies. We should, in principle, be able to detect these welfare reductions by comparing monopsonized constituents to their peers from more internally competitive communities. Consequently, Lebanese Sunnis and Yemeni Zaydis should be broadly comparable to one another and should differ in predictable ways from their co-nationals who enjoy competition for their political support. The core expectation, then, is that Lebanese Sunnis and Yemeni Zaydis should receive more modest material payoffs than their respective co-nationals.

The first major test of this expectation looks for variation in constituents' access to basic infrastructure and government services. Specifically, it examines electricity and piped water coverage, two basic utilities that citizens of the developed world can take for granted but residents of the developing world cannot. In Lebanon and Yemen, rare are the individuals who do not encounter interruptions in their supply of basic utilities on a near-daily basis. The first test examines whether community membership helps to explain the frequency of service interruptions, controlling for other, plausible determinants of access. The data reveal that, all else equal, Lebanese Sunnis and Yemeni Zaydis go without electricity and water more often than their co-nationals – but with an important caveat connected to their patrons' discretionary capacity to target payoffs.

Targeting is, of course, a central dynamic in clientelistic politics. Another central hypothesis that falls out of the overall argument claims that monopsonists, due to their insulation from competitive pressures, are relatively free to exercise discretion in where and to whom to target rewards. Greater scope for discretion, in turn, frees them to deploy their patronage resources with greater efficiency, serving only select subsets of their nominal constituencies. Consequently, we should expect monopsonists to concentrate their dispensations of club goods

---

the northern province of Saada, the location of the on-again, of-again Houthi insurgency. Technically, excluding Saada makes the survey less representative of the national population, but the province itself is sparsely populated and would have contributed only a small handful of respondents to the sample. Moreover, there are several other provinces in the sample that are heavily Zaydi and heavily tribal, so the inferential concerns should be minimal. Ultimately, the provinces sampled were Aden and Hadramawt (both formerly in the southern republic), Taiz, Ibb, Hajjah, Hudayda, Dhamar, Amran, Marib, and Sanaa city. Stratification was based on preliminary figures from the 2004 census down to the village or city neighborhood level, with respondents sampled via a random walk pattern.

in discrete, homogeneous localities where the benefits accrue only to supporters without risk of dissipating them on non-supporters. Moreover, we should also expect monopsonists to swap out club goods in favor of privately consumed rewards such as jobs in mixed areas, reserving the latter for localities in which they prefer to target clients more precisely.

The public utilities data, in turn, reveal patterns of interruption consistent with the expectations about targeting. For the electricity and water supply, it is indeed the case that Lebanese Sunnis and Yemeni Zaydis get poorer services – in the urban areas. Their rural cosectarians, meanwhile, have their services interrupted relatively less often. Rural constituents are, in key respects, better clients. In addition to being easier to monitor, most villages tend to be homogeneous and, consequently, are attractive locations to deploy club goods. Hence, efficient monopsonists leverage patronage economies of scale – and clients' lowered expectations – by targeting modestly better services to the rural areas.

I find additional evidence of targeting in Lebanon, for which I have more detailed data on the locations of constituent concentrations derived from voter rolls. First, the data reveal that Sunni dominant electoral districts suffer more interruptions to their utilities than do other districts. While particular villages may escape the worst of the monopsony penalty, the districts overall suffer from neglect. Second, Sunnis living in homogeneous neighborhoods are less likely to hold government jobs than their cosectarians living in mixed neighborhoods. The latter finding substantiates the expectation that the monopsonist has greater discretion to toggle between club and privately-consumed rewards as needed, with the former going to homogeneous areas and the latter to mixed ones.

The luxury that hegemonic patrons enjoy to target payoffs also changes the relationship dynamics between patrons and clients in a subtle but important way: who is competing to impress whom. The final working hypothesis posits that monopsonized constituents must compete with one another for patronage more explicitly than must their peers in competitive communities. Dominant politicians, largely freed from electoral pressure, do not need votes from all of their nominal constituents to retain office and, consequently, can be selective in which clients they patronize. The result is perverse competition: constituents must demonstrate why they, as opposed to their neighbors, should be granted a share of the largesse. Empirically, we should observe Lebanese Sunnis and Yemeni Zaydis making special efforts to attract the attention of their patrons in pursuit of a small share in the spoils.

I use a novel behavioral measure to capture constituent efforts to attract patronage: whether or not they proclaim their loyalty to their patron by publicly displaying a poster or other political symbol outside their homes.[37]

---

[37] See Kitschelt and Wilkinson (2007a) for a brief discussion of public displays of political loyalty. Cammett (2014) uses a similar technique. See also Corstange (2012a) for other uses of iconographic displays to communicate.

1.5 Plan of the Book

The poster data, in turn, align with the general patterns described earlier. In particular, Lebanese Sunnis and Yemeni Zaydis are much more likely than their co-nationals to display such posters the stronger they believe that they need political connections to secure a government job, one of the classic patronage rewards. Meanwhile, there is no evidence that their co-nationals in the more competitive communities display posters for this instrumental reason. The poster evidence suggests that monopsonized constituents in both countries compete with one another for patronage rewards, while their peers in other communities do not.

1.5 PLAN OF THE BOOK

The plan of the rest of the book is as follows. Chapter 2 develops the book's theoretical framework. Although clientelism is pervasive in the developing world, the chapter begins by examining barriers to clientelistic exchange between politicians and their constituents. It argues that patrons and clients can reduce their transaction costs by exploiting ethnic social networks to keep monitoring costs low and the credibility of their promises to each other high. This reliance on ethnicity to facilitate clientelistic transactions, however, creates imperfectly competitive vote markets that are segmented along ethnic lines. The chapter then distinguishes between internally competitive ethnic constituencies in which multiple elites vie for their coethnics' support, and constituencies dominated by a single, hegemonic leader – *ethnic monopsonies*. It argues that internal competition bids up the value of constituents' support, while unity enables the dominant leader to neglect group members' needs in the absence of competitive pressures. The chapter closes with observable implications of the theory.

Chapters 3 and 4 examine the book's empirical venues of Lebanon and Yemen in detail, leaning heavily on qualitative evidence gleaned from elite interviews, local scholarly work, and newspaper coverage. These chapters chart the historical background to the different communal cleavages in the two countries and elaborate on the degree of within-group political competition found within each community. They show that, historically, within-group competition was more the norm than the exception in both countries, but that major shocks to their systems such as civil wars and foreign intervention allowed hegemonic leaders to establish their dominance in some communities but not others. Once established, these monopsonies could use control over state resources for patronage purposes to reinforce their positions.

Again leaning heavily on the qualitative evidence, chapter 5 elaborates on the mechanisms of clientelistic exchange in Lebanon and Yemen as facilitated by communal linkages. It first discusses party programs and ideologies in the two countries, and shows that large swaths of the populations discount platforms and dismiss parties as untrustworthy. Most people, instead, engage in personalized politics via patron–client relationships. The chapter then shows how both politicians and their constituents make use of communal networks, and especially extended families, to facilitate clientelistic transactions by making them cheaper and more reliable. It finishes by detailing the development and deployment of political machines by the parties in order to organize these exchanges.

While the empirical chapters up to this point have relied on qualitative evidence to tell the elite side of the story, chapter 6 switches over to quantitative evidence to examine what regular people get out of these clientelistic exchanges. This chapter uses data from the Lebanon and Yemen surveys to investigate people's access to two basic government services: electricity and piped water. The survey data make two core points. First, members of politically-dominated communities receive poorer services than do their counterparts in the internally-competitive communities. Second, dominant leaders disproportionately favor rural constituents with club goods to take advantage of geographical clustering and the lower demands of rural voters.

Chapter 7 builds on the targeting story introduced in Chapter 6 and examines how patrons deploy different kinds of patronage rewards – club goods versus privately-consumed goods – in different contexts. This chapter relies on the Lebanese survey data, which contain richer information about district and neighborhood diversity. First, consistent with the book's competition argument, members of dominated communities receive poorer services than their peers when living in homogeneous districts – dominant leaders face no competitive pressures to do better in service provision. As districts become more diverse, however, the gap between communities shrinks as dominant leaders adjust to the competitive pressures emanating from other communities. Second, consistent with a targeting logic, dominant leaders reserve private payoffs – here, government jobs – for supporters living in mixed neighborhoods where club goods such as infrastructure would be wasted on members of other communities.

Chapter 8 examines another of the empirical implications of the book's theory: who competes for whom. More specifically, I had argued that politicians compete against each other for votes in internally-competitive communities, but in constituencies dominated by a single, hegemonic leader, voters compete against each other for patronage. This chapter again makes use of the Lebanon and Yemen survey data, and specifically, a behavioral measure contained within them: people's public display of political iconography outside their homes. These data show that, first, members of the politically-dominated communities display political imagery much more frequently than do their counterparts in the other communities. Second, decisions to make these public displays have an instrumental motive: people do it because they see it as a tool to secure patronage rewards. This instrumental motive is, however, evident only among members of the dominated communities.

Chapter 9 concludes the book by evaluating its arguments and findings in the the broader context of democratic and authoritarian governance in the diverse societies of the developing world. It reviews the scope of the argument, and then considers the book's ramifications for the study of ethnic politics, clientelism, and democratic governance.

2

Ethnic Constituencies in the Market for Votes

2.1 INTRODUCTION

How can ethnic favoritism coexist with ethnic neglect? We often observe scarce resources allocated politically along ethnic lines in the diverse societies of the developing world. In many cases, however, the mass constituents whose votes put their coethnics in office receive only meager rewards for their political support – raising the question of how favorable "ethnic favoritism" actually is for regular people. What can explain this dual dynamic? Why would people vote for coethnic leaders if they get little for their trouble? Why would they tolerate meager rewards rather than shop their votes around? How can elites get away with offering such payoffs?

The academic literature on ethnic politics focuses heavily on explaining ethnic favoritism and competition *between* communities. In contrast, it remains relatively silent about the distribution of resources *within* ethnic constituencies, whether in terms of how lucrative the payoffs are or how many people they reach. Commonly cited mechanisms that purport to explain the appeal of ethnic constituencies – whether due to shared tastes, information networks, or strategic selection – suffer from non-trivial conceptual holes and leave important questions unanswered. Moreover, these mechanisms offer no explanation for variation in reward size and quantity – why votes are cheap in some communities and dear in others.

This chapter develops a transactions-based theory of ethnic constituencies. It argues that ethnic links facilitate clientelism by reducing both uncertainty and transactions costs in exchange relationships. Efficient exchange, in turn, drives patrons and clients to prefer transaction partners within their own communities. Strategic selection of coethnics, however, segments the electorate and transforms these constituencies into protected vote markets for communal elites. Under such conditions, *intra*ethnic competition between dueling patrons raises both the value of the vote and the quantity of votes demanded. In contrast, constituencies that unify behind a hegemonic patron trap their members in a vote monopsony that demands few votes and pays out meager rewards for them.

The rest of this chapter proceeds as follows. It begins by examining mechanisms that link politicians with their constituents in the market for votes. It highlights clientelism, examines barriers to patron–client exchange, and describes common tools such as machines and brokers that help to streamline transactions. Next, the chapter offers an information-based explanation for how ethnicity helps to reduce transaction costs in clientelistic exchange. It then argues that ethnicity induces imperfect competition in the vote market. Subsequently, the chapter builds the idea of the ethnic monopsony, in which hegemonic patrons dominate their communities. It ends by exploring the empirical ramifications of different competitive environments within different communities.

2.2 TRANSACTIONS IN THE MARKET FOR VOTES

Much of politics revolves around the ceaseless contest over how to allocate society's scarce resources – the "who gets what, when, and how" questions that have animated political debate across both time and space (Lasswell, 1935). Societies, both contemporary and historical, have used a wide range of mechanisms to handle this distribution, but elections, whether free and fair or clearly fraudulent, have increasingly become the procedure of choice.[1] When elections structure the political allocation of resources, politicians and their constituents interact in a market for votes by exchanging rewards for political support. Rewards, of course, can take on a great many forms, ranging from policy outcomes to symbolic payoffs to material benefits. Likewise, political support can include a number of activities such as campaign work and rally attendance, but for most people centers on the vote itself.

In principle, a wide variety of linkage mechanisms exist that can connect politicians to their constituents. They run through a menu of options such as ideologies, party programs, charismatic authority, kinship ties, religious injunctions, and patron–client relationships.[2] These mechanisms provide various forms of structure to the relationship between politicians and voters.

---

[1] We can make broad distinctions between elections that allocate the authority to hold office and subsequently allocate resources, and elections that merely allocate resources (cf. Gandhi and Lust-Okar, 2009; Hyde and Marinov, 2012; Magaloni and Kricheli, 2010). We see the former in democratic elections where the results are legitimately uncertain, and the latter in electoral autocracies where elections do not serve as tools to change office holders, but rather to allocate patronage resources (Blaydes, 2011; Lust, 2009; Lust-Okar, 2009b; Magaloni, 2006).

[2] Kitschelt (2000, 2010); Kitschelt and Wilkinson (2007a).

2.2 Transactions in the Market for Votes

They also define what each side of the bargain may reasonably expect of the other, as well as who is accountable to whom.

Most studies of the advanced industrial democracies use programmatic linkages as their conceptual point of departure. In the canonical version of the "responsible partisan model," parties bundle their policy commitments into campaign platforms, voters choose the program that most closely aligns with their own preferences, and the winning party implements its promised policies after the election. Voters reward competence and fulfilled promises by reelecting parties, and punish failures by voting them out of office in the next election.[3] The reality of electoral competition is, of course, not so neat and tidy, even in institutionalized democracies where non-trivial amounts of non-programmatic policking occur in the form of pork-barrel appeals and patronage spending.[4] Even so, this simplifying abstraction serves as a useful benchmark against which to gauge deviations from the idealized form of programmatic competition that, according to our stylized facts, emphasizes the provision of public goods.

Despite the canonical model's appealing normative connotations – generous public goods provision and accountable politicians among them – programmatic linkages do *not* predominate in much of the developing world. In particular, the responsible partisan model assumes that voters believe campaign platforms to be credible and that parties keep such promises after the elections. Neither assumption is tenable in the developing world where programs usually provide cheap talk rather than policy commitments. In these environments, platforms and ideologies are generally vague, uninformative, indistinguishable between parties, and sometimes simply nonexistent.[5] In any event, parties have difficulty making credible commitments to their programs, so voters do not expect politicians to implement their platforms after the elections. Consequently, people rarely vote for parties or hold them accountable on the basis of their programmatic appeals.

2.2.1 Patron–Client Linkages

Unable to commit credibly to their programs, politicians in the developing world turn instead to a number of other linkage mechanisms to connect with their constituents. Perhaps the two most prominent and frequently studied alternatives to programs are clientelism and ethnicity, often deployed in tandem. The observed empirical connection between these two mechanisms is not accidental; I will argue in this chapter that ethnic links facilitate clientelism. First, though, I describe the stylized version of clientelistic exchanges,

---

[3] Downs (1957); Kitschelt (2000, 2010); Lipset and Rokkan (1967).
[4] See Stokes (2009); Stokes et al. (2013) and the collected contributions in Kitschelt and Wilkinson (2007b).
[5] Keefer (2007, 2010); Keefer and Vlaicu (2008); Kitschelt (2000); Kitschelt and Wilkinson (2007b); Stokes et al. (2013).

and subsequently explain how ethnicity helps to streamline the transactions between patrons and clients.

Compared to the canonical accounts of programmatic party competition, there is less consensus on how clientelism works.[6] Used colloquially, the term provides a shorthand pejorative for institutions and relationships that are "somehow less than ideal."[7] Numerous attempts to conceptualize this mechanism have focused on different characteristics of the transaction, including direct and affective relationships, exchange between asymmetrically endowed parties, emphasis on targeted and private goods, connections to pork-barrel politics, and so on.[8] Nonetheless, there is growing scholarly agreement on clientelism as the contingent, direct exchange of rewards for political support.

The distinguishing feature of clientelism is its emphasis on the quid pro quo element.[9] Understandably, most scholars focus on the contingency of the payoffs to clients: in stylized terms, patrons only distribute benefits to compliant voters. Hence, patrons offer rewards to a subset of the electorate whose defining characteristic is simply: "do you support me politically?"[10] The flip side of the

---

[6] Compare, for example, Auyero (1999, 2001); Hicken (2011); Kitschelt and Wilkinson (2007a); Magaloni (2006); Stokes (2007); Stokes et al. (2013); Weitz-Shapiro (2014).

[7] Hicken (2011, 290); see also the extended discussion in Stokes et al. (2013, ch. 1).

[8] Early work that drew from sociological and anthropological traditions emphasized direct, personal relationships and affective ties between patrons and clients of unequal status and resource endowments (Lemarchand, 1972; Lemarchand and Legg, 1972; Powell, 1970; Scott, 1969, 1972; Weingrod, 1968). Later generations of studies, meanwhile, have moved away from the affective dimensions and toward greater emphasis on brokers and monitoring (Kitschelt, 2010; Kitschelt and Wilkinson, 2007a; Stokes, 2007; Stokes et al., 2013; Wantchekon, 2003), although recent work has revived arguments about reciprocity (Finan and Schechter, 2012; Lawson and Greene, 2014). Earlier work tended to conflate the structure of the exchange relationship with the types of rewards that patrons typically provided. More recent studies have subsequently abstracted away from particular reward types in favor of focusing on the contingent element of the exchange (Hicken, 2011; Stokes, 2007; Stokes et al., 2013).

[9] The contingency of the exchange is what distinguishes clientelism from other, seemingly similar dynamics such as constituency services or pork barrel politics (Hicken, 2011; Stokes, 2009; Stokes et al., 2013). Elected officials who provide individual services directly to constituents may engage in good politics, but they do *not* engage in clientelism provided that they make such services available to constituents independent of partisan leanings or political support. Pork-barrel politics, even though it targets club goods to narrowly defined and potentially idiosyncratic groups, supplies those goods on the basis of group membership and not on the basis of political support. Nor are privately consumed rewards necessary or sufficient components of clientelist exchange. Benefits such as social security or unemployment insurance are consumed by private individuals but are programmatic policies. Meanwhile, club goods targeted to key demographics (or geographies) may represent "collective clientelism" (Hicken, 2011) if distributed on the basis of some proportion of the collectivity providing its support to the patron.

[10] Stokes (2007, 606). I will qualify this simplifying claim later when discussing monitoring: patrons *wish* to reward only compliant voters, but cannot observe compliance perfectly. Instead, patrons may tolerate some "false positives" if, in the main, rewards primarily reach the compliant.

quid pro quo, meanwhile, is that clients only supply votes to patrons who fulfill their promises of rewards.[11] Patron–client relationships are, consequently, more explicitly transactional than are relationships between parties and voters linked by programs.

Clientelism does not eliminate the need for credibility and accountability so much as it restructures them. First, accountability becomes more clearly reciprocal between patrons and clients than it is under programmatic linkages. Modifications to the vote market in the advanced democracies grant important privileges to voters that do not extend to politicians. In particular, innovations such as an enforced secret ballot make it possible for voters to hold politicians accountable for their promises through the electoral mechanism, but *prevent* politicians from holding voters accountable for their vote choices. Clientelism, meanwhile, rests not only on the ability of clients to sanction patrons by withdrawing their political support, but also on patrons' capacity to police voters and punish noncompliant clients by withdrawing rewards. Mutual accountability is normatively unappealing, prompting Stokes (2005) to call it "perverse accountability." Nonetheless, it reinforces the exchange relationship by giving both parties to the transaction recourse when their partners renege on the bargain.

Moreover, the credible commitments problem does not disappear simply because politicians link to voters via clientelism rather than ideologies or party programs. Patrons must still convince clients that the rewards they promise will, in fact, materialize. If anything, credibility bites harder under clientelism because the rewards that are typically offered are more tangible and easier to verify than the nebulous "policy goods" offered by programmatic parties. Mutual accountability further complicating matters: clients must also be able to make credible commitments to patrons to convince the latter that the promised votes will, indeed, be cast. There are, in other words, non-trivial barriers to clientelist exchange which patrons and clients must overcome if they are to transact in the vote market.

2.2.2 Barriers to Clientelistic Exchange

Transactions in the vote market are not inherently self-enforcing, regardless of whether the linkages between politicians and voters are programmatic, clientelistic, or some other form. Black-boxing enforcement issues – such as in

---

[11] Hence, if affective ties, expressive interests, or ethnic solidarity provide the deciding (rather than contributing) factor in a "client's" vote choice, then the voter's relationship to the "patron" is not clientelistic. This distinction does not preclude affect, expression, or solidarity from entering voters' calculations, of course. Indeed, we should expect patrons to cultivate these considerations among their clientele in order to subsidize the material component of the exchange by compensating clients partially with non-material rewards. I return to this point later in the chapter.

	Patron	
	Reward	Withhold
Client — Vote	Bargain	Patron Opportunism
Client — Stay Home	Client Opportunism	No Exchange

FIGURE 2.1: Patron–Client Exchange as a One-Shot Prisoner's Dilemma

the responsible partisan model – consequently assumes away one of the core components of the exchange. There are, however, multiple impediments to clientelistic exchange which patrons and clients must overcome if they wish to engage in mutually beneficial transactions. Two key barriers are, first, incentives for opportunistic behavior, and second, imperfect observability.

Patrons and clients transact against a backdrop of opportunism without recourse to a third-party enforcer; exchanges are "full of opportunities for defection and betrayal."[12] Rewards-for-support bargains are not legally enforceable contracts and, depending on the terms, may, in fact, be illegal. The parties to the transaction cannot expect a neutral state to enforce such a bargain, so must find ways to enforce it themselves. First, the two sides have unaligned interests in one-off exchanges, as depicted informally in Figure 2.1. Both benefit from concluding a bargain, but each has a self-evident incentive to renege on it. In particular, the patron prefers to win the client's vote but withhold the promised payoff, while the client prefers to pocket the reward but stay home on election day – or, worse still, vote for someone else. The structure of the exchange environment is, consequently, a one-shot prisoner's dilemma. Both sides benefit from a transaction, but the dominant strategy for each is to renege on the other. The familiar outcome is the "socially" undesirable one: no exchange occurs.[13]

---

[12] The quote comes from Stokes (2007, 608); see also Dixit (2004); Ostrom (1990); Williamson (1985) on exchanges without third-party enforcers.

[13] The no-exchange outcome is "socially" undesirable in the sense that the "society" of two (the patron and the client) gains collectively from a concluded transaction relative to no transaction. To the degree that clientelistic exchange misallocates resources, of course, the ability of patrons and clients to conclude such bargains is itself socially undesirable from the standpoint of the larger society (in the more usual sense of the term).

2.2 Transactions in the Market for Votes

One of the well-known resolutions to the prisoner's dilemma is to iterate it: under the right conditions, repeated interactions can alter incentives enough to make mutual cooperation an equilibrium outcome. Given the inherent limitations of one-shot transactions in the vote market, then, patrons and clients typically embed individual exchanges in ongoing, iterative relationships.[14] Doing so leverages the shadow of the future to dissuade opportunistic behavior through fear of losing the benefits of future interactions. Provided that both patron and client value the future enough, iterative relationships help make promises of exchange in the present more credible and, hence, worth entertaining. Likewise, iteration helps to resolve the time-inconsistency problem inherent in vote market transactions. Patron–client exchange is more typically sequential than simultaneous – providing incentives for the patron (client) to withhold the reward (vote) after first securing the vote (reward). Iteration, again, helps to guard against this temptation to opportunism through the threat of losing benefits from forgone future interactions.

The threat of opportunism is one significant barrier to clientelistic exchange. The other major impediment is imperfectly observable behavior, which makes it difficult for both patrons and clients to verify that their partners have fulfilled their promises. Neither side to the exchange observes the other's actions with complete certainty, although electoral procedures such as the secret ballot primarily hamper the patron's capacity to observe behavior. Despite this asymmetry, the patron's uncertainty is still the client's problem, because the latter cannot sell what the former will not buy. In order to facilitate transactions in the shadow of imperfect information, both parties must make their "unobservable" actions observable – at least probabilistically – to each other. Hence, both patrons and clients must be able to monitor and police their transaction partners.[15]

Contingency defines clientelistic exchanges, so patrons must have some capacity to condition payoffs on clients' political support. By design, however, the secret ballot disrupts this relationship by preventing patrons from observing vote choices. Patrons may, of course, simply work to subvert the secret ballot, or at least cultivate uncertainty about its secrecy.[16] Complementing these efforts,

---

[14] For canonical discussions of the iterated prisoner's dilemma in the abstract, see Axelrod (1984); Kreps et al. (1982). See Hicken (2011); Stokes (2007) for iteration in clientelistic exchange.
[15] As Ostrom (1990, 45) observes, people cannot make credible commitments to each other unless they can resolve their monitoring problem.
[16] An empirical literature on vote trafficking has documented an impressive range of techniques parties use to sidestep the nominally secret ballot (Bratton, 2008; Brusco et al., 2004; Corstange, 2012b; Stokes, 2005). Moreover, survey evidence on perceptions of ballot secrecy in the United States shows that roughly 25 percent of Americans believe that parties can observe their ballot choices against their will (Gerber et al., 2013). Insofar as American electoral regulations generally provide adequate ballot secrecy, one can only wonder what voters in the developing world think where regulations are less stringent. Fundamentally, of course, the *perception* of ballot secrecy is more important than its reality for vote choice – fearful voters act on their

patrons can also look for indirect indicators of political support, while clients can send costly signals of the same. Hence, patrons can track who turns out to rallies, who puts up political posters, and who bothers to learn otherwise obtuse party slogans or ideological formulae.[17] They may be unable to observe vote choice with complete certainty, but they can observe support probabilistically. As long as their educated guesses are sufficiently accurate, patrons can tolerate some "false positives" if they can still transact with reasonable efficiency.

Understandably, most studies of clientelism focus on patrons' efforts to monitor their clients' behavior. Nonetheless, the contingency in clientelistic exchanges is reciprocal, and clients also need to confirm that patrons are fulfilling their pledges and providing rewards that are as valuable as promised. Clients may be able to verify certain types of tangible payoffs, such as consumer goods or cash handouts, with relative ease. Other rewards, however, may be much harder to verify, such as intercessions with the police, a post in the civil service at some point in the indefinite future, or medical assistance to be held in reserve until needed. Should a client receive a reduced sentence or fine for a traffic violation, for example, it may or may not be due to the patron's unobserved efforts. Moreover, the penalty may or may not be as low as it could have been had the patron exerted more influence (such as to dismiss the offense altogether). The patron's good word may or may not help the client move up the queue in the wait for a civil service job, and more effort may secure more interesting work or a better salary. Promises of assistance to be called upon at a later date may or may not be honored, and the scope of that assistance may or may not fulfill the spirit of the transaction in the absence of a written contract spelling out the terms. Clients may need to make credible commitments to patrons in order to secure rewards, but patrons must also make credible commitments to clients to secure their votes. Their efforts to do so make transacting clientelistic exchanges costly.

2.2.3 Tools to Reduce Transaction Costs

In practice, then, patrons and clients cannot transact costlessly. Instead, they must factor in two sets of considerations when negotiating an exchange. The first component is, of course, the intrinsic value of the rewards and votes to be traded. The second factor is the cost of doing business – the expenses that arise from the act of exchange itself. These transaction costs accrue from the efforts of both patrons and clients to monitor and police each other. Monitoring may

---

perceptions that parties can observe their votes regardless of whether or not the parties actually have that capacity (Chandra, 2004).

[17] Compare Havel (1978); Kitschelt and Wilkinson (2007a); Szwarcberg (2012, 2014); Wedeen (1999).

require non-trivial expenditures of time and resources which may, in turn, be sufficiently onerous to preclude clientelistic exchange.

Both patrons and clients face incentives to reduce transaction costs. Patrons, however, hold an encompassing interest in doing so. The stylized clientelistic relationship is dyadic at base, but the quantity of exchanges on either side of the dyad is highly asymmetric. Clients focus on a single exchange – or at most a few if entertaining offers from multiple patrons – while patrons typically transact with a great many clients. Patrons thus multiply any reduction of unit transaction costs by the number of exchanges they conclude, yielding a powerful incentive to invest in the machinery to streamline clientelistic transactions. Patrons' encompassing interests in minimizing transaction costs may, in fact, cause them to subsidize those expenses borne by *clients* in order to stimulate more clientelistic exchanges. One common example of this phenomenon is the well-orchestrated get-out-the-vote efforts to transport voters to the polls on election day in an effort to reduce the latter's turnout costs.

Early-generation studies of clientelism emphasized the traditional, personalized nature of relationships between patrons and clients. Later studies, meanwhile, implicitly acknowledged that "modern" patrons could not conceivably maintain their clientele through personal ties alone, and so build up organizations to mediate relationships with their clients.[18] Patrons have typically invested in their own political machines to reduce transaction costs, subcontracted out to local notables who internalize those costs, or a combination of both methods. Although nominally called political parties, these organizations perform different functions than their counterparts in advanced democracies that are engaged in programmatic competition. Whereas the latter aggregate and express interests and policy preferences, the former organize to reduce transaction costs in clientelistic exchange. In practice, they serve primarily to monitor, police, and distribute rewards to voters.

Patrons rely on intermediaries and brokers who embed themselves deeply in clients' social networks. These agents – who Wang and Kurzman (2007b) call "walking encyclopedias" of localized knowledge – help to ameliorate information imperfections and uncertainty in the local vote market. Such individuals cultivate intricate and extensive connections within the community which they leverage to distribute benefits to existing clients, recruit new ones onto the network, and monitor people's behavior to verify their compliance with the quid pro quo. Their informational advantages help brokers to reduce clientelistic transaction costs significantly.[19]

---

[18] The localized, small-scale patrons of the early-generation studies, in fact, resemble the brokers highlighted by later studies (Auyero, 1999, 2001; Kasara, 2007; Powell, 1970; Scott, 1969, 1972; Stokes, 2007; Stokes et al., 2013; Weingrod, 1968).

[19] Brokers and intermediaries almost immediately bring to mind the ward bosses and precinct captains of American urban machines such as Tammany Hall in New York City, the Republican Organization in Philadelphia, or the Daley Machine in Chicago (Despres, 2005; Erie, 1992;

The patron's local agents provide a mechanism to distribute rewards directly to clients. Moreover, brokers can leverage their localized knowledge to tailor benefits to the idiosyncratic needs of individual clients rather than rely on one-size-fits-all rewards. Further, the broker's connections in the social network serve an important recruitment function. Distributing needed benefits to clients promptly advertises the patron's reliability and responsiveness on the social network and helps recruit new clients by convincing fence-sitters of the value of supporting the patron. Hence, as a notorious ward boss for Tammany Hall illustrated:

If a family is burned out ... I don't refer them to the Charity Organization Society, which would investigate their case in a month or two and decide they were worthy of help about the time they are dead from starvation. I just get quarters for them, buy clothes for them if their clothes were burned up, and fix them up till they get things runnin' again. It's philanthropy, but it's good politics, too – mighty good politics. Who can tell how many votes one of these fires bring me? The poor are the most grateful people in the world, and, let me tell you, they have more friends in their neighborhoods than the rich have in theirs.[20]

Brokers provide the benign face of clientelism by distributing benefits to clients, but also act as its policemen by monitoring client behavior. The patron's intermediaries tap the information-rich environments within which they embed themselves to observe a wide variety of direct and indirect indicators and costly signals of political support. Such indicators, as described earlier, include attendance at rallies, demonstrations, and meetings, public displays of political paraphernalia such as campaign posters and flags, knowledge of party slogans, fluency in revolutionary jargon, and so forth. Due to their intimate familiarity with clients, brokers also claim the ability to "look people in the eye" in order to judge who has sincerely complied with the quid pro quo – although their actual efficacy remains open to question.[21]

Golway, 2014; Kurtzman, 1935; McCaffery, 1993; Riordon, 1905). More contemporary examples from the developing world include *punteros* in Argentina and *qabaday*s in Lebanon (Auyero, 1999, 2001; Johnson, 1986). Intermediaries often, but not always, benefit from informal social standing as shaykhs, heads of extended families, or local notables – making them the local focal points and clearinghouses for clientelistic exchange (Kasara, 2007). Machines typically employ a large number of intermediaries, so brokers need not command particularly expansive networks – in fact, patrons have reason to discourage the cultivation of too wide a network around any broker for fear that a lieutenant may evolve into a rival. Nonetheless, patrons must contend with significant principal–agent problems in monitoring and disciplining their *brokers*, as Stokes et al. (2013) explain.

[20] The speaker is George Washington Plunkitt – see Riordon (1905, 27–28 *et passim*).
[21] Auyero (1999, 2001); Brusco et al. (2004); Schneider (2015); Stokes et al. (2013); Szwarcberg (2012, 2014). They can also use their embeddedness to wheedle additional information out of network members about behavior that the broker does not observe directly – in effect, spreading the monitoring duties throughout the network.

Reliance on rich information flows in social networks also serves a complementary, but less-frequently acknowledged, function: it provides a mechanism through which *clients* can monitor their *patrons*. Distributing benefits within social networks serves not only to advertise the patron's largesse and recruit new clients, but it also facilitates the efforts of existing clients to verify that the patron pays out rewards as promised by drawing on the accumulated experiences of network members with past payouts. This information advantage becomes particularly important for non-tangible rewards and those to be paid out at an indefinite date in the future. Increasing clients' access to information about past transactions reduces the uncertainty surrounding the exchange relationship with the patron. Compare the stylized model of dyadic relationships between patrons and clients who transact in an informational vacuum. In such a scenario, the clients' information about the patrons rests solely on their past personal experiences of exchange, which may be limited in both quantity, type, and duration. By tapping a network of clients in similar circumstances, however, each client can leverage the network's accumulated experiences over a much larger and varied number of exchanges to form a composite expectation of the patron's reliability.

Hence, embedding intermediaries deeply in social networks facilitates clientelistic exchange by reducing transaction costs. This observation begs an additional question, however: in which networks do patrons choose to embed intermediaries? Put another way, which networks do patrons choose to cultivate? As I argue later in this chapter, patrons utilize networks that help them minimize transaction costs. Ethnicity provides a linkage mechanism that makes ethnic networks particularly well-suited to reduce the costs of transacting.

2.3 ETHNICITY AND TRANSACTION COSTS

The previous section developed an argument about clientelistic exchange in the vote market; this section theorizes about how ethnicity facilitates transactions between patrons and clients. I previously suggested that, when politicians cannot make credible programmatic appeals to the electorate, they link to voters via other means such as clientelism. Clientelistic exchange does not, of course, eliminate the need for credible commitments; patrons and clients must be able to hold each other to the terms of the bargain. Typically, they do so by embedding individual transactions in an ongoing relationship of exchange and relying on information flows in dense social networks to monitor compliance. Why, though, do patrons and clients tap *ethnic* networks so frequently?

Early studies of politicized ethnicity tended to conceptualize ethnic identity as a primordial given that people naturally felt to be important and on which they acted accordingly. In contrast, subsequent scholarship has emphasized that identities are multiple rather than monolithic, context-driven in their importance, and often motivated, at least partially, by instrumental calculations rather than by pure affect. Contemporary studies have, in turn, drawn from this larger body of work on identity politics to identify several broad families of mechanisms to account for the formation of ethnic constituencies. Some works emphasize direct demand for identity goods, while others posit derived demand for material benefits.[22]

In contrast to demand-based accounts, I argue that ethnicity is itself a linkage mechanism that facilitates clientelistic exchange by reducing transaction costs. In particular, ethnically based networks often provide more efficient and reliable information flows to tap than their alternatives, while ascriptive membership rules inhibit members from disrupting the networks by switching between them. Patrons and clients therefore prefer to transact over ethnic networks because such links facilitate exchange rather than because of an intrinsic preference for interacting with coethnics. Because the cost of making credible commitments is higher across ethnic networks compared to within them, people strategically select coethnic partners for clientelistic exchange – producing an equilibrium strategy that we observe as "ethnic favoritism."[23]

2.3.1 Demand-Based Mechanisms

The first set of mechanisms cited to explain the formation of ethnic constituencies draws on demand-side accounts of people's tastes. Which tastes trump others, in turn, differs from narrative to narrative. Some studies underscore direct demand for symbolic identity goods, while others emphasize derived demand for tangible material benefits. Although frequently portrayed as competing motivations, the "identity versus materialism" debate is something of a false dichotomy – it is more likely that people value both kinds of benefits, but vary in their elasticities of demand for the two categories of goods.[24]

Hence, ethnic constituencies may satisfy people's direct demand for intangible, but nonetheless valued, psychological benefits. Politically influential ethnic constituencies can help satisfy demands for identity goods such as dignity and recognition, and even the desire to "bask in the reflected status of the patron." Voting their ethnicity may, in turn, provide people with expressive benefits. Finally, at a basic level, people may simply derive satisfaction from homophily: interacting with other people who are like themselves. Whether framed as ethnocentrism, personal expression, or demand for identity goods, this family

---

[22] For summaries of the broad conceptual debates over the three main *-isms* – primordialism, instrumentalism, and constructivism – see Chandra et al. (2001); Varshney (2003, 2007). Compare Bates (1974); Birnir (2007); Chandra (2004); Habyarimana et al. (2009); Horowitz (1985); Kasfir (1976); Ordeshook and Shvetsova (1994); Posner (2005); Shils (1957).
[23] Compare Bowles and Gintis (2004); Fafchamps (1992); Fearon and Laitin (1996); Greif (1994, 2006); Habyarimana et al. (2009).
[24] See Bratton et al. (2012); Chandra (2004); Corstange (2013).

of arguments draws its inspiration from an extensive line of inquiry in social psychology on intergroup relations.[25]

Alternately, ethnic constituencies may satisfy people's derived demand for material benefits – the desirable but scarce "goods of modernity" such as infrastructure or modern-sector jobs. One common narrative positing clustered tastes implies that coethnicity is coincidental rather than causal for the formation of political constituencies. Here, tastes cluster within groups but differ between them, so a vote for material interests is observationally equivalent to a vote for ethnicity. Tastes may, in fact, cluster ethnically, such as over the language of instruction in schools. Many of the "goods of modernity" may also cluster *geographically*, such as with infrastructure projects; given that ethnic groups tend to cluster residentially, a vote for "local interests" may in turn be observationally equivalent to a vote for ethnicity. Hence, coincidental tastes arguments provide a seemingly rationalist alternative to narratives stressing direct demand for identity goods.[26]

Citing derived demand for material benefits based on clustered tastes does not also explain why the key clusters should be ethnic; tastes may correlate with group membership, but do so on many dimensions besides ethnicity. As such, the "coincidental tastes" mechanism is descriptive rather than explanatory and does not tell us why people select ethnically based constituencies rather than, say, class-based alternatives. That is, this mechanism assumes that ethnicity trumps other dimensions of political difference rather than explains why it does so. Moreover, the material resources themselves are the same regardless of the identities of the politicians that supply them or the voters that consume them. Hence, to the degree that people care about the identity of their co-constituents, there must be auxiliary demand for ethnicity independent of the material resources pursued.

Demand-based arguments also implicitly posit that people in ethnic constituencies demand collective benefits. Insofar as club goods share some of the properties of public goods for everyone in the club – particularly the non-excludability property – the provision of these benefits should suffer from debilitating collective action problems.[27] Identity goods such as dignity and recognition accrue to all members of the group irrespective of individual efforts

---

[25] The "reflected status" quote is from Chandra (2004, 12). See also Horowitz (1985); Varshney (2003, 2007) on the social psychological component of ethnic politics and demand for identity goods, and Cutler (2002) for an example of homophily with ramifications for electoral behavior. For general reviews of the vast social psychological literature on intergroup relations, see Brewer and Brown (1998); Green and Seher (2003); Hewstone et al. (2002); Huddy (2001, 2003); Monroe et al. (2000); Tajfel (1982).

[26] The "goods of modernity" quote is from Bates (1974). Compare the arguments in Ferree (2006) on the observational equivalence of ethnic and material demands. Compare Alesina et al. (1999, 2000); Miguel and Gugerty (2005) for examples of arguments based on material demands.

[27] Corstange (2013); Green and Seher (2003); Ostrom (1990).

to secure the collective benefits. The material "goods of modernity," in turn, tend to be club goods such as paved roads or piped water that benefit the people who live in the region through which they run. Yet, because collective identity and material benefits are non-excludable in practice, we would expect free-riding to be rampant in the absence of mechanisms to police individual contributions to their supply – mechanisms about which the demand-based claims are silent.

Lastly, demand-based arguments imply that politicians can make credible commitments to the collective welfare of their ethnic groups. To make these mechanisms bite, voters must be able to verify that coethnic politicians actually share their group's policy preferences, monitor compliance with their campaign promises once in office, and punish politicians who shirk on those promises. Each of these tasks requires non-trivial effort on the part of individual voters on behalf of a collective benefit – the politician's accountability – and as such represent another collective action problem for the ethnic group. Hence, even if they share identity and material interests, voters have little reason to believe a coethnic politician's promises to pursue those interests solely on the basis of coethnicity. Consistent with these weaknesses, several studies find little empirical support for tastes-based arguments.[28]

2.3.2 Transactions-Based Mechanisms

Despite their intuitive appeal, demand-side accounts of ethnic constituencies do not, by themselves, resolve the problems of collective action and credible commitments that otherwise debilitate constituency maintenance. In contrast, an alternate family of mechanisms deemphasizes ethnicity's influence on tastes in favor of its impact on transacting. Hence, rather than focus on *what* people want, these accounts concentrate on *how* people get what they want. First, an "information technology" mechanism suggests that ethnic networks facilitate inexpensive and reliable information flows among members. Second, a strategic selection argument posits a self-reinforcing equilibrium strategy of cooperation between coethnics and non-interaction across ethnic groups.[29]

The information technology mechanism emphasizes the informational advantages of dense social networks within ethnic groups. According to this explanation, people engage in many more interactions with coethnics than they do with non-coethnics. Consequently, people have access to more and better information about members of their own ethnic group than they do about those of other ethnicities. Moreover, the networks embed individual

---

[28] Ferree (2006); Habyarimana et al. (2007a, 2009); Keefer (2010).
[29] For convenience, I use the mechanism terminology in Habyarimana et al. (2009), although different authors have referred to conceptually similar dynamics by different names (Bowles and Gintis, 2004; Chandra, 2004; Fearon and Laitin, 1996; Greif, 1994, 2006; Hammond and Axelrod, 2006; Horowitz, 1985; Landa, 1994; Posner, 2005).

2.3 Ethnicity and Transaction Costs

interactions in iterated, varied, and reinforcing relationships that lengthen the shadow of the future and motivate people to cultivate personal reputations for cooperation. People consequently prefer to transact within ethnic networks rather than across them because the networks provide tools for members to monitor each other and sanction misbehavior.[30] One weakness of information-based arguments, however, is that they commonly assert that ethnic networks are dense without elaborating on *why* they are dense or how they stay that way – points I take up later when discussing group boundary restrictions.

The most prominent transactions-based alternative to the information technology mechanism focuses on the strategic selection of interaction partners. This account rests on people's beliefs that members of the same ethnic group cooperate with each other but members of different groups do not. These expectations, in turn, drive equilibrium behavior as people seek out coethnics with whom to interact while avoiding non-coethnics. Hence, the strategic selection mechanism effectively rests on a self-fulfilling prophecy.[31] People turn to ethnicity because it facilitates transactions by helping them select reliable partners with whom to deal.

The strategic selection mechanism also suffers from weaknesses as an explanatory tool. First, it does not account for its own origins. Strategic selection implicitly rests on repeated interaction to make cooperative behavior viable, but does not explain why people began interacting in the first place. Second, the mechanism does not explain how the strategic selection equilibrium sustains itself against incentives for opportunism. A within-group cooperative strategy is a valuable club good for all coethnics, but is, therefore, subject to free-rider problems in its provision. It also suffers the threat of collapse in the absence of an enforcement mechanism. Without means to police compliance with the cooperative strategy, people have incentives to exploit their coethnic partners in each interaction while free-riding on the collectively supplied expectations for cooperation among coethnics. As such, the strategic selection equilibrium requires auxiliary mechanisms to account for its origins, maintenance, and enforcement.

2.3.3 Transacting in Ethnic Networks

Combined, the information technology mechanism and its strategic selection counterpart provide the microfoundations for ethnically based clientelism.

---

[30] Although Habyarimana et al. (2009) introduced the "information technology" moniker, numerous scholars have argued for dense social networks within ethnic groups (Bowles and Gintis, 2004; Fearon and Laitin, 1996; Greif, 1994, 2006; Landa, 1994; Rauch, 2001).

[31] Compare Fearon and Laitin (2000, 856 fn. 31) on cultural equilibria and Hilton and von Hippel (1996, 244) on self-fulfilling prophecies. On the strategic selection mechanism more generally, see Axelrod et al. (2002); Chandra (2004); Cohen et al. (2001); Greif (1994, 2006); Habyarimana et al. (2009); Hammond and Axelrod (2006); Horowitz (1985); Posner (2005).

As I argue later in this chapter, small-scale units within ethnic groups have dense social networks of strong ties while connecting to each other via weak ties. Ascriptive-like membership rules, in turn, help to keep networks intact by raising the costs of switching networks to prohibitive levels. Cheaper and more reliable monitoring on the network makes within-group transactions less costly relative to off-network transactions across groups. These information-based transactional advantages underpin the strategic selection mechanism, which in turn reinforces the informational advantages enjoyed by ethnic groups. Put together, these mechanisms imply that patrons and clients cannot make credible commitments to just anyone – they can only make them to people that they can police efficiently, which, in practice, means coethnics.[32]

Information-based accounts often cite dense social networks among coethnics, but, on its face, the "dense networks" claim is difficult to sustain at the macro level. When defined inclusively, large-scale ethnic groups can easily include millions of people. At this level of aggregation, such groups are not social networks, but rather imagined communities in Anderson's (1991, 6) sense that "members ... will never know most of their fellow-members, meet them, or even hear of them, yet in the minds of each lives the image of their communion." Consequently, it strains credulity to suppose that a "dense social network" connects millions of community members to each other.

It is, however, considerably less difficult to imagine social networks linking people together within the smaller-scale units that pyramid within ethnic groups.[33] Disaggregating down to constituent units such as tribes, clans, parishes, branches, and extended families reduces the extent of the networks that members must labor to cultivate. As the collectivities get smaller in scope, the connections between people within them become less costly to maintain. They also increasingly approximate the dense social networks about which we theorize, with members interacting repeatedly in a wide variety of social exchanges.[34]

Small groups use a variety of mechanisms to maintain the density of their local networks.[35] In practical terms, many groups concentrate residentially;

---

[32] Compare Ostrom (1990, 45) argument that people cannot make credible commitments until they first solve the problem of monitoring.

[33] For arguments related to the pyramiding of smaller scale groups within ethnic groups, compare Horowitz (1985, 59) and Dixit (2004, 65–66 *et passim*). There are some broad parallels here to anthropology's old segmentary lineage theory (Caton, 1987; Dresch, 1988; Gellner and Munson, Jr., 1995; Kuper, 1982; Smith, 1956). My intent is not to revive this model, but rather to note the flexibility in seemingly rigid group membership rules based on putative descent. In particular, people can make the criteria for ascriptive membership inclusive or exclusive in order to imagine larger or smaller collectivities (Corstange, 2012a; Roccas and Brewer, 2002).

[34] Bowles and Gintis (2004); Fafchamps (1992); Hoff and Sen (2006); Ostrom (1990).

[35] Compare computational models of cooperation among agents that concentrate either spatially or "diasporically" (Axelrod et al., 2002; Cohen et al., 2001; Hammond and Axelrod, 2006).

2.3 Ethnicity and Transaction Costs

multiple generations of the same family may cohabitate in shared houses, extended families populate villages and neighborhoods, and larger units such as clans or tribes frequently claim a territorial base. Moreover, members interact across multiple domains – not just transacting in a market or a workplace, but also gathering for family functions and holidays, weekly religious services and subsequent family time, leisure activities and club events, and many other day-to-day interactions that put members in repeated and close proximity with one another. Further, many such groups self-insure economically and share risks by diversifying their income streams across generations and space, thus tying individual welfare strongly to collective welfare.[36] Members not only have access to detailed information about each other's past histories and track records, but also strong incentive to monitor each other to make sure that no members shirk their family obligations and to punish those that do.[37]

Ascriptive membership, meanwhile, helps to stabilize the network's composition by making it difficult to leave one network and join another.[38] In principle, of course, descent-based rules make it impossible to switch groups: one is either born into the group or is not. In practice, however, switching is simply costly – perhaps prohibitively so – but occasionally occurs through such recognized procedures such as adoption, conversion, intermarriage, and so on.[39] Ascription therefore deters switching by imposing personal, social,

---

[36] See Bates (1983a, 1990, 2001); Fafchamps (1992); Platteau (1991); Scott (1976). In societies with weak law and order institutions, family also provides physical security, as in the institution of the feud or vendetta (Fearon and Laitin, 1996; Hardin, 1995).

[37] Enforcement is itself a collective good subject to free-rider problems. However, groups that are sufficiently small in number are much more likely to overcome these barriers (Hardin, 1982; Olson, 1965; Ostrom, 1990). In addition, individual enforcement costs are often modest. Dense networks considerably reduce the cost of monitoring members. Punishment, in turn, often takes the form of social ostracization or cutting off offending members from group benefits for a period of time.

[38] Work in social psychology notes that ascribed identities are "quite difficult to change" rather than impossible (Huddy, 2003, 536); changing identities has long been central to constructivist arguments about ethnic politics (Chandra, 2006; Chandra et al., 2001). Nonetheless, people may adopt beliefs about natural or unchanging social categories – what Fearon and Laitin (2000, 848) call "everyday primordialism" – and behave *as if* the categories are unchanging.

[39] In Yemen, for example, tribesmen who switch tribes or tribes that switch confederations engage in the process of "fraternization" (my imperfect gloss for *mu'akha* – more literally, "becoming brothers"). The process is not particularly common, but sufficiently so that people still distinguish between the original tribes of the Hashid and Bakil confederations and those that "Hashidized" or "Bakilized" (*mutahashida* and *mutabakila*). See Abu Ghanim (1985, 35, 74–76) and Abu Ghanim (1990, 219) for details. Consider the many kinship idioms that we use unthinkingly: blood brothers, brothers in arms, sorority sisters, joining Mother Church to become a brother in Christ, and so on. Consider also the Latin roots of commonly used terms such as *affiliate*, *matriculate*, or *fraternize*, each of which bears biological connotations. Poignantly for this book, also consider the Latin root behind *patronize* and *patron*.

and transactional costs on the switcher.[40] Further, it also deters opportunism within existing networks by lending weight to threats of ostracization.

Dense networks within the smaller-scale units facilitate clientelism by reducing transaction costs and making exchanges between patrons and clients more secure. The information flows within these units generate common knowledge on the network – everyone knows what everyone else is doing, everyone knows that everyone knows, and so on in an infinite regress. Network-based common knowledge, in turn, reduces the cost of monitoring and enforcing clientelistic bargains.[41] First, it provides intermediaries with rich and easily accessible information about voter behavior, as well as the idiosyncratic needs of individual clients, hence reducing patrons' monitoring and distribution costs. Second, it pools voters' personal experiences and helps them to verify patron largesse and reliability in many interactions besides their own – hence facilitating clients' efforts to monitor their patrons.

Superior information technology makes transactions on the network more efficient than those across networks. Neither affect nor an intrinsic desire to interact with coethnics for its own sake need enter either party's considerations; informational advantages are sufficient to elicit preferences for coethnic partners. Nonetheless, social psychological processes can reinforce these information-based mechanisms rather than compete with them. Affinity, homophily, and ethnocentrism facilitate transactions by creating shared expectations and directing similar people to the same networks. By providing additional incentives to interact within-network, they increase the differential in the cost of transacting on versus off the network – making coethnic partners even more attractive.[42]

Ethnicity facilitates clientelism by reducing transaction costs between coethnics, but it also *constrains* clientelism by placing limits on who can make credible commitments to whom. In particular, ethnicity's informational advantages reduce the cost of transacting within ethnic groups relative to transacting across them. Dense networks create common knowledge within

---

[40] Switchers may, for example, lose friendships or social connections from their old networks. They must also pay the costs of developing personal reputations on the new network, which they enter without a track record and so represent risky transaction partners. To develop a record for trustworthiness to which network members can refer, new entrants may need to transact on less favorable terms or otherwise send costly signals of their new fidelity.

[41] See Chwe (2001) and Patel (2007, chs. 2–3) on the creation of common knowledge. Williamson (1985, 29) cites the importance of economizing on measurement costs, while Ostrom (1990, 36) highlights how social capital reduces transaction costs.

[42] The relationship between ethnocentrism and ethnic network-based clientelism is likely endogenous – ethnocentrism may contribute to people using their ethnic networks, but the benefits of such transactions may, in turn, make people more ethnocentric (compare Hardin 1995 on constrained epistemologies). To the degree that there are other, auxiliary reasons to prefer coethnics – that is, not due to the benefits of transacting – these processes complement the information-based mechanisms.

groups rather than between them. Politicians, therefore, lack the informational resources to monitor voters off the network, while the latter only pool their experiences within-network when monitoring the former's compliance.[43] Consequently, patrons and clients select partners strategically by seeking out coethnics with whom to transact. Information advantages and strategic selection combine to hamper the ability of patrons and clients to make credible commitments across ethnic lines, thus concentrating clientelistic exchange within ethnic groups and retarding it between them.

2.4 ETHNICITY AND PROTECTED VOTE MARKETS

In one sense, patrons and clients both benefit from ethnic links – they facilitate clientelistic exchange where it might otherwise be very costly. Yet reliance on ethnic links also alters the structure of the vote market within which the parties transact. In particular, ethnicity encourages market segmentation, with each segment serving as a protected market for its communal elites. Client welfare, in turn, depends crucially on the competitive environment *within* communities – whether multiple patrons must compete for support, or whether a single patron dominates it. Ethnic monopsonies are thus a form of market failure that yields undesirable outcomes from the viewpoint of constituents. How, though, might vote markets fail in the first place? Once they fail, why might the markets not self-correct? The former question asks about the origins of monopsony, while the latter asks about its persistence.

2.4.1 Origins of Monopsony

Many studies of ethnic politics focus on between-group competition and make the simplifying assumption, implicitly or explicitly, of within-group unity. The usefulness of such an abstraction depends, of course, on the model that invokes it. Yet, empirically, the assertion of ethnic group unity is frequently inaccurate; within-group competition is more common than the simplifying assumption implies. For ethnic groups, factional competition often manifests in both day-to-day politics and the more extreme conditions of civil wars.[44] Within-group

---

[43] Compare Bowles and Gintis (2004); Calvo and Murillo (2013); Fearon and Laitin (1996).
[44] Ethnographic work often emphasizes factional disputes beneath the veneer of ethnic group unity; earlier generations of anthropological studies worked to develop variants of segmentary lineage theory, which focused conceptually on group factionalism. On ethnic factionalism in civil wars, see Asal et al. (2012); Christia (2012); Cunningham (2011); Cunningham et al. (2012); Cunningham and Weidmann (2010); Pearlman and Cunningham (2012); Staniland (2012). We commonly make analogous assumptions about party unity when studying political parties, even as we acknowledge internal factions and party wings. See, e.g., Aldrich (1995); Cox (1997); Grzymala-Busse (2007); Magaloni (2006); Scheiner (2006). Note also arguments about factionalism within ethnic groups that manifest as competing political parties (Fearon and Laitin, 2000; Horowitz, 1985; Lijphart, 1977; Rabushka and Shepsle, 1972).

competition is not rare; what political dynamics, then, lead to the emergence of monopsonies?

One potential path to market failure is that one of the factions subdues its rivals by winning a decisive electoral victory over them. We might also envision a group of factions allying against other factions, of course, but, as I describe later in this chapter, such a cartel would be internally competitive and unstable given incentives to cheat allies. We can imagine several possible paths to victory: a highly attractive electoral platform, access to state resources to dispense as patronage, use of the security apparatus to harass opponents, and so on. Yet we can also raise objections to these possibilities. Where programs are non-credible, it is difficult to believe that an electoral program could be the key to a decisive victory; contrariwise, where programs are credible, it is unclear why at least some factions would not run to the ethnic group's median voter. Distributing state patronage and deploying the security apparatus may indeed aid a faction in crushing its rivals – such tools have helped many dominant parties win victories throughout the developing world. But citing access to state resources to explain victory does not explain how the victorious faction, and not its rivals, achieved that access in the first place.

Alternately, conflict with other ethnic groups could motivate within-group factions to form an alliance to counteract threats from rival communities. Such threats could be about physical security, as with riots or militia fighting in civil wars, but could also be about access to resources or less tangible desirables such as prestige or status. It is unclear, however, that competitive pressures from out-groups are sufficient to close in-group ranks, or keep fractious alliances stable in the context of temptations to defect. Perceived threats from other ethnic groups may indeed stimulate demand for ethnic group unity, but the threats themselves offer no guidance over which elites should lead the unified group. Hence, we might expect conflict with other groups to provoke ethnic outbidding among elites maneuvering for influence – that is, *more* rather than less within-group competition.

Were elites to cobble together an alliance, moreover, they would face temptations to cheat their allies, as is the case with cartels more generally. We might expect the factional components of the cartel to jockey for preeminence within the alliance and for favorable positions from which to compete against their erstwhile allies in future elections. Further, each faction also faces incentives to defect and ally with an out-group in order to defeat its internal rivals. Hence, out-group competition may indeed increase demand for unity. Yet, in the absence of preexisting unity, we may expect elite factions to compete over how best to achieve that goal and who should lead the unified community.

Electoral victory so decisive as to eliminate subsequent factional competition may, therefore, be impractical to achieve in the absence of preexisting dominance that could render such a victory possible in the first place. Alternately,

2.4 Ethnicity and Protected Vote Markets

then, monopsony may emerge from competition conducted through physical force – one faction eliminates its coethnic rivals via coups, assassinations, or some form of paramilitary action. At the extreme end, one might expect civil wars to heighten demand for ethnic unity to counter perceived existential threats from other ethnic groups. In practice, however, within-community factionalism frequently persists against the backdrop of the larger war, and rival militias often inflict huge losses on each other in internecine fighting. Such fighting provides incentives for the factions to seek out allies from other communities or foreign powers in the hopes of subduing coethnic rivals, but such alliances often provoke ethnic outbidding and reactionary interventions.[45]

Physical force may therefore eliminate some or all of a group's elite factions, particularly if outside parties intervene to tip the balance of power between the factions. If one faction defeats the others – or if all factions collapse, leaving a vacuum – market failure occurs because rivals compete via extraconstitutional means. Hence, the vote market ceases to exist in even approximate form because votes no longer allocate authority.

2.4.2 Monopsony Maintenance

Monopsonies emerge out of vote market failure. We might wonder, however, whether monopsonies, once they emerge, can be self-sustaining, or whether the vote markets will self-correct. At the mass level, why would constituents tolerate the lack of choice; what prevents them from selecting a different patron? At the elite level, why would new rivals not emerge to challenge the monopsonist?

Elites have several tools available to perpetuate monopsony once it exists. First, elites can take the lead in policing their community's social boundaries

---

[45] Lebanon's long civil war provides numerous examples of within-community fighting. Rival Christian forces frequently attacked each other as the emerging Lebanese Forces militia sought to liquidate its rivals in the early period of the war, while the Lebanese Forces fought destructive battles against Michel Aoun's Christian army units at the war's end. Amal and Hizballah, the two largest Shia militias, fought long-running and deeply destructive battles against each other as each attempted to establish its hegemony over the Shia community.

Yemen's civil wars reveal analogous factionalism among ostensibly united groups. The 1962–1970 civil war in the north pitted Zaydi tribes against each other in the battles between royalists and republicans. The 1994 war in united Yemen, meanwhile, showcased southern factionalism between Ali Salim al-Baydh's secessionist forces and the Ali Nasser partisans who had lost the south's 1986 civil war and fled to the north. On ethnic factionalism and ethnic outbidding in civil wars more generally, compare Asal et al. (2012); Christia (2008, 2012); Corstange and Marinov (2012); Cunningham (2006, 2011); Cunningham et al. (2012); Cunningham and Weidmann (2010); Fearon (1998); Horowitz (1985); Rabushka and Shepsle (1972); Staniland (2012).

and try to exert control over their constituents' networks.[46] Well-policed boundaries benefit both patron and client by facilitating within-group exchange, but several factors give elites an encompassing interest in boundary maintenance. Patrons typically transact with many clients, so multiply transaction cost savings across each voter. Moreover, patrons benefit from segmented vote markets, so policing boundaries helps to forestall exit by dissatisfied voters. And, by exerting control over community networks – such as by organizing cultural clubs, infiltrating syndicates, or controlling news media – hegemonic patrons can make it more difficult for voters to coordinate on an alternative leader from within their community.

When policing boundaries, elites can, of course, extol the self-serving virtues of ethnic unity – advantageous when coethnic rivals have already been eliminated and solidarity serves to reinforce their own authority. Elites can also manipulate conflicts with other communities to stimulate demand for group unity. Maintaining conflicts allows elites to encourage vulnerability concerns in their constituents, whether in the form of physical insecurity in the context of violent conflict, or status insecurity in less extreme forms of competition. Vulnerability, in turn, makes constituents more amenable to monopsony. Perceptions of heightened competition with other groups encourages people to emphasize zero-sum, comparative outcomes in which they focus on differentials between groups, even at their own expense. Moreover, vulnerability concerns can induce constituents to trade off material resources for physical security or non-tangibles such as status affirmations.[47]

Elites can also perpetuate monopsony by cultivating an aura of electoral invincibility by building oversized coalitions and turning out supporters to the polls even in the absence of real electoral competition.[48] First, broadcasting the image of invincibility helps to deter defections from the patron's coalition. Overwhelming margins, whether real or manufactured, demonstrate to constituents that challengers stand no chance of winning at the polls and help to persuade voters not to waste their votes on non-viable candidates. Second, electoral invincibility helps to deter defections from *brokers* and local notables. To the degree that the latter deliver votes in blocs, they have the capacity to coordinate voters around alternate candidates. Convincing brokers that no viable alternatives exist mitigates the temptation to defect to opponents.

---

[46] Many studies examine how political entrepreneurs push public discourse to focus on nationalist and ethnic identities in order to carve out constituencies based on these social categories. Compare Anderson (1991); Birnir (2007); Chandra (2004); Eifert et al. (2010); Fearon and Laitin (2000); Gellner (1983); Hobsbawm (1990); Posner (2005).

[47] Compare Brewer and Brown (1998); Green and Seher (2003); Horowitz (1985); Huddy (2001, 2003); Tajfel (1982).

[48] Compare Blaydes (2011) and especially Magaloni (2006) on the aura of invincibility. For an example of an extreme case surrounding a cult of personality, see Wedeen (1999) for the mobilizing efforts of the Syrian regime.

Moreover, cultivating an aura of invincibility helps monopsonists to co-opt potential rivals by convincing the latter that their political careers are better served as junior partners in the monopsony rather than as rivals to it. By offering attractive positions in the parliament, bureaucracy, or diplomatic corps, monopsonists can buy off many careerist rivals. If, however, competitors refuse co-optation, patrons can instead crush them electorally with well-organized and better-financed political machines. This implicit threat, in turn, helps to deter rivals from mounting challenges to the monopsonist. The deterring effect of massive resources and political organization, in turn, implies that dominant patrons rarely need to mobilize their resources fully.[49]

In sum, internal competition for community leadership is not uncommon, although vote markets sometimes fail. Once a monopsony emerges, market failure can persist as elites use a variety of tools to perpetuate political dominance in their communities. Hegemons can police boundaries to raise the cost of crossing ethnic lines and manipulate conflict to increase demand for group unity. By cultivating an aura of invincibility, they can prevent defections and deter new rivals from emerging – in effect, channeling people's strategic choices in their favor.

2.5 IMPLICATIONS

This theory of ethnic constituencies yields three sets of observable implications about the structure of the vote market, its ramifications for voter welfare, and strategic behavior by elites. First, internal political competition should increase the volume and value of clientelistic transactions. Second, voters should receive better rewards when their votes are in high demand, but may need to compete with one another for patronage in uncompetitive environments. Third, elites should try to select institutions strategically and eliminate internal competitors in order to secure market power. I elaborate on each of these points next.

2.5.1 Market Power

Electoral competition, or the lack thereof, influences the balance of market power in clientelistic exchanges. One can broadly situate this dynamic within the context of a Rubinstein-style bargaining model between a patron and client. Loosely, competitive pressures shorten the former's time horizon because failure to conclude the bargain means the risk of losing the election; the lack of competition, in contrast shortens the latter's time horizon because failure to conclude the bargain means the value of the ballot disappears after the election.

---

[49] The deterence of candidate entry works analogously to the resolution to the chain store paradox (Selten, 1978; Trockel, 1986).

As Rubinstein-style models show, the more patient party – the one with the longer time horizons – gets better terms in equilibrium.

Hence, electoral contestation between dueling patrons bids up the value of the vote within their community. People have credible options from which to choose, so competitive pressures compel politicians to reach out to more, and more expensive, voters. Hence, hegemonic patrons are better positioned to set the value of their rewards than are politicians in internally competitive communities. Moreover, they are also better positioned to pick and choose which clients to patronize. Insofar as hegemonic politicians do not need active support from all of their nominal constituents, they can select voters making modest demands and price discriminate between them.

2.5.2 Which Voters?

All else equal, politicians prefer cheaper voters to their more demanding counterparts. One of the most frequently made observations in studies of clientelism, in fact, is that political machines prefer to target *poor* voters. One common rationale for this preference is the declining marginal utility of income: a poor person derives more benefits from a reward of a given value than does a rich person. Consequently, modestly valued rewards may satisfy poor constituents, whereas their richer counterparts may demand much costlier payoffs. An alternative rationale is that poor voters have shorter time horizons than do their wealthier peers and place greater value on cheaper benefits in the present than on more lucrative payoffs in the future. In either case, we expect poor people to have lower reservation prices – the value below which they will not trade their support – than richer voters.[50] Moreover, we might expect all politicians to prefer small payouts to large ones, but that patrons who dominate their own communities will be better able to minimize the number of expensive payoffs they make.

Reservation prices are not the only factor behind vote cost, however. As argued earlier, transaction costs are lower within communities than across them, which, all else equal, makes patrons prefer coethnic clients over non-coethnics. Transaction costs may also vary *within* constituencies, however. In particular, voters that are easier to monitor and police should be less costly and, therefore, more attractive to politicians.

Due to cost differences, politicians, if given the choice, may prefer to distribute scarce patronage resources among rural voters rather than their urban counterparts. First, as a stylized fact, residents of rural areas tend to be poorer

---

[50] Compare arguments in Blaydes (2011); Magaloni (2006); Stokes et al. (2013); Weitz-Shapiro (2014). Gans-Morse et al. (2014) show, theoretically, conditions under which parties may be willing to patronize richer voters, while Chubb (1982, ch. 4) provides empirical evidence that clientelistic parties frequently patronize middle class voters.

than their urban counterparts and, as such, may make more modest demands. Second, given the geographic concentration of ethnic groups, villages tend to be more homogenous than cities. Insofar as they work with a diversified portfolio of patronage benefits, politicians have incentives to allocate club goods and private payoffs to supporters in different areas. Patrons may thus be able to leverage economies of scale and distribute club goods to rural residents, while reserving privately consumed benefits such as jobs to supporters in mixed areas, where they need to exercise more precise targeting. Moreover, more homogenous localities may, in turn, have denser social networks – which help to reduce monitoring and policing costs. Villagers' relative lack of mobility further contributes to low monitoring costs, and their limited outside options make them especially subject to capture.

Electoral competition affects not only how much voters get for their support, but also how many voters get anything at all. Competitive communities should enjoy lively vote markets, while monopsonized markets should provide little impetus for patrons to mobilize their constituents en masse. Insofar as voters have no credible outside options, hegemonic patrons can pick and choose the clients to whom they distribute rewards. As such, we should expect to observe perverse accountability – and perverse competition – in dominated communities: rather than candidates competing for votes, clients compete for patronage.

2.5.3 Elite Strategies

Although competition may improve voter welfare, patrons clearly prefer monopsonistic vote buying to competitive clientelism. As such, they face strong incentives to restrict electoral competition. Broadly, strategic elites can manipulate institutions to raise the political salience of ethnicity in order to give themselves access to protected vote markets segmented along ethnic lines. Doing so, however, implies some degree of collusion, implicit or explicit, between elites from different communities. This collusion may take constitutional forms as with federalism, community quotas, or, more explicitly, consociationalism – a "cartel of elites," to use Lijphart's choice phrase.[51] We might also expect elites to collude over electoral rules and districting. Threats of electoral violence and demands by voters for descriptive representation – that they be represented by "one of their own" – serve as ready justification for gerrymandered districts dominated by one community or another. Aligning *electoral* constituencies with *ethnic* constituencies, however, serves the double purpose of protecting local vote markets from between-group competition that would require costly mobilization efforts by patrons.

---

[51] See Lijphart (1969, 1977, 1981, 2001). More broadly on institutional engineering, compare Andeweg (2000); Birnir (2007); Brancati (2006, 2009); Horowitz (1991); Rabushka and Shepsle (1972); Reilly (2006); Steiner (1981).

Elites also face incentives to reduce the degree of competition within their own communities. As argued earlier, they may attempt to collude with coethnic rivals to form communal "unity coalitions" or "solidarity fronts," or else co-opt weaker competitors. To the degree they can achieve within-community dominance, we can expect them to try to deter entry by new opponents by cultivating auras of invincibility and crushing incipient rivals before the latter can establish themselves.

Hegemonic patrons that dominate their communities position themselves as the only credible partners for clientelistic exchange. As such, they approximate the "single machine" ideal type that faces only opponents making programmatic rather than clientelistic appeals to voters. In these circumstances, hegemons can take steps to keep the programmatic opposition weak and divided.[52] Broadly, they can stake out the amorphous middle of the policy space to remain as ideologically inoffensive as possible to as many voters as possible while splitting the opposition into rival ideological poles. Moreover, they can perpetuate splits in the opposition by selectively incorporating factions of the latter in short-term alliances.

2.6 CONCLUSION

This chapter started with a conceptual puzzle: how can ethnic favoritism and ethnic neglect coexist? Empirically, we often observe politically allocated resources flowing along ethnic lines, and yet mass constituents often receive meager rewards for their political support. Existing accounts in the academic literature on ethnic politics tend to focus on ethnic favoritism, but usually fail to address how lucrative or miserly "favoritism" turns out to be. In contrast, this chapter developed a transactions-based theory of ethnic politics that explains both why resources flow along ethnic lines *and* when the flow is a deluge or a trickle.

Clientelism links politicians and their constituents when politicians cannot make credible programmatic promises. Tools such as machines and brokers help to overcome barriers to clientelistic exchange by enabling patrons and clients to make credible commitments to each other. Ethnic networks, in turn, facilitate clientelism by reducing both the uncertainty and costs of transacting. Reduced transaction costs drive both patrons and clients to prefer coethnic partners for clientelistic exchange.

Strategic selection, however, segments the vote market into ethnic constituencies with prohibitively high barriers to entry and exit. Electoral competition between dueling patrons drives up the value of the vote and the number of votes demanded. Communities that unify behind a single, hegemonic patron, meanwhile, trap their members in monopsonies with minimal payoffs to

---

[52] See Lust-Okar (2004, 2005); Magaloni (2006); Stokes (2009).

2.6 Conclusion

political support. Efforts to streamline clientelistic exchange produce the phenomenon of ethnic favoritism, while efforts to restrict within-group competition yield ethnic neglect.

From here on, subsequent chapters delve into the data to test some of the observable implications of the book's theoretical claims. The next chapters introduce the book's main empirical venues, Lebanon and Yemen, and describes the diverging competitive environments found in the two countries' various communities. It then explores several of the observable implications about elite behavior as leaders try to restrict competition within their own constituencies. Subsequent chapters turn to mass-level implications to answer the questions "who gets what?" and "how much?" These latter chapters explore differences in clientelistic exchange between internally competitive and uncompetitive communities from the client's point of view.

3

Communal Politics in Lebanon

3.1 INTRODUCTION: AN ELECTORAL PUZZLE

Lebanon held parliamentary by-elections in August 2007 to replace two assassinated deputies from the western-leaning ruling coalition – one from the Sunni community, and another from the Maronite Christian community. Although held on the same day in districts that were scarcely more than ten kilometers apart, the elections differed dramatically in both the intensity of their campaigns and the closeness of their results.[1] Despite repeated attempts in the preceding months to find a consensus candidate for the Christian seat – including a proposal to award the seat to the assassinated deputy's father by acclamation – government- and opposition-aligned Christians put forward candidates for the fiercely contested seat. The former nominated former President Amin al-Gemayel against a candidate from Michel Aoun's opposition-aligned Free Patriotic Movement, the largest Christian faction in parliament. Taking on added gravity, at the time of the by-election, local observers saw Gemayel and Aoun as rivals in the upcoming presidential elections scheduled for later in the year.

In contrast, no uncertainty lingered over the outcome of the Sunni contest, in which the candidate of the Future Movement ran virtually unopposed. According to local election monitors, the nominee's two main "opponents" were, in fact, his own campaign manager and deputy campaign manager, who, according to the monitors, submitted their candidacies in order to hire three sets of "candidate representatives" instead of one. No other factions bothered to

---

[1] The by-elections were held to fill Walid Eido's Sunni seat in Beirut and Pierre al-Gemayel's Maronite seat in the Metn district immediately to the east of Beirut. The latter was assassinated in November 2006, and the former in June 2007, as part of a string of unsolved murders of anti-Syrian politicians over the preceding two years.

3.1 Introduction: An Electoral Puzzle

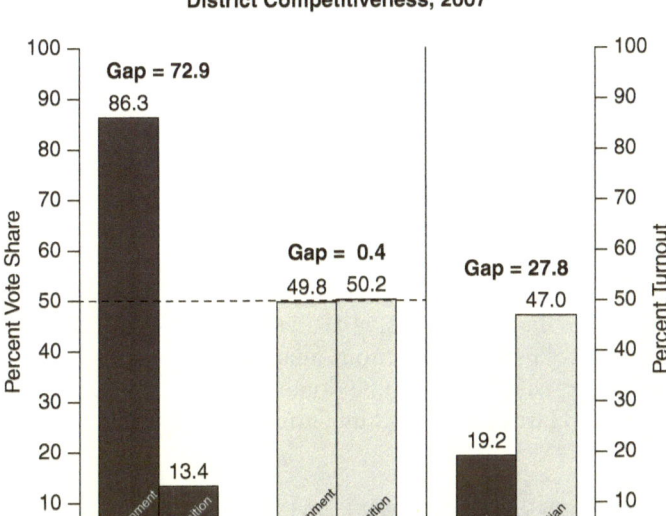

FIGURE 3.1: 2007 By-Election Results: Sunni Landslide, Christian Cliffhanger

register because they knew they had no chance of winning. Reflecting the lack of opposition, campaigning for the Sunni seat barely registered in the public consciousness and received virtually no coverage in the press.[2]

In contrast, boisterous campaign rallies for the two Christian candidates drew thousands of enthusiastic supporters and attracted widespread media coverage and seemingly endless political analysis. Election results, as summarized in Figure 3.1, reflected the diverging competitiveness of the races. Less than 20 percent of the electorate turned out in Beirut, and the Future Movement's Sunni candidate won his seat in a landslide with some 86 percent of the vote – more than six times that of his closest "rival." Meanwhile, turnout doubled for the Christian contest, and although Gemayel took the majority of Maronite votes, the opposition candidate won the seat by only a handful of ballots – less than one-half of 1 percent of the vote – due to stronger support from other Christian constituencies in the district.[3]

---

[2] According to senior officials in the Lebanese Association for Democratic Elections (LADE), the country's premier election monitoring organization, the Future Movement registered three candidates for the seat and then withdrew two of them after the official withdrawal deadline. Interviews, Beirut, July 2008.

[3] For a breakdown of the vote by precinct, see "Fierce confrontation in Metn draws new political contours: Aoun wins election by 418 votes and Gemayel reaps the Maronite majority," *al-Nahar*, 6 August 2007.

These contests, as with *any* elections, mixed idiosyncracies with more general patterns. Yet the possibility that the observed differences between them may generalize makes them intriguing. How did these two sectarian communities arrive at a point where their elections could differ so dramatically in competitiveness? Were these outcomes merely peculiarities of the districts involved, or do they reflect systematic differences between the communities? This chapter addresses these questions by exploring the political evolution of the main sectarian constituencies in Lebanon. In doing so, it attempts to establish the broad differences found in their internal competitive environments. It demonstrates that competition in the Christian community extends throughout the country, even as the two main Shia parties, Hizballah and the Amal Movement, closed ranks to form a collusive but fractious alliance. It then traces how the Sunni community progressively came to be dominated by a single faction under the leadership of the Hariri family and its Future Movement.

3.2 INSTITUTIONS AND COMMUNALISM

Religious identities have long been central to Lebanese public life, and the country has experimented with various power-sharing arrangements over the years to regulate conflict and cooperation between its religious communities.[4] Originally a minor tax farm with shifting borders inside the Ottoman Empire's Syrian provinces, Mount Lebanon began to acquire the antecedents of its power-sharing practices when Christian–Druze conflicts in the mid-nineteenth century attracted intervention by several European powers. Reforms imposed at the time laid the basis for various institutions and the principles of communal representation that received greater elaboration in the European colonial period.

After the collapse of the Ottoman Empire at the end of the first world war, France established the state of Greater Lebanon by attaching parts of its Syrian mandate to Mount Lebanon, including Beirut and Muslim-dominant areas to its north, south, and east. Although Christian demands for an economically viable entity provided the pretext for the new borders, attaching Muslim-heavy areas also enhanced Christian dependency on France by reducing them to a bare demographic majority in the new state. France governed the mandate for the next two decades with variations on the basic power-sharing institutions that granted communal representation and attempted to coax Muslim opponents of the new state, particularly in the Sunni community, to participate in its affairs.

---

[4] A number of general as well as specialized histories of Lebanon exist (e.g., Akarli, 1993; Firro, 2003; Makdisi, 2000; Traboulsi, 2007). As Salibi (1988) observed in the midst of the civil war, however, much of Lebanese history is itself contested. I do not attempt to enter into these debates in this brief historical overview, which serves the much more modest purpose of providing some of the basic institutional context within which to consider competition – or the lack thereof – between and within Lebanon's sectarian communities in the contemporary period.

3.2 Institutions and Communalism

Lebanon achieved independence in 1943 and adopted a series of power-sharing practices that built upon those used in the mandate period. The written constitution and unwritten National Pact divided key executive positions and other senior state posts between the confessional communities, allocated positions in the civil service proportionally between the sects, and, reflecting the supposed demographic weight of the communities at the time, allocated seats in parliament on a 6 : 5 ratio between Christians and Muslims.[5] Lebanon adopted a variety of different electoral laws from independence up to the 1960s when the law stablized for three straight elections, but each version rested on the same basic principles. Aside from occasional forays into single-member districts, most laws specified multimember districts with quota-based plurality voting. Each seat was allocated by confessional community: only cosectarians could run for a given seat, although all voters registered in the district voted for all seats, irrespective of sectarian affiliation. Hence, the electoral system reinforced the political centrality of sect that had been enshrined in the constitution and national pact, but attempted to build in incentives for leaders to build electoral alliances across communities in what Hudson (1968, 213) called a "mutual coattail effect" as electoral list members encouraged their cosectarians to vote for their list mates.[6]

Lebanese elections became increasingly clean and competitive over the years, but two major challenges threatened state institutions in the lead-up to the start of the civil war. First, the Palestine Liberation Organization (PLO) became increasingly active in Lebanon in the late-1960s and early-1970s, particularly after being expelled from Jordan in 1970. The PLO had widespread support among Lebanon's Muslim – and especially Sunni – population, and began to operate with increasing impunity along the country's southern border with Israel, which came to be known as "Fatahland" after the dominant faction

---

[5] The controversial 1932 census – never since repeated – found a demographic majority of Christians to Muslims on a rough 6 : 5 ratio, although a number of manipulations may have inflated the ratio in favor of Christian residents (Maktabi, 1999). Although parliamentary representation followed this 6 : 5 ratio, the cabinet composition itself followed the principle of parity between Christian and Muslim ministers. Note that, as is commonly observed, the national pact allocated, by custom, the presidency to a Maronite Christian, the premiership to a Sunni Muslim, and the speakership to a Shia Muslim, but the latter custom took slightly longer to institutionalize than the former two – Lebanon had a Greek Orthodox speaker for nearly six months in its first year of independence.

[6] Compare Corstange (2010); el Khazen (2000); Hudson (1968). To clarify with an example, consider a hypothetical district with three seats: one Maronite seat, one Druze seat, and one Shia seat. Only Maronites could run for the Maronite seat, only Druze for the Druze seat, and only Shia for the Shia seat, but all voters in the district would cast votes for all three seats. In practice, politicians created electoral alliances – often temporary in nature – to form a single electoral list and urged their cosectarians to vote for their allies on the list. In principle, this feature limited the electoral viability of extremist politicians, at least in heterogeneous districts, because they would have difficulty finding willing list mates, and also because extreme chauvinism could induce voters to vote for a competitor instead.

in the PLO. Second, the country's power-sharing arrangements failed to keep pace with demographic changes that favored its Muslim communities, causing many in the latter to advocate replacing Lebanon's sectarian institutions with a "secular" system, by which they generally meant ending the allocation of offices and seats by sect. Many of the political parties formed militias as tensions mounted in the 1970s and then spilled over into civil war in 1975 as an alliance of Lebanese progressive parties and the PLO confronted the state and a coalition of Christian militias.

As the civil war progressed, the party militias overran various parts of the country and began to offer services – rudimentary at first, and then increasingly intricate – to residents. Although the civil war was frequently portrayed in simplistic terms as Christian versus Muslim, the militias frequently turned to violence against rivals in their own communities in order to eliminate opponents and establish their own dominance. Meanwhile, a number of foreign powers, most importantly Syria and Israel, intervened at various stages in the war. Although militias in the Christian, Shia, and Druze communities survived to the end of the war, the Sunni community's fighting forces and allies in the PLO were destroyed by the middle of the war through a combination of attacks by Israeli, Syrian, and, later, Lebanese militia forces. After years of false starts and attempts at international mediation, the surviving members of parliament signed the Taif Accord in 1989 to end the war.

In addition to a variety of provisions – some of which, such as the abolition of sectarianism, were never implemented – the Taif Accord retained the state's basic institutions, but reallocated power between the sectarian communities on a parity basis between Muslims and Christians while strengthening the powers of the Sunni prime minister and Shia speaker. It also legitimated a major role for Syria in Lebanese domestic politics, and most elected politicians and governments were, accordingly, "pro-Syrian" to one degree or another. In this context, Rafik al-Hariri emerged from the Sunni political vacuum at the end of the civil war and began the process of rebuilding the country, along with a political constituency within his own community. Tensions increased over time between Hariri and the Syrian authorities, however, until the former's assassination in 2005, allegedly at Syrian behest, sparked massive demonstrations against the continued Syrian presence in the country. These ongoing protests, accompanied by strong international pressure, compelled Syria to withdraw its remaining forces later that spring, and the country held its first post-Syrian elections that summer.

In simplified terms, the 2005 (and, subsequently, 2009) elections pitted parties and politicians from the anti-Syrian March 14 alliance against their counterparts in the pro-Syrian March 8 alliance – named after the days on which massive anti- and pro-Syrian demonstrations occurred, respectively. The March 14 forces represented a fractious group of Sunni, Druze, and Christian politicians, while the two main Shia parties, Amal and Hizballah, formed the core of the March 8 forces. Although March 14 won a parliamentary majority in 2005, one of the biggest anti-Syrian factions had, in fact, run *against* the March 14 forces, and eventually allied itself with March 8. Despite some changes in composition, the core of the two alliances persisted through the 2009 elections, which again returned a March 14 majority.

This brief overview of Lebanon's institutional history aims not for completeness, but rather to provide context for the discussions in the next several sections about competition *within* the country's sectarian communities rather than between them. First, it has noted how power-sharing arrangements between the sects have been mainstays of Lebanese public life since well before the European colonial period. These institutions, in turn, have perpetuated the importance of religious identities and religious groups in Lebanese politics. Second, it has introduced, however briefly and incompletely, some of the key political parties and politicians in the contemporary period. The next few sections expand on these latter points by tracking the development of political competition – or the lack thereof – in Lebanon's Christian, Shia, and Sunni communities.

3.3 CHRISTIAN COMPETITION

The Christian community is the most electorally competitive of Lebanon's confessional groups, at least in the contemporary period. These internal dynamics contrast with the Hizballah–Amal cartel among the Shia, and the dominance of hegemonic leaders within the Sunni and Druze communities. Competition between rival Christian politicians has been the norm rather than the exception throughout modern Lebanon's history, and this internal competitiveness has persisted into the post-Syria period. Prominent Christian leaders have aligned themselves with both the March 14 and March 8 alliances, and Christian voters array themselves at roughly even levels between the two alliances and independents. As such, their internal competitiveness makes the Christian community the "linchpin" of post-Syrian electoral politics.[7]

3.3.1 Competing Factions in the Independence Era

The French Mandate gave Christians privileged access to state authority, a distribution of formal power that Lebanon's independence-era institutions mirrored. Insofar as these institutions concentrated disproportionate power in the presidency of the republic – a post reserved, by convention, for Maronite Christians – factional competition and alliance building revolved around control of that post, election to which occurred within the parliament. Although

---

[7] Interview, think tank director, Beirut, July 2008.

several presidents attempted, unsuccessfully, to arrogate power and extend their own terms in office, their elections became increasingly competitive in the independence period up through the last presidential campaign before the start of the civil war.[8]

As tensions with the PLO and Lebanese Muslim politicians grew in the 1970s, most of the Christian parties formed militias and, initially, joined their separate forces in a loose coalition – the Lebanese Front – against a mainly-Muslim alliance that threatened to overturn the sectarian power-sharing system that buttressed Christian preeminence in Lebanon. Even the existential crisis of civil war failed to unify the rival Christian forces, however, and the constituent members of the front soon began to fight among themselves for supremacy in the Christian community. The Lebanese Forces (LF), the militia outgrowth of the Kataeb Party, came closest to achieving this goal, but assassinations, internal leadership struggles, and confrontations with the Christian component of the Lebanese army prevented the militia from unifying its ostensible constituency under LF leadership.

As a Kataeb party activist explained, the LF commander, Bashir al-Gemayel, "tried to unite all Christians under one banner, and thus massacred the other, smaller forces," but "then he got assassinated just as he united all the Christians." Nothwithstanding the LF's attempt at enforced unification, the community remained factionalized. In addition to forces loyal to other political leaders, the Kataeb activist acknowledged that "after the assassination, the Kataeb and the [Lebanese Forces] were halfway merged. Some wanted to split them again, and some wanted to merge them fully. Over the next eight years or so they did split again." Samir Geagea and Eli Hobeika eventually overthrew Gemayel's successor in the LF, and Geagea subsequently ousted Hobeika.[9]

---

[8] The most prominent Maronite Christian leaders under the French Mandate were Emile Eddé and Bishara el-Khoury, the latter of whom was the Christian partner to the National Pact and the country's first independence-era president. Subsequently, competition among Maronites revolved around Eddé's son Raymond, Camille Chamoun, Pierre al-Gemayel, Suleiman Frangieh, as well as other leaders with military and technocratic backgrounds such as Fouad Chehab and Charles Helou. Khoury and Chamoun both maneuvered unsuccessfully to extend their mandates. Suleiman Frangieh won the 1970 presidential elections by a single vote in parliament over his eventual successor, Elias Sarkis, the former governor of the Bank of Lebanon.

[9] Bashir al-Gemayel, son of Kataeb Party founder Pierre al-Gemayel, was elected by parliament to the presidency of the republic in 1982 but was assassinated before taking office; his brother, Amin, was subsequently elected in his place. The quoted Kataeb activist argued that Geagea and Hobeika overthrew Bashir's successor in the LF for the latter's close ties to Amin – reflecting an ongoing rivalry between the established leadership of the Kataeb and the rising leadership of the LF (cf. Entelis, 1974; Snider, 1984). Interview, Kataeb Party activist, Beirut, July 2008. Geagea ousted Hobeika after the latter signed the Tripartite Agreement with the militia leaders of the (Shia) Amal Movement and (Druze) Progressive Socialist Party in 1985 designed to end the civil war. Hobeika reemerged after the civil war as head of the Wa'ad Party, won elections in 1992 and 1996, and served in several ministerial roles.

3.3 Christian Competition

Although Geagea and the LF supported the Taif Accord designed to end the civil war, they faced opposition from the Maronite commander of the army, Michel Aoun, who opposed the accord and waged a destructive campaign against the LF and the Syrian armed forces until forced into exile.[10]

Hence, the Christian community emerged factionalized from the civil war. Many of its leaders were, moreover, subject to repression by the Syrian and Lebanese security forces as Syria consolidated its authority in Lebanon and cracked down on Christian factions critical of the Syrian role in the country. Hence, key figures resided in exile (Gemayel, Aoun, Eddé), languished in prison (Geagea), or boycotted elections (Chamoun) stacked in favor of Damascus-leaning politicians (Hobeika, Frangieh). Several political parties and movements were banned (the Lebanese Forces, and what eventually became Aoun's Free Patriotic Movement) or taken over by pro-Syrian figures (the Kataeb under Pakradouni). Notwithstanding some independents tolerated by the Syrian leadership, most of the politically active Christian politicians that participated in government were viewed as collaborators.[11] Rafik al-Hariri himself dismissed these figures, claiming that "the Christians in power represent no one. Michel Aoun in exile and Samir Geagea in prison have more popular support than they do."[12] Hence, partly because no faction had defeated its rivals in the civil war, and partly due to repression, the Christian community remained disunited throughout the post-war period – no dominant leader could, or did, emerge.

---

[10] In the context of his campaign against the Lebanese Forces militia, Aoun, then acting prime minister in a parallel administration to the government of Salim al-Hoss, launched what he called a "war of liberation" against the Syrian armed forces occupying large parts of the country and tasked with helping the Lebanese government implement the Taif Accord (Laurent, 1991; Salem, 1991).

[11] Aoun fled the country after Syrian forces overwhelmed his "War of Liberation" in the waning days of the civil war and remained in exile until 2005. Amin al-Gemayel, head of the Kataeb Party, left for exile after his presidential term ended in 1988 but attempted to direct the party from abroad, returning to Lebanon in 2000. Figures more amenable to the Syrian government subsequently took over the party's official leadership and caused a split between the "Legitimate Kataeb" (the Pakradouni faction) and the "Real Kataeb" (the Gemayel faction). Samir Geagea, head of the Lebanese Forces, received life imprisonment in 1994 on politically motivated charges; the Lebanese government dissolved and banned the Lebanese Forces as a political organization, although it continued to operate. Raymond Eddé remained in exile until his death in 2000; leadership of his National Bloc subsequently passed to his nephew, Carlos Eddé, who had been living in Latin America. Dory Chamoun's National Liberal Party boycotted the elections of 1992, 1996, and 2000. A loose coalition of Christian opposition figures formed the Qornet Shehwan Gathering in the early-2000s (el Khazen, 2003); the gathering lacked anything approximating an electoral machine but was influential in the development of the subsequent March 14 alliance.

[12] Interview with journalist Ghassan Charbel (2008, 240). The irony in this statement, of course, is that Hariri himself collaborated, if unenthusiastically, with the Syrian regime through most of the post-war period prior to his 2005 assassination.

3.3.2 Rivalries and Splits in the Independence Intifada

Aside from the small pro-Syrian groups, the vast majority of Christians participated in the anti-Syrian uprising that emerged in the wake of Rafik al-Hariri's 2005 assassination. Political miscalculations and the venerable Lebanese practice of forming temporary electoral alliances, however, disrupted the fractious unity between the Christian factions. The 2005 elections, as in previous years, occurred in four rounds, each a week apart, in different regions of the country. For the first round, held in Beirut, Druze leader Walid Jumblatt and Hariri's son and political heir, Saad, reached electoral agreements with Hizballah and Amal.

Although March 14's Christian leadership acquiesced to this accommodation with the core March 8 parties – its leaders "thought, naïvely, that it would allow Amal and Hizballah to come to grips with the rest of the country," as one activist explained[13] – Michel Aoun's Free Patriotic Movement (FPM) objected to being frozen out of the agreement. Upon his return from exile, Aoun argued that March 14's Muslim leaders were simply looking to secure as many seats as possible for themselves, and were willing to freeze Christian leaders out of the decision-making process in order to do so. Angered and alienated, Aoun formed electoral alliances of his own with pro-Syrian politicians elsewhere in the country. As a senior official in the FPM explained:

> There was no such thing as March 14 [the movement]. It was just a headline, but not the spirit. The quartet alliance of Hizballah, Amal, Jumblatt, and Hariri – it's object was to fight Aoun. Hence, there was no possible alliance between us and March 14.[14]

Ultimately, the Free Patriotic Movement and its allies won landslide victories throughout the Christian heartland in the 2005 elections. A senior official in one of the March 8 parties observed that, "March 14 Christians have tried to jump on the Sunni bus so they can win on other sects' votes" implying that that the only "Christian" seats that March 14 won were those in which large numbers of Sunni or Druze voters buttressed their Christian allies; in purely-Christian districts, the solid majority voted with Aoun.[15] Six months after the election, Aoun aligned himself openly with Hizballah and Amal in parliament – a remarkable about-face even in the Lebanese context of shifting alliances.

March 14 leaders attributed Aoun's electoral victories to voter disenchantment with the former's alliances. A member of the Christian Qornet Shehwan Gathering, whose unsuccessful candidates bore the brunt of the Free Patriotic Movement's success, explained that:

---

[13] Interview, senior March 14 activist, Beirut, July 2008.

[14] Interview, senior Free Patriotic Movement official, Beirut, July 2008. The irony in this statement, of course, is that Hizballah and Amal's decision to ally with the March 14 parties in the elections did not stop the Free Patriotic Movement from aligning with Hizballah and Amal a few months after the elections.

[15] Interview, senior March 8 official, April 2009.

Our big problem was Aoun's comeback. The people were saying, "March 14 betrayed its ideals, but we have a good example of a March 14 leader in Aoun." They saw him as a good, clean, March 14 guy, not like the others.

The FPM victory, he continued, was "a vote of sanction against the betrayal of March 14" for its accommodations with Hizballah and Amal:

They voted for the guy who, at the time, was asking to disarm Hizballah, implement UN 1559 and the U.S. Syrian Accountability Act, and so on. And they discovered what happened afterwards [when Aoun allied with Hizballah].[16]

3.3.3 Intensifying Factional Rivalries

Most observers interpreted Aoun's decision to ally with the March 8 Shia parties as part of his overall strategy to become president, the goal of ambitious Maronite politicians since independence. Aoun, by common consent, has long aspired to the presidency, and many of his detractors accuse him of megalomania in pursuit of the office – hence the unflattering nicknames such as "Napoleaoun."

Parliament, rather than a popular vote, elects the president, requiring candidates to gain the consent of MPs from other sectarian communities – a mechanism designed to empower moderate politicians and handicap those that lacked cross-sectarian support. Although March 8 lacked a majority in parliament, Aoun's accession gave the bloc the numbers to deny quorum and prevent the election from occurring. Hence, as a March 14 strategist observed:

Aoun joining the opposition was a calculation to win the presidency. His thought was that [he's] going to block the majority, and to unblock it they must make [him] president.[17]

March 8 did, indeed, block presidential elections for months in 2007–2008, and again from 2014 onwards inducing a constitutional vacuum each time as the presidency remained unoccupied in the interval. Consistent with his dramatic reversals of policy positions, Aoun's alliances appeared to reflect not principled decisions, but rather pursuit of office.

These policy and alliance reversals did not, however, go unchallenged in the Christian community. A senior official in the Free Patriotic Movement, for example, admitted that his party's alignments had caused serious disquiet among its constituents:

---

[16] Interview, member of the March 14 general secretariat, Beirut, July 2008. United Nations Security Council Resolution 1559 called for the complete withdrawal of the Syrian armed forces from Lebanon and the disarmament of all militias in the country, the latter clause of which clearly referred to Hizballah's armed wing.

[17] Interview, Beirut, July 2008.

There's a lot of trust in General Aoun. We faced some difficulties, though, in explaining it ... Our supporters support Aoun and the memorandum [of understanding with Hizballah], not Hizballah itself.[18]

As this official acknowledged, his party's supporters were particularly wary of Hizballah, especially given the latter's close ties to the Syrian and Iranian regimes. This choice of alignments presented many Christians with unappealing options. A former FPM leader explained that the party's supporters comprised "people who did not like the [Lebanese Forces] and the other Christian militias because they suffered from them in the war." As a member of the March 14 general secretariat observed, however, Aoun's choice of allies presented Christians with a stark choice:

For the Maronites, if the question is "do you like [Lebanese Forces leader Samir] Geagea," it's a good question for Aoun. But if the question is "do you like [Iranian President Mahmoud] Ahmadinejad," it's very difficult for Aoun.[19]

Although Lebanese politicians commonly forge cross-sectarian alliances at the elite level – indeed, they must in order to participate in government – Aoun's choice of allies opened him up to unrelenting criticism from his detractors for betraying both the political principles he formerly espoused as well as the independence movement.

Allying with Hizballah, in particular, made the Free Patriotic Movement vulnerable to communal outflanking by other leaders seeking to capitalize on fears that Aoun had sold out the Christians. After the FPM announced that it sought to build Lebanon's "Third Republic" after the 2009 elections, for example, the Lebanese Forces responded with the billboard reproduced in Figure 3.2. On the left is the Lebanese flag with the caption "Second Independence," referring to the 2005 uprising that pushed Syria out of the country. On the right, with the caption "Third Republic," is a distorted version of the flag with an FPM-orange cedar on top of a Hizballah-yellow background. Hence, this ad played on Christian anxieties of losing the country to Hizballah and, by extension, Syria and Iran.[20]

Campaign advertising from other March 14-aligned Christians hammered on similar themes. The Kataeb Party, for example, posted billboards declaring that "order is our program, and parliament is our weapon" – invoking Hizballah's armed takeover of Beirut in 2008. Carlos Eddé, who nearly defeated Aoun himself in the Kesrouan district, posted billboards contrasting "change" and "reform" (namechecking Aoun's "Change and Reform" parliamentary bloc)

---

[18] Interview, senior Free Patriotic Movement official, Beirut, July 2008.
[19] Interviews with a former senior Free Patriotic Movement official and with a member of the March 14 general secretariat, Beirut, July 2008.
[20] The Taif Accord reforms produced what is commonly called Lebanon's "Second Republic." The Free Patriotic Movement's "Third Republic" would, in turn, be a post-Taif system. On this billboard, see Corstange (2012a).

3.3 Christian Competition

FIGURE 3.2: Lebanese Forces Campaign Billboard, 2009: (Left) Second Independence, (Right) Third Republic

with "principles" and "morals," while another set of ads contrasted "resistance" and "weapons" (referring to Hizballah's militia, the "Resistance") with "the state" and "the army."

3.3.4 Real if Uninspiring Choice

Most Christians were euphoric after the 2005 uprising seemed to offer them a new, more principled Lebanon – t-shirts on sale in Beirut at the time trumpeted "Lebanese Democracy 2.0" – as well as a revived role for their community in government. Over time, however, many have become discontent with their leaders and disillusioned by the political divisions within their community. A civil society activist, for example, bemoaned her community's leadership:

I can't believe ... we're back to the Aoun–Geagea saga [from the end of the civil war]. One was in exile, and the other in jail, and 15 years later we're back to this. It's hard for Christians to get new elites. It was very intelligent on the part of the Syrians. [Assassinated March 14 MP] Gebran Tueni could have been a new one, and they killed him. [Assassinated Kataeb MP] Pierre al-Gemayel was a new kind of leader and brought in new ideas and started to get the youths excited in the Kataeb again, and they killed him. I could have followed a [assassinated journalist] Samir Kassir party, and they killed him. Now what do you have? Chamoun or Amin al-Gemayel? They're not inspiring, and so we're left with Aoun and Geagea.[21]

---

[21] Interview, Beirut, July 2008. The "Aoun–Geagea saga" to which the activist referred was the fighting at the end of the civil war between the Lebanese army, then headed by Michel Aoun, and the Lebanese Forces led by Samir Geagea. Gebran Tueni, assassinated in late-2005, was a prominent member of the Qornet Shehwan Gathering and the March 14 movement, the editor of Lebanon's flagship daily *al-Nahar*, and a member of parliament. Pierre al-Gemayel, the son of former president Amin al-Gemayel, was twice elected to parliament and was assassinated in

More generally, people found the choice between Aoun and Geagea to be a distasteful one. Many were uncomfortable with the former's political reversals, but found the alternatives equally unpalatable. A former Aoun supporter turned March 14 activist, for example, expressed his disillusionment with Aoun, but then quickly stated that "Geagea could never represent me because I can't be a fascist, and the [Kataeb is] even worse." Detractors commonly level charges of fascism against Geagea and the Lebanese Forces, while the Kataeb itself originated in the 1930s on a model of the European fascist parties. Even so, another activist argued, "the LF is the most left wing of the LF–Kataeb–[Chamounist] line," with the latter comprising "the biggest paramilitary folks."[22]

Even allowing for hyperbole and the indignation of the disenchanted, these comments illustrate some of the discursive themes found in the post-2005 Christian community. First, some members, largely activists, were disappointed that their leaders had not delivered on their promises of change. Many people turned to Aoun in 2005 when the other March 14 Christian leaders appeared to compromise themselves; many others abandoned Aoun when he, too, compromised himself with his alliance choices. As a Christian March 14 leader described his interactions with disenchanted Aounists, "at the end of our conversations, we always have a very difficult moment when they say, 'how could I be so stupid?'"[23] One such former Aounist, in turn, described a changing, less principled constituency for the Free Patriotic Movement:

It's the Christians of the margins ... [those] that still support Aoun do so for personal reasons, because they don't like Geagea, have "middle manager" plans to be candidates for parliament, local elections, and so on. There is no movement today; there are no principles.[24]

By and large, the idealism of 2005 quickly evaporated and gave way to the less savory aspects of Lebanese politics, in which few politicians – successful ones, at any rate – offer the consistent articulation of principle that motivate idealists. Arguably, of course, the Christian leaders that reemerged in 2005 were less able than their counterparts in other communities to position themselves as *patrons*. Initially, then, competition between them put more emphasis on programmatic promises and communal outbidding. Over time, however, the competing parties reestablished their organizations and gained access to more

---

late-2006. Samir Kassir, assassinated shortly after the 2005 elections, was a professor, a founding member of the Democratic Left Movement, and a prolific anti-Syrian columnist. These three assassinations, along with several others that occurred around the same time, are widely believed to be the work of Syrian intelligence agents, although the cases have never been resolved.

[22] Interviews with a March 14 activist and a Kataeb activist, Beirut, July 2008.
[23] Interview, member of the March 14 general secretariat, Beirut, July 2008.
[24] Interview, former senior Free Patriotic Movement official, Beirut, July 2008.

state and foreign resources to distribute to their constituents, and so patronage politics became increasingly prominent.[25]

In addition to unhappiness with their choices in leaders, many Christians were also frustrated that those leaders could not – or would not – forge a united political front. One common rhetorical trope held that Christians needed to unify in order to reclaim their role in the country's political life. Building off of this trope, for example, an election monitor attributed Aoun's success in 2005 to the fact that "he represented himself as a powerful Christian leader against other strong confessional leaders like Hariri and Jumblatt."[26] As such, numerous entities, most prominently the Maronite patriarchy, sponsored ongoing efforts to "reconcile" the community's competing politicians. Numerous satirical cartoons riffed off of this theme – one, for example, depicted a man asking a genie for "Christian reconciliation" and watching in bemusement as the genie leaps back into his lamp, while another depicted fighting children exclaiming that "we're playing Christian reconciliation!"[27] Put together, the caricatures denounce the intra-community competition as both childish and insoluble.

In short, there was demand for, but not supply of, political unity. Unsurprisingly, one impediment was simply the community's diversity of political views. There was nothing approaching consensus among Christians about which community was the "enemy" – the Shiites? the Sunnis? the Druze? the Syrians? – nor about the degree of threat. A complementary impediment, of course, was communal competition over leadership. In the context of the discursive battle over Christian public opinion, both camps alleged that the other was weakening the Christian position vis-à-vis the other sects and urged "Christian unity" – behind their own camp, of course. Most Christian elites would be only too happy to unify if their political opponents were to accept a subordinate role.

Despite the periodic calls for unity, at least some Christian politicians and civil society activists took pride in the ongoing contest between the community's different camps. One official in the March 14 alliance, for example, acknowledged that some members of his community saw Christian competition as a "sign of weakness," but that "for me, [it's] a sign of vitality."[28] Similarly, a March 8-aligned competitor lauded the community's competitiveness:

Historically, the Christians were never one bloc. It's a healthy state to have competition. It's an unhealthy situation in the other sects without competition. For example, the

---

[25] Compare Cammett (2014); Corstange (2012b). Rhetorically, of course, *all* parties, Christian or not, made programmatic promises. The promise that "we'll buy your votes," although uncharacteristically truthful, would have been decidedly out of place.
[26] Interview, senior official in the Lebanese Association for Democratic Elections, Beirut, July 2008.
[27] See the caricatures in *al-Nahar*, 8 and 10 October 2008.
[28] Interview, March 14-aligned official, Beirut, July 2008.

Sunnis can't be against Hariri without being against the whole community. Among Christians, you can dislike Aoun and it's okay.[29]

Christian constituents, in turn, benefit from high demand for their political support. Given the competition, the overarching need to win over voters obligates both the March 14 and the March 8 alliances to cater to the Christian community.

3.3.5 Christians in Demand

Since 2005, nearly all Sunnis have aligned with Hariri's Future Movement and the March 14 forces, while nearly all Shiites sided with Amal and Hizballah in the March 8 alliance. Given the demographic parity between Lebanon's two main Muslim communities, competition between the rival Christian camps has played a central role in determining which of the two alliances speaks for the country's "real majority."[30] Going into the 2009 elections, the Christians were, in the words of a former Free Patriotic Movement official, the "swing vote." After citing polling evidence (always a dubious proposition) that gave 25 to 30 percent of the Christian vote each to Aoun and the March 14 parties, he observed that:

> The majority is in no one's hands ... The tipping point is entirely on these [voters]. They're disappointed with March 14 Christian leaders. They're disappointed with Aoun. How will they vote? No one knows.[31]

The pervasive uncertainty about which way the Christian electorate would swing meant that none of the Christian parties, nor either alliance more generally, could take Christian voters for granted.

With the community split down the middle between the two alliances, both sides campaigned actively to attract Christian voters. Consequently, "both sides are trying to woo the Christians ... the Christians are the linchpin," as one observer remarked.[32] Wooing the Christians, in turn, obliged the Muslim components of both blocs to make concessions to their Christian allies who, as one disgruntled leader observed, were locked in "a competition ... over who is more Maronite" than the other.[33] Both alliances, for example, had to jettison

---

[29] Interview, March 8-aligned official, Beirut, July 2008.
[30] Discourse on the "real majority," the "new majority," and the "missing majority" derive from claims that Aoun's post-2005 defection to March 8 tipped the electoral balance in the latter's favor even as March 14 exploited its parliamentary majority to form the government. For examples of this discourse, see, for instance, "Jumblatt: We are the Real Majority," *Daily Star*, 6 May 2006; "Lebanon's future: Bending toward Hezbollah or leaning to the West?" *New York Times*, 22 September 2006; and "Hezbollah chief defiant at huge rally," *Washington Post*, 23 September 2006. For more details, see also International Crisis Group (2008).
[31] Interview, former Free Patriotic Movement official, Beirut, July 2008.
[32] Interview, think tank director, Beirut, June 2008.
[33] Interview, senior March 14 leader, Beirut, June 2008.

moderate, less confrontational Christian candidates in favor of more strident partisans.[34]

In summary, then, the Christian community has been Lebanon's most competitive constituency throughout the contemporary period. Inspiring or not, Christians have split into two competing camps: first, Michel Aoun's Free Patriotic Movement and its allies, and second, the less well-organized March 14-aligned Christians. Rhetorically, both camps make frequent calls for Christian unity, and yet neither is willing to cede authority to the other. The seeming paradox, of course, is that the community's divisions have, if anything, made it more, rather than less, focal in Lebanon's political life. Ultimately, internal competition has meant that Christian voters cannot be taken for granted by either their own leaders or their allies in the other sectarian communities.

3.4 SHIA CARTEL

In contrast to the open political competition between Christian elites, the two main Shia parties, Amal and Hizballah, have forged a working alliance in the post-war and, especially, post-2005 period. This collusive behavior has restricted competition and deterred the emergence of other Shia politicians, but, at the same time, offers constituents credible patronage alternatives between the two cartel members. Amal and Hizballah's decisions to coalesce have largely been driven by circumstance. Syria compelled the civil war rivals and erstwhile opponents to form electoral alliances throughout the post-war period, and the March 14 movement pushed them to extend their coordination into the post-Syrian period. By colluding, the two Shia parties shored up their bargaining leverage with their March 14 opponents, protected their own vote and seat shares, and prevented alternate Shia political leadership from emerging.

3.4.1 Emerging Competition in the Independence Era

At independence, the Shia community was, in fact, among the *least* competitive confessional groups in Lebanon. Concentrating largely in the rural hinterlands, Shiites were, on average, the country's poorest and most marginalized inhabitants. Throughout the 1940s and 1950s, a small number of notable families with large landholdings – often termed "feudalists" in both the academic

---

[34] As one March 14-aligned list leader explained, independent and moderate Christians had lost ground to the Lebanese Forces and Kataeb Party; his own parliamentary bloc had sacrificed several members. "I don't like it, but it's not a question of personal feelings," he complained. "Gemayel and Geagea are greedy, more than greedy." Interview, Beirut, April 2009. Hizballah and Amal, in turn, faced pressure to grant the Free Patriotic Movement greater say about the composition of their joint electoral lists. The latter ever ran a list against its ally Amal in the Jezzine district when the two parties could not reach agreement over the share of the seats.

literature and by their political detractors – dominated the Shia population in the south and the Bekaa valley in the east. So firm a political grip did these notables hold over their constituents that the latter regularly voted in the former's electoral lists by wide margins despite receiving little in exchange; in his heyday, the most notorious such leader boasted that he could get his cane elected to parliament if he wished.[35] These traditional notables rarely competed directly with one another; each maintained his own ancestral bailiwick, with gentlemen's agreements not to encroach on each other's territory. As such, they faced few incentives to attend to the needs of their impoverished constituents.[36]

Given the lack of competitive pressures on their representatives, the Shia areas of the country remained, unsurprisingly, the poorest and most bereft of basic government services and infrastructure. Evocatively, Ajami (1986, 67), who grew up in the country's Shia heartland in the south, articulated a bitter protest against the traditional notables:

Peasants were peasants, Ahmad Bey [al-Asa'ad] thought. Schools, roads, clinics had to be denied them if the world and its familiar landmarks were to remain the same. To a delegation of villagers who came to plead for the establishment of a school, Ahmad Bey gave one of his vintage answers. There was, he said, no need for a school for he was educating his son Kamel Bey for all of them.

Critics, in turn, decried how the traditional leaders – and, consequently, the state – neglected the Shia population. For example, Musa al-Sadr, a religious scholar who sought to mobilize his community for political action, complained that "the rate of illiteracy among [the Shia] is greater than any other sect in Lebanon, perhaps by more than double ... and the number of villages without mosques or schools is very great."[37] More broadly, he observed, most Shia villages lacked even basic infrastructure and services such as electricity, water, or roads – even large towns might get piped water only once every two weeks,

---

[35] Ajami (1986, 63–64) provides this anecdote and notes that, at his height, the most politically powerful Shia leader (Ahmad al-Asa'ad, and then his son, Kamal) headed a bloc that accounted for nearly 20 percent of parliament – a huge delegation by Lebanese standards. Ajami further observes that, "there wasn't much that men from a backward community could accomplish when elected to the Parliament. Every now and then one of them would stand up and make the 'perennial demand' of their community for justice. As always, the government promised benevolence."

[36] See Chalabi (2006); Corstange (2013); Hess, Jr. and Bodman, Jr. (1954); Hottinger (1966); Hudson (1968); Shanahan (2005).

[37] Musa al-Sadr interview with *al-Usbua' al-Arabi*, 26 May 1969 (Sadr, 2000a, 54–58, quoted at 55). Note that, in this context, Sadr likely mentions the absence of mosques not in his capacity as a religious scholar, but because they commonly offered Quranic schools (*kuttabs*) which provided people with a basic, traditional education – usually rote memorization of Quranic verses.

"then the water may come on for an hour, then it would cut off for another two weeks."[38]

Against this backdrop of localized dominance and neglect by the notable families, a new set of Shia elites began to emerge in the 1960s under the leadership of Musa al-Sadr, the charismatic religious figure cited earlier.[39] Poverty in the rural hinterlands of the south and Bekaa valley drove many Shiites to the "misery belt" of slums around Beirut and to seek their fortunes abroad. Migration from the villages, although it did not sever people's ties to their traditional notables, did at least weaken the connection and exposed migrants to alternative forms of political organization.[40] According to Muhammad Shams al-Din (2002, 34), another religious leader working alongside Sadr, the community experienced a "renaissance in education" from the 1950s onward as members began to enroll in schools and, "little by little, formed an advanced, educated elite." Over time, the core of this emerging elite, buttressed by support and funding from the expatriate Shia community, began to challenge the political dominance of the traditional notables.

Sadr and others repeatedly denounced the notable families for their inattentiveness to the underdeveloped Shia regions that they represented. He and others also criticized them for being unaccountable to the people who lived under their authority and whose welfare they ignored:

> What saddens me is that the reason [for the deprivation] is due to the *lack of pressure*, because the south was making appeals, gently and earnestly, without troubling officials' minds ... The other regions [in Lebanon] would never stand for what the south bears daily.[41]

Hence, prior to the emergence of Sadr and his supporters, the traditional notables, largely insulated from competitive pressures, had little incentive to attend to the needs of their constituents. By the end of the 1960s, however, the new elites attempted to create an institutional alternative to the notable families by forming the Supreme Shia Council, although subsequently abandoned that effort after the notables undermined it in the lead-up to the civil war.[42]

---

[38] Musa al-Sadr interview with *al-Jamhur*, 4 June 1970 (Sadr, 2000a, 142–156, quoted at 148–149). The specific town to which the quote refers is Bint Jbeil, one of the largest towns is the southern district of Nabatieh.

[39] For details, see Ajami (1986); Fadlallah (1997); Gharib (2001); Madini (1999); Norton (1987).

[40] Compare the argument in Deutsch (1961). Most migrants, whether to the cities or abroad, had family members that continued to live in the villages who were still subject to, and dependent on, the traditional notables. Moreover, given Lebanon's electoral regulations of requiring people to vote where they originated rather than where they lived, migrants had to return to their villages to cast their votes there.

[41] Musa al-Sadr interview with *al-Muharrir*, 10 October 1974 (Sadr, 2000a, 373–384, quoted at 380). Emphasis added.

[42] In particular, see the description of events in Shams al-Din (2002, 36–46), one of Sadr's associates who helped to establish the council.

Sadr and his associates next launched the Movement of the Dispossessed which, like most of its contemporaries, formed a militia, Amal, in the lead-up to the civil war.[43] Initially a rag-tag force, Amal played only a minor role early in the war, and cabinets formed after the first round of fighting continued to allocate ministries to the traditional Shia notables. Sadr himself disappeared in Libya in 1978, and leadership of the movement fell to its militia leaders.[44] As the war continued and Amal improved its organizational and fighting capacity, the movement eclipsed the traditional notables, who lacked comparable forces. Hence, as one scholar observed, "it was the civil war, and the associated growth of extralegal organizations, that conclusively rendered these political personalities anachronistic, if not irrelevant in the Lebanese political system."[45]

Up until the Iranian Revolution of 1979 and the Israeli occupation of the south in 1982, Amal was, as Gharib (2001, 207–219) argues, on the verge of dominating the Shia community. Amal was, however, an umbrella movement that combined disparate constituencies; as party leader Nabih Berri later recalled, "just as in all movements and parties, there was a moderate faction and an extreme faction ... even when Sadr was around."[46] After the Iranian Revolution, however, Amal experienced increasing strains between mainstream Shiites and revolutionaries inspired by Iranian revolutionary doctrine. "Islamic Amal" split off from the main body in the early-1980s, and then Hizballah itself emerged as a separate organization opposed to Amal and sponsored by the Iranian regime, which included funding, training, and personnel. The rival militias fought internecine battles at various stages of the civil war as they competed for supremacy within the Shia community. Neither force, however, was able to eliminate the other, although the pitched battles between the two at

---

[43] Acronyms are rarely used in Arabic, but "Amal" is a pseudo-acronym for *afwaj al-muqawama al-lubnaniyya* – the "Battalions of the Lebanese Resistance." Literally, *amal* translates to "hope." The Movement of the Dispossessed eventually became subsumed in its own militia.

[44] The first round of fighting lasted from 1975 to 1976, followed by attempts to restore peace with the help of the Arab Deterrent Force. Sadr, for example, criticized the first Hoss government of 1976, denouncing the "traditional positions" toward the cabinet that failed to grant him any representation. By allocating the Shia share to the traditional notables, the government "perpetuated a failed past" that was "neglectful of the nation and its citizens." Musa al-Sadr, interview with *al-Anwar*, 27 December 1976 (Sadr, 2000b, 236–247, quoted at 238). Most people presume that the Libyan regime under Muammar al-Qaddafi killed Sadr, but some Lebanese Shiites refuse to believe that Sadr is dead. Emphasis on his "disappearance" plays into Twelver Shia millenarian doctrine on the hidden imam who will one day reemerge to bring justice to the world.

[45] Quoting Norton (1987, 49). Arguably, had the civil war ended after the first round of fighting in 1975–1976, the traditional notables may have been able to preserve their political influence in the Shia community against the upstart but unconsolidated Amal Movement. As the war continued, however, militia elites from Amal (and later Hizballah) supplanted the community's traditional leadership – a process with broad parallels in the Christian community.

[46] Nabih Berri interview with Ghassan Charbel (2008, 164–165).

the tail end of the war allowed Hizballah to consolidate its position in Beirut's southern suburbs. Hence, the Shia community exited the war divided primarily between the two militias.

3.4.2 Constrained Rivalry in the Post-War Era

After the war, most observers expected Amal and Hizballah to continue to compete directly with each other, albeit via elections. Syria's armed forces and intelligence apparatus remained in Lebanon after the civil war ended, however, and the Syrian leadership retained final authority over many domestic Lebanese matters. Given Syria's strategic relationships with both parties, as well as Iran, the Syrian authorities sought to regulate the degree of open contestation between Amal and Hizballah; competition between the latter two could never become so sharp as to cross the "Syrian red line" (Madini 1999, 178–179; cf. Gharib 2001, 205).

In particular, the Syrian authorities imposed electoral alliances and shared electoral slates on the two parties in each of the three parliamentary elections held during the Syrian period. The imposition of these alliances reflected, in part, Syria's strategic calculations in the ongoing conflict with Israel: Hizballah's militia retained its weapons to fight the Israeli occupation in the south, originally the core of Amal's support base. Electoral coordination imposed on the parties prevented open breaks between them as well as consolidated their holds over Shia parliamentary representation by shutting out alternative Shia politicians unaligned with Damascus.

Perhaps more importantly, however, imposing the electoral alliances on Amal and Hizballah reflected Syrian efforts to prevent any leaders or parties from becoming dominant in their sects. Writing at the time, one scholar observed that "Syria has no interest in seeing Amal or Hizballah (or any other political force) triumph in Lebanon," while the International Crisis Group subsequently acknowledged that "Syria systematically sought to protect [Amal's] interests and ensure that [Hizballah] not achieve a hegemonic position over the Shiite community."[47] Echoing a number of other interviewees, one youth movement leader argued:

> Syria used to behave in such a way as to prevent a single sectarian figure from becoming the single, dominant leader to lead his sect alone. Compare the Shia. Syria used to be very favorable to Amal, then supported Hizballah, but didn't allow Amal to die out ... it was very intelligent: they're all competing with each other for Syrian favor.[48]

---

[47] See Norton (1999, 11) for the former quote and International Crisis Group (2010, 11, fn. 89) for the latter. See also analogous commentary on the competition between the two parties in Charbel (2008).
[48] Interview, Beirut, July 2008.

Hence, competition between the two Shia parties persisted throughout the post-war years, even as Syrian influence regulated that competition and prevented either side from achieving total victory.

3.4.3 Closing Ranks After the Independence Intifada

After the withdrawal of Syrian forces from Lebanon in 2005, "it had been assumed that, with Syria gone, Hizballah and Amal would have fought it out for dominance of the Shiite community at the first available opportunity," as one long-time correspondent wrote (Blanford, 2006, 168). But Syria's influence had buttressed the two Shia parties in Lebanon's domestic politics, for which they were deeply implicated, and organizing the March 8 demonstrations to "thank Syria" had publicly aligned Amal and Hizballah – and, by extension, the Shia community – with the Syrian regime against much of the rest of the population. Consequently, the Syrian withdrawal weakened the two parties' bargaining leverage with the other Lebanese factions, and particularly the leaders of the March 14 movement. Amal and Hizballah, previously reluctant allies that coalesced only after Syrian prodding, now closed ranks against the burgeoning anti-Syria movement from which they were estranged. Several factors help to account for the parties' decision to coalesce.

First, the Amal–Hizballah alliance helped the parties retain their vote and seat shares by deterring entry from potential competitors among independent Shia elites. As described previously, the March 14 alliance, rather than capitalize on 2005's window of opportunity to cultivate the Shia community, formed short-term electoral accommodations with Amal and Hizballah – depending on one's interpretation, either to allow the latter two parties "to come to grips with the rest of the country" or "because they were afraid of [Hizballah's] arms." With the benefit of hindsight, however, a member of March 14's general secretariat acknowledged the short-term accommodation to be an ill-conceived one, because "March 14 joining Hizballah killed the new, secular Shia leaders." Similarly, an independent candidate for parliament called the decision "a great catastrophe," and belated efforts to help alternative Shia leaders "too little, too late."[49] After Amal and Hizballah consolidated their holds over the Shia districts in 2005, they were able to build upon their advantages in organization and patronage resources.

Amal and Hizballah have not relied solely on resource advantages to overwhelm their competitors, but have also used intimidation to deter potential opponents as well – particularly those that could offer viable alternatives to themselves. An independent electoral list coordinator, for example, explained that:

[49] Interviews, Beirut, July 2008 and April 2009.

Hizballah is clever when facing an opponent with no chance: it won't give any trouble. But credible candidates like [one of my list members] face real problems from Hizballah. He's on our list and can't ... even leave his house.[50]

A March 14 activist, in turn, argued that:

We shouldn't have elections until we solve the guns problem. It's unfair, and I'm speaking from the Shiite context. Could an independent Shiite run against [Amal leader Nabih] Berri and win? Not in the presence of guns.[51]

More broadly, many independent Shia activists have complained of acts of intimidation directed at them and their families – allegations which, unsurprisingly, Amal and Hizballah officials deny.[52]

Hence, March 14 failed to support independent Shia elites when the latter had a window within which to make inroads against Hizballah and Amal. By colluding, the Shia parties have been better able to prevent viable, third-party alternatives from emerging. Significant patronage disadvantages and intimidation both contribute to deter candidate entry among unaffiliated elites. By handicapping the emergence of competitors, Amal and Hizballah have restricted the menu of options from which their constituents can choose and prevent unaligned voters from coordinating on an alternative.

By all accounts, the two main Shia parties commanded the majority of their community's votes around the time of the Syrian withdrawal. Hizballah does enjoy legitimate popularity among many Shiites, as does Amal to a lesser degree. However, the alliance maintains the acquiescence among many less enthusiastic constituents through a combination of patronage spending and intimidation. In addition to the chilling effect of Hizballah's heavy security presence in party-controlled areas, individual voters contend with implicit threats from both parties to withdraw needed services or employment.[53]

Nonetheless, many Shiites do not align with either of the two parties. Numerous observers have suggested that a sizeable minority of the Shia community remains unattached. On the low end, one think tank director estimated that 15 to 20 percent of Shiites – the "secular forces and the middle class who think this is bullshit" – oppose Amal and Hizballah, but have opted for silence in the absence of a credible alternative. On the upper end, one publisher, citing his own polling data, claimed that upwards of 40 percent of Shiites – again, "the middle class, educated bourgeoisie" – are "unaligned, voiceless."[54] Hence, a non-trivial minority of Shia voters remain outside the

---

[50] Interview, Beirut, April 2009.   [51] Interview, Beirut, July 2008.
[52] Interviews, Beirut, April 2009. See also Corstange (2012b). Compare Smyth (2011) for evidence from the Wikileaks documents.
[53] Interviews, various parties and civil society activists, Beirut, July 2008 and April 2009. For more details, see Corstange (2012b). Compare also Deeb (2006); Norton (1999) on unaffiliated Shiites living in Hizballah strongholds.
[54] Interviews, Beirut, June and July 2008. Abd al-Khaliq (2006, 74) estimates that, going into the 2005 elections, some 30 percent of the Shia did not align with Hizballah or Amal.

FIGURE 3.3: Amal–Hizballah mural: "We all resist" (Beirut, Summer 2008)

ambit of the Amal–Hizballah alliance, but have largely been untapped – and, if the latter have their way, untappable – by unaligned or opposition politicians.

The post-Syrian discursive environment in Lebanon has further complicated matters for independent Shiites by heightening the emphasis on sectarian solidarity. By closing ranks, however, the two Shia parties have been able to police social boundaries and cultivate the view that opposition within the community is an act of betrayal. Consequently, Shiites opposed to Hizballah and Amal cannot realistically align themselves with March 14. Even those figures that acknowledge supporting March 14's general principles recognize how damning that label has become in their own community, and prefer to identify as independents instead.[55]

For an illustration of the discourse, consider Figure 3.3. It depicts a streetside mural that went up shortly after the March 8 parties' armed takeover of West Beirut in May 2008, ostensibly in response to cabinet decisions that threatened Hizballah's militia.[56] The mural portrays a Lebanese cedar – similar to the one on the national flag – colored in with the green Amal logo on the trunk and lower branches blending seemlessly into the yellow Hizballah logo on the top. Written above the cedar in large text are the words "we all resist," simultaneously invoking "the Resistance" (Hizballah's militia) and asserting that everyone in the community supports the Amal–Hizballah alliance.[57]

---

[55] See Smyth (2011). [56] For a quick overview of the May 2008 events, see Salem (2008).
[57] The smaller text on the banner along the bottom is boilerplate anti-American rhetoric: "beware of America, enemy of peoples and instigator of wars." Unfortunately, the singsong, rhyming Arabic loses something in the translation. The extremely high quality of the workmanship makes

The parties' used a similar slogan, "resist with your vote," in the 2009 election campaign, and other, self-serving discourse emphasized the importance of community unity and safeguarding Hizballah's arms from "traitors" – sometimes directed at non-Shia leaders that wanted to disarm Hizballah, but implicitly directed at any Shiites that might agree.

3.4.4 Uneasy Alliance

Hence, collusion between Amal and Hizballah hamstrings potential competitors within the community and keeps independent Shiites uncoordinated and demobilized. But the mural depicted in Figure 3.3 also hints at a second major goal of the alliance: to paper over differences between the two erstwhile competitors and militate against defections. Both parties benefit from the collusive agreement, but both also have incentives to act opportunistically. The alliance offers a controlled way for the parties to divvy up their constituents. Amal gets to preserve its support base and its representation in government against Hizballah encroachment. Hizballah, in turn, gets to prevent Amal from breaking away to serve either as March 14's Shia partner or as the Shia component of a non-aligned bloc unaffiliated with March 14 or March 8.

During the post-war Syrian period, Amal operated analogous to a "ruling party" in the Shia community. Its leader, Nabih Berri, has served as speaker of parliament uninterruptedly since the 1992 elections, the party always held seats in the cabinet, and it serviced its constituency largely through access to state patronage and civil service jobs. As a think tank director explained:

> Amal maintains its constituency via government patronage. Almost the entire Shia component of the civil service and army, tens of thousands, I don't know how many, comes from Berri.[58]

Relatedly, one of the party's critics explained that "Amal gets about a billion dollars a year from the state in unpaid electricity bills, social security benefits, jobs in the state, and so on" that it distributes among its supporters.[59] More generally, the party distributes state resources, packs the civil service with its supporters, and intervenes in the justice system on behalf of its partisans – all classic tools used by political machines to service a constituency.

Hizballah, meanwhile, abstained from participating in government and instead focused on resistance to Israeli occupation and consolidating its "state-within-a-state."[60] Although its parliamentary delegation was always similar in size to Amal's, it neither contested the speaker's chair nor participated in the cabinet, at least throughout the Syrian period. Rather than rely on state

it unlikely that the mural was, as it claims, "presented by the youth of the district" who, judging by the crudely spraypainted graffiti on nearby walls, lacked the skill to compose such a display.
[58] Interview, Beirut, June 2008. [59] Interview, senior March 14 activist, Beirut, July 2008.
[60] See, among many others, Madini (1999); Norton (1999); Saad-Ghorayeb (2002); Yadav (2013).

patronage to shore up its constituency, it turned instead to massive annual subventions from Iran and other funding sources to finance party-operated charities and run a parallel administration in party-controlled regions. The party, in turn, employs huge numbers of Shia in its agencies – estimates run to around 50,000 people – and some officials suggest that it is the second largest employer in Lebanon behind the state itself.[61]

By all accounts, however, Amal's voting bloc is smaller than Hizballah's, as well as more fragile. Most observers also acknowledge that Amal has been losing supporters to Hizballah for years. Further, evidence from local and syndicate elections in which the two parties have not coordinated shows support shifting to Hizballah as well.[62] A publisher cautioned, however, that:

[Many Shiites] defend Hizballah as providing an alternative, but it's not really the one they would like. Amal is not an alternative because of [party leader Nabih] Berri. He's a crook and surrounded by a bunch of crooks. Amal does not enjoy good standing even in its own constituency.[63]

On its own, then, Amal is the weaker of the two parties and, given perceptions of the pervasive corruption within its ranks, the one more vulnerable to the erosion of its support base. For Amal, then, the collusive alliance offers it a reprieve from an all-out competition with Hizballah that could significantly cut into the size of its parliamentary bloc, representation in government, and access to the state patronage resources that are the mainstay of its political machine.

Given the disparities in strength between the two parties, many people presume that Amal retains its relevance only at the whim of Hizballah's leaders. One think tank director, for example, went so far as to argue that:

Because Hizballah has won among the Shia, it doesn't mind Amal having its own constituency. If Hizballah became displeased with Amal, they're done in a day.[64]

---

[61] See Smyth (2011) for a sampling of what the Wikileaks cables revealed about Hizballah's massive stock of resources with which to service its constituency. The documents also repeat long-standing assertions – denied by Hizballah, of course – that the party engages in racketeering and drug smuggling networks to fund itself. See also Deeb (2006); el Khazen (2002); Harik (2004); Madini (1999); Norton (1999).

[62] For example, el Khazen (2002, 133) observes that, despite firm popular bases for both parties, Hizballah had been widening its influence at Amal's expense, especially in the south. Amal and Hizballah competed head-to-head for the first time in 2004's municipal elections. Hizballah won landslide victories in its stronghold in Beirut's suburbs, as well as in the Bekaa; it also did well in the south, traditionally an Amal area. See Blanford (2006, 96–97).

[63] Interview, Beirut, July 2008. After describing Berri as a "crook," he paused and then sheepishly observed that, "you might want to change that word when you print it." I leave the word as it is because it is consistent with prevailing views about corruption in Amal; I have heard Berri called far less polite things than "crook" – and, presumably, Berri has, too. In the same vein, Norton (1999, 9) observes that Berri "is now privately derided for his pocket-stuffing and publicly feared for his control of a patronage system that few [Shiites] can afford to slight."

[64] Interview, Beirut, June 2008.

Although clearly the stronger of the two parties, however, Hizballah does not hold all of the bargaining leverage in their relationship. Amal retains the implicit threat to break the alliance and find an accommodation with March 14 or, more plausibly, join a "centrist bloc."[65] Hence, as Blanford (2006, 191) observed, Hizballah struck the alliance with Amal "in a bid to retain them as allies and defenders of the resistance [Hizballah's militia], rather than turn them into opponents through competition at the ballot box." Instead of permitting its opponents a credible entrée into the Shia community via Amal, Hizballah must sacrifice the electoral gains it could make at its ally's expense to safeguard its leverage in the institutions game – particularly with respect to its militia.[66]

Hence, the collusive alliance between Amal and Hizballah benefits both parties by deterring entry among unaligned Shia elites and denying the March 14 forces a credible partner in the Shia community. Nonetheless, the erstwhile opponents are mutual hostages: Hizballah can almost certainly out-compete Amal among the Shia, but Amal can retain its influence by partnering with leaders in other communities. In the meantime, each must guard against the other poaching supporters and upending the internal balance of power between them. Furthermore, both face strong incentives to cultivate the non-trivial bloc of Shia voters unattached to either party. Hence, Shiites do not enjoy a fully competitive vote market. Nonetheless, neither party can take their constituents for granted, either.

3.5 SUNNI MONOPSONY

Elites compete with cosectarian rivals in some of Lebanon's confessional communities, whether openly as with the Christian factions or under the surface of a collusive alliance as with the main Shia parties. The Sunni community, however, stands in contrast to its counterparts. Formerly one of the country's most internally competitive constituencies, Sunnis in post-war Lebanon have mostly lined up behind a single, powerful leader. Filling a political vacuum in the community at the end of the civil war, Rafik al-Hariri methodically built a political movement that came to dominate the Sunni community. After Hariri's assassination, his son and and political heir, Saad, extended the movement's reach in the post-Syria era, although financial strains and the ongoing struggle with the March 8 parties have begun to open up opportunities that Sunni competitors might exploit.

---

[65] In the lead-up to the 2009 elections, many interviewees speculated on the formation of a "centrist bloc" revolving around various combinations of Druze leader Walid Jumblatt, President Michel Sleiman, Tripoli Sunnis Najib Mikati and Muhammad Safadi, and, somewhat less frequently, Amal leader Nabih Berri. One of Berri's senior Christian allies forthrightly suggested that Berri and Jumblatt could break off together. Interviews, Beirut, 2008 and 2009.

[66] On dual games, see Cammett (2014); Mainwaring (2003).

3.5.1 Pre-War Competition

Before the civil war, and in contrast to the post-war period, Lebanon's Sunni community was among the most internally competitive in the country rather than among its least. Traditional notables and, later, Arab nationalists vied for Sunni support in the main cities and the hinterlands of the north and Bekaa valley.[67] The National Pact of 1943 reserved the premiership for the Sunni community, so political competition among Sunni leaders ultimately centered on the office of the prime minister.

The idiosyncracies of Lebanon's governing institutions, however, required aspirants to the premiership to achieve a delicate balancing act between their Sunni constituents and their Christian partners at the elite level. The former, whose votes sent their elites to parliament, responded enthusiastically to the pan-Arab nationalism then sweeping through the Arab world; Sunni politicians were constantly exposed to communal outbidding. Their Christian partners, in contrast, opposed pan-Arabism, and the Maronite president enjoyed the constitutional prerogative to appoint the prime minister. Hence, Sunni politicians with ambitions to the premiership could neither ignore Arab nationalism nor embrace it unreservedly. In practice, most Sunni elites struck a balance by offering their constituents patronage payoffs along with the obligatory nods to pan-Arab rhetoric.[68]

Hence, traditional notables, especially those based in Tripoli and Beirut, competed with one another for influence within the Sunni community in order to attract enough popular support to justify appointment to the premiership. In the three decades between independence and the start of the civil war, fifteen different Sunni politicians served as prime minister. In that time, no fewer than five credible Sunni leaders competed for support in Beirut alone. Abdallah al-Yafi, for example, held the premiership on six separate occasions, while Sami al-Sulh and Sa'ib Salam both served four times each – not counting other members of their families who also held the post. Meanwhile, Rashid Karami, the most prominent notable in Tripoli, served as prime minister six times before the civil war and twice more after the war started.[69] Hence, Sunni leadership rotated quickly as notables vied for their community's top executive position.

---

[67] Lebanon's Sunni community had traditionally been more urbanized than its counterparts, although the disparities have diminished over time as members of the other sectarian communities urbanized. Sunni urban populations concentrate in Tripoli, Beirut, and Saida, while the rural population spreads throughout the hinterlands of the north and parts of the Bekaa valley. The contemporary population is approximately one-third rural (Tannouri, 1998, 431).
[68] Compare Hudson (1968); Johnson (1986).
[69] For details, see Malhah (2003) and Johnson (1986, 47–49, 163). Note that Karami's father, Abdul Hamid, briefly served as prime minister in the early post-independence period, and his brother, Omar, served twice in the post-war period.

In addition to the frequent changes in premiership, parliamentary elections produced significant turnover in Sunni deputies from session to session. Like their Christian counterparts, Sunni elites waged competitive campaigns that became increasingly close over time. In particular, electoral returns from the pre-war period showed that Christian constituencies were no more competitive than their Muslim counterparts, and even hinted that the closest contests occurred in the Sunni districts.

Across the 276 electoral contests in the six elections from independence through 1964, the winner's average vote share among Christians was 62 percent, 61 percent among Sunnis, and 60 percent among Shiites. Based on fifty-four contests in single-member districts between 1953 and 1964, the average Christian winner's vote share was 66 percent, the average Shiite's was 61 percent, and the average Sunni's was 55 percent. The latter comparison hints that the Sunni contests may have been slightly more competitive than those in other communities, although the small number of observations does not provide enough information to detect reliable differences between communities. In 1972, the last election before the civil war, competition was fierce in Beirut's heavily Sunni third district. Out of four Sunni seats, the last winner received 12,872 votes against the first loser's 12,264 – a difference of just 608 votes.[70] Even incumbent prime ministers regularly lost their seats in parliament, only to return during the next election cycle. Members of their electoral lists, in turn, saw their fortunes rise and fall similarly.[71]

3.5.2 Wartime Vacuum

As elections became more competitive, the traditional Sunni notables also faced increasing pressure from Arab nationalists and other self-styled "progressive" forces throughout the 1960s and early-1970s, including the Palestine Liberation Organization (PLO). Unlike their counterparts in the other sectarian communities, the Sunni notables did not organize militias in the lead-up to the civil war. Instead, some Sunni-based, Arab nationalist organizations, most notably the Mourabitoun, began to militarize and undermine the established clientelistic system in the 1970s. Many of the brokers and "electoral keys" in the Sunni community started to operate independently of the notables under the patronage of outside, revisionist actors such as the PLO, and the Libyan and Iraqi governments. Hence, as one scholar observed mid-war, the early stages of

---

[70] These data come primarily from Hudson (1968, 225–231), who shows that elections across all communities became increasingly competitive from independence through the mid-1960s; el Khazen (2000), in turn, shows that this trend continued up to 1972, the last pre-war election. For the 1972 Beirut third district data, see Johnson (1986, 47–49).

[71] Abdallah al-Yafi, for example, won elections in 1943, 1947, 1951, and 1953, lost in 1957, 1960, and 1964, won again in 1968, and then lost in 1972. Sami al-Sulh, in turn, won a seat in parliament in consecutive elections from 1943 to 1957, lost in 1960, won again in 1964, and lost again in 1968. See Johnson (1986, 47–49).

the civil war brought the PLO and Mourabitoun to prominence and marked "the final collapse of the [traditional notables'] clientelist system" (Johnson, 1986, 183 *et passim*).

In contrast to the other sectarian militias that fought on to the end of the civil war, the Sunni-based fighting forces were destroyed by the war's midpoint. As one scholar observed at the time, "the decimation of [the Sunni] militias has left many Sunnis with the conclusion that an armed Palestinian presence in Lebanon is their only hope." In effect, "the Sunni militia *was* the PLO, and as the fortunes of the PLO have waned in Lebanon, so have those of the Sunni community."[72] The PLO, however, was liquidated as a fighting force by the Israeli invasion of 1982, Syrian attacks on Arafat loyalists in the north, and the "war of the camps" that Amal launched in 1984 in the Palestinian refugee camps. The Mourabitoun, much smaller and less effective than the PLO, was forcibly disarmed when Shia and Druze militias, allied with Syria, occupied Sunni West Beirut in 1985.[73] In summary, then, the PLO and the other Lebanese Sunni militias were effectively eliminated by foreign forces – both Israeli and Syrian – with the residuals subsequently finished off by local militias.

Hence, nearly all Sunni political organizations had collapsed by the middle of the civil war. Put together, the destruction of the militias, the sidelining of the traditional notables, and the deaths of many other Sunni figures created a political vacuum in the community. As one scholar summarized, the initial phase of the war "all but destroyed" the power of the existing Sunni leaders, the rise of the Mourabitoun "marked [their] final collapse," and the routing of the PLO and Mourabitoun meant that "in a political sense, the Sunnis were the war's main casualty" and that "as a political entity, [they] were to all intents and purposes destroyed." A Tripoli-based think tank director concurred that this vacuum left community members unprotected, fragmented, and marginalized to the point that "Sunnis largely were excluded from political life" for the remainder of the war.[74]

3.5.3 The Post-War "Money Militia"

Hence, by war's end, the Sunni community, "the war's main casualty," was both fragmented and effectively leaderless. Into this political vacuum stepped Rafik al-Hariri, a self-made billionaire from humble origins in Saida who had made his fortune in construction in Saudi Arabia. Hariri had, in fact, been active behind the scenes in the latter years of the war, providing aid to charities,

---

[72] Quotes from Norton (1987, 136, 137), emphasis added.
[73] Around this time, Syrian forces and their Lebanese allies also disarmed a smaller Sunni fighting force, the Islamic Unity Movement (*Harakat al-Tawhid al-Islami*), in Tripoli (Humphrey, 1989).
[74] The former quotes come from Johnson (1986, 2, 105, 183, 214), and the latter from an interview with the director of Tripoli's Cultural Centre for Dialogue and Studies, in International Crisis Group (2010, 2).

occasionally underwriting the Lebanese government, and trying to facilitate a peace agreement.[75] He entered Lebanese politics at the end of the war in the image of a "savior" with "sweeping, nearly total support" – a figure who was neither a militia warlord nor a scion of the elite political families, much to the resentment of the latter.[76]

As Lebanon shifted back to peacetime politics, the wartime militias in the other sectarian communities hastily converted themselves to political parties. The Sunni-based forces had, as described earlier, been scattered and destroyed during the war. Instead, Hariri relied on what one of his former advisors called the "Money Militia" (Farshakh, 2006, 405). As one journalist observed, Hariri's massive personal wealth and latitude to dispense Saudi aid "allowed him to create his own political constellation and finance social, educational, and charity associations that provided him with valuable patronage ability and enhanced his popularity."[77] Working deliberately, Hariri's charitable foundation and nascent political organization, which eventually became the Future Movement, mobilized mass constituents and distributed benefits to them.[78] In the process, he systematically cultivated a clientele via patronage politics, as a think tank director explained:

Rafik al-Hariri coopted all of Beirut, neighborhood by neighborhood, going family by family. This guy's an engineer? Get him a scholarship. Get this other guy a job.[79]

In sum, Hariri relied on massive financial resources to build a political machine from the ground up.

Hariri's influence in the Sunni electorate waxed over time, which, in combination with institutional reforms, enabled him to hold the premiership for stretches unprecedented in length in Lebanese history. The tenure of pre-war prime ministers was usually counted in months, whereas Hariri held the office

---

[75] See interviews with Hariri in Charbel (2008) and one of his advisors in Farshakh (2006).
[76] Blanford (2006, 46) observes that "the traditional Sunni elite, the powerful families of Beirut, [Saida] and Tripoli, resented the intrusion of this immensely wealthy Saudi-backed newcomer." The "savior" characterization comes from Charbel (2008, 261), a journalist who had interviewed Hariri on multiple occasions. The "sweeping support" remark comes from Hariri advisor al-Fadl Shalaq (Farshakh, 2006, 273).
[77] Young (2010, 82). By the late-1990s, Hariri's fortune exceeded $4 billion; he estimated that he spent around $200 million a year on charities and personal expenses (Charbel, 2008, 221, 235). In 2008, Forbes estimated his son and political successor Saad's net worth at $3.3 billion; 6 of the 13 billionaires of Lebanese descent are Rafik Hariris heirs. See www.forbes.com/lists/2008/10/billionaires08_Saad-Hariri_4R2O.html and http://yalibnan.com/site/archives/2008/03/forbes_names_13.php. For a sense of proportion, Lebanon's 2008 gross domestic product was approximately $29 billion; Hariri's personal fortune amounts to more than 10 percent of his country's gross domestic product. See www.cia.gov/library/publications/the-world-factbook/geos/le.html.
[78] See, for example, Cammett (2011, 2014); Cammett and Issar (2010); International Crisis Group (2010).
[79] Interview, think tank director, Beirut, June 2008.

continuously from 1992 to 1998, and then again from 2000 to 2004.[80] Syria, however, sought to counterbalance Hariri's growing influence, in line with its strategy of blocking the emergence of unrivaled leaders in any of the sectarian communities. In coordination with its Lebanese allies, these efforts included gerrymandered electoral districts, the cultivation of alternative centers of Sunni influence, and forcing through the appointment of rivals to the premiership.[81] Hence, one Future Movement activist observed that the Syrian leadership "supported Hariri from time to time, but also kept the Hoss and Karami cards" to play when Hariri displayed too much independence.[82] Building on the card metaphor, one journalist observed that, "with Syria always looking over his shoulder, Hariri usually won his hands with three aces, never four" (Young, 2010, 24). In other words, Hariri's main constraint was not competition from rivals in his own community, but rather externally imposed by Syria.

Despite efforts to curtail his influence, each subsequent election further extended Hariri's dominance of the Sunni electorate. After Syria and its Lebanese allies pushed him out of the premiership in 1998, Hariri marshalled his resources and staged a "countercoup" by scoring an "unprecedented victory" for himself and his allies in the 2000 elections – causing one local scholar to observe that "never before was there such a wide gap in votes as between Hariri's lists and the other lists, and particularly their leaders" (el Khazen, 2000, 218, 235). In particular, Hariri's list crushed that of Salim al-Hoss, the sitting prime minister, who retired from politics in the aftermath.[83] As another local scholar observed, the residual popular bases for the remaining Sunni leaders subsequently melted away, to the point where the traditional notables, at least in Beirut, were unable to form any nucleus of competition

---

[80] See Malhah (2003) for the tenures of all the successive Lebanese governments. Note, however, that there was an important institutional difference between the pre- and post-war periods, with the prime minister responsible to the president in the pre-war period, but to the parliament in the post-war period.

[81] Syrian and Lebanese intelligence agencies had, for example, promoted the activities of al-Ahbash and the reemergence of the Mourabitoun (Blanford 2006, 82, 177; compare also the discussion in Charbel 2008, 123–124, 141). Syria allegedly gerrymandered the 2000 electoral districts to shrink Hariri's parliamentary bloc; colloquially, the 2000 electoral law was known as the "Ghazi Kanaan law" after the head of the Syrian security apparatus in Lebanon who allegedly wrote it. Hariri was, moreover, also pressured to accept pro-Syrian figures on his electoral lists.

[82] Interview, Future Movement activist, Beirut, July 2008. Salim al-Hoss held the premiership from 1998 to 2000 at the behest of President Emile Lahoud, a close Syrian ally, despite having no parliamentary bloc of which to speak. Omar Karami, also lacking a parliamentary bloc, became prime minister in late-2004 after Syria pushed through a controversial constitutional amendment to extend Lahoud's term in office.

[83] The election of Emile Lahoud, a close Syrian ally, to the presidency in 1998 provided the constitutional opportunity to replace Hariri as prime minister, given that post-war institutional reforms made the premier responsible to the parliament rather than the president. After the Hariri government submitted its resignation in 1998, Lahoud appointed Hoss as formateur, and parliament subsequently gave its confidence to the latter's cabinet.

3.5 Sunni Monopsony

(Abd al-Khaliq, 2006, 62). Syria and its allies again pushed Hariri out of office in late-2004 after forcing through a constitutional amendment to extend the sitting president's term. After resigning the premiership, Hariri subsequently began to prepare his "electoral juggernaut" for another landslide victory in the 2005 elections (Blanford, 2006, 115, 119).

In the midst of the debates over the electoral law, however, Hariri was assassinated in February 2005, sparking popular demonstrations on an unprecedented scale that, in combination with intense international pressure, pushed Syria to withdraw its forces from the country. The 2005 elections, which began a month after the Syrian withdrawal, returned a sweeping victory for Hariri's son, Saad, and his allies. The combination of a virtually unbeatable electoral machine and the massive outpouring of communal solidarity deterred virtually all potential opponents from running. The transitional prime minister, Najib Mikati, had agreed not to run and even went so far as to nominate Hariri as his successor; his predecessor, Omar Karami, dropped out of the race citing "unfair competition" and complaining that "the elections aren't elections, they are simply appointments."[84]

As a local election monitor observed, there was, by this point, "no real contender to [the Future Movement] in the Sunni community" because "no one had the scope to contend."[85] Hence, "the field cleared completely," as one local scholar concluded, "except for a sole player: the Future Movement and its allies." In the aftermath of the elections, as another observed, Hariri enjoyed the "uncontested leadership" of the Sunni community.[86]

3.5.4 Maintaining Dominance

Since the 2005 electoral landslide, Hariri has worked to consolidate his dominance of the Sunni community. As one element of the strategy, he and his allies have emphasized the need for Sunni unity in the context of the ongoing conflict with Syria and, especially, Hizballah. The confrontation with the latter, largely over its militia, has grown more intense over time and accelerated after Hizballah laid siege to the prime minister's headquarters and took over the Sunni areas of West Beirut by force in 2008. As one of Hariri's advisors recalled in the lead-up to the events, "Beirut's Sunni residents were in a state of shock: they were surrounded by Shiites. Hizballah had taken control of all of Beirut, including its Sunni neighborhoods" (International Crisis Group, 2010, 13).

---

[84] The Lebanese branch of the Muslim Brotherhood cited similar reasons as Karami when it also dropped out of the race. See "Lebanese PM Mikati nominates Saad Hariri as his successor," *Ya Libnan*, 18 May 2005, and "Lebanon's former Prime Minister Omar Karami quits race," *Ya Libnan*, 21 May 2005. Muhammad Safadi, a member of the Tripoli Bloc, won his seat as a Hariri ally. Hariri's aunt and a local rival, Osama Saad, won seats by acclamation in Saida.
[85] Interview, board member, Lebanese Association for Democratic Elections, Beirut, July 2008.
[86] Quotes from Abd al-Khaliq (2006, 62), and Dhahir (2008, 83).

Many observers speculated at the time that Hariri's inability to protect his constituents would drive Sunnis to the Salafi movement; other observers noted the Future Movement's increasingly immoderate rhetoric that stressed sectarian conflict. By emphasizing the "existential threat" facing the Sunni community, though, Hariri and his allies helped to perpetuate the notion that "any expression of dissent was viewed as betrayal."[87] Ultimately, nearly all Sunni elites allied under Hariri's umbrella for the 2009 elections, which again returned huge majorities to the Future Movement and its allies.[88]

Sectarian rhetoric made it difficult for other Sunnis to run against Hariri, and his financial and organizational advantages further deterred potential rivals. Hariri complemented massive financial resources – his own, as well as Saudi support – with the largest political machine in his community by far (Abd al-Khaliq, 2006, 84). These assets deterred many would-be competitors, enabled him to co-opt some elites with local power bases, and eliminated others as viable electoral challengers. Omar Karami, for example, for a time the most plausible alternative to Hariri, dropped out of the 2005 elections and suffered a resounding defeat in 2009. As one of Hariri's allies in Tripoli explained, "Karami is no longer a power. He's a local player. We're not seriously concerned about him."[89] Karami enjoyed dwindling prestige in his hometown, but lacked a comparable organization and the resources needed to contend.

To illustrate, Figures 3.4 and 3.5 show two billboards displayed in Tripoli, Karami's home base, in the summer of 2008. Both attempt to shore up Karami's dwindling support and take thinly veiled shots at Hariri in the process. Figure 3.4 plays on the former's name with the caption "dignity (*karama*) is more precious than money." It simultaneously condemns Hariri for using his extensive patronage resources to buy supporters in Tripoli, while indirectly acknowledging that Karami lacks the means to compete on those terms.

Figure 3.5, meanwhile, suggests what Karami *can* offer: his lineage as a local notable. It depicts Karami (on the left) next to his brother and father, both highly respected former prime ministers. Along the top, the billboard reads "the Karamis: a family with roots" – that is, roots in Tripoli. It implicitly criticizes Hariri's origins in a non-notable family from the southern city of Saida while reminding Tripolitans that generations of Karamis have served the city and the country in public office.

Few doubt that patronage forms the core of Hariri's appeal to his constituents. One of his March 14 allies sheepishly acknowledged that the Future Movement's hegemonic position in the Sunni community rests heavily on "money, money, a huge amount of money" – almost word for word the

---

[87] Interviews, Beirut, June–July 2008, April 2009. The quoted passage is from International Crisis Group (2010, 14); see also Dhahir (2008).
[88] The only Sunni elites of note to run against Hariri lists in 2009 were Osama Saad in Saida and Omar Karami in Tripoli; both lost by huge amounts.
[89] Interview, Hariri-allied member of parliament, Beirut, July 2008.

3.5 Sunni Monopsony

FIGURE 3.4: Omar Karami Billboard: "Dignity (*karama*) is more precious than money" (Tripoli, summer 2008)

complaint levied against Hariri by many of his critics.[90] These seemingly unassailable resources, in turn, hamper electoral contestation because, in the words of a high-ranking opposition official, "We simply don't have the money. We don't have Hariri's money. You can't fight Hariri's money."[91]

Some figures, of course, do have significant financial resources; both Najib Mikati and Muhammad Safadi in Tripoli, for example, are billionaires and operate charities in that city. Both, however, have only localized power bases, and neither has a machine to rival Future's organization. Mikati, for example, "is not a ground operator, and has no grassroots," as one pollster explained.[92] Neither could hope to supplant Hariri nationally, at least alone.[93] In essence,

---

[90] Interviews, Beirut, July 2008, April 2009.
[91] Interview, senior March 8 official, Beirut, July 2008.   [92] Interview, Beirut, July 2008.
[93] Both Mikati and Safadi, however, defected from Hariri's bloc when Hizballah brought down Hariri's unity government in 2011, events which are described more fully in the book's conclusion chapter. Mikati became prime minister in a centrist–March 8 coalition, but eventually resigned, after which a new unity government formed under Tammam Salam, a member of Hariri's parliamentary bloc. Safadi, allegedly maneuvering to secure the premiership for himself, has subsequently announced that he would not run in the next parliamentary elections. On the latter point, see "Safadi's choice not to run sends mixed messages to rival coalitions," *Daily Star*, 6 October 2012.

FIGURE 3.5: Omar Karami Billboard: "The Karamis: A family with roots" (Tripoli, summer 2008)

non-Hariri governments – whether the father or the son – have formed only when imposed by forces outside the Sunni community, whether Syria or Hizballah.

3.5.5 Sunni Dominance in Comparative Perspective

As described previously, the competitive environments in the Christian and Shia communities contrast sharply with that in the Sunni community, which progressively came to be dominated by Rafik al-Hariri and, after his assassination, his son, Saad. Public opinion data, in turn, reveal systematic differences in the configuration of the partisan environments in Lebanon's three largest confessional communities. Drawing from original survey data as well as the 2009 and 2010 Pew Global Attitudes Project, Figure 3.6 plots party identification in the fall of 2005 and again in 2009–2010.[94]

---

[94] The Pew Global Attitudes Project (www.pewglobal.org) bears no responsibility for the interpretations presented or conclusions reached from my analysis of their data. Pew began to ask its respondents for their party preferences starting in 2009. At the time of writing, Pew has made data from the 2009 and 2010 waves publicly available. For these figures, I have combined the two waves; for my purposes here, the aggregate differences in party choice between 2009 and 2010 are modest enough to be inconsequential, except where noted. Unfortunately, Pew did not

3.5 Sunni Monopsony

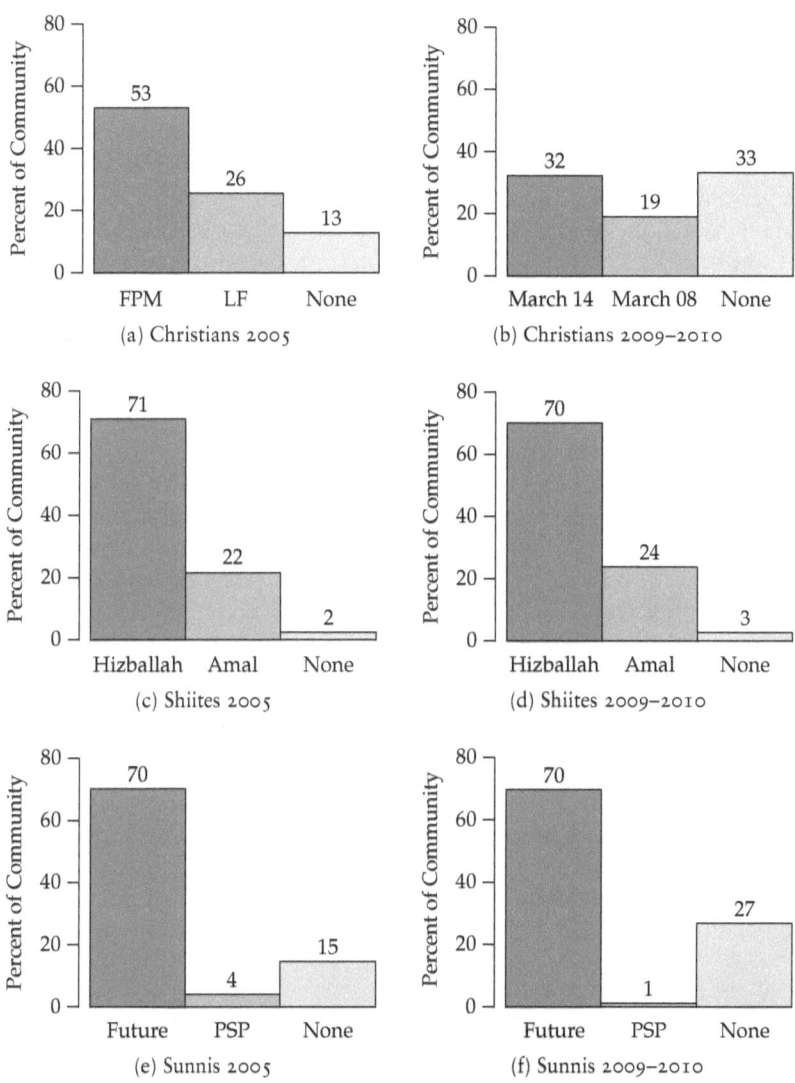

FIGURE 3.6: Parties' Popular Support by Sect, 2005 and 2009–2010

As described previously, these data confirm the competition among Christian elites: Figure 3.6a shows that the two most-cited parties in 2005 were Michel Aoun's Free Patriotic Movement and Samir Geagea's Lebanese Forces (53 versus 26 percent), with a large number of other parties and leaders cited as well.

ask for party identification before 2009, so there is no way to track a time series of support using the same question wording.

The Pew data in Figure 3.6b, meanwhile, reveal qualitatively similar degrees of competition in 2009–2010: about 20 percent chose one of the parties allied with March 8, a third selected a March 14 party, and another third chose not to identify with either bloc.[95]

Shia public opinion, meanwhile, shows the expected tilt in favor of Hizballah, but also steady minority support for its alliance partner and erstwhile competitor, Amal. Figure 3.6c shows that some 71 percent of Shiites favored Hizballah in 2005 against another 22 percent that identified with Amal, with very few unaffiliated voters. Figure 3.6d, in turn, shows virtually identical levels of support in 2009–2010, with 70 percent identifying with the former and 24 percent with the latter. Hence, these data demonstrate a clear popular advantage for Hizballah but, contrary to several elite interviewees' expectations, a sizeable and stable support base for Amal.

Sunni public opinion differs qualitatively from its counterparts. Figure's 3.6e and 3.6f show that Hariri's Future Movement claimed a steady 70 percent of popular support in the Sunni community in both 2005 and 2009–2010 – on par with Hizballah's level of support among Shiites. In contrast to the Shia community, however, in which Amal accounted for nearly a quarter of the voters, the second-most common answer for the party or leader with whom Sunnis identified was, in fact *no one* – 15 percent in 2005, rising to 27 percent in 2009–2010. Even more poignantly, the questions did not even offer respondents a "don't know" or "no one" category – "no one" was a conscious choice on their part.[96]

Reinforcing the Future Movement's dominance is the fact that the next most popular parties actually named by Sunni respondents were not even Sunni. In 2005, the Progressive Socialist Party (PSP) of Druze leader Walid Jumblatt, allied at the time with Hariri, received the next most support at 4 percent, followed by Hizballah at 3 percent, before any Sunni leaders were cited at all. The most "popular" Sunni alternative was Osama Saad of Saida (3 of 316 Sunnis), then Najib Mikati, the transitional prime minister, who was named by

---

[95] March 8 identifiers mostly chose Michel Aoun's Free Patriotic Movement; a small portion chose the Marada Movement or the Tashnaq. March 14 identifiers chose Samir Geagea's Lebanese Forces or Amin al-Gemayel's Kataeb Party, with a few choosing Dory Chamoun's Free Nationalists. Note that the 2005 figures come from *before* the 2006 announcement of the memorandum of understanding that Aoun signed with Hizballah, so it was not, strictly speaking, relevant to discuss a March 8-affiliated Christian party in 2005.

[96] The 2005 question used an open-response format, with a prompt reading, "please tell me which political party, political movement or gathering, or political leader you feel closest to politically." Note that I have combined the following three responses into the *None* category: active citations of "no one," *don't know*s, and *non-responses* (22, 4, and 20 Sunni respondents respectively). For the 2009–2010 data, Pew uses a force-choice response, but does *not* read the "none" option to respondents. Note here that what I report as "none" includes true "none" responses along with "refuse to answer." In 2009, most of the *nones* were true "none" responses; in 2010, about 40 percent were refusals to respond. Whether or not this change is indicative of growing opposition to Hariri is an open question.

one respondent.[97] Not only did Hariri command the large majority of support within his community, but no one else commanded *any*. The 2009–2010 data confirm the pattern: the second-most popular party among Sunnis was, again, the Druze PSP at 1 percent; those that did not support Hariri had no viable alternatives to which to turn.

In summary, then, the Sunni community, formerly one of Lebanon's most internally competitive, has largely aligned with a single, dominant leader in the post-war period. Rafik al-Hariri filled his community's civil war-era political vacuum and built up a formidable political machine, which his son inherited and extended. By deploying patronage resources, cultivating sectarian conflict, and co-opting localized elites, the Future Movement came to dominate the Sunni community. Although unrivaled in his own community, Hariri's ascendence is neither absolute nor without weaknesses, however. Lebanon's power-sharing institutions obligate leaders to form cross-sectarian alliances in order to govern, leaving Hariri vulnerable to challenges from opponents in other sects.

3.6 CONCLUSION

As this chapter has demonstrated, Lebanon's sectarian communities vary along a continuum of internal competitiveness. Rival politicians have contested the leadership of the Christian community in both the pre- and post-war years, vying with one another for popular support in their community. The Shia community, in turn, began Lebanon's independence era beholden to their traditional notables, but a new generation of leaders began to displace the old just as the civil war erupted. After eclipsing the notables, the wartime militias in the Shia community forged an uneasy, two-party cartel in the post-war era and controlled most of the representation in the Shia community.

Hence, Christian voters enjoy a number of alternatives when deciding which party to support, while Shiites select from a more limited menu of options.

Sunni voters, in contrast, have little choice available to them, at least in practical terms. Although their community had been among Lebanon's most competitive before the civil war, wartime losses eliminated many of their leaders or else left them ineffective. Rafik al-Hariri filled the political vacuum at the end of the war, and progressively built a strong political machine while co-opting or defeating his remaining rivals in the Sunni community. His son, Saad, subsequently extended the reach of this machine after 2005. The lack of competition within the Sunni community leaves this constituency with few options: to support Hariri, whether enthusiastically or grudgingly, to support candidates compromised by their cooperation with Hizballah, or to support no one at all.

---

[97] In addition to Saad and Mikati, one respondent each named Muhammad Safadi, Hariri's ally in Tripoli, and the al-Ahbash association. No one named Omar Karami, prime minister at the time of the Hariri assassination.

4

Communal Politics in Yemen

4.1 INTRODUCTION

As the previous chapter demonstrated, Lebanon's communal constituencies vary considerably in the degree to which they are internally competitive: elites compete vigorously for political support in some communities, but are sheltered from competition in others. As one would expect, Yemen's communal groups evolved in a different historical, institutional, and demographic context from their counterparts in Lebanon. Although the contextual details differ between the two societies, they have experienced similar patterns in the development of their communal constituencies: political competition inside some of them, but not in others.

Lebanon's communal divisions are not absolute, of course, and Yemen's are also more contingent than simple dichotomies would imply. Partially overlapping cleavages based on tribe, sect, and region suffuse Yemeni society, with different people placing differing degrees of weight on each element. Political contestation has exacerbated these divisions since the 1990 unification of the northern and southern republics, however. In particular, the ruling party and opposition compete – albeit on an uneven playing field – for supporters within the less tribalized Sunni communities of the midland and southern provinces that constitute the country's demographic majority. Over time, however, Zaydi tribesmen gravitated to the ruling party in response to the push of Salafi assertiveness in the Sunni community and, more importantly, the pull of patronage payoffs to their shaykhs. Hence, the ruling regime progressively established its ascendency over the tribes in the Zaydi community – a dominance eventually ruptured by the shock of the Arab Spring and the opportunistic defection of key allies among the tribes.[1]

---

[1] The ruling regime began to cut patronage payoffs to many of the shaykhs in response to a decline in government resources in the late-2000s, due in part to dwindling oil reserves. Disgruntlement

4.2 Institutions and the Politics of Unification

This chapter runs roughly in parallel to the previous one, which examined the evolution of competition within Lebanon's sectarian communities. Here, I trace how Yemen arrived at a point where competition differed substantially within its Sunni and Zaydi constituencies. The chapter begins with an overview of governance in Yemen pre- and post-unification, focusing on the collusive bargain between the northern and southern ruling parties that ultimately ended in a civil war from which the northern ruling regime emerged victorious. Whereas the Lebanese civil war created a political vacuum in that country's Sunni community, the Yemeni civil war disrupted the balance of power among the Yemeni political parties and enabled the ruling party to consolidate its authority at the expense of its erstwhile partners by poaching the latters' supporters. Next, the chapter examines the competition between the regime and opposition for support from different elements of the Sunni community, including mainstream voters from the midlands, doctrinal radicals among the Salafis, and disgruntled southerners. Finally, it details how the Zaydi community – internally competitive at the beginning of the unity period – defected en masse to the ruling party in the elections after the civil war.

4.2 INSTITUTIONS AND THE POLITICS OF UNIFICATION

The modern Republic of Yemen emerged from the surprise merger of the Cold War-era northern and southern states in 1990. Although the governing elites in the two republics ruled in the name of different ideologies, they shared the experience of governing weak states with minimal administrative capacity. United Yemen introduced a new, multiparty system in the process of amalgamating the two states, but also inherited cleavages that spilled over into civil war in 1994, from which the north emerged victorious. This section provides historical context on the Cold War-era Yemens and the early unity period, highlighting the continuing importance of social divisions based on tribe, sect, and region.

4.2.1 Two Yemens

Prior to the revolutions in the 1960s, the northern and southern regions of what is today Yemen were separate states. Notwithstanding two periods of partial Ottoman occupation, a 1000-year old Zaydi Shia imamate ruled the northern regions, although government was personalized, offered virtually no services, and was largely restricted to the urban areas. Only in the twentieth century did an aspiring dynasty put together the basic elements of a centralized state that enabled it to extend its writ, however tenuous, over wide swaths of territory. The government neither kept statistics nor conducted censuses, but the

---

on the part of these intermediaries likely contributed to their abandonment of the regime in the Arab Spring events of 2011.

northern regions appeared to split evenly between Zaydis and Sunnis following the Shafai rites. The former concentrated in the marginally productive northern mountains and on the desert fringes where the tribal system dominated day-to-day life in the absence of a central government. The latter, in turn, predominated in fertile midland areas and along the coastal plains where the tribal system was weaker. Zaydis were, nominally, the ruling sect, although latter-day imams selectively employed Sunni jurisprudence to counter inconvenient Zaydi doctrine to legitimize the shift to dynastic rule.[2]

While the imamate formed the kernel of centralized rule in the northern regions, the more sparsely populated areas of southern Yemen, with the partial exception of parts of the Hadhramawt, enjoyed even less governance before the advent of British colonial rule in the mid-nineteenth century. Britain initially restricted its attention to the port of Aden, located strategically on the Suez-to-India sea lanes, and then gradually extended into the hinterlands through treaties with local rulers – some of whom Britain effectively created – in order to minimize the material cost of governance. British forces also made efforts to suppress the endemic tribal warfare in the region in order to safeguard supply routes to the port.[3]

Revolution against imamic rule broke out in the north in 1962, sparking an eight-year civil war that served as a proxy battle in the "Arab Cold War" between Egyptian troops on the side of the republic and Saudi money on the side of the imamate.[4] The Shafais of the midland regions largely supported the republic and formed the core of its progressive factions, while the Zaydi tribes of the north split between the warring factions. Important elements of the Hashid tribal confederation sided with the republican government, others sided with the imam, and still others fought for whichever side paid better – hence the well-traveled quip that the latter were "royalist by day, republican by night."[5] The civil war eventually ended after the Egyptian forces withdrew and Saudi Arabia brokered a settlement that established a conservative, republican state in which Zaydis retained key positions in the government and military, while the tribes and local notables continued to exercise wide authority in local affairs.[6]

At roughly the same time, a doctrinaire and explicitly anti-tribal Marxist party took power in South Yemen after the 1967 revolution against British rule. The new regime deposed the British-installed petty sultans, eliminated tribal

---

[2] See Abu Ghanim (1985, 1990); Corstange (2007); Dresch (1989, 2000); Haykel (2003); Serjeant (1982).
[3] See Dresch (2000); Gavin (1975); Hamilton (1942); Luqman (1986); Zahiri (2004).
[4] The "Arab Cold War" pitted leftist republics led by Egypt against conservative monarchies led by Saudi Arabia (Kerr, 1971). Yemen was a major battleground as Saudi Arabia opposed Egyptian attempts to extend onto the Arabian peninsula.
[5] See Corstange (2007); Dresch (2000); O'Ballance (1971).
[6] See Burrowes (1987); Mansour (1999); Zahiri (1996).

4.2 Institutions and the Politics of Unification

shaykhs, often violently, and enacted policies to impose scientific socialism and stamp out tribalism. Despite repeated pronunciations in favor of unification between the two republics, and occasionally convening summits to discuss the matter, the north and south fought two major border wars in the 1970s. The southern state also sponsored a long-running leftist insurrection across the border in the northern republic. The northern government, in turn, mobilized Zaydi tribal forces to fight the largely Shafai insurrectionists in the midlands, who comprised many of the progressive elements frozen out of the Saudi-brokered peace agreement. Doctrinal differences were not, however, a salient part of the conflict, and the north's Muslim Brotherhood and nascent Salafi groups also opposed the insurrectionists.[7]

4.2.2 United Yemen

After a quarter century of false starts and half-serious rounds of negotiation between the two Yemens, the northern and southern republics unified in 1990 – much to the surprise of most Yemenis and foreign observers. Among the most plausible explanations for the decision include the collapse of Soviet aid to the south, joint interest in exploiting newly discovered oil fields straddling the north–south border, and collusion between northern and southern elites. During the transition period, the northern and southern ruling parties – the General People's Congress (GPC) and Yemeni Socialist Party (YSP), respectively – shared power equally as they merged their parliaments and civil services but retained control over their own militaries and security services.[8]

Both republics had restricted partisanship in the pre-unity era, with the south operating a one-party state and the north prohibiting all parties and permitting only a series of state-controlled "mass political organizations." The transitional government, however, ushered in a period of unprecedented political liberalization by lifting restrictions on press freedoms, granting greater rights to association, and legalizing political parties. In response, more than forty parties established themselves in the months after the declaration of unity, with half of them going on to contest the country's first multiparty elections in 1993. Some of the parties were new groups, while a number of others emerged from the spectrum-spanning GPC umbrella. Many of the self-styled progressive parties joined the YSP, allied with it, or established separate organizations – as with two Baathist parties and up to nine Nasirist factions, three of which won seats in 1993.[9]

---

[7] See Burrowes (1987); Corstange (2007); Dresch (2000); Halliday (1974).
[8] Compare Abu Talib (1994); Burrowes (1991); Carapico (1993b,c); Dresch (2000); Dunbar (1992); Mansour (2004).
[9] See Burrowes (1987); Carapico (1993a,c, 1998); Farah (2005); Mansour (2004); Muhammad (1998); Sarraf (1992); Zahiri (2004).

The most important faction to split off from the GPC, however, was the Islah Party, which combined diverse trends with, for lack of better terminology, "conservative" views – one of the few unifying features was a general opposition to "leftists" and "secularists," particularly those in the YSP. The party formed what observers called a "marriage of convenience" between key tribal leaders with power bases in the countryside, the urban-based Muslim Brotherhood and some of its Salafi proponents, and a number of prominent businessmen. Early commentary described the party as having two "wings" – a tribal wing and a Muslim Brotherhood wing – although this description became increasingly inaccurate over time as the tribal wing shrank; by the time of my own interviews, Islah officials openly scoffed at the idea and explicitly cited the exodus of tribal leaders from their party to the GPC. Many Islah figures retained close ties with the former northern regime and, in the early unity period, Islah was often indistinguishable from the GPC.[10]

Yemen held its first multiparty elections for parliament in 1993, using plurality electoral rules in 301 single-member districts, the same basic system it employed in subsequent elections. The 1993 campaign was broadly fair and very competitive, and no party emerged with a clear mandate. The GPC won some 29 percent of the popular vote nationwide, which translated into 41 percent of the seats due to plurality-based disproportionality. The YSP won slightly more of the popular vote than did Islah (19 versus 17 percent), although the latter won slightly more seats than the former (21 versus 19 percent).[11] The YSP retained its preeminence in the south, where it won nearly 75 percent of the region's 56 seats, with most of the remainder going to independent candidates. Although it also polled competitively in several northern provinces along the old border, southern seats accounted for less than 20 percent of the seats in parliament, and so threatened to restrict the party to permanent minority status.[12] Much to southern leaders' anxiety, Islah and the GPC together won

---

[10] Consistent with the distaste that many Yemenis, particularly religiously devout ones, share for the ideas of partisanship, Islah is formally a "congregation," although, in practice, most people refer to it as a "party" (i.e., as a *hizb* rather than a *tajammu*). Cooperation between tribal figures and the Muslim Brotherhood had its origins in the "Islamic Front" that fought against the leftist insurgency in the early-1980s. Note that the tribal leaders were principally Zaydi, the Muslim Brotherhood included both mainstream Shafais and more extreme Salafis, and the businessmen were often those from traditional business families originating in the Shafai regions. Carapico (1993c, 3) refers to the "marriage of convenience," a description consistent with the prevailing view in the academic literature of the period, while Dresch and Haykel (1995) report the "two wings" description without endorsing it. I conducted most of my own interviews with Islah officials in 2005–2006. For various aspects on the development of the party, see Dresch and Haykel (1995); Mansour (2004); Maqalih (1998); Muhammad (1998); Said (1995); Schwedler (2004, 2006); Yadav (2013).

[11] For data, see Farah (2005) and www.al-bab.com/yemen/pol/election1993.htm (accessed 1 August 2012).

[12] The YSP won 41 of the 56 southern seats, independents captured 12, and the GPC won the remaining 3. Based on the popular vote, it also polled competitively in several border provinces

61 percent of the seats in parliament – albeit on only 46 percent of the popular vote – and cooperated, tacitly or openly, in a large number of districts.[13]

The three parties ultimately formed a unity government, but this time with the GPC as the senior partner and the YSP relegated to a junior role on par with Islah. The unity project continued to teeter as outnumbered and outmaneuvered southern leaders absorbed their loss of influence in united Yemen and faced growing waves of violence directed at YSP officials. Civil war broke out in 1994 after YSP leaders declared the south's secession, but the northern military forces routed their southern counterparts. With most of its leaders in exile, its properties confiscated, and many of its supporters eventually losing their jobs in the civil service or armed forces, the war destroyed the YSP and marked its collapse as a major political party.

As in Lebanon, a civil war upended the competitive environment in Yemen and effectively destroyed one of the main contenders. Unlike in Lebanon, however, the war did not leave a vacuum in any community – southerners still had choices, as the GPC and Islah both rushed into the south to compete for its voters. After crushing the YSP in the civil war, however, the GPC could treat Islah not as a partner and counterweight to the southern leaders, but as a rival. Consequently, the collapse of the YSP freed the GPC to chip away at Islah's support base. Although it made inroads among all communities, the GPC was particularly effective at buying off most of the tribal shaykhs in the Zaydi community – points to which I now turn.

4.3 COMMUNAL POLITICS IN UNITED YEMEN

As Chapter 3 described, communalism in Lebanon centers on religious sect, with sectarian identities written into the constitution and electoral laws, and, as a practical result, into the political parties as well. Communal politics are also highly salient in Yemen, although they are less straightforward to describe insofar as Yemen has not written power-sharing mechanisms into its formal institutions and does not officially recognize communal groups as Lebanon does. On the contrary, and consistent with efforts in other developing world countries with salient ethnic cleavages, the political parties law forbids the

---

and won a quarter of its seats in the latter. Independent candidates, meanwhile appeared to be equally strong in the southern and northern provinces. Whether broken down by seat or province, there is no detectable difference between the two regions in the probability of an independent victory. As before, see data from www.al-bab.com/yemen/pol/election1993.htm (accessed 1 August 2012).

[13] Hence, Dresch and Haykel (1995, 407) report that upwards of 70 Islah candidates withdrew in favor of GPC candidates, while 30 people elected on the GPC ticket were, in fact, Islah supporters. Given the porous boundaries between the parties, the official results are merely rough approximations because, as Dresch and Haykel argued, "precise calculation is pointless where the categories are ill-defined."

establishment of parties based on region, sect, tribe, and race – a largely symbolic attempt to disrupt communal politicking in a society characterized by precisely those cleavages.[14] Partially overlapping distinctions based on tribe, religious denomination, and regional origin are all politically salient, and each dimension figures into shared narratives about Yemeni politics. A key, recurring theme in these narratives, however, is the central importance of the Zaydi tribes from the northern regions to Yemen's political life throughout its history and, more recently, as a key constituency for the ruling regime.

Yemenis belong to several politically salient social categories at the same time, but differ in the degree of importance they place on their memberships, both situationally and in the abstract. One indication of this diversity of views comes from a question posed to survey respondents about their most important group membership aside from nationality. In the aggregate, some 20 percent of the sample identified themselves by sect, another 23 percent by tribe, and the rest by their economic circumstances. More interesting, however, are the differences between the main religious communities, which break down in informative ways (Figure 4.1).[15]

Figure 4.1a summarizes Zaydi and Shafai self-categorizations, which indicate that the two communities barely differ in their degree of identification with their religious denominations, but diverge sharply in the weight they place on tribal identities. While indetectably different on the former dimension, Zaydis are more than two and a half times more likely than are Shafais to identify with their tribes. Moreover, the former are also more likely than the latter to place importance on their tribal affiliations. In the aggregate, about half the sample declared their tribal memberships to be unimportant, while the other half considered them either somewhat or very important (28 and 23 percent, respectively). As Figure 4.1b shows, however, well over half of Shafais place no value on their tribal affiliations – more than two and a half times as many as their Zaydi counterparts. Zaydis, in turn, are over two and a half times more likely as Shafais to declare their tribal links to be very important.[16]

---

[14] See Mansour (2004, 165 *et passim*) for details.
[15] I originally designed the question to be open response, but, upon implementation, the survey team categorized responses into religious denomination, tribe, and economic circumstances only – meaning that I cannot distinguish other categorizations, the most important of which would have been region. Although not ideal, these data are still informative in that they give us the relative likelihoods that respondents would choose one of these three categories. The question wording reads: "We have spoken to many Yemenis and they have all described themselves in different ways. Some people, for example, describe themselves in terms of their religion, some in terms of their tribe, some in terms of where they live, and others describe themselves in economic terms, such as working class, middle class, or a farmer. *Besides being Yemeni*, which specific group do you feel you belong to first and foremost?"
[16] All respondents received the following prompt: "Many people in Yemen are members of a tribe, and for some people this is a very important part of their lives while for others it is not very important. I'll ask you first if you are nominally part of a tribe, and then how important that

4.3 Communal Politics in United Yemen

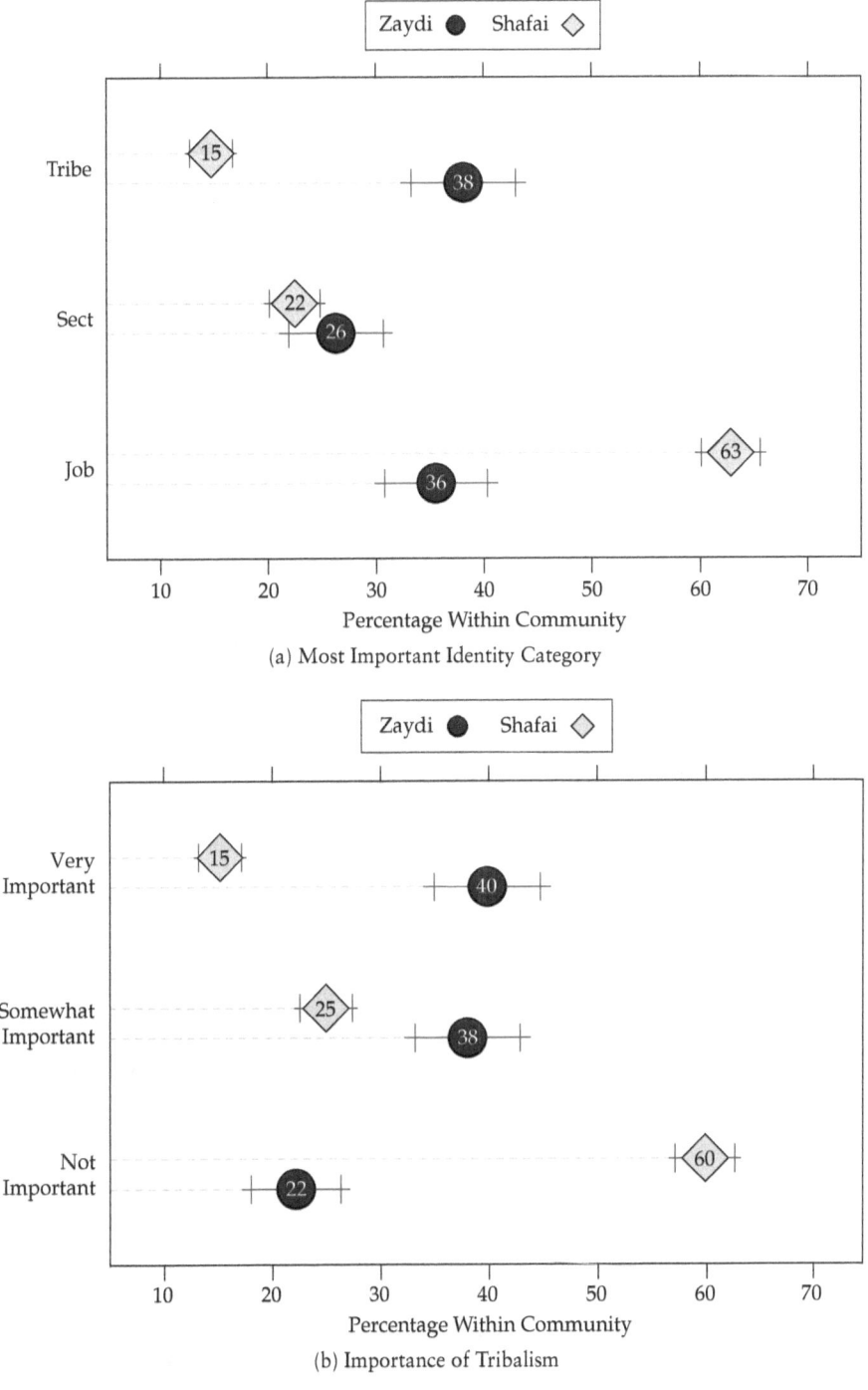

FIGURE 4.1: Yemeni Self-Identification

Yemen's Zaydi population resides almost entirely in its northern provinces; most southerners, in turn, follow the Shafai rites. Southern Shafais are indistinguishable from their northern counterparts in the importance they place on tribalism, whether measured via the group membership question or the question on the importance of tribal affiliation.[17] In contrast, southerners are more than three times as likely as northern Shafais to identify themselves by denomination (49 versus 16 percent, respectively). This difference, however, most likely reflects the lack of a regional category with which to identify (see Note 15) – given the long-standing association of Zaydism with the north (on which see later in this chapter), denomination provided the most effective means of the options available for southern respondents to declare their difference from the north. Put together, then, southerners differed very little from their Shafai cosectarians in the northern provinces; both these constituencies, in turn, put far less weight on their tribal identities than did Zaydi northerners.

Differences in religious denomination, in *doctrinal* terms, is important to a minority of the population – arguably a growing one – that ascribe to Salafism or Zaydi revivalism.[18] Mainstream Yemenis do not, however, draw sharp distinctions between each other based on doctrinal content. Doctrine and practice in Zaydism – sometimes called the fifth school of Sunni Islam – broadly resembles its Shafai counterparts, although the appearance of similarity may be a product of the lack of salient difference as much as a cause.[19] One Zaydi scholar, for example, illustrated this convergence by relating an anecdote about how "even [President] Salih and [Shaykh Abdullah] al-Ahmar now pray like Shafais."[20] That the president and the paramount shaykh of the Hashid tribal confederation, both Zaydis and the country's two most powerful individuals, should adopt the observable trappings of Shafai rituals must surely have

---

membership is for you." They were then asked: "Regardless of how important it is to you, do you consider yourself affiliated with a tribe?" And then: "How important is this membership to you?" I include people who declared themselves as non-tribesmen in the "not important" category.

[17] Some 13 percent of southerners selected tribe in the group membership question, as compared to 15 percent of northern Shafais; the 2 percentage point difference is indetectably different from 0. Northern Shafais placed slightly more importance on their tribal affiliations, but these, too, were too small to detect reliably. Some 65 percent of southerners declared their tribal links to be "not important" against 59 percent for northern Shafais; the figures were 11 and 16 percent, respectively, for "very important." Overall, the differences are indetectable at conventional levels of significance ($\chi_2^2 = 3.31, p = .19$).

[18] On Salafism and Zaydi revivalism, see Bonnefoy (2011); Haykel (1995, 1999); vom Bruck (1999, 2010); Weir (1997).

[19] The "fifth school" terminology refers to the four recognized schools of Sunni Islam – the Hanafi, Hanbali, Maliki, and Shafai rites. On doctrinal similarities, see Burrowes (1987); Haykel (2003); vom Bruck (2010); Wenner (1967); Zabarah (1982).

[20] Interview, Sanaa, August 2005. The interviewee was not a Zaydi revivalist aghast at this practice: he related this anecdote to illustrate the convergence rather than to derogate it.

been good politics in a religiously observant, Shafai-majority society. Yet the convergence of practice, and the secondary importance of doctrinal differences per se, meant that the political trade-offs for doing so were relatively mild.

Instead, religious denomination overlaps with, and sometimes serves as a synonym for, distinctions based on region and tribe – especially given the degree to which Yemenis believe that "northern Zaydi tribesmen" run the country. Hence, as one opposition leader observed:

> The Zaydi–Shafai competition is now becoming an issue of region, as in "the region that used to, and still does, control the country" ... Shafais look to the north, to the Zaydis, and see that they [i.e., Shafais] are suffering all the time, and are second-class citizens.[21]

Similarly, another scholar remarks that "the residents of northern Shafai cities ... share the southern feeling of being marginalized by the elites who monopolize power and wealth in the Zaydi highlands."[22] For many Yemenis, then, sect is a shorthand political category used to distinguish – not always accurately – between those presumed to be politically influential or not. This rough-and-ready political classification has, in turn, taken on an additional dimension of salience in the light of mounting Salafi attacks on Zaydi doctrine and a corresponding reaction of Zaydi revivalism, points to which I return later.

Having established the basic context within which Yemenis make communal distinctions, the next two sections contrast the competitive environments for political support within the country's Sunni communities to the progressive loss of competition for the support of the Zaydi tribes.

4.4 COMPETITION FOR SUNNI SUPPORT

In addition to opening up the country to multiparty electoral competition, unification also significantly altered Yemen's demographic profile. Zaydis and Sunnis populated the north in roughly equal numbers, while the south was almost entirely Sunni. Hence, united Yemen's demographic balance tilted toward its Sunni component, which accounts for two-thirds to three-quarters of the country's population. Therefore demographic realities gave parties strong incentives to cultivate this expansive and diverse group of citizens.[23]

Simply aggregating to a demographic majority does not mean that there is a single, united, self-aware bloc of "Sunni voters," of course. Instead, the Sunni population subdivides into at least three partially overlapping, sometimes

---

[21] Interview, Sanaa, August 2005.   [22] Quoting Day (2008, 430); see also Day (2012).
[23] The north also hosted tiny populations of Ismailis and Jews, neither of which held any demographic weight or political influence. The population of the former northern republic was roughly three times that of the south as of unification. Censuses do not break down the population by sect due to political sensitivity, so estimations of community size rely on educated guesswork (Bonnefoy, 2011; Dresch, 2000).

conflictual components. These segments include the mainstream majority of the population that follows the rites of the Shafai school of jurisprudence and a growing minority of people who follow conservative Salafi teachings that many of their detractors describe as regressive or intolerant. The southern population partially crosscuts this division of schools. As in the north, Shafais account for the mainstream majority, but Salafis have also made evangelizing inroads into the south – much to the chagrin of many southerners, whether they consider themselves "progressive" or follow religious practices that the Salafi groups consider heterodox.[24]

4.4.1 Conservative and Progressive Voters

Given the unity-era shift in demographics toward Sunnis, virtually all of Yemen's political parties have attempted to cultivate the support of these voters. The GPC and Islah both ramped up their mobilization efforts in the highly contested midland and southern provinces, both before and after the civil war. Likewise, the YSP focused on expanding from its southern base up into the midland provinces, especially those along the border with large urban and progressive constituencies, where it polled competitively in the 1993 elections. Various Nasirist factions and other progressive parties, many of whose leaders had been active in the leftist insurgency sponsored by the YSP in the early 1980s, also drew on support bases in the midlands, particularly in the heavily populated province of Taiz.

Residents of the midlands and south were and are, of course, heterogeneous in their political leanings. In addition to sizeable constituencies receptive to the progressive parties, these areas also include large numbers of conservative Sunnis for whom the loosely articulated appeals to secularism, socialism, and Arab nationalism do not resonate. Islah, via its Muslim Brotherhood and Salafi components, has made explicit appeals to religiously conservative voters, and the GPC, even less ideologically coherent than its peers, has also competed directly for the same constituents. Competition between the latter two parties intensified over time for Salafi supporters in particular, albeit in a roundabout way. Both parties want the voters that key Salafi leaders can mobilize, but both also recognize the distaste that many Yemenis have for the Salafis – and so accuse each other of cultivating and protecting "extremists," as discussed later.[25]

---

[24] Some southerners, particularly in the Hadhramawt province, follow Sufi teachings, which are anathema to Salafi groups. See Bonnefoy (2011) on the Salafi movement and Buchman (1997); Knysh (2000, 2001) on the Sufi movements.

[25] Not all Salafis are politically active, and some Salafi leaders argue that participation in elections is religiously forbidden – a few have even gone so far as to declare other Salafi leaders apostates for participating in partisan life. Other Salafi leaders, such as Abd al-Majid al-Zindani, have participated actively in public and party affairs and are actively cultivated by Islah and the GPC. Compare Bonnefoy (2011); Said (1995); Yadav (2013).

4.4.2 Retribalizing Voters

In addition to religious conservatives, Islah and the GPC also courted social conservatives by cultivating tribal links in Sunni areas where the tribal system had traditionally been weaker, as in the midland provinces, or repressed, as in the south under the YSP. Part of the rationale for doing so in the early days of unity was to build counterweights to the progressive parties, whose leaders made little secret of both their disdain for tribalism and their angst that northern shaykhs were attempting to revitalize the tribal system further south. Hence, otherwise mild-mannered officials in the YSP repeatedly lamented how "the tribes have returned, the shaykhs have returned," and some became visibly agitated when denouncing "the tribesmen that rule now," who were "backward" and had "no rationalism in their minds."[26] Although not always expressed in such denigrating terms, discourse on "retribalization," even if exaggerated, has become common among Sunnis in light of the heavy emphasis on tribalism in Yemeni politics.

Although no longer needed as counterweights after the YSP's post-civil war collapse, the tribes continue to be convenient tools for dispensing patronage to clients – as one economist remarked, "the state is building tribes ... along with infrastructure."[27] As people became disillusioned with the parties' failures to deliver on their programs, many responded pragmatically by organizing, or at least trying to organize, to lobby for a share of state largesse. Hence, the head of a GPC-affiliated NGO, himself an urban sophisticate, described his efforts to revitalize the moribund Mathhaj tribal confederation in the Sunni areas, and a development specialist from the midland province of Taiz explained that "people are rebuilding their tribal links in order to get better deals from the government."[28]

By no means have all, or even most, midland and southern Sunnis retribalized to the point that they can rival their Zaydi counterparts in the north in organization, cohesion, or influence. Nonetheless, when the government negotiates with tribal groups and acquiesces to their demands, "the people from ... the Shafai areas and the people without tribes [become] extremely angry, saying 'we need to get our own tribes,'" as an opposition party leader remarked.[29] Hence, at least some people, particularly in the rural areas, have chosen to cultivate their family and tribal linkages in order to bargain with the government for material resources.[30]

---

[26] Interviews, senior YSP leaders, Sanaa, November and December 2005.
[27] Participant, qat chew roundtable, Sanaa, November 2005.
[28] The two most influential tribal confederations are the Zaydi-dominant Hashid and Bakil confederations; Mathhaj has traditionally been weaker and less able to organize its members to act collectively. Interviews with an NGO director and a Yemeni official in a western development agency, Sanaa, November 2005 and March 2006.
[29] Interview, Sanaa, August 2005.
[30] Compare also Baylouny (2006, 2010); Cammett (2014) on privatizing welfare provisions via kinship and communal links.

4.4.3 Southern Voters

Southerners, at roughly a quarter of the population, represent an especially salient bloc of voters. The YSP retained the bulk of the south's electoral support through the 1993 elections, in large part because it still had influence over civil service and military appointments, as well as other patronage resources. After the YSP's collapse, however, Islah and the GPC made significant inroads in the south, and southern polemics turned increasingly against "internal colonialism" and the perceived exploitation of the south by the "northern tribesmen" running the government and armed forces.[31]

Criticism of "northern" governance is widespread. One southern NGO director complained, for example, that the government was "building mosques, but they're not building schools," while a technician with a flair for the histrionic remarked that government services in the south had collapsed under northern rule:

> Previously, there were schools ... now, there are none. Previously, the hospitals were clean. Everything was clean, even the ground. Now, it's falling apart: filth, cockroaches, and insects.[32]

Many other southern interviewees waxed nostalgic for what they described as the order and rationality of the southern republic – and, poignantly, even the British colonial period – against which they compared the "chaos" and "backwardness" of the north's "tribal regime."[33] More concisely, or at least less melodramatically, a sympathetic western diplomat echoed southern activists in observing that "the northern [tribesmen] are basically exploiting [southerners] and taking everything they can."[34] Hence, many in the south subscribe to the local conventional wisdom of regional exploitation by the "north" – which, in this context, usually means the "north of the north," that is, by northern Zaydi tribesmen.

There is little doubt that the south is poorly governed. But, then again, so is the rest of the country: few Yemenis in *any* region receive good services. As a senior figure in Islah argued, "the south is suffering because of ... bad administration, and not because they're southerners."[35] More generally, as Longley and al Iryani (2008, 5) observe:

> While southerners often claim their marginalization is the product of regional discrimination, if one examines the socio-economic situation in the north, it becomes clear that

---

[31] Compare Alley (2010b); Day (2008, 2010, 2012); Longley and al Iryani (2008).
[32] Interview with human rights activist, Aden, September 2005; participant, qat chew roundtable, Aden, September 2005.
[33] To be sure, *fawda*, *takhalluf*, and *al-sulta al-qabiliyya* (or *al-nizam al-qabili*) were all terms used by northerners as well, although less frequently and less pointedly.
[34] Interview, Sanaa, March 2006.
[35] Note, however, that this official is from the north – the more polemically oriented of his southern counterparts might disagree. Interview, Sanaa, September 2005.

[the government] is an equal opportunity discriminator. Rural peasants, tribesmen, and city dwellers in [the north] beg the regime for basic necessities: sewage systems, clean water, electricity, agricultural support, and access to basic healthcare and education.

In short, the government provides poor services *everywhere*. Rather than discriminating against the south, there are, instead, important reasons why the government may, in fact, devote special attention to its residents, at least in relative terms. In particular, the regime cannot afford to ignore southern citizens in the light of the many parties and movements competing for their support. Despite polemics to the contrary, southerners have not categorically rejected the "northern" parties: both Islah and the GPC have made concerted efforts to cultivate clienteles in the southern provinces. In addition, the rump YSP – by default the only "southern" party in the country – and southern movement activists also vie for popular support among the region's residents by pushing for southern rights.[36]

Moreover, the ruling regime must compete against advocates of secession by convincing southerners that Yemeni unity is, in fact, good for the southern population. Part of the rationale is, of course, symbolic and nationalistic – the GPC, and President Salih himself, have staked a great deal of their prestige on the historic achievement of Yemeni unity. More practically, however, the ruling regime cannot afford to lose the oil revenues flowing from the southern provinces. Government statistics on oil production and budgeting are notoriously opaque in Yemen. Interviewees estimated, however, that oil revenues cover 70 to 90 percent of the government budget. Most interviewees, moreover, argued that the northern oil fields are drying up, so that the growing majority of Yemen's oil comes from the south. Hence, "unity is more than a sentimental attachment or a historic achievement; it is the cornerstone of [the regime's] survival."[37]

The GPC, in particular, has been keen on extending the trappings of government into the south and has taken a number of symbolic measures to highlight southern integration by appointing southerners to highly visible positions in the state, such as the vice presidency and premiership.[38] More practically, and

---

[36] Compare Day (2008, 2010, 2012); Longley and al Iryani (2008); Wedeen (2008).

[37] The quoted passage comes from Longley and al Iryani (2008, 12); see also Colton (2010). Compare Phillips (2008, 2011) on the opacity of oil and budget figures, and official Yemeni data more generally. Most interviewees acknowledged that oil production has shifted increasingly into the southern provinces (especially Hadhramawt and Shabwa), while the northern oil fields in Marib have been producing decreasing quantities. Tellingly, however, some northern officials insisted that oil revenues are not declining, and that the majority of production comes from the north. Interviews, Sanaa, 2005–2006.

[38] For example, Abd al-Qadir Bajammal served as prime minister for six years in the 2000s, and then became the GPC's secretary-general. Yemen's long-time vice president, Abd Rabbuh Mansour al-Hadi, was a southern military strategist widely credited with the victory in the 1994 civil war. He succeeded Ali Abdallah Salih to the presidency when the latter was finally pushed out of office in 2012 by the Arab Spring-inspired revolt. In the early unity period, most southern officials hailed from the faction of the YSP that won the south's 1986 civil war. After

inconsistent with polemics about discrimination, the government has tried to build infrastructure and extend government services in the southern provinces. A reformist in the ruling party, for example, acknowledged that "people are complaining about the use of unity," and argued that "the whole issue is to improve the standard of living" in the south in order to "give people hope that unity is good for everyone."[39] Another political analyst, often quite critical of the government, concurred on both its efforts to provide services in the south and the political rationale for doing so:

> The government is now putting a lot of money per capita into infrastructure in the south, three to four times more than in the north ... The political imperative comes first and foremost, to prove to the southern population that they're better off in a united Yemen than to secede.[40]

The political imperatives to woo the southern population have, in fact, often trumped efforts at rational development planning – itself never high on the list of the regime's priorities. For example, a technocrat in the Ministry of Planning, himself a southerner, objected that the government was excessively fixated on addressing southern complaints:

> North–South issues aren't really a big issue for us [in the Ministry]. I'm from the south, and I don't see it [i.e., discrimination against southerners]. Sometimes, I think it's the other way around as we try to do too much for southern "equality."[41]

Again, services and infrastructure are generally poor throughout all regions of Yemen, and a strong case could be made to deploy more resources in many of the impoverished *northern* areas that the government has largely ignored. Foreign aid agencies such as USAID and GTZ have, in fact, specifically targeted several of the northern provinces – heavily populated by Zaydi tribesmen – because the government has neglected them.[42] Instead, the ruling regime has put more effort into cultivating the southern population, whose loyalties are by no means secure. It has adopted a number of symbolic measures in order to sooth anxieties about loss of influence, but has also deployed significant material resources in trying to win over – or at least mollify – the southern population.

In summary, then, both the GPC and the opposition parties actively compete for support from Sunni voters in the midlands and the south – not because they are Sunni per se, but because they represent the country's demographic center of gravity and are open to mobilization. Although the parties engage

---

united Yemen's 1994 civil war, these officials were largely supplanted by the losing faction from 1986, many of whom had fled to the north (the "Ali Nasser faction"). Later still, many from the Ali Nasser faction were replaced by southerners more directly linked to the ruling party. The personalities and factional politics can be both Byzantine and sordid; see Alley (2010b); Day (2008, 2010); Longley and al Iryani (2008) for more details.

[39] Interviews, senior GPC official, Sanaa, February and June 2006.
[40] Participant, qat chew roundtable, Sanaa, November 2005.   [41] Interview, Sanaa, May 2006.
[42] Interviews, donor officials, Sanaa, 2005–2006.

in some programmatic competition, particularly in the urban areas, many citizens have become disillusioned by the parties' repeated failures to implement those programs. Consequently, as one opposition leader observed, many people "still feel that the old system of sects and tribes is stronger than the political parties," and have cultivated such links in order to bargain for a cut of the patronage.[43] Whether voting on the basis of communal ties or programs, however, voters in the Sunni regions at least have multiple options from which to choose.

4.5 STAGNANT COMPETITION FOR ZAYDI SUPPORT

While Sunni citizens continued to attract competitors for their political support throughout the unity period, their counterparts in the Zaydi community enjoyed less and less competition for their support over time. Such a disparity was neither anticipated nor a foregone conclusion in the early days of unity, when Zaydis spread their votes widely between several political parties that contested their support just as avidly as they contested the Sunni vote. After the civil war, however, the bulk of Zaydi voters shifted their support to the ruling party – abandoning these other contestants along the way. Both push and, especially, pull factors contributed to this shift. For the former, Salafi evangelism and threats against Zaydis pushed the latter to seek the dubious protection of the ruling regime given the lack of viable alternatives. More importantly, however, state patronage enabled the ruling party to buy off the bulk of the tribal shaykhs in the Zaydi community. Only with the sharp drop in patronage resources and the systemic shock of the Arab Spring did the Zaydi tribes defect from the regime in large numbers.[44]

As with their Sunni counterparts, there is no single, self-aware bloc of "Zaydi voters." Some fringe leaders and militant groups operating extraconstitutionally, most notably the Houthi movement, sometimes claim to speak on behalf of "the Zaydis" as a whole.[45] More in the mainstream, and more in keeping with the importance of the tribal system in the Zaydi community, the paramount shaykh of the Hashid tribal confederation occasionally tried, with minimal success, to position himself as the paramount shaykh of all of Yemen's tribes – but even then, the register he used was tribal rather than denominational. Hence,

---

[43] Interview, Sanaa, August 2005. Compare also Baylouny (2006, 2010).
[44] Compare, for example, Phillips (2011); Yadav (2013). I take up ramifications of the lead-up to the Arab Spring protests and their aftermath in the book's concluding chapter.
[45] The Houthis are, of course, influential insofar as they can field a tenacious fighting force capable of waging an on-again, off-again insurgency since 2003 – and, spectacularly, overran the capital in 2014 and evicted the transitional government. Although their level of popular support is virtually impossible to guess, they were, at least prior to the Arab Spring, "marginal" insofar as they commanded a few thousand insurgents in a country of approximately 30 million people. Hence, their influence stems from their capacity for violence rather than a burgeoning mass movement.

the Zaydi population pyramids on top of its constituent tribal components.[46] These tribes attend not to "Zaydi interests" per se, but rather their own tribal interests. "Tribal interests," certainly in the way that interviewees used the phrase, are generally material rather than ideological, which makes them particularly receptive to clientelistic exchange relationships.

4.5.1 Early Unity-Era Competition

Although their fortunes would change in the years to come, many parties and politicians competed for political support among the tribes in the Zaydi-dominant regions in the early period of Yemeni unity. The two most prominent competitors were the GPC, the north's former ruling party, and Islah, under its president, the paramount shaykh of the Hashid confederation, which had split off from the GPC after the legalization of political parties. The Iraqi branch of the Baath Party, headed by another senior shaykh from Hashid, won seven seats in 1993, although its support base collapsed in subsequent elections. Even the avowedly anti-tribal YSP flirted off and on with the Bakil tribal confederation – its erstwhile Hashid rival had strong influence in both the GPC and Islah – but with few tangible results.[47] Two small parties, al-Haqq and the Union of Popular Forces, focused primarily on the Zaydi electorate without emphasizing tribal links; the former party won two seats in 1993, which it subsequently lost in 1997.[48] Further reflecting the state of flux among Zaydis, a substantial proportion of the electorate chose independent candidates, some of whom subsequently joined one of the parties' parliamentary blocs.

As described earlier, Islah was founded on a "marriage of convenience" between important tribal figures and the Muslim Brotherhood. Although it polled well in the 1993 elections, its victories came mostly from its shaykhly candidates in the countryside, while its Muslim Brotherhood-affiliated candidates performed poorly in the cities.[49] The party also coordinated with the GPC in a number of electoral districts, and its leaders retained strong links with the latter.

---

[46] Compare the arguments in Dixit (2004); Fafchamps (1992); Horowitz (1985) on large groups pyramiding down to lower levels of aggregation. Most tribes belong to one of the major confederations, and subdivide into smaller segments that tend to be more salient in the day-to-day affairs of their members. Compare Abu Ghanim (1985, 1990); Dresch (1988, 1989); Sharjabi (1986, 1990).

[47] The YSP's efforts to cultivate links to the Bakil confederation reflected the attempt to counterbalance the GPC. For their part, Bakil leaders contemplated an alignment with the YSP to counterbalance the Hashid tribal confederation. Interview, senior shaykh in the Bakil confederation, April 2006.

[48] Among al-Haqq's two MPs was Hussein al-Houthi, the original leader and namesake of the Houthi movement.

[49] See Carapico (1993a,c); Dresch and Haykel (1995); Farah (2005); Mansour (2004).

4.5 Stagnant Competition for Zaydi Support

GPC–Islah coordination deteriorated soon after the civil war, however. Once the GPC no longer needed Islah to counterbalance the YSP, Islah itself became the GPC's chief rival. Although the two parties formed a coalition government after the war, the GPC began to undermine Islah almost immediately by siphoning off its support base among the tribes, discussed later in the chapter, and cultivating other religious organizations as counterweights to the Muslim Brotherhood, including leaders of al-Haqq and a number of Salafi groups. As a high-ranking official in Islah argued, the government exerted substantial effort to weaken his party by interfering with Yemen's "Islamic trend" by encouraging "Wahhabism" (the local pejorative for Salafism) and by supporting al-Haqq – which, he contended, attracted the more extreme Zaydis.[50]

4.5.2 The "Wahhabi" Push

While building its own links to various Salafi groups in the country, the GPC simultaneously emphasized the extremism of the Salafis within Islah, cultivating Yemeni anxieties about religious militants among both Zaydis and mainstream Shafais. In addition to detaching Zaydis from Islah, this emphasis on Islahi extremism hampered coordination between the various opposition factions. Hence, even one of the main architects of the umbrella opposition alliance, the Joint Meeting Parties (JMP), expressed some skepticism over Islah's control of its Salafi elements. As he observed,

> We don't really have sectarian conflict over doctrinal issues in Yemen, but rather the use of sect for political purposes. Yemenis are generally not fanatical about religion.

Within the parties, he explained, "there's not really too much ... tension over denominations," but immediately qualified these claims by cautioning that, "the only place where it's an issue is Islah, where ... many supporters are Salafi." These Salafis, he continued, are "fanatical" people who "don't accept others, don't accept others' religions, nor other Muslims."[51]

Pressing an advantage, the ruling regime has made a point of emphasizing Islah's links to the Salafi movement. A political cartoon in a GPC party newspaper, for example, illustrates the rhetoric by depicting Islah as a two-headed party – the friendly face, "for export," is smiling, clean-cut, and sports a trim beard, while its snarling counterpart, "for domestic consumption" and complete with the bushy beard favored by Salafis, depicts the party's militant face, which it uses to appeal to religious extremists.[52] They refer to Islah's attempts to cultivate a moderate image to foreign observers and embassies while maintaining a militant image for its local Salafi constituents. Islah's opponents

---

[50] Interview, Sanaa, September 2005.
[51] Interviews, senior opposition alliance activist, Sanaa, August and September 2005. On the origins of the Joint Meeting Parties, see Browers (2007, 2009); Burrowes and Kasper (2007); International Crisis Group (2012).
[52] See the caricature in 22 *Mayo*, 24 November 2005.

often make the analogous criticism that the party puts forward a moderate face to win over skeptical voters while revealing its militant face for the Salafi audience. This image, and the line of rhetoric behind it, seeks to dissuade citizens from accepting the moderate image that the mainstream Muslim Brothers have put forward, and to remind them of the militant Salafis within Islah's ranks.

Salafi activities in the northern provinces touched off tensions with Zaydi residents and contributed to a small but growing Zaydi revivalist movement.[53] Activists complain of Salafi evangelism, as well as threats against Zaydis – up to and including declarations of apostasy, a sin punishable by death in some doctrinal interpretations.[54] Using the same "Wahhabi" pejorative for the Salafis common among Zaydi activists, the former secretary-general of al-Haqq remarked:

> Look, Saudi Arabia is pouring lots and lots of money into Yemen to promote its own version of Wahhabist Islam. This is actually an irrational and uncompromising version of our religion, which we can do without. So, we need to counter those efforts ... and to fight intellectual advances by Wahhabism into Yemen.[55]

Many other members of al-Haqq complained of "Wahhabi" intimidation and threats, with Salafis "going around excommunicating people, and slaughtering Zaydis ... for being apostates."[56] Although al-Haqq has always been a small party, these declarations reflect significant anxiety among Zaydis about the apparent impunity with which Salafi groups may operate and target their community.

In addition to stoking anxieties among Zaydis, the ruling party has also attempted to split the opposition by emphasizing the Salafi influence in Islah. As alluded earlier, various representatives of the other parties in the JMP alliance – both secular and Zaydi-oriented – expressed anxiety about partnering with Islah due to their prior experiences with the Salafi faction in the party.[57] Most

---

[53] On the Salafis in Yemen, Zaydi revivalism, and the Salafi–Zaydi conflict, see Bonnefoy (2011); Glosemeyer (2004); Haykel (1995, 1999); International Crisis Group (2009); Makhlafi (2004); Said (1995); Salmoni et al. (2010); vom Bruck (1999, 2010); Weir (1997).

[54] More specifically, some Salafis engage in the act of *takfir* – declaring someone an apostate – which serves as justification for the killing of the offending individual. Considerable controversy surrounds *takfir*, especially about what constitutes sufficient grounds for declaring it, who has the authority to do so, and who may enforce such declarations. Some of my interviewees – pious Muslims, as far as I could tell – had been declared apostates by opponents who disliked their politics. Even Abd al-Majid al-Zindani, the controversial figurehead of Islah's Salafis, had been declared an apostate by another Salafi preacher for his partisan activities. Compare Wiktorowicz (2000); Yadav (2013).

[55] Sayyid Ahmad al-Shami interviewed by the *Yemen Times* in 1992 (cited in Dresch and Haykel, 1995, 412). Salafi movements became increasingly active in northern Yemen in the 1970s and began operating more openly after unification; many receive generous financial backing from the Saudi state and private foundations.

[56] Officials in al-Haqq, qat chew roundtable, Sanaa, January 2006.

[57] Interviews, Sanaa, 2005–2006.

4.5 Stagnant Competition for Zaydi Support

recognize, of course, the ruling regime's attempts to divide them. One senior official in the YSP, for example, acknowledged that:

> The Muslim Brotherhood was able to sideline ... the Salafis. Now, [the latter are] closer to [President Salih] than to the rest of Islah. All the crazy Salafi talk is ... now from the security services. They're trying to force a split in Islah, but Islah realizes this.[58]

Hence, the ruling party utilizes the Salafi threat as a tool to disrupt coordination among the opposition – a tactic of which party elites are well aware.

Nonetheless, not all of Islah's allies in the JMP were so sanguine about the party's capacity to control its Salafi elements. One of the leaders of al-Haqq remarked that "we're concerned about the Wahhabism in Islah. We're concerned about the sectarian politics of pitting one denomination against another."[59] More broadly, many Zaydis have grown increasingly nervous about the influence of the Salafis. As a journalist specializing in tribal affairs explained, Islah had been targeting Zaydis more and more as the Salafi influence grew within that party. Consequently, he continued, Zaydis, and especially the tribes, were taking refuge in the ruling party in ever-increasing numbers.[60]

In summary, the ruling regime has expended considerable effort in cultivating anxiety about religious extremism among both Zaydis and mainstream Shafais. The GPC stimulated the perception of a Salafi threat while simultaneously offering itself as the most practical alternative that could offer protection to anxious constituents. These anxieties and concomitant demands for protection, in turn, made people more susceptible to ruling party dominance by making their political support more inelastic – people were more willing to tolerate shoddy services for the sake of protection.

4.5.3 Eliminating Zaydi Alternatives

While emphasizing the threat of "Wahhabi" extremists, the ruling regime simultaneously worked to eliminate other viable options for voters by repressing other parties and movements. Hence, the government made concerted efforts to eliminate other rivals in the Zaydi community. Two small, Zaydi-oriented parties in the JMP, al-Haqq and the Union of Popular Forces, have been harassed repeatedly by the government, had their offices closed and party papers shuttered on various occasions, and even been subject to a phenomenon known locally as "cloning." The ruling regime has, in the past, supported pro-government factions inside a number of small parties to mount internal coups

---

[58] Interview, senior YSP official, Sanaa, December 2005. The official explicitly cited Abd al-Majid al-Zindani, the controversial Salafi figurehead in Islah, who President Salih had made special efforts to cultivate. The efforts appear to have paid off – Zindani denounced the opposition alliance reform plan of 2005, and endorsed Salih for president against an opposition-backed candidate in 2006.
[59] Interview, senior official in al-Haqq, Sanaa, January 2006.
[60] Interview, tribal correspondent, Sanaa, August 2005.

(a) Party Paper of the (Legitimate) Union of Popular Forces

(b) Party Paper of the (Cloned) Democratic Union of Popular Forces

FIGURE 4.2: Cloning in Yemen: Mastheads of the UPF's *al-Shoura* Newspaper

against the existing leadership. Once undermined, such parties typically offer public support for the GPC or the faux-opposition alliance – the latter itself viewed as government-supported effort to split the opposition. As one YSP leader explained, the regime does "everything possible to weaken opposition and dissent. There are 14 'parties' that support the GPC's tribal regime. They're not really parties, just parties on paper."[61]

In more extreme cases, the regime simply clones a party by setting up a parallel organization with a very similar name, party paper, program, and so on. Hence, in 2006, the regime sponsored the formation of the "Democratic Union of Popular Forces," a clone of the JMP-aligned "Union of Popular Forces." To illustrate the degree of mimickry involved, Figure 4.2 reproduces

---

[61] The YSP official went on to observe that such parties are usually comprised of "just the leader, who gets a key job in the state, like the head of the Syrian Baathists, who is the deputy speaker of parliament." Interview, YSP leader, Sanaa, December 2005. On the government-preferred National Council of the Opposition and its relationship to the JMP's precursor, the Supreme Coordinating Council of the Opposition, see Mansour (2004, 366–370 *et passim*).

the mastheads from the two party papers. On the top is the logo of the legitimate UPF's paper *al-Shoura* ("Deliberation"). On the bottom, in turn, is the cloned DUPF's paper masthead for *Manbar al-Shoura* ("Pulpit of Deliberation"). The logo shape, fonts, and colors (the original is green) are all virtually identical; even the Arabic *manbar* in buried inside the original *al-Shoura* to deemphasize the difference.[62]

Another small, Zaydi party, al-Haqq, also faced growing pressure from the regime and the security forces. Ostensibly, these repressive efforts stem from the party's association with, and accused sympathy for, the Houthi rebel movement that originated in the northern mountains of the Saada province; Hussein al-Houthi, the movement's founder, won a seat in parliament in 1993 as a candidate for al-Haqq. According to numerous interviewees, the GPC encouraged al-Haqq's establishment as a counterweight to Islah in the early unity period, although interviewees in al-Haqq disputed this claim. Some of al-Haqq's leaders, however, eventually turned on the GPC as the regime also provided support to Salafi groups seeking to convert Zaydis and threatening to excommunicate those who did not. These leaders, Hussein al-Houthi most prominent among them, eventually left al-Haqq and formed an armed militia – ostensibly to protect Zaydis from Salafis – that repeatedly clashed with the state's armed forces from 2003 onwards in the northern province of Saada.[63]

The government, in turn, denounced both the insurgents and al-Haqq, declaring both to be "imamists" seeking to overthrow the republic and restore the Zaydi imamate. Such rhetoric had its origins in the north's pre-unity days when progressives and other republican officials routinely denigrated the traditional social class system that privileged Zaydi descendants of the Prophet – a class from which many of al-Haqq's leaders hailed.[64] Consistent with this line of criticism, various ruling party and government spokespersons reminded people, ad nauseam, about the oppression and backwardness of life under the imams – allegedly, the life that al-Haqq and the Houthis were seeking to restore. As an example of this rhetoric, the Ministry of Culture republished, shortly after the outbreak of the insurgency, a collection of revolution-era poetry under the not-so-subtle title of *The Imamate and its Danger for Yemeni Unity*. The book jacket inscription, attributed to President Salih himself, offered

---

[62] *al-Shoura*'s editor, Abd al-Karim al-Khaywani, had been subject to repressive efforts in the past due to his writings critical of the government; these repressive efforts include jail sentences in 2005 and 2008 for which he was later pardoned.

[63] Hussein al-Houthi and al-Haqq's other MP eventually left the party to organize the "Believing Youth" militia (i.e., the Houthis). Interviews, Sanaa, 2005–2006. On the Houthi insurgency in Saada, see International Crisis Group (2009); Makhlafi (2004); Salmoni et al. (2010); Weir (1997).

[64] Collectively, this was the *sayyid* class (less frequently referred to as *sharif*s or *hashemi*s) whose members enjoyed great social prestige, if not always wealth, and who staffed many of the key government posts under the imams. See Burrowes (1987); Dresch (1989); Sharjabi (1986).

the volume to "the new generations that did not live in the dark and oppressive days of the imamate" which "some imamists" seek to restore:

> The imamate was the most backward system in the world. It was based on a sectarian regime ... There were no hospitals, no schools, no roads, and no universities ... Nothing at all, except ignorance, sickness, and fear.[65]

More generally, this rhetoric contrasted the injustices of the pre-revolutionary era to the material improvements in Yemeni life under the republic – in which some schools, roads, and hospitals, however humble, were decidedly better than none.

Given its alleged ties to the Houthi insurgency, al-Haqq faced sustained scrutiny and numerous attempts at repression. As one senior figure in the party complained, the common pretext for attacking his party and the military campaign in the north was "Zaydi separatism," and, increasingly, "it's practically as if it's forbidden to buy a book on Zaydi thought."[66] At one point in 2007, the party's secretary-general even dissolved the party, apparently under government pressure – which came as a surprise to the rest of his colleagues in the party's leadership, who had not been consulted on the decision and continued to operate the party on their own.[67]

In summary, then, the ruling regime has exerted considerable efforts to marginalize its competitors for Zaydi constituents. Analogous to its rhetorical attacks on the Salafis in Islah, the GPC has, rightly or wrongly, depicted the Zaydi parties and Houthi insurgents as religious extremists seeking to drag Yemen back to the dark ages of the imamate, while offering itself as the only reasonable alternative to these extreme views. Hence, it has hemmed in its Zaydi constituents between fears of the Salafi threat against them and the unpalatable options offered by the revivalists and "imamists."

Nonetheless, party repression and voter anxiety can only be *parts* of the story behind the differing degrees of competitiveness in the Zaydi and Sunni communities: repression and anxiety affect both communities in broadly similar ways. While the regime has certainly attempted to marginalize Zaydi parties such as the UPF and al-Haqq, it has also sought to do the same to parties with Sunni constituencies – most notably the YSP, which has been subject to on-and-off persecution since the civil war, but also others such as the Nasirists and Baathists, alternative factions of which operate under the umbrella of the government-approved, faux-opposition alliance described earlier. Moreover,

---

[65] The book in question was a compilation of poetry by the the revolutionary Muhammad al Zubayri (2004). On the importance of poetry as a form of political expression in Yemeni public life, compare Caton (1990).

[66] Interview, senior official in al-Haqq, Sanaa, January 2006. To the degree that the state was indeed suppressing Zaydi religious tracts, one of the main reasons may have been the inconvenient point of Zaydi doctrine that legitimizes rising up against unjust authority (i.e., *al-khuruj*). The latter-day Zaydi imams, of course, also tried to deemphasize that point in favor of Sunni interpretations that emphasize obedience to the ruler (Haykel, 2003).

[67] "Political Parties Affairs Committee Abolishes al-Haq Party," *Yemen Observer*, 20 March 2007.

4.5 Stagnant Competition for Zaydi Support

anxiety over Salafi activity extends beyond Zaydis to affect mainstream Shafais as well, particularly the progressives and secularists that have traditionally been targeted by religious militants. Even were these phenomena to affect Zaydis disproportionately, party repression and voter anxiety would only contribute to, rather than define, the differences in competitiveness between the Zaydi and Sunni communities.

4.5.4 The Patronage Pull

Anxiety about extremists and repression of alternatives no doubt contributed to the Zaydi shift to the ruling party, but more central to the GPC's hold over these constituents was the patron–client relationships it maintained with the tribes, and, especially, their shaykhs. Although it has extended patronage to Zaydis and Sunnis alike, tribal links are, on average, much stronger among Zaydis, and their shaykhs are better able to serve as intermediaries between the state and the tribes. Consequently, the ruling party was better able to buy off the tribes in the Zaydi community – and because the opposition largely lacked the means to extend into the countryside, those that were bought tended to stay bought.

At the beginning of the unity period, the GPC's primary competition for votes among the Zaydi tribes came from independent candidates – themselves usually shaykhs – and, especially, Islah. As described earlier, the GPC began to chip away at Islah's support among the tribes after the civil war. It did so by targeting the shaykhs as the party's entrée into the tribes themselves. As one academic explained, "most of the [GPC's] supporters are influential people from the traditional classes. The regime doesn't have legitimacy from the population, so it goes for influential traditional leaders [i.e., shaykhs]."[68] Given that many tribes vote in blocs – a point I take up in a subsequent chapter – winning over the shaykhs meant winning over the tribes as well.[69]

Hence, the GPC began to poach Islah's supporters in the rural areas by cultivating the tribal shaykhs that had initially sided with the latter party. Moreover, it also converted many "independent" MPs to GPC members. A pivotal senior shaykh in the Bakil confederation, for example, described how he and his peers among the other shaykhs decided to join the ruling party:

We made the decision to bring Bakil into the GPC. We sat and talked with a number of shaykhs and said, look, we share so many interests with them that it is silly to stay in the opposition. So we all moved into the GPC.[70]

---

[68] Participant, qat chew roundtable, Sanaa, November 2005.
[69] Not all tribes vote perfectly in bloc, of course, and the tribes also vary in the degree of autonomy granted to the shaykh to make partisan decisions on behalf of his tribe. However, even in those tribes that arrive at more consensual partisan choices through deliberation, the shaykh retains important agenda-setting and coordinating powers – notwithstanding his ability to dispense patronage and adjudicate in local disputes. Compare also Baldwin (2010, 2013, 2014).
[70] Interview, senior shaykh in the Bakil confederation, Sanaa, April 2006.

Acknowledging this instrumental shift to the ruling party, a prominent shaykh in the Hashid confederation criticized the GPC as "a collection of opportunists" pursuing their "personal interests." He went on to explain how the ruling party increasingly relied on "notables, high-ranking state officials, and shaykhs" – often the same people – in order to win elections.[71] The GPC could thus bank on these influential figures both to deliver votes and to serve as conduits to and from their constituents.

The departure of many shaykhs from Islah for the GPC, in turn, flipped the composition of the former's parliamentary bloc and support base. As a member of a notable Zaydi family explained:

Most of Islah's support in [the early elections] came from the countryside, and not the cities, since so many shaykhs won as Islahis. After 1997, however, the GPC went and bought off the shaykhs in the countryside, and now they're GPC MPs. Thus, [there] was a reversal – Islahi MPs are now primarily from the urban areas instead of the rural.[72]

The Bakil shaykh just cited explicitly confirmed this flip, acknowledging that "yes, a lot of shaykhs left Islah after the 1997 elections to join the GPC."[73] When the shaykhs left, so did the votes of their tribes.

Patronage politics, in turn, explain the success with which the ruling party snapped up the tribes. A senior official in Islah confirmed how his party hemorrhaged its tribal support base after 1997 and, more importantly, the material motivations behind the defections:

When Islah formed, we got about 20 percent of the shaykhs. But they all pulled out of the party. Most of the shaykhs left Islah for the GPC. Why? Because of [material] "interests." The GPC could give resources and money to the shaykhs and the tribes.[74]

Confirming this overriding emphasis on patronage resources, another interviewee observed that "tribal interests are focused on the billions found in Sanaa."[75] Hence, the "interests" cited by so many interviewees that motivated the switch to the ruling party are, in practice, *material* interests – whether collective goods such as paved roads or personalized payoffs such as jobs.[76] The ruling party, in short, bought off the bulk of Islah's support among the tribes of the countryside.

Over time, then, Islah, initially characterized by its tribal and Islamist wings, saw its tribal component contract significantly in size. One of the party's former ministers, in fact, dismissed this traditional, "two wing" description of Islah as "an old story" that no longer reflected the party's constituency after the 1990s. As he explained, "we have a homogeneous membership, and we don't have these wings ... the shaykhly leadership within Islah is declining in

---

[71] Interview, Sanaa, June 2006. [72] Participant, qat chew roundtable, Sanaa, May 2006.
[73] Interview, Sanaa, February 2006. [74] Interview, Sanaa, August 2005.
[75] Participant, qat chew roundtable, Sanaa, September 2005.
[76] "Interests" is my gloss for the Arabic term *maslaha* – which interviewees normally qualified as "personal" (*shakhsi*) or "tribal" (*qabili*).

importance, and [the party is] becoming more about ideas and programs." Consistent with this assessment, a member of Islah's consultative council indicated that this "shaykhly leadership" had shrunk to little more than Abdallah al-Ahmar, Hashid's paramount shaykh, and his allies. "The 'tribal wing' within Islah is really just ... Ahmar's supporters," he argued, speculating that "once Ahmar dies, that will be the end of the 'tribal wing' in Islah." More bluntly still, another senior party leader remarked that Ahmar "doesn't have a wing within the party." When pressed for details on Ahmar's role in the Islah, the interviewee responded disinterestedly that "he's a shaykh" and simply stopped without bothering to mention Ahmar's nominal position as party president.[77]

Implicitly, these officials acknowledged a common criticism of Islah's dwindling tribal component: that the party's remaining shaykhs were not committed to the party's vision or programmatic ideals, but were, rather, using Islah for their own purposes. This tension within the party is not surprising given that the "marriage of convenience" has become less convenient for the shaykhs, whose interests lie in extracting state resources rather than principled opposition to the ruling regime. As Dresch (1995, 39) noted just after the civil war and before the mass defection of shaykhs to the GPC, "tribesmen involved with Islah generally dislike the fundamentalists and the fundamentalists dislike the tribesmen" due to disagreements over how to run the state which reach up to "the party's highest levels." The remaining shaykhs largely used the party for bargaining leverage vis-à-vis the ruling regime – although formally outside of the GPC, many are part of the president's patronage network, which transcends the ruling party apparatus.[78]

Abdallah al-Ahmar, for example, remained the titular head of Islah and speaker of parliament up until his death – although he repeatedly won his parliamentary seat by acclamation between the GPC and Islah, and retained the speakership even after the GPC won an absolute parliamentary majority in 1997.[79] He also helped get a number of his sons and other relatives elected to parliament with a diversified slate of partisan affiliations – some as GPC candidates, some as Islahis, and some as independents – to form what one interviewee sarcastically called the "Ahmar bloc."[80] He retained close ties

---

[77] Interviews, Islahi leaders, Sanaa, February 2006, December 2005, and August 2005, respectively.
[78] Compare arguments in Alley (2010a); Phillips (2008, 2011).
[79] Republic of Yemen (2004, 233), for example, devotes an entire page to describe this idiosyncratic arrangement in the 2003 elections.
[80] By the numbers, the "Ahmar bloc" tied with the YSP for the third-largest bloc in parliament at seven members after the 2003 elections. Interview, senior YSP official, Sanaa, November 2005. Two of his sons, Hussein and Himyar, won seats in 2003 as GPC candidates, while two more, Hamid and Mathhaj, won as Islahis (Republic of Yemen, 2004, 229–230, 246). Two other sons served on President Salih's personal security detail (http://bigthink.com/waq-al-waq/the-al-ahmar-family-whos-who, accessed 28 August 2012). His eldest son, Sadiq, had won a seat as an independent in earlier elections (Farah, 2005, 60), and was later appointed to the upper chamber – eventually taking a position within the GPC, from which he resigned during the Arab Spring revolt.

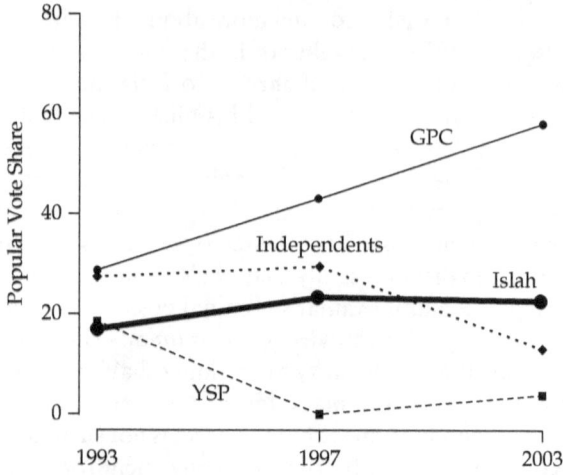

FIGURE 4.3: Popular Vote Share in Parliamentary Elections, 1993–2003

with the president, with whom he bargained over the allocation of power and resources, and openly supported each of Salih's presidential bids, including in 2006, when Islah had nominated a different candidate – with the result that the head of the country's largest opposition party campaigned on behalf of the ruling party's candidate. Although he retained his affiliation with Islah, Ahmar and his remaining allies bucked the party when it suited them. As one of his ostensible allies in the opposition argued, "Ahmar needs Islah. It keeps him separate from the state. Without Islah, he's just a shaykh of the tribes."[81]

4.5.5 Zaydi Stagnation and Sunni Competitiveness

Islah's shrinking tribal component had important ramifications for the make-up of its popular constituency – and for what it means about the competitiveness of the Zaydi and Sunni communities. As previously discussed, the party's tribal contingent accounted for most of the party's victories in the 1993 elections, but its representation flipped from rural to urban after 1997 when the bulk of its shaykhly supporters defected to the GPC. As Figure 4.3 reveals, however, Islah's share of the popular vote remained steady at around 20 percent over successive elections – meaning that, as the party lost its Zaydi supporters, it replaced them with Sunni voters.[82]

---

[81] Interview, opposition leader, Sanaa, September 2005.
[82] While the GPC was the primary beneficiary of the YSP's decision to boycott the 1997 elections, it's additional gains in 2003 came almost entirely at the expense of independent candidates – many of whom, in the past, had been tribal figures.

The shift away from the rural-based shaykhs led to a corresponding shift toward the urban-based Islamists. The changing balance of influence has meant, as one of the party's top leaders acknowledged, that "Islah is increasingly coming to represent Sunni thought" – and Sunni constituents.[83] Moreover, the shift away from the the older generation in the party altered Islah's alliance-making decisions. As one of the JMP alliance's architects explained, the party's old guard retained close ties with the ruling regime. However:

> [The new generation in Islah has] started to feel that the enemy is not the YSP or the others, but the GPC. They're starting to get closer to the YSP and the Nasirists ... especially because [those parties] come from the Shafai areas. They feel that the ruling clique comes from one area and is against the people from other areas.[84]

As the shaykhs from the Zaydi areas shifted their support to the ruling party, Islah moved more openly into the opposition to represent constituencies from elsewhere in the country.

Competition for support in Yemen's Sunni communities persisted – despite the ruling party's privileged access to the state – even as competition among the Zaydi tribes stagnated. As one Islahi leader explained:

> In the elections, the GPC relies heavily on tribal figures who have nothing to do with democracy. They go into elections with public money ... pushing people to vote for them not because they have [support] but because they have influence. The old school is tribal and the GPC has them. The new generation belongs to us. The ones who believe in the ballot box come to us and the other parties.[85]

Patronage-based competition may, of course, be central to Yemeni politics – but it is *more* competitive for some Yemenis than for others.

4.6 CONCLUSION

After unifying the former northern and southern republics in 1990, Yemenis faced the task of integrating different, partially overlapping constituencies based on region, tribe, and sect into a single body politic. In the hopeful early days of the unity period, parties contested popular support among all of these groups. This competition became decidedly uneven over time, however, as the former ruling party of the north consolidated its influence and Yemen slipped back into electoral autocracy. Notwithstanding the uneven playing field, several parties continued to vie for support among the various Sunni constituencies, but competition for support among the Zaydi tribes of the north waned as their shaykhs, attracted by state patronage, shifted en masse into the ruling party.

This emphasis on patronage politics extends well beyond the tribal shaykhs, of course – clientelism pervades nearly all aspects of Yemeni politics. True to

---

[83] Interview, senior Islah official, Sanaa, September 2005.
[84] Interviews, opposition party leader, Sanaa, August and September 2005.
[85] Interview, Sanaa, February 2006.

its origins, the ruling party continues to operate a classic, catch-all machine that crosscuts sects, tribes, and regions. Rather than aggregate and express constituents' policy preferences, it maintains its otherwise unwieldy coalition with patron–client politics at the local level. As in many other electoral autocracies, however, the party apparatus serves as just one of several tools for the ruling regime to use when dispensing patronage. This multiplicity of options gives regime elites a number of channels through which to service non-partisan clients and co-opt members of the opposition.

The ruling regime makes heavy use of local notables to serve as go-betweens with regular constituents. Although their capacity to deliver votes can vary, tribal shaykhs can act as brokers in the patronage system – particularly among Zaydis in the rural areas of the north where the tribal system is most vibrant. Although local notables provide a simple, cost-effective way for the regime to extend its reach into the countryside, farming out broker duties to the shaykhs implies a lack of control over local agents. Doing so leaves regime elites and the ruling party vulnerable to defections by their brokers if the former fail to fulfill their end of the clientelistic bargain.

While the ruling regime could maintain its clientele in relatively flush times, mounting fiscal problems in the late-2000s depleted the stock of patronage resources and made it increasingly difficult to service its clients. The ruling party was able to retain support among the Zaydi tribes for as long as it did not because the shaykhs or tribesmen were particularly happy with the GPC (by and large, they were not), but because they lacked viable alternatives. The events of the Arab Spring, however, provided a systemic shock around which many of the tribes coordinated to defect on the ruling regime – led by opportunistic tribal elites acting for their own purposes. I return to these recent, ongoing events in the conclusion chapter.

5

Contemporary Clientelism

5.1 INTRODUCTION

Clientelism is pervasive in Lebanon and Yemen. Despite a veneer of party politics and an abundance of ideological rhetoric, day-to-day politicking in both countries centers on clientelistic rather than programmatic linkages. Patrons and clients do not link up haphazardly, however. Instead, they seek each other out largely from within their communal groups rather than across them.

People in both societies often lament this emphasis on communalism. One respected religious figure in Lebanon, for example, complained that:

We don't have Lebanese in Lebanon, we have Maronites working on behalf of Maronites, Orthodox on behalf of Orthodox, Druze, Shiites, Sunnis, and so on. They know they're not getting anything except via their sects.[1]

Analogously, a senior opposition party leader in Yemen bemoaned how political competition in his country revolved around:

[It's] all the old divisions: mountains versus cities, Zaydi versus Shafai, North versus South. Everyone's searching: where's the money? ... They're not interested in good government or the good of the country.[2]

---

[1] Muhammad Fadlallah, July 1992 interview with *al-'Ahd* (Fadlallah, 2001, 238).
[2] Interview, senior Islah Party leader, Sanaa, September 2005. "Mountains versus cities" is a long-standing trope in Yemeni politics that refers to divisions between the Zaydi tribesmen who are concentrated in the northern mountains and the Shafai populations with weaker tribal ties that are concentrated in the cities and the midland provinces. "North versus South," in turn, sometimes refers to divisions between the former northern and southern republics, and sometimes to the "North of the North" (the northern mountains) against the midland provinces. In either case, people usually mean northern *tribesmen* versus everyone else.

These two statements, and many others like them, illustrate a pervasive and much-lamented phenomenon found in both countries: people rely on their community links to facilitate access to scarce material resources.

This chapter elaborates on the linkage strategies that elites and their constituents use in Lebanon and Yemen. Consistent with findings from many other parts of the developing world, ideologies and programs fail to animate most politicians or inspire their supporters. Parties and leaders lack programmatic brand names; instead, they cultivate reputations as credible sources of patronage. Moreover, they use their community links to facilitate clientelistic exchange with their supporters. In doing so, they rely on intermediaries such as local notables, family heads, and shaykhs to dispense rewards and monitor voters.

5.2 PARTIES AND PROGRAMS

Party programs in Lebanon and Yemen are, for the most part, hypothetical: documents consisting of dubious promises to the electorate that few people take seriously. Parties typically couch their platforms in generalities about valence issues such as "good governance" that are light on implementation details, with the result that programs on paper do little to distinguish one party from another. Given their lack of content, few voters pay attention to platforms, which in turn gives politicians little incentive to invest in programmatic linkages. Instead, politicians cultivate reputations as reliable patrons in order to attract and service their constituencies.

On paper, there are many parties competing for Lebanese and Yemeni votes, ostensibly advocating "comprehensive" and "detailed" programs of "reform" that offer "salvation" for their countries. In neither country do rhetoric and practice line up, however. Few of the many dozens of parties, rallies, gatherings, blocs, and electoral alliances bring well-established brand names to the menu of options facing voters.[3] Fewer still have built their reputations on the basis of political programs, relying instead on services and clientelistic linkages with their constituents to win votes. As such, a prominent Lebanese scholar has observed that Lebanon has a multiplicity of parties, but no party *system*

---

[3] More than forty parties rushed to declare themselves in the first year after Yemeni unification, many of which drew most of their members from a single tribe, village, or sect. Some twenty-two parties contested the first elections, fifteen continued to "operate" after by-laws to the law on political parties went into effect in the mid-1990s, and the number of parties has fluctuated since then (Farah, 2002, 83, 92; Mansour, 2004, 119, 423). Given the overlapping and shifting nature of the parties, parliamentary blocs, and temporary electoral alliances in Lebanon, it is difficult to hazard a count beyond "indeterminately many" (Dhahir, 2008; el Khazen, 2000, 2002, 2003; Hashishu, 1998). Many of the parties, however, operate as nothing more than an organizational label for one politician's electoral campaign, in turn contributing to the proliferation of one- or two-deputy "blocs" in parliament.

5.2 Parties and Programs

based on programmatic competition; Yemeni scholars, in turn, make analogous claims about party life in their country.[4]

Despite a veneer of programmatic rhetoric, few political organizations win adherents on the basis of their policy positions, and the main parties do not compete with one another in a comprehensible issue space. One scholarly member of parliament in Lebanon, for example, bluntly observes that "parties do not have programs, neither govern nor oppose, and are neither right nor left."[5] Another MP echoed this point by observing that:

> There are practically no issue politics here. There's no real concept of left, right, and center. It's undefined: what are you in the center of? The concept doesn't exist.[6]

Aside from a few "left"-leaning Lebanese parties with small popular support bases, most parties are catch-alls rather than ideologically driven organizations. At best, parties stand for communities; more accurately, they stand for *politicians*, who often find policy stances a hindrance in Lebanese politics.

Many Yemeni elites, in turn, concurred with their Lebanese counterparts. One Adeni intellectual stated bluntly that "there is no party life in Yemen, full stop. There are no party programs."[7] A newspaper editor, meanwhile, digressed slightly from this "full stop" to make the acerbic observation that "we've got electoral programs here, but no one reads them ... [pauses for effect, looks at me meaningfully] except maybe academics."[8] Although he chose his phrasing in part as a friendly jibe at me, his larger point still stands. Few people beyond academics or party activists know or care what the platforms say.

More generally, platforms exist because "everyone has to have one," but they are almost always vague in both policy prescriptions and details of implementation, relying instead on "generalities and enigmatic slogans."[9] In Yemen, for example, a western diplomat complained that, for all their well-intentioned effort to push for a reform agenda, the opposition alliance

> needs an actual, detailed program. People talk a lot about big issues and big ideas here, but don't have an actual plan. It's difficult to get people here to be precise.[10]

One of his colleagues, in turn, expressed admiration for the opposition's broad intentions, but noted that,

---

[4] el Khazen (2002, 67) provides the assessment about Lebanon. Farah (2002), Mansour (2004), and Mutawakkil (2004) make similar observations about Yemen.
[5] See el Khazen (2002, 166), who is an independent MP aligned with Michel Aoun's Change and Reform bloc in parliament.
[6] Interview, March 8-aligned member of parliament, Beirut, April 2009.
[7] Qat chew roundtable, Aden, September 2005.
[8] Qat chew roundtable, Sanaa, February 2006.
[9] See, for example, el Khazen (2000, 126–127 *et passim*) on Lebanon and Afandi (2003, 83–85 *et passim*) and Mansour (2004, 233 *et passim*) on Yemen.
[10] Interview, western diplomat, Sanaa, August 2005.

If [the opposition alliance] ever got to power, it would be clear that they couldn't hold it together. [The ruling party], with some merit, says that the reason [the opposition] doesn't have a candidate, an economic reform program, [and a] platform is because they can't.[11]

Although some party officials gamely tried to sell their political programs when interviewed, relatively few expanded beyond stock talking points. Illustratively, a senior Lebanese party leader proclaimed that his movement "believes in a group of ideas and a program" and wants voters "to rely on the program and know it's not about [the leader] himself." When pressed for some of the details about the program's contents, he eventually responded that "we're a reform movement: change and reform" – and, fitting deeds to words, promptly changed the subject. Not coincidentally, "Change and Reform" was also the name of his parliamentary bloc. To be fair, however, members of the other parties had similar trouble describing their programs; this official's response was merely more poignant than most.[12]

In addition to their imprecision, platforms are also remarkably similar from party to party. To the degree that there is indeed "no real concept of left, right, and center," then there is any obvious issue space within which parties can position themselves. Rather than compete on issue positions, then, parties instead emphasize valence appeals – outcomes that are universally desired ("social justice") or reviled ("corruption") by the electorate. Lebanese parties, for example, contest elections in the name of "sovereignty," "unity," and "reform."[13] Yemeni parties, in turn, commit themselves to "comprehensive development," strengthening of modern state institutions, and "encouraging" women's participation. One Yemeni scholar's detailed analysis of the parties' written platforms, in fact, revealed them to be similar to the point of using the same section divisions, sentences, expressions, and rhetorical tropes (Mansour, 2004, 216–233 *et passim*).

Programs and ideologies do attract some "true believers," but these principled partisans often express disappointment in their parties as well as the lack of real choice between platforms. A member of parliament from the Islah Party, the largest faction in the Yemeni opposition, argued that

---

[11] Interview, western diplomat, Sanaa, May 2006.
[12] Interview, senior Free Patriotic Movement official, Beirut, July 2008.
[13] For additional examples of these "vague slogans," see, for instance, Abd al-Khaliq (2006, 61). Landau (1961, 136–137), in turn, illustrates the "grandiloquent pathos" of Lebanese sloganeering with text lifted directly from different electoral platforms. One advocates "liberty, satisfaction, love and equality for all." Another lauds a candidate for having "a clear purity, a sharp decisiveness and a noble patriotic credo" and for his ability to get to the core of "complex problems, be they social, economic or political." Although these latter illustrations come from 1960, the imprecision and emphasis on valence issues persists through today, even if the language tends to be less cloying.

5.2 Parties and Programs

Marxism failed. Arab nationalism failed. What we need to try now are the Islamic groups. The Islamists are, anyway, using the same terms as the Marxists and the nationalists.[14]

One of his frustrated colleagues on Islah's Consultative Council, meanwhile, complained that the party no longer inspired him, but that none of the other opposition factions did, either:

> The other parties are parties of the past, [like] the Socialists and the Baath. There are now five Nasirist parties or factions. They base themselves on [former Egyptian President Gamal abd] al-Nasir, but he's dead and has been dead for over 30 years.[15]

The other opposition factions, he argued, offered only out-of-date ideas that were far removed from Yemen's political problems.

Many of those activists who join parties out of conviction become cynical over time as they realize that their parties either cannot or will not implement their promised platforms. During Lebanon's 2009 electoral campaign, for example, a strategist for one of the March 14-aligned parties remarked bitterly that:

> My personal opinion is that March 14 will disappear [the day after the elections]. It's a big joke. It's composed of people who hate each other. They don't have a common project, they have a common enemy.

He went on to argue, however, that a March 14 win would be symbolically important because:

> They have a minimum of principles to safeguard the country and democracy. March 8 is not showing these minimal principles. Therefore it's important that the principles of March 14 win even if the alliance falls apart afterwards.[16]

In essence, he acknowledged his disenchantment even as he expressed diminished expectations of what he hoped to achieve: the election of politicians with nothing more than "a minimum of principles" to recommend them. One of his electoral opponents, however, an old hand in Lebanese politics, dismissed the activist's concerns with programs and principles:

> Most Lebanese talk about ... a fateful election between two blocs and ideologies, good versus evil, and so on. For us, they are elections. This is not the destiny or future of Lebanon. Not much is going to change with the elections. Just some of the faces are going to change.[17]

---

[14] Interview, Taiz, August 2005.
[15] Interview, member of Islah's Consultative (*Shoura*) Council, Sanaa, December 2005. The Yemeni Socialist Party long positioned itself as a Marxist vanguard party, while the Baath and Nasirist factions all espoused one form of pan-Arab nationalism or another. At one point, Yemen had up to nine Nasirist factions that claimed to be operating (Mansour, 2004). Gamal abd al-Nasir was the leading figure of Arab nationalism in the 1950s and 1960s.
[16] Interview, senior campaign strategist for a party in the March 14 alliance, Beirut, April 2009.
[17] Interview, March 8-aligned member of parliament, Beirut, April 2009.

Another old hand across the aisles in March 14 concurred, conceding that, "I don't think these elections are crucial. If we win it's a moral boost. But nothing will change." He did, however, acknowledge that, "I can't say this publicly because my allies will say I'm a traitor."[18] The broader point, on which both interviewees subsequently elaborated, was simple: parties do not implement programs, and voters, by and large, do not expect them to do so.

Put together, then, most parties do not contest elections on the basis of their ill-defined and largely interchangeable programs, so voters do not bother to read them, and so the parties do not expend much effort to propagate them.[19] Numerous Yemeni elites dismissed party programs as irrelevant, arguing that it made no difference what the parties wrote down when they never implement what they write. A reformist in the ruling party, for example, conceded that:

> In our part of the world, writing is so easy. It's very easy to put ideas down on paper, but implementing [them] is very hard ... We're no better or worse than the [opposition]: we also talk and don't do much.

The ruling party and the opposition alliance, he concluded, were "mirrors of themselves." Both faithfully wrote platforms to be ignored by all but the most faithful – who, in turn, would be disappointed when the platforms did not get implemented.[20]

Consistent with this refrain, a Lebanese cabinet member discounted platforms as "not important" and asked, rhetorically, "why would people believe me if I say that you'll be better off tomorrow if you elect me today?"[21] Even firebrand, "programmatic" organizations have deemphasized (as opposed to moderated) their ideological appeals over time in pursuit of votes.[22] One disenchanted former official of a self-styled "reform" movement scoffed that its leader had withdrawn the party program from public circulation:

> How can you do that? It's a contract you signed with your constituents! We were fighting the old system, an archaic system. And now he's more feudal than they are! Feudal just like the rest.[23]

Rather than fulfill the promises made in its electoral platform, the party had, in this activist's view, simply begun to behave like every other political organization in the country: by cutting deals and building up its clientele.

---

[18] Interview, March 14-aligned member of parliament, Beirut, April 2009.
[19] el Khazen (2002, 162–163); Mansour (2004, 232).
[20] Interview, senior ruling party official, Sanaa, April 2006.
[21] Interview, March 14-aligned minister, Beirut, July 2008.
[22] Although the Muslim Brotherhood provided much of the ideological content of Yemen's Islah Party, it emphasized services and public sector employment while in power, and subsequently non-state patronage after moving into the opposition (Farah, 2002; Mansour, 2004). Hizballah, in turn, continues to attract adherents via its program, but much of its electoral strength comes from service provision and employment in its parallel "state" institutions (Cammett, 2011, 2014; Cammett and Issar, 2010). On a related debate about the "inclusion–moderation" hypothesis, see Schwedler (2006).
[23] Interview, former senior Free Patriotic Movement official, Beirut, July 2008.

When this activist denounced his former leader as *feudal just like the rest*, he was, in effect, condemning clientelism and machine politics. "Feudalism," in Lebanese parlance, is a popular pejorative term used to express disdain for the country's political "bosses," sometimes referred to as the "whales" or "octopuses" of money. The imagery is not, of course, Lebanon-specific; in its heyday, Tammany Hall's bosses were often depicted as octopuses with their tentacles dipping into the public administration and ensnaring judges, public officials, and voters. Lebanese use the term "feudalism" to describe the manner in which politicians and their supporters – that is, *patrons and clients* – interact. "Feudalism," in other words, both invokes and condemns clientelism as a political linkage mechanism.[24]

5.3 PERSONALIZED POLITICS

Given the general disregard for policy promises, most parties cannot build collective brand names on the basis of their programs. Instead, they build track records as distributive machines, while individual politicians cultivate *personal* reputations for assisting their clients. Consequently, party loyalties tend to be weak and contingent on access to rewards and services. Many elites, in turn, affiliate only loosely with parties, while others do not bother to join them or choose to run for election under party labels.

Hence, in Lebanon, the country's highest offices are usually filled by non-partisans. Historically, most presidents and prime ministers have not belonged to parties, and the same was true of the speaker until after the civil war. Moreover, partisans have, historically, held less than a third of the seats in parliament, while independents accounted for the supermajority. Party representation rose from about 20 percent of deputies in the 1950s to just over 30 percent by the last pre-war elections in 1972 in what el Khazen (2002, 77–82 *et passim*) calls Lebanon's "golden age of parties." It dropped again in the post-war elections, reaching 25 percent by 2000 (el Khazen, 2000). Calling the parties "schizophrenic," a senior official in the Lebanese Association for Democratic Elections elaborated further on their lack of appeal to politicians:

---

[24] An elaboration on the "whales" and "octopuses" comes from a member of a blue-ribbon commission tasked with designing a new electoral law for the country. Interview, Boutros Commission member, Beirut, July 2008. Approximating how the terms are used in practice, I have translated *qutb/aqtab* and *za'im/zu'ama'* as "bosses." The former term glosses as "axis" or "pole" and refers to the biggest bosses, while the latter translates more literally as "leader" and can refer to both the "big" and "small" bosses. Note that Yemenis also use the term "feudal," albeit not as frequently as their Lebanese counterparts. In Yemen, the shaykhs in the middle provinces were often described as "feudal" because the tribal system was not as strong there, allowing the shaykhs (sometimes state-appointed) to behave more like large land owners and less like the tribal leaders of the northern mountain tribes. Yemenis from the southern provinces sometimes refer to the former petty sultans from the British protectorate era – and their contemporary descendants – as "feudal."

Electoral programs are irrelevant in the current system. Ideological parties exist, but are hindered by this system. Here, you need a strong clientele. Political party affiliation is sometimes a hindrance. Parties control the politics of the streets, but they're a minority in parliament.[25]

Consequently, many independent candidates form electoral alliances with established parties to draw on the latters' mobilizational capacity rather than out of commitment to a shared programmatic vision. With a few, partial exceptions, party and bloc discipline is weak, and parliamentary politics revolves around shifting alliances. Most deputies, as one commentator caustically observed, "have no taste or color [here: views or principles] and lean whichever way the balance of power leans."[26]

Similarly, in Yemen, many elites choose to contest parliamentary elections – and win them – as independents. In the first unity-era elections of 1993, non-affiliated candidates accounted for nearly three quarters of contestants. When aggregated countrywide, independents nearly tied the ruling party for first place in the popular vote (cf. Figure 4.3 in the previous chapter). Non-partisans actually increased their share of the popular vote in the 1997 elections; they continued to attract popular support, albeit at a more modest level, in subsequent elections. When they win, most of these independents join one of the parties' parliamentary blocs – usually the ruling party's – when they get to the capital.[27] In explaining the lackluster performance of the parties and the continued success of independent candidates, one senior ruling party official estimated that about three quarters of the population is unaffiliated, with "no more than 20 to 30 percent ... with [the opposition and the ruling party] put together."[28] That is: few people vote for partisans out of ideological commitment to a party program; a large majority choose candidates, instead, for more prosaic reasons – especially access to services and other material benefits.

More generally, the very concept of partisanship bears strongly negative connotations among both elites and the electorates in both countries. In

---

[25] Interview, board member of the Lebanese Association for Democratic Elections, July 2008.
[26] Newspaper commentary in pan-Arab daily *al-Hayat* from May 1992, reprinted in Sulayman (1998, 166). "Color," as used locally, usually refers to political or sectarian diversity – "multicolored" districts are diverse, while their "monochrome" counterparts are dominated by one group or another.
[27] Independents won more than 27 percent of the popular vote in 1993, about a percentage point less than the GPC, and significantly more than the YSP or the Islah Party. The independent vote share actually increased to 30 percent in the 1997 elections – reflecting, in part, individual YSP candidates running as independents despite the party's official boycott. Electoral rules forbid parties from running more than one candidate per district; many aspiring politicians who fail to win the ruling party's nomination run, instead, as independents and, if victorious, join the party's parliamentary bloc (Farah 2002, 92, 97, 148 *et passim*; Mansour 2004, 124, 390, 414–424 *et passim*) – a dynamic observed in other electoral autocracies as well (Blaydes, 2011; Lust-Okar, 2009a,b).
[28] Interview, Sanaa, April 2006.

5.3 Personalized Politics

Yemen, parties were, in fact, illegal up until the unification of the northern and southern republics, and many elites continue to denigrate partisanship in the unity era.[29] Referring to the commonly cited Quranic dichotomy between the "party of God" and the "party of Satan," one leader of the opposition Islah Party explained that, "the idea was that parties were the work of Satan," and, now, the contemporary understanding of partisanship is negative and "one of extremism."[30] Some prominent Salafi figures have, in fact, gone so far as to declare partisans to be apostates who may, accordingly, be executed with impunity.[31]

Many Lebanese, in turn, hold grim views about political parties. According to local conventional wisdom, parties advocate extremism and narrow interests at the expense of Lebanon as a whole; one prominent scholar observes that the word "party" has been transformed into a "vile word" for many Lebanese. A civil society activist, for example, echoed her peers when she stated, bluntly, that "political parties are very scary ... I won't ever join one." A parliamentary candidate, in turn, explained how he would never join a party or a bloc "because it's not for Lebanon," but rather works for its, and its leader's, "own interests."[32] Nearly all of the parties have experienced crises in the post-civil war period with dropping membership figures and alienated electorates. Post-war polls, for example, showed that the majority of Lebanese identified as independents and saw the parties themselves as one of Lebanon's most important political problems (el Khazen, 2002, 60–61, 149–150).

---

[29] See, for example, Muhammad (1998). More precisely, the northern constitution forbade all parties, while the southern constitution forbade all parties other than the ruling socialist party. In practice, the northern ruling regime constructed a series of "mass political organizations" modeled loosely on their Egyptian counterparts that served to mobilize voters when desired and provided a limited amount of controlled political representation. The ruling General People's Congress was the last such organization before unity; it persisted into the unity period after several parties split off from it to declare their own, separate existence.

[30] Interview, Sanaa, September 2005. Quranic verses separate mankind into the "party of God" (e.g., verse 58:22) and the "party of Satan" (e.g., verse 58:19). This dichotomy, in turn, provides doctrinal justification for a one-party state for ideologues willing to pursue this line of reasoning – the only virtuous party is the party of God, as a Muslim polity may never submit to the party of Satan. The literal translation of "party of God" is *hizb allah*; the Lebanese party of that name in fact incorporates Quranic verse 5:56 into its banner – approximately rendered into English as "verily, the party of God shall be victorious." Illustrating the widespread resonance of the trope, an unrelated *hizb allah* operated in northern Yemen during that country's revolutionary decade of the 1960s (Corstange, 2007).

[31] These declarations follow from the notorious practice of *takfir* (literally, declaring someone an apostate). Salafi figures were especially active in declaring socialist party members to be apostates in the lead-up to, and during, the 1994 civil war. Others, however, have gone so far as to denounce other Salafis for legitimizing political parties. Most prominently, Abd al-Majid al-Zindani, a prominent Salafi who holds a senior position in the Islah Party, was denounced as an apostate by other Salafi figures. Interviews, Aden and Sanaa, 2005–2006. See Bonnefoy (2011); Schwedler (2006); Yadav (2013).

[32] Quotes from el Khazen (2000, 130) and interviews, Beirut, July 2008 and April 2009.

5.4 PARTISANSHIP IN COMPARATIVE PERSPECTIVE

Lebanese and Yemenis are not alone in their disillusionment with parties and the emphasis they place on personalized politics. Public opinion data from the first wave of the Arab Barometer project reveals that Arab mass publics in general hold low opinions of their political parties. One battery of questions asks respondents from seven Arab societies – including Lebanon and Yemen – how much trust they place in a variety of state institutions.[33] In the aggregate, respondents were extremely distrustful of parties and were, in fact, far more skeptical of them than of any other institution listed. Half the respondents in the sample stated that they did not trust parties at all, and nearly a quarter more expressed not much trust.[34] Meanwhile, fully 75 percent of the seven-country sample trusted parties the least when compared to the prime minister, parliament, the courts, and the police.[35]

Figure 5.1 summarizes the trust figures as broken down by surveyed country. Grey circles report the percentage of each society's sample that reported having no trust in parties. Yemen sits at the seven-country median at 52 percent, while Lebanon is at the maximum at 62 percent. Adding on respondents who reported having "not very much trust" in the parties (not plotted), meanwhile, puts both countries in the middle of the list at 75 and 78 percent, respectively – lower than the two North African countries and above the rest.[36]

The black squares in Figure 5.1, meanwhile, report the percentage of respondents that trust the parties least out of all the options listed to them. Distrusters

---

[33] These data come from the first wave of the Arab Barometer (www.arabbarometer.org), which was conducted between 2006 and 2008 and included surveys in Algeria, Jordan, Kuwait, Lebanon, Morocco, Palestine (West Bank and Gaza), and Yemen. Question 201 asks respondents about their degree of trust in a variety of institutions: the prime minister, the courts, parliament, the police, and political parties. Respondents score these bodies on a four-point scale. The full question text reads: "I'm going to name a number of institutions. For each one, please tell me how much trust you have in them. Is it a great deal of trust, quite a lot of trust, not very much trust, or none at all?" Note that I drop non-responses from these analyses – a non-trivial choice, but one that simplifies this overview enough to justify their exclusion.

[34] More precisely, 50 percent stated no trust and another 21 percent expressed "not much trust." The item non-response rate for the "trust parties" question was 11 percent in the seven-country sample.

[35] In the seven-country sample, median responses were "quite a lot of trust" (the third point) in the prime minister, the courts, and the police, "not very much trust" (the second point) in parliament, and "none at all" (the bottom point) for political parties. For my purposes here, respondents that "trust parties least" are those who reported that they trusted parties as little as or less than each of the remaining institutions on the list (75 percent, index non-response 16 percent).

[36] For Lebanon, 62 percent of respondents expressed no trust in the parties, and another 16 percent expressed "not very much trust" in them for a total of 78 percent distrusting the parties. The corresponding figures for Yemen are 52 and 23 percent for a total of 75 percent. On this metric, Lebanon and Yemen sit below Morocco and Algeria (81 and 80 percent, respectively) and above Jordan, Kuwait, and Palestine (63, 63, and 52 percent).

5.4 Partisanship in Comparative Perspective

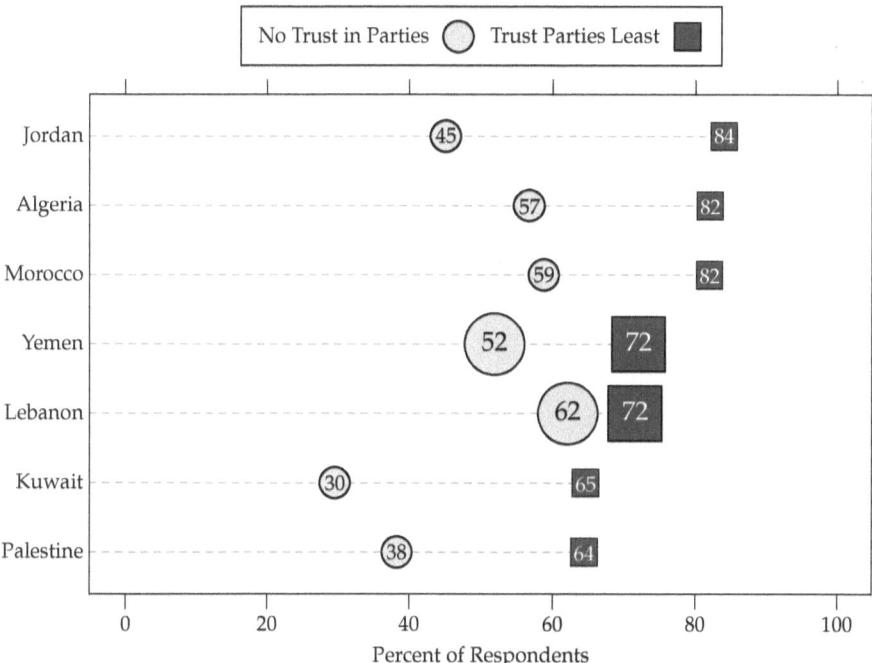

FIGURE 5.1: Trust in Parties (Arab Barometer, First Wave)

accounted for 75 percent of the seven-country sample, ranging from a low of 64 percent in Palestine to a high of 84 percent in Jordan. Lebanon and Yemen, meanwhile, sit in the middle of the list at 72 percent each, below three peer countries and above two. Hence, both the absolute and relative measures show that distrust in parties is very high in the Arab world. Correspondingly, Lebanese and Yemeni citizens distrust their parties at high rates. At the same time, these data reveal that neither Lebanon nor Yemen are outliers, but rather fall in between the other Arab countries in the aggregate extent of their distrust.

These data indicate that large majorities of Arab citizens distrust political parties – encouraging politicians and their constituents to find alternate means to connect. The Arab Barometer project also provides comparative evidence of the importance regular people place on having "connections" (i.e., the infamous *wasta*). In the aggregate, respondents placed great importance on connections. One behavioral question asks people whether or not they have used *wasta* to resolve problems affecting them personally; nearly a third of the seven-country sample acknowledged doing so.[37] Meanwhile, another battery of questions

---

[37] Question 226 asks people: "during the past five years, have you ever used wasta to achieve something personal, family related, or a neighborhood problem?" In the aggregate, 30 percent of respondents answered affirmatively; the item non-response rate was low at 4 percent.

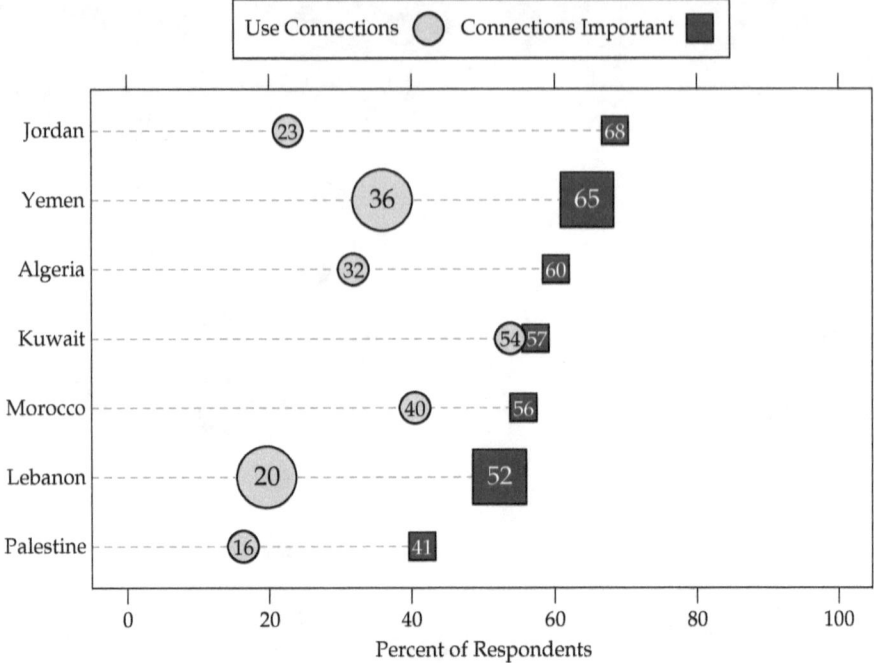

FIGURE 5.2: Importance of Connections (Arab Barometer, First Wave)

inquires about beliefs in the importance of connections in acquiring a government job – one of the classic payoffs in patronage-based political systems. Over three quarters of the sample believed that connections of some form or another were more important that qualifications for getting such a job.[38]

Figure 5.2 reports the connections figures broken down by participating society. Grey circles report the behavioral measure, that is, the percentage of each country's sample that reported actually employing their connections to solve a problem. Against a range of 16–54 percent, Lebanon (20 percent) and Yemen (36 percent) fall within the interior of the list. Hence, many Lebanese

---

[38] Question battery 506 asked: "what is the importance of a person's professional qualifications in obtaining a government job in [country name] relative to other factors?" It then directed respondents to "indicate whether each is more important, equally important, or less important as a person's experience and professional qualifications." In the full sample, 17 percent of respondents believed that "a person's political affiliations" were more important than qualifications, and another 21 percent considered them equally important. The corresponding figures for "a person's family or tribal affiliation" were 18 and 19 percent; for "the quality of a person's personal connections or wasta," the figures were 30 and 15 percent. Overall, 57 percent believed that at least one of the three types of connections listed was equally or more important than qualifications; the index non-response rate was 10 percent.

and Yemenis have used their connections, and yet they are not outliers compared to their Arab peers.

Meanwhile, the black squares in Figure 5.2 report the attitudinal measure: the percentage of each country's sample that believes connections of some form are more important than qualifications to get a government job. Some 57 percent of the full seven-country sample cited the importance of connections in this domain, ranging from a low of 41 percent in Palestine to a high of 68 percent in Jordan. Although spread out, Lebanon (52 percent) and Yemen (65 percent) again fall within the interior of the list.[39] Hence, large majorities in each Arab society sampled attest to the importance of having connections; Lebanese and Yemeni citizens look broadly similar to their counterparts elsewhere in their assessments.

Put together, then, the qualitative evidence from Lebanon and Yemen, buttressed by the comparative Arab Barometer data, suggest that politicians and their constituents rely heavily on personalized connections rather than party programs. Many Lebanese and Yemeni politicians choose to run as independent candidates, and many people denigrate the very idea of "partisanship." Survey data, in turn, shows that large majorities of citizens distrust political parties. Instead, they view personal connections as important tools to fix problems and acquire benefits.

5.5 PATRONS AND CLIENTS

Most voters – and even many party activists – are skeptical of the policy pledges enumerated in party platforms. Most such promises end up broken or unimplemented, so people justifiably discount them as cheap talk. Few politicians, in turn, can hope to mobilize enough popular support to win elections on the basis of their rhetorical appeals alone. Rather than rely on programmatic linkages, then, politicians instead use clientelism to attract supporters.

Many politicians maintain that their constituents care more about favors and services than about policy. Sounding distinctly more like a Tammany Hall-style ward boss than an ideologically driven partisan, for example, a Lebanese deputy laughed off questions about his policy positions. Instead, he emphasized that his reelection bid hinged on the personal services that he performs for his constituents:

---

[39] More precisely, 23 percent of Lebanese believed that "political affiliations" were more important than qualifications, while another 18 percent believed they were equally important. The corresponding figures for Yemenis were 20 and 25 percent. Some 19 percent of Lebanese and 19 percent of Yemenis considered "family or tribal affiliation" more important than qualifications, and another 16 and 22 percent, respectively, believed them to be equally important. Lastly, 34 percent of Lebanese and 37 percent of Yemenis considered "personal connections or wasta" to be more important than qualifications; the figures for equal importance were 14 and 15 percent, respectively.

There's no accountability. No one asks what I've done for the last four years. It only matters whose list I'm on, that I went to funerals, that I got someone out of jail, and so on. No one cares about my voting record.[40]

His constituents, in other words, ignored his fidelity to, or deviation from, the party's policy line – assuming, probably heroically, that they even knew what that line was. Instead, they focused almost entirely on the personal benefits they could extract from their representative.

The importance of services is a common refrain among politicians; many, in turn, express exasperation at the demands their supporters make of them. Another MP complained that:

Here, constituents count on MPs to render them services. If they need a job, they come to you, [and the same] if they want to register their kids in school, [or] if they're pregnant and need to get into a hospital. It's everything, from A to Z.[41]

Similarly, an opponent from across the aisle explained that:

[Future Movement leader Saad al-] Hariri is willing to assist with the development of certain regions and to help people who are in need. But they prefer to remain unproductive and completely rely on Hariri. Many people expect the Future [Movement] to do everything for them.

The MP went on to illustrate with a letter from a constituent asking Hariri to pay off his debts.[42] More prosaic scholarly studies, in turn, echo these deputies' observations. Among Lebanese and Yemeni voters, programs and policies generally play the smallest role in voting decisions, while services and material rewards play the largest role.[43]

Politicians and their operatives perform various services and distribute a breathtakingly wide array of material benefits to cultivate their constituencies. In addition to money, payoffs include a wide range of consumer goods such as food, alcohol, clothing, gasoline coupons, and mobile phone recharge cards. Rewards also include subsidized school fees, scholarships, underwritten medical care, free prescription drugs, and "forgiven" utility bills. Politicians, even poorly endowed ones, can also provide valuable services to constituents by cutting bureaucratic red tape, granting licenses and permits, providing preferential access to government benefits to which all citizens are nominally entitled, bailing people out of jail, and "fixing" parking tickets. They also steer public

---

[40] Interview, March 8-aligned member of parliament, Beirut, April 2009.
[41] Interview, March 8-aligned member of parliament, Beirut, July 2008.
[42] Future Movement MP, interview cited in International Crisis Group (2010, 18).
[43] el Khazen (2000, 41, 196–197); Mansour (2004, 233). More generally, these observations are consistent with the argument that parliamentarians in clientelistic and authoritarian systems do not act as policymakers, but rather as conduits of services and other patronage benefits (Lust, 2009; Lust-Okar, 2009a,b).

resources toward supporters through targeted public works projects or by hiring people onto the public payroll.⁴⁴

State resources provide the most obvious, although by no means the only, set of benefits for politicians to distribute to constituents. The Yemeni ruling party, like many of its peers in the electoral autocracies of the developing world, blurs the line between state and party resources.⁴⁵ As a frustrated opposition activist grumbled,

> When we contest elections here, we're not facing the ruling party, we're facing the state ... If we face the state, they win. If we face the party, we win.⁴⁶

More generally, a common refrain among party officials in the Yemeni opposition was the complaint against an unequal playing field when competing with the ruling party, that "you're not facing a party, you're facing the state," – ironically enough, the same complaint made by Lebanese opponents of Hizballah facing the latter's "state-within-a-state."

The blurring of lines between the ruling party and the state has, unsurprisingly, inspired some colorful satire. A bemused European election observer, for example, related the following anecdote upon returning from a trip to the field:

> One of the [Yemeni] drivers was asking what the Arabic word for "government" was – he knew the English word but not the Arabic. When we told him [what the word was], he asked, "you mean it's not 'GPC' [i.e., the ruling party]?"⁴⁷

The driver in question was almost certainly being facetious, but this common form of black humor illustrates the degree to which the ruling party makes use of state resources for its own ends. For example, a political cartoon, one of many, lampoons the government's discretionary power to determine who does, and who does not, get access to the spotty provision of public services such as water and electricity. It caricatures a paunchy, balding government official exclaiming to a bemused reporter, "electricity and water and roads and health and education and *and AND*! I mean, we turn them on when we want and turn them off when we want!"⁴⁸ Although hyperbolic, the caricature expresses the

---

44 The academic literature on clientelism is vast and full of sordid examples. The payoffs described in the text come from Auyero (1999, 2001); Bates (1981); Blaydes (2011); Cammett (2011, 2014); Cammett and Issar (2010); Chhibber and Nooruddin (2004); Chubb (1982); Corstange (2012b); Jamal (2007); Remmer (2007); Robinson and Verdier (2013); Rose-Ackerman (1999); Schaffer (2007a); van de Walle (2007); Weitz-Shapiro (2014).
45 Alley (2010a); Phillips (2008, 2011).
46 Interview, opposition-aligned Nasirist official, Sanaa, March 2006.
47 The word the driver used was *al-mu'tamar*, literally "Congress," but used as an English-speaker would use the acronym "GPC" to refer to the "General People's Congress." The observer relating the anecdote had worked in Yemen for months and spoke Arabic; by no means did this person fit the common stereotype of the bumbling and clueless "election tourist" easily taken in by the "wily locals." Qat chew roundtable, election observer, Sanaa, January 2006.
48 See caricature in *al-Nass*, 20 March 2006.

common view that officials prioritize basic services to some people and areas over others.

Lebanese parties, in turn, make extensive use of state resources to maintain their constituencies and win votes. One MP complained that a sitting minister, who was running for the former's seat in parliament, was using his powers to sway voters by doling out ministry jobs and building new facilities in select villages for the convenience of his supporters.[49] More generally, the Lebanese Transparency Association has documented how cabinet members running for parliament become much more active in dispensing ministry services than they were before the campaign season. Officials explained how more than half the cabinet ran for seats in 2009, and those that did were *"much* more active before they [became] candidates" in order to distribute benefits to voters while sidestepping campaign finance regulations.[50] Several technocrats, in turn, railed against what they saw as the perverse misallocation of state resources, which they felt prevented them from performing their duties effectively. One official, for example, complained how a minister might demand that his agency build an unplanned school in a given district and require them to move money from one place to another to do it. The technocrats could not mention this on-the-fly reallocation in their reports, of course, "but that's the reality of how it works in Lebanon."[51]

Yemeni technocrats told analogous stories. One presidential advisor, for example, remarked that "there's a bunch of western-educated Young Turks trying to get reforms going ... and the ministers are up in arms." Many were enraged at the mere prospect of an independent tendering board, which would limit their discretionary powers to award contracts. But, laughed the advisor, "how is some political appointee, sitting there scratching his balls, supposed to know about the technicalities of building an airport?" Meanwhile, one of the aforementioned "Young Turks" in the Ministry of Planning recounted how the president had warned him not to get carried away with reforms "because you're in Sanaa now, not the United States."[52] Although the technocrats recognized the perversity of the system, their ability to push through reforms depended on the acquiescence of the very politicians who benefited most from this perversity.

State resources are not, however, the only rewards that politicians may distribute or for which they may claim credit. They also tap into non-state resources provided by wealthy supporters, diaspora communities, party-controlled charity networks, and "aid" from foreign governments. Yemen's Islah Party, for example, is both well-organized and well-financed by business interests, wealthy party members, and foreign donations from party supporters,

---

[49] Interview, March 14-aligned member of parliament, Beirut, April 2009.
[50] Interview, senior officials in the Lebanese Transparency Association, Beirut, April 2009.
[51] Interview, official in the Council for Development and Reconstruction, Beirut, July 2008.
[52] Interviews, Sanaa, May and June 2006.

5.5 Patrons and Clients

religious groups, and (allegedly) from private Saudi citizens and the Saudi government itself. These funds, in turn, allow it to run an efficient and extensive charity network that reaches many Yemenis.[53] These non-state resources help the party to service its clientele with material rewards rather than just programmatic appeals. As one cynical party detractor observed:

> Islah's appeal is all money. They go to poor areas and distribute money. If the money went away, so would Islah. Islah is a party that uses Islam as a cover.[54]

Programmatic appeals in the form of a vague "Islamism" may inspire the party's activists, but fail to motivate many ordinary people – and so service provision helps the party cultivate its mass support base.

Likewise, parties in Lebanon have access to resources coming from private, charitable, and foreign sources. Several politicians, most notoriously Saad al-Hariri, are billionaires and use their personal wealth to fund their political campaigns. As with Yemen's Islah Party, Lebanese political movements also tap into the charitable organizations with which they affiliate, and often control. Examples include the Hariri Foundation and the *Maqasid* in the Sunni community, Hizballah's various charity branches in the Shia community, and party-affiliated institutions that the Christian parties are reviving in the post-Syria period.[55]

In addition to private funds and charity networks, Lebanese politicians draw on foreign funding for their political activities to a greater degree – or at least more openly – than their counterparts in Yemen. The sources of foreign funding shift with regional alignments, and the amounts are kept secret. A member of the Boutros Commission tasked with drafting a new electoral law, for example, complained that, for campaign funding,

> There's no law and no transparency. Hizballah is funded by Iran. Future is funded by Saudi and some of Hariri's money. [For Jumblatt, it] depends on his phase, but currently it's probably Saudi. [For Aoun, it also] depends on his phase, but currently Iran or Qatar.[56]

---

[53] For an overview of the party-affiliated Islah Charitable Society, see Clark (2004, ch. 4). These points about Islah's funding came up repeatedly in discussions about the party in interviews and qat chew roundtables with journalists, academics, civil society activists, and western diplomats. Party supporters, of course, stressed the role of private Yemeni business interests and charity donations. Detractors of the party, meanwhile, stressed the role of foreign funding, that money coming in from "religious" groups actually comes from Salafi and "Wahhabi" organizations, and that the "wealthy businessmen" in question had built their fortunes illicitly through corrupt dealings with the state.

[54] Interview, newspaper editor, Aden, September 2005.

[55] See Cammett (2011, 2014); Cammett and Issar (2010); Deeb (2006); International Crisis Group (2010); Johnson (1986); Norton (1999).

[56] Interview, Boutros Commission member, Beirut, July 2008. Walid Jumblatt is the preeminent political leader of the Druze community. Note that, at the time of the interview, he was still a leading member of the Saudi-backed March 14 alliance; he left March 14 after the 2009 elections and has, presumably, switched foreign funding sources as a result. Michel Aoun, in

Other Christian parties, such as the Lebanese Forces and the Kataeb Party, are rumored to receive funds from Saudi Arabia and Kuwait. Hence, most parties receive foreign funding in one form or another, but, by their nature, the flows and sources are unverifiable, with magnitudes that are subject to wide speculation.

The party with the most pronounced links to a foreign sponsor is, of course, Hizballah. The party's long-standing relationship with Iran provides it with massive annual subventions for its militia and its services branches. As a senior March 14 activist observed, the party "is influential because it is a social service provider, which is how it maintains its constituency." In contrast to its ally and erstwhile rival, Amal, the parliamentary speaker's party which relies on state resources to service its clientele, Hizballah receives the bulk of its funds from the Iranian government, as well as from private donations, the party's business interests and investments, and religious tithing.[57] Although the amount of funding is kept secret, by all accounts it is a massive and influential injection of resources:

> Iran alone dumps in 500 million dollars, and it means that a little less than 50 percent of the Shiites are with Hizballah. Give me that much money and I can make half of London pro-Hizballah.[58]

The amount cited is probably an exaggeration, but most informed guesses seem to fall within the interval of 100–300 million dollars annually – although neither Iran nor Hizballah release figures, of course. Whatever the true size of the subvention to fund Hizballah's "state-within-a-state," the influx of funds often provoked March 14 activists to ask, "how can you have a free election when one of the competitors is a state?" As described previously, these remarks parallel, almost word-for-word, the complaints that Yemeni opposition activists level against the ruling party's use of state resources.

In addition to distributing material resources to supporters, politicians use their influence to facilitate people's interactions with both the state apparatus and with non-state entities. Hence, another option for politicians is to act as ombudsmen or "fixers" that help constituents navigate mazes of bureaucratic procedure – procedure which, perhaps not coincidentally, the politicians themselves have helped to put in place.[59] They may, for example, use their influence

---

turn, is the leader of the Free Patriotic Movement. His main rivals, Amin Gemayel of the Kataeb Party and Samir Geagea of the Lebanese Forces, were widely rumored to be receiving funding from Kuwait in the run-up to the 2009 parliamentary elections.

[57] Interview, senior March 14 activist, Beirut, July 2008. Note that Hizballah's secretary-general is the official religious deputy in Lebanon of Iran's supreme leader Ali Khameini. Hence, religious taxes are also funnelled to Hizballah for use in its charitable service branches.

[58] Interview, publisher, Beirut, July 2008. A senior March 14 figure put the figure somewhat lower at $300–400 million a year. Interview, Beirut, July 2008.

[59] Baldwin (2010); Benstead (2008); Lust (2009); Lust-Okar (2009a,b).

5.6 Communal Clienteles

to help constituents jump the queue to access overstressed public services to which they are already legally entitled, but which have long wait periods or co-pays – and then claim full credit for services that the state renders or underwrites.[60] Hence, even politicians from resource-poor parties can act as "service deputies." Although these activities are somewhat analogous to "constituency service," there is neither a tradition nor an expectation of disinterested services in either country: politicians and voters each assume a quid pro quo. In this capacity, politicians provide an interface to the state apparatus as well as to non-state actors such as employers or charity organizations via personal connections – in local terms, the infamous and omnipresent *wasta* of Arab societies.

5.6 COMMUNAL CLIENTELES

Neither Lebanese nor Yemeni voters put much stock in the promises that parties make to them in the form of political programs – a rhetorical veneer which people justifiably discount as cheap talk. Instead, politicians and voters rely on clientelistic linkages to trade rewards for political support. Nonetheless, such transactions still require politicians and voters to make credible commitments to each other. The simplest conceptualizations of patron–client relationships envision personalized, dyadic interactions conducted in a social vacuum. In practice, however, patrons and clients frequently embed their exchanges in social networks to reduce transaction costs. Due to their dense information flows, such networks help the transaction partners monitor each other and police deviations from their rewards-for-support bargains.

As described in Chapter 2, clientelistic exchange is neither self-enforcing nor self-policing. Instead, patrons and clients transact against a backdrop of opportunism. But transaction costs can preclude such exchanges if patrons and clients cannot make credible commitments to each other to fulfill their respective ends of the bargain. One common step that the parties take is to embed individual transactions into ongoing relationships of exchange in order to forestall opportunistic deviation by leveraging the shadow of the future. Another strategy employed, as mentioned earlier, is to embed these relationships in social networks to facilitate the distribution of rewards and to monitor compliance with responsibilities. In Lebanon and Yemen, communal groups facilitate clientelism by embedding exchange relationships in dense, low-level units such as extended families and clans, which, in turn, aggregate up to broader, more encompassing groups.[61]

---

[60] Cammett (2011, 2014), for example, reports that Lebanese parties help supporters access health services to which all Lebanese are entitled, cover the costs of the modest co-pay, and then claim credit for the entire service – even though the Lebanese state pays for most of the fees.

[61] Compare Dixit (2004, 65–66), Fafchamps (1992), and especially Horowitz (1985, 59) on the "pyramiding" of small groups into larger ones, and Hardin (1982); Olson (1965) on the federation of small groups within large ones.

Families play a central role in Lebanese social life, and, consequently, they also condition political choices as well. A former Free Patriotic Movement leader, for example, explained that:

> People are not in parties because of principles, but for personal reasons. If you're born into this family, who votes for this guy, you're for this guy. It's like how you choose a basketball team.[62]

A Kataeb Party member, in turn, illustrated the phenomenon with his own upbringing:

> For me, it was [always] "Kataeb, Kataeb, Kataeb." The first, most important tie in Lebanon is family. You can't let down your father and mother, or your family.

Similar to the basketball analogy, he went on to explain that joining a party is "like if someone's father goes to [such-and-such a university]: he wants to go to [that university] as well so his father won't be disappointed."[63] More generally, Lebanese scholars emphasize that partisanship is "inherited" – parties renew their membership bases via "biological growth" as members' children reach voting age.[64]

What "personal reasons," as invoked earlier, might compel people to adopt their parents' political affiliations? Why should people feel pressure not to "let your family down?" Personal welfare correlates within extended families, which help to secure job opportunities and provide a social safety net for members. Political participation, in turn, also correlates within families as they trade their collective support for jobs, subsidized health care, scholarships, and other services directed to members of the family.[65] Consistent with these impetuses, a senior official in the Lebanese Association for Democratic Elections explained that "families usually sit together and choose candidates, and vote almost entirely as a bloc." Moreover, "you get a higher price if you vote as a bloc," which effectively simplifies the exchange and transfers many of the monitoring and policing tasks to the clients themselves.[66] This willingness and capacity to vote in blocs makes families particularly attractive to candidates.

In practice, Lebanese family networks tend to be tightly linked. Moreover, the overwhelming majority of Lebanese have single-sect families, and most people's social networks concentrate within their own sect. Among my survey respondents, 95 percent had parents of the same sect – and 94 percent of their parents' parents were also from the same sect.[67] All told, 88 percent of

---

[62] Interview, Beirut, July 2008.   [63] Interview, Beirut, July 2008.
[64] See, for example, el Khazen (2002, 61–62) and Khashan (1992).
[65] Compare Baylouny (2006, 2010); Cammett (2011, 2014); Fafchamps (1992); Hoff and Sen (2006).
[66] Interview, Beirut, July 2008.
[67] That is, 95 percent of the sample's paternal grandparents and 93 percent of maternal grandparents were from the same sect.

people had both parents and all four grandparents from the same sect. When asked to cite the sect of their five closest friends, 58 percent of the sample indicated that *all* of them were from the same sect, and 91 percent indicated that the majority of their friends were from the same sect.[68] Family- and friend-based networks, in other words, scale up into more encompassing, sect-based networks.

Family and tribal linkages are also central to many Yemenis' daily lives, especially in the rural areas where the presence of the state is modest at best. Analagous to their counterparts in Lebanon, Yemenis commonly vote in blocs. "Collective voting," as a local NGO official described it, means that "if you know the clan, you know that *all* the votes are going to such-and-such a party."[69] A tribesman, in turn, emphasized that most Yemenis "think in terms especially of tribes." He went on to illustrate with his own experience, stating that, "if I'm Khawlani [a large northern tribe] and I'm [personally with the GPC] but my tribe is Islah, I vote Islah, and vice versa."[70] The practice of collective voting, as these interviewees explained, can therefore override personal vote choice, especially in the rural areas where tribal links are strongest.

Bloc voting does not, however, imply enduring loyalty to the party which receives the votes. Yemenis routinely remark that people's first loyalties are to their tribes rather than to political parties.[71] A high-ranking shaykh in the ruling party, for example, explained, matter-of-factly, that tribal loyalties trump political affiliations whenever the two conflict, stating that, "if you ask someone to choose between loyalty to a party versus a tribe, 99 percent will go with the tribe."[72] While many Yemenis vote collectively, the "slogans and banners" of the parties are rarely the key motivating factors. Instead, their loyalty is commonly contingent on the provision of material benefits, and may be transferred if the tribe decides to bestow its support elsewhere.

"Tribal loyalties" can apply to multiple groups, however. When speaking in general terms, many Yemenis use the catch-all term "tribe" to denote everything from the largest tribal confederations that include millions of Yemenis down to the clans and extended families that might populate a rural hamlet and include just a few dozen people. As a prominent shaykh from the Hashid confederation observed, to whom people give their tribal loyalty varies because it varies by context – which sometimes means the most encompassing units, and sometimes the smaller ones, down even to the level of the family.[73]

---

[68] For these statistics, I have aggregated the various Christian sub-denominations into a single category.
[69] Qat chew roundtable, official in democracy promotion NGO, Sanaa, January 2006.
[70] Interview, Dhamar, May 2006.
[71] Qat chew roundtable participants, Aden, Sanaa, Taiz, 2005–2006.
[72] Interview, Sanaa, February 2006.   [73] Interview, Sanaa, June 2006.

Lower-level units are, in turn, usually more salient for local issues such as service provision than are the larger groups within which the smaller ones nest. Given the challenges of coordinating and policing within the more encompassing tribal collectivities, practical loyalties tend to follow the day-to-day networks in the smaller groups, whether extended families or the villages in which they live.[74] Survey evidence, in turn, suggests that Yemenis default to identifying with lower-level units rather than the larger ones. When asked an open-ended question about their tribal affiliations, over 60 percent of respondents identified themselves as tribal, and, in the process, cited more than 500 unique "tribes" – of which more than 80 percent had only one representative in the sample. In contrast, miniscule numbers identified themselves with the larger tribes or confederations.[75] These responses suggest that most Yemenis think first in terms of their extended families; only when context demands it do they think about the larger units to which their families belong.

Extended families and clans, in turn, facilitate clientelistic exchanges. Aside from the possibility of inherited programmatic commitments, family members have additional, tangible reasons to support the same party or patron. First, as mentioned previously, families have correlated welfare – payoffs to one member benefit the others. Hence, a medical clinic or new school constructed in a village benefits the entire family (and their neighbors, of course). Subsidies for doctor's bills or educational fees, meanwhile, nominally pay off only the beneficiary, but, in practice, the money saved remains in the household budget for the whole family to use. Here, I am simplifying voters' calculations to consider *only* the material payoff from subsidized medical care and schooling. More realistically, however, it is plausible that patrons also benefit from the gratitude that a family would feel for, say, easing a grandmother's pain from arthritis or providing school books for a child. That is: the utility value of the reward could easily be greater than its nominal, monetary value.

---

[74] Interview, Khawlani tribesman, Dhamar, May 2006. Village identity may, in turn, create a unit out of several lineage groups, perhaps the most notorious of which Bayt al-Ahmar (no relationship to Hashid's paramount shaykh), the home village of President Salih and many important members of the security services (for some of the sordid but difficult to confirm details, see Phillips 2011, 87–100). More generally, see Abu Ghanim (1985, 1990); Dresch (1989); Sharjabi (1986, 1990); Zahiri (1996, 2004).

[75] The question wording reads, "Many people in Yemen are members of a tribe, and for some people this is a very important part of their lives while for others it is not very important. I'll ask you first if you are nominally part of a tribe, and then how important that membership is for you." Respondents first answered, "Regardless of how important it is to you, do you consider yourself affiliated with a tribe?" If yes, respondents then answered the open-response question, "which tribe is that?" That is, they did not choose from an established list of tribes, but simply gave whichever answer they considered appropriate. Some 61 percent of the sample (873 people) identified themselves as tribesmen, and went on to cite 552 unique "tribes," 454 of which had only one member in the sample. Eight people explicitly identified with Bakil, and 14 with Hashid. These figure contrast sharply with the few dozen commonly cited in academic studies.

Public employment, a classic patronage tool, affects the welfare of entire families as well. Although ostensibly targeted to individual supporters, the salary and benefits from civil service jobs accrue at a minimum to the nuclear family, and often extend to more distant relatives. Numerous studies reveal that patrons and parties expect such jobs to deliver not just the jobholder's vote, but also votes from the jobholder's entire family, members of the extended family, and, possibly, from the jobholder's network of friends as well.[76] To illustrate, a Lebanese think tank director estimated that "Hizballah has 50,000 individuals on its payroll. If the average family size is 7, that's already 350,000 people supporting you."[77] Whole families benefit from politically allocated jobs, and many vote accordingly – whether out of gratitude for the income, out of fear that the job could be withdrawn, or, more likely, both.

Correlated welfare alone does not account for why families should be particularly well-equipped to strike bargains with politicians, however. Aside from *demand* for coordination on a patron, families also enjoy transaction cost advantages in monitoring and policing the clientelistic exchanges to which they commit themselves. Dense information flows within families helps members monitor each other's behavior. Moreover, the composition of family networks changes very little except through open, deliberate procedures that regulate membership. Hence, under normal circumstances, entry into the network comes from birth, marriage, or, much less frequently, adoption – a procedure that, itself, builds on the birth metaphor.

Families can also enforce collective decisions by subjecting deviating members to social pressure, ostracizing them, or otherwise punishing them by cutting them off from family aid and family-controlled assets. For example, a Lebanese activist with long-term family ties to the Kataeb Party explained how "my uncle went for [Free Patriotic Movement leader Michel] Aoun, and he was immediately ostracized." When asked how often such family splits occur, he shrugged and replied that, "sure, these things happen, but it's very rare."[78] Because family members have correlated welfare, they commonly have aligned interests in fulfilling their responsibilities in the collective bargains the families may strike with parties and patrons. Fear of being cut off from family networks, in turn, helps to dissuade members from defying collective decisions. Hence, individual family members enjoy less independence in their vote choices than the "one person, one vote" principle implies.

Family heads and tribal shaykhs, in turn, help to coordinate members on exchanges with their chosen parties and politicians. Consistent with prior research on the role of local notables, these figures often serve as intermediaries

---

[76] See, for example, (Chubb, 1982; Kurtzman, 1935; Robinson and Verdier, 2013). Compare also the discussion on kinship linkages as risk diversification strategies in Bates (1990, 2008).
[77] Interview, Beirut, June 2008.   [78] Interview, Beirut, July 2008.

between mass clients and their patrons.[79] As one part of this role, local leaders negotiate with politicians for payoffs. One of the electoral reform commission members in Lebanon described a dynamic in which "the head of a family says, 'I have 60 votes, pay me for them,'" at which point, the patron "can use charitable donations and all the clientelistic stuff" to meet the family's demands. The family head, of course, "keeps the lion's share of the money for the votes he sells ... [and] of course he's not giving anything to his nephews or his nieces for their votes."[80] Analogously, family leaders in Yemen exploit younger voters; one of the most frequently observed forms of electoral fraud in the country is, in fact, underaged registration and voting. Children are attractive "voters" because they are especially pliable, and family heads can be confident in their votes. Unsurprisingly, children receive virtually nothing, at least directly, from their families for their votes – often no more than a candy bar or a plastic toy.[81]

Family heads and tribal leaders also serve a complementary role, as a Yemeni roundtable participant explained: "first, the shaykh represents the tribe to the state," as in the preceding example of presenting demands to politicians, and "second, the shaykh represents the state to the tribe."[82] In the former sense, the shaykh makes demands of the state (or a patron) on behalf of his tribe, bartering for their support. In the latter sense, the shaykh serves as a conduit through which state officials and other patrons can allocate benefits and services to members of the tribe.

Patrons can effectively sub-contract out intermediary responsibilities to family heads: not only do they act as clearinghouses for patronage rewards, but they take responsibility for delivering the vote. Families, in effect, internalize the transaction costs of clientelistic exchange. Family leaders, meanwhile, cultivate their own personal reputations for delivering votes to patrons and rewards to members that make them valuable go-betweens in subsequent exchanges. In effect, the local shaykh or patriarch acts akin to a "family whip" that turns out the vote while also parcelling out the payoffs for those votes.

Given their transactional advantages, families often collude to sell their votes in blocs – a dynamic confirmed by numerous Lebanese and Yemeni interviewees. Hence, an unsuccessful candidate for the Lebanese parliament, running a campaign built, quixotically, on a political program, illustrated the point when he described his experiences with electioneering:

---

[79] Baldwin (2010, 2013, 2014); Kasara (2007); Keefer (2007); Scott (1969, 1972). See also Alesina and Spear (1988); Cremer (1986); Stokes (1999) on arguments about overlapping-generations organizations; here, family dynasties are *literal* rather than figurative overlapping generations.
[80] Interview, Boutros Commission member, Beirut, July 2008.
[81] Interviews, election monitors, and participant observation, election registration monitoring, Sanaa, al-Bayda, and Dhamar, April 2006.
[82] Qat chew roundtable participant, mixed gathering of shaykhs and party officials, Sanaa, June 2006.

5.7 *Machines in Motion*   143

Communities and family leaders organize to *sell* votes ... I would go into neighborhoods and give my spiel. They would come up to me afterwards and say, look, we've got 260 votes and we need money. If you can't give it to us, we don't want to waste your time.[83]

He attributed his electoral loss to his decision to run a policy-oriented campaign rather than one based on clientelistic payoffs and service provision. Rather than attract supporters with his program – which they largely ignored – he failed to peel away individual voters from the family blocs, whose ballots offered more when traded for services than for hypothetical policy positions.

5.7 MACHINES IN MOTION

Theoretical accounts of clientelism often posit dyadic relationships between patrons and clients who interact in a social vacuum. Such abstractions help us to understand the basic incentives to which both parties respond. They also skip over other features of the relationship that facilitate exchange between the two sides – either a virtue or a vice, depending on which part of the exchange one is most interested in understanding. My emphasis on communalism moves the story to networks and intermediaries as tools to help patrons and clients transact. Electoral machines and brokers in a wide array of countries have developed creative techniques to help politicians and voters make credible commitments to each other.

As described previously, intermediaries perform a key role as monitors and information clearinghouses about the behavior and needs of voters.[84] This information helps parties to observe – or, at least, infer – voter compliance, and to target payoffs efficiently. Intermediaries and party minders therefore make it their business to obtain detailed information about constituents in their bailiwicks. Hence, one famous Tammany Hall boss boasted that:

You have to go among the people, see them and be seen. I know every man, woman and child in the Fifteenth District, except them that's been born this summer – and I know some of them, too. I know what they like and what they don't like, what they are strong at and what they are weak in, and I reach them by approachin' at the right side.[85]

---

[83] Interview, Beirut, July 2008.
[84] This emphasis on direct, personal knowledge of constituents recurs throughout the academic literature on clientelism. Compare Auyero (1999, 2001); Brusco et al. (2004); Gosnell (1937); Johnson (1986); Powell (1970); Scott (1969, 1972); Stokes (2005, 2007); Stokes et al. (2013); Wang and Kurzman (2007a,b); Weingrod (1968); Weitz-Shapiro (2014).
[85] From George Washington Plunkitt's impromptu lecture "To Hold Your District: Study Human Nature and Act Accordin'," (Riordon, 1905, 25). Plunkitt reiterates the centrality of information gathering in a diary entry about a meeting with district captains: "each captain submitted a list of all the voters in his district, reported on their attitude toward Tammany, suggested who might be won over and how they could be won, told who were in need, and who were in trouble of any kind and the best way to reach them" (Riordon, 1905, 92–93). Meanwhile, a political scientist, in the process of conducting a field experiment decades before such tools achieved popularity, observed how great was the amount of effort that ward bosses and their lieutenants expended to canvass their districts and obtain this sort of information (Gosnell, 1927).

Similarly, a boss in the Philadelphia Republican machine – one of Tammany's contemporaries – observed that:

> If I have got a man in my ward who does not know every man by his first name who lives in his division, who does not know when that man is in trouble, who does not know when there is want and privation visiting a household – if he sees one man moving out and another coming in and he does not know it, he is no good to me.[86]

Machines, via their operatives, gather information about voters in a variety of ways. Party-controlled charity organizations may, for example, perform "needs assessments" among potential and current beneficiaries, as when Hizballah-affiliated charities dispatch workers on house calls to assess potential charges and monitor their "progress" – ostensibly non-partisan activity, but one might forgive beneficiaries who doubt the absence of a quid pro quo.[87] More generally, party operatives may pay social calls, participate in local celebrations and religious gatherings, track attendance at rallies, and monitor observable displays of partisanship – not to mention following informal word-of-mouth and gossip about their constituents.

5.7.1 Observing and Inferring Voting Behavior

For electoral politics, parties and patrons ultimately seek confirmation of client behavior at the polls – turnout, and, ideally, ballot choice. Consequently, their lieutenants pay special attention to election day.[88] On its face, the secret ballot would seem to forestall the possibility of observing actual vote choice. Nonetheless, electoral machines have developed a wide array of techniques to overcome the inconvenience of the secret ballot – often with the connivance of the voters themselves.

Voters behave according to their *beliefs* about ballot observability, not whether or not their votes are technically or truly untraceable. Perhaps unsurprisingly, then, parties throughout the developing world cultivate uncertainty about the sanctity of the vote. Nor can ballot secrecy be taken for granted even in well-established democracies; recent research demonstrates that roughly a quarter of the American electorate believes that officials can trace vote choices to individuals without their consent.[89] Accordingly, a Lebanese election

---

[86] Kurtzman (1935, 30).
[87] See, for example, Cammett (2011, 2014); Cammett and Issar (2010); Deeb (2006).
[88] One ongoing debate in the academic literature on vote trafficking is whether patrons attempt to buy turnout, actual votes, or both (Corstange, 2012b; Cox and Kousser, 1981; Gans-Morse et al., 2014; Nichter, 2008; Stokes, 2005; Stokes et al., 2013).
[89] Compare Chandra (2004) on cultivating beliefs about the uncertainty of ballot secrecy. Research in the United States shows that many voters do not believe that their votes are private: in addition to the quarter of the electorate that believes that electoral officials can trace their vote choices, up to three quarters believe that they are voting publicly because they tell others their vote choices (Gerber et al., 2013). One can only imagine the proportions of developing-world electorates

5.7 Machines in Motion

monitoring official explained that many of the parties sought to instill doubts about the secrecy of the ballot among voters:

> There's lots of ... intimidation, where [party operatives] tell voters that they can see everything and they had better vote for them or there will be trouble. They try to make voters afraid.[90]

More generally, machines cultivate the belief that their operatives can discover who their constituents support and how they vote, along with the fear that the wrong choices can result in retribution.

Yemeni patrons have numerous ways to observe voter behavior and cultivate the belief among constituents that their operatives can observe vote choice. Moreover, the opportunities to do so are especially pronounced in the far-flung rural areas that are difficult and costly for the media and civil society to access. Hence, election monitors observed that, in the rural areas, people often need to travel very far to register or to vote – sometimes hours, sometimes a full day.[91] Consequently, intermediaries can observe the costly efforts that voters make to turn out. Parties can also reduce turnout costs for voters with the classic machine tactic of providing transportation to the polls – which, conveniently, keeps people in close proximity to their party minders.

Members of a democracy promotion NGO described a wide variety of ways that patrons and their clients circumvented the regulations that protect ballot secrecy. As one commented:

> You're supposed to go into voting booths, but lots of times they don't enforce this. If you were going to vote for [the "right" party], why do it in secret?[92]

In other words, election officials sometimes treat the use of voting booths as a *right* rather than a *responsibility* – and, implicitly, anyone choosing to exercise that right must be doing so to cast the "wrong" vote. Misapplied electoral regulations may, of course, reflect a lack of training on the part of election officials, but it also reflects subversion of local commissions, especially in the rural areas that opposition parties and civil society organizations lack the resources to monitor. Party agents often serve as the official election commissioners in voting centers, gun-toting soldiers charged with keeping "order" mill about the room, and domestic intelligence officers maintain oversight as "security commissioners."[93]

---

that hold similar beliefs where basic electoral regulations cannot be taken for granted and where parties actively cultivate the impression that they can trace ballot choices.

[90] Interview, senior official in the Lebanese Association for Democratic Elections, Beirut, July 2008.
[91] Group session, NGO voter registration monitoring team, Sanaa, April 2006.
[92] Qat chew roundtable, members of a democracy promotion NGO, Sanaa, January 2006.
[93] The particular branch of domestic intelligence to which interviewees most frequently referred was the Political Security Office (PSO) – the famed *mukhabarat* so frequently cited in the Arab world. One set of election observers noted that "there were PSO officers everywhere, acting like PSO." Another set of observers believed that the PSO was spying on them and that their driver

Another election observer explained how parties exploit Yemen's low levels of literacy – over half the population is illiterate – to provide "help" when marking ballots. Use of this tactic is particularly acute among women, among whom illiteracy is especially common. Hence, as one monitor described, women often "will claim illiteracy and want the shaykh's wife to help her mark the ballot. This is even though you just mark the photo of the candidate." Reward-seeking voters may "seek help" in order to help brokers confirm their vote choices, but others may be intimidated into accepting "assistance." Accordingly, an election observer explained that:

> Lots of times, the shaykhs' wives will stand outside the women's voting areas. [They'll say,] "you know that plot of land your husband owns? Vote for my husband or we'll see about that piece of land."[94]

Combined, monitoring and intimidation compel many voters to cast their ballots as directed rather than risk repercussions.

Nor can Yemeni civil society organizations do much to counteract efforts to monitor and intimidate voters. Most independent groups, usually urban-based, lack the membership bases or the financial resources to send out more than a handful of observers, and, even then, the organizations cannot operate on a sustained basis. Many other groups have partisan and financial links to the political parties (especially the ruling party). A senior official at a democracy promotion NGO explained that:

> NGOs are still very weak here ... They don't have a tradition of membership bases. When they need members, they scurry out and look for [them] wherever they can find them, and this usually means members of political parties.[95]

Another election monitor, freshly returned from a disappointing field visit to observe the voter registration process, reported that, perversely, problems with the NGO observer teams were worse than with the election commissions themselves, because most of the NGOs were "effectively [ruling party]-affiliated," and their members were "only interested in the money, and the only questions they ask are about the *per diem*s."[96] Party-aligned NGOs may, in other words, send out election monitors, but many people suspect that they are monitoring *voters* on behalf of the parties rather than the process on behalf of voters.

---

worked for the PSO. When I asked them what made them think so, one replied, "well, [he] told us he was PSO." Touché, sir. Group session, NGO voter registration monitoring team, Sanaa, April 2006.

[94] Qat chew roundtable after an election monitoring field trip, members of a democracy promotion NGO, Sanaa, January 2006.

[95] Interview, senior official at the National Democratic Institute's Yemen field office, Sanaa, April 2006.

[96] Qat chew roundtable after an election monitoring field trip, members of a democracy promotion NGO, Sanaa, January 2006.

5.7 Machines in Motion

Lebanese politicians, even more so than their Yemeni counterparts, have developed sophisticated techniques to monitor constituent behavior.[97] As in Yemen, parties engage in the classic machine practice of transporting voters to the polls. Doing so, in turn, takes on extra importance in a country where people vote in their families' ancestral villages rather than where they reside. The practice, which parties have used for decades, took on renewed vigor – and a touch of the absurd – in the 2009 elections when the competing blocs flew in supporters from abroad in order to vote in some of the key, closely contested electoral districts.[98] The classic "ride to the polls" service both reduces people's turnout costs, gives party minders close observational access to voters, and provides an opportunity to distribute voting materials to a captive audience. Some of these "materials" are innocuous and legal, but parties also abuse their access to voters by distributing benefits and organizing variants on the Tasmanian Dodge.[99]

Machine operatives enjoy many other opportunities to observe vote choice – and to intimate to voters that their "secret" ballots are not so secret. Despite increasing pressure from civil society groups, Lebanese politicians have retained the country's traditional ballot design of *no* ballot design: Lebanon does not use pre-printed ballots. Instead, election officials provide voters with a blank sheet of paper on which they can write the names of their choices; voters may

---

[97] I am basing the text for the next few paragraphs off of participant observation as well as interviews with officials at the Lebanese Association for Democratic Elections (July 2008; April, June 2009) and with foreign technical experts brought in to provide technical assistance for the 2009 elections (April, June 2009).

[98] Representatives from both blocs accused each other of flying in supporters to the "hot" districts where the gap separating winners and losers was just a few hundred votes. Bloc members estimated that it cost anywhere from $2,000 to $10,000 to bring in such voters. Interviews, Beirut, April 2009. Anecdotally, I sat next to such a voter on my flight into Beirut in June 2009 to observe the elections. I was reading a newspaper story about party leader X, and my seatmate leaned over to say, "that's my guy." I asked him if he was excited about the election; he responded that he had no idea what the issues were, but that he was using this opportunity to get a ride home so he could lay on the beach for a week. As of the 2009 elections, Lebanon had no provisions for expatriate voting, and hence the parties took the "ride to the polls" practice to its logical extreme. See Corstange (2012b).

[99] In the variant that Lebanese observers described to me, party X gets a hold of official ballot envelopes. The party collects voters' registration cards prior to election day and returns them at the polling place, along with an official envelope stuffed with a "suggested" ballot. Voters queue up, get another official envelope at the polling place, deposit the first envelope in the ballot box, and return the empty second envelope to party operatives to prove they had voted as directed. Other times, parties slip a "suggested" ballot into one envelope and the payoff into another envelope and hand them to voters at the polling stations. Officials in the Lebanese Association for Democratic Elections explained, with bemused chuckles, how voters occasionally drop the wrong envelope in the ballot box – with the result that, at counting time, officials open up "ballots" that contain gasoline coupons, mobile phone recharge cards, and the like. One may wonder if voters who drop the wrong envelope do so intentionally to register a protest at this form of electioneering. For their part, LADE officials found this possibility less plausible than simple mistakes on the part of the voters.

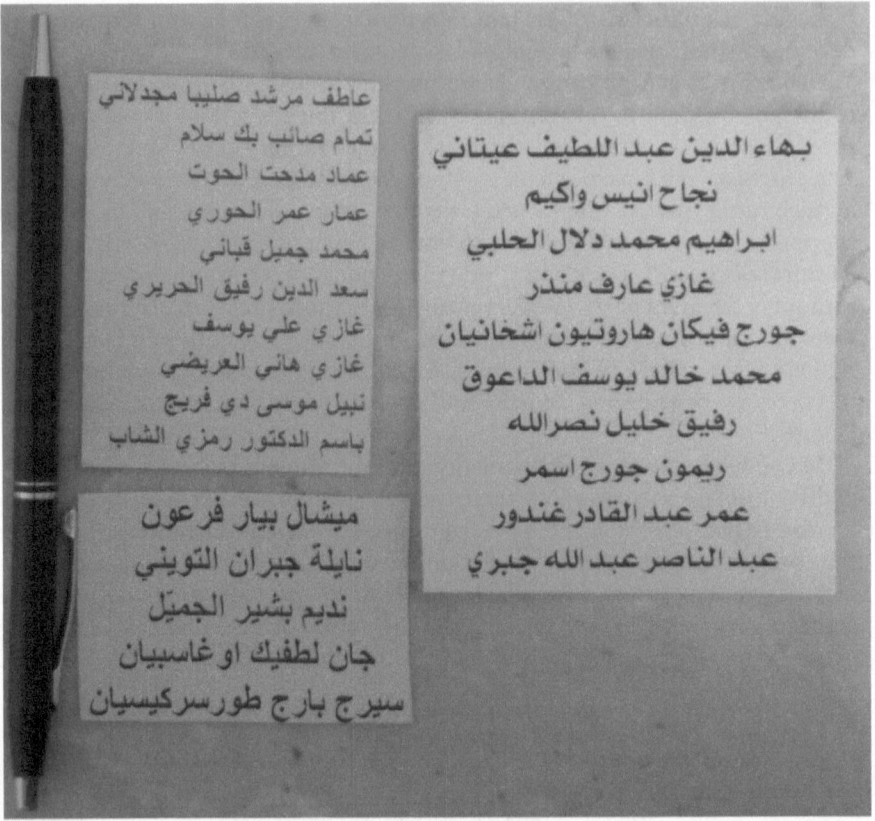

FIGURE 5.3: Party-Distributed Ballots, Beirut (2009)

alternately bring in their own, previously prepared ballots. Naturally, few people use the blank papers, and instead opt for one of the party-prepared ballots distributed by the omnipresent operatives – examples of which are reproduced in Figure 5.3.

The "suggested" lists of candidates (Lebanon uses multimember districts) provide several ways for brokers to infer voters' choices. As a civil society activist observed, the most obvious indication – with analogues to straight-ticket voting elsewhere in the world – is that:

If you use the whole suggested list, you come out of the booth quickly because you did not need the time to change names. You can cross out names and write in new ones, but it takes more time [so people will know you're up to something].

Party-prepared ballots, however, offer opportunities for observation beyond the simple timing of voters in the voting booth. Obvious markings such as Xs or

5.7 Machines in Motion

writing the voter's name on the ballot are not permitted, but many other manipulations are admissible under existing electoral rules. Careful manipulation of the ballot contents, along with systematic variation of these manipulations, enables brokers to follow vote choices with precision.[100]

To illustrate, a senior official in the Lebanese Association for Democratic Elections (LADE) described, in sordid detail, how parties and voters exploit the absence of the pre-printed ballot to make vote choice easy to verify:

> The candidate representative gives 20 identical lists to a family head of 20 people. Between family blocs of voters, you change the list order. You change the font. You change the font size. You can add or leave off the candidate's father's name. You can add or leave off titles.

The official then illustrated the point with an example from the 2007 by-election in which former President Amin al-Gemayel ran against a Free Patriotic Movement challenger:

> You could write "His Excellency the President Shaykh Amin Pierre al-Gemayel." [You could write it] with or without "Pierre." With or without "Shaykh." With or without "President." Either "President" or "His Excellency the President." You can even do "Gemayel" or "al-Gemayel."[101]

Intermediaries distribute different permutations of the "suggested" ballot to different families in a systematic fashion. Consequently, as another LADE board member observed, brokers "know that this ballot is for family A, this one is for family B, and this one is for family C."

Ballot booth assignments and counting procedures, in turn, complement the absence of the pre-printed ballot. Extended families cast their votes in the same – or just a few – ballot boxes; a foreign technical expert elaborated that:

---

[100] See Corstange (2012b). Although I have never heard of anyone employing the following tactic, one could, in principle, write a voter's name on the ballot quite legally – by having voters submit write-in votes for themselves. Very few write-ins occur in practice, but they are legal and electoral commissioners accept them as a matter of course. At least two factors presumably dissuade parties from exploiting this loophole. First, candidates may only run for a seat allocated to their sect, so voters could only write themselves in if they belonged to a seat's sect. Second, and probably more importantly, voters may cast ballots for, at most, the total number of seats in the district; any extra vote would invalidate the entire ballot. Consequently, voters could vote for, at most, $K - 1$ members of a list if they were to write themselves in – that is, the list would lose a vote.

[101] Election commissioners would even accept ballots written out in Arabic script or transliterated into the Latin alphabet. The latter does not appear to be a common tool, but I observed a commissioner telephone election authorities during ballot counting to confirm that a ballot written with Latin characters was, in fact, valid. One can only imagine the number of permutations that Latinization would open up were it more widely practiced, especially as there is no one canonical or legally recognized transliteration scheme. Many Lebanese use French conventions – hence "al-Gemayel," although people sometimes drop the "al-" prefix. The English-speaking scholarly convention, in contrast, uses a simplified version of the system laid out by the *International Journal of Middle East Studies* that transliterates "al-Gemayel" as "al-Jumayyil."

Families have a family number with, say, 250 [people] listed on that family name. You find individuals on the registration list by family. Families are assigned to polling stations by family.[102]

Ballot counting occurs immediately after the polls close in the room in which they were cast. The head polling commissioner magnifies each ballot on an overhead projector so that everyone in the room, including the various candidate representatives, can inspect each ballot in detail. Election monitors, in turn, noted that voters appeared to prefer to have votes counted locally because it made the process more transparent.[103]

Ultimately, a LADE board member summarized Lebanon's collective electoral regulations by stating that, "there's a backwards, archaic system for a purpose ... As a candidate, I can know within a person or two in a family [how] they voted." In other words, the country's electoral system makes voting very transparent, but not in the normatively appealing way we tend to use the term. Instead of making the electoral *process* transparent to voters, the act of voting makes *ballot choices* transparent to parties.

Although observations of direct support in the form of votes may be the clientelistic gold standard, parties need not limit themselves to monitoring outcomes on election day only. Instead, they can watch for other, indirect evidence of political support indicating that clients will vote as directed when election day rolls around. Voters can, for example, signal support by attending rallies, memorizing party slogans (the more absurd, the better), prominently displaying party iconography, and engaging in public sycophancy – points I take up in greater detail in Chapter 8.[104]

5.7.2 Rural Clientelism

Clientelistic linkages connect politicians and voters throughout both Lebanon and Yemen. Such relationships are, however, especially pervasive in the rural areas where monitoring is easier, social pressure from family and tribe members greater, and people are poorer. An official from a democracy promotion NGO in Yemen, for example, acknowledged that "[of course] we're interested in the

---

[102] "Polling stations" here are typically classrooms in a local school; the school, in turn, would house multiple polling stations. LADE officials confirmed that polling stations rarely had more than 350 voters assigned to them. Very large families might, by administrative necessity, be split into multiple polling stations. Customarily, men and women vote in separate polling stations. Polling stations are effectively segregated by sect not because of explicit legal provisions, but because families are almost all single-sect, and polling stations are assigned by family.

[103] At least in 2009, candidate representatives were well-supplied with laptops kept open to spreadsheets of the voter registration list. The spreadsheets allowed them to check off when people voted and, presumably, check off when the "right" ballot turned up. Candidate representatives presumably used paper copies of the voter rolls in earlier elections before laptops became pervasive.

[104] See, for example, Auyero (1999, 2001); Cammett (2011, 2014); Kitschelt and Wilkinson (2007a); Szwarcberg (2012, 2014); Wedeen (1999).

urban areas, but for electoral systems, the real problem is in the rural areas," due to minimal development, high illiteracy, and various other challenges impeding clean elections in the rural areas where more than two-thirds of the population lives.[105] What difficulties the organization faced countrywide in promoting free and fair elections were most acute in the rural areas where, not coincidentally, patron–client relationships were strongest.

Lebanon presents an interesting variation on this theme. Much of the country's population *resides* in urban areas. However, due to a curious provision in the voter registration laws, people return to their ancestral villages to cast their ballots. Consequently, many Lebanese live in cities but vote in their villages, as officials from a local democracy promotion NGO explained:

> You don't vote where you live, but where you're from. I, for example, don't vote where I live, but in the village where my grandfather was from – not me, or even my father ... There's no genuine mobility for the electorate: you vote where you originate. Changing your registration place is one of the hardest things to do in Lebanon. For example: half of the Lebanese live in Beirut, but most Beirutis don't vote here.[106]

Although this residency provision persists, in part, due to popular anxieties about upsetting the sectarian demographics throughout the country – especially concerning Christians – it means that a large proportion of the urban population returns to the rural areas on election day.

The profusion of rural constituencies helps to perpetuate patron–client relationships. First, rural voters are typically easier to track than their urban counterparts, hence reducing monitoring costs for patrons. Among the most enduring images of "machine politics" are the ward bosses of the great American urban machines such as Tammany Hall in New York City, the Republican Organization of Philadelphia, and the Daley machine in Chicago (cf. Erie, 1992).

Arguably, one of the reasons why these leviathan-like machines became so elaborate in their organizational structures is because they *had* to be. To win elections consistently, the machines had to keep track of huge numbers of highly-mobile voters in dynamic urban environments. Individual villages and hamlets, in contrast, house fewer voters that are also less mobile, and who, by dint of local social networks, cannot slip into urban autonomy. Villagers who migrate to urban areas for work typically stay rooted in their villages due to family links with members who remain behind. Some people make the daily commute into the big city, others take cheap lodgings and return to their villages regularly to be with spouses and children, and still others maintain close relationships with parents, siblings, and other members of the extended family in the villages even after moving semi-permanently to urban locations.[107]

---

[105] Interview, senior official in the National Democratic Institute's Yemen field office, Sanaa, April 2006.
[106] Interview, senior LADE officials, Beirut, July 2008.
[107] These strong emphases on family ties are common in less-developed societies that lack well-developed markets for risk and obligate people to self-insure by investing in kin networks to spread risk among extended families (Bates, 1990, 2001).

The relative ease with which patrons can monitor rural voters implies that clientelistic transaction costs are lower in the villages. Hence, according to election monitors, detailed information on rural voters is easy to obtain in Lebanon:

> In a small village, everyone knows everyone. Someone can do a detailed report on what you did on election day. It's easier to keep track of vote buying in rural areas because it's a smaller community.[108]

Analogously, election monitors also noted that Yemeni villagers are easy to track:

> In the countryside, there's no anonymity. Everyone knows everyone, so you can expect voting officials to know everyone [and to] pressure them to cast the "right" vote.[109]

Patrons, consequently, can conserve on resources by operating rural electoral machines or farming out monitoring duties to local notables.

In addition to the ease of monitoring, families and tribes typically exert greater pressure on individual voters in the villages than in the cities to conform to collective family decisions on which candidates to support. A Yemeni democracy promotion activist I cited earlier had said, "if you know the clan, you know that *all* the votes are going to such-and-such a party." These voting dynamics, which he described as "a tribal thing," contrasted somewhat with electoral politics in the cities, where voters were less subject to pressure from their tribes.[110] A senior member of one of Yemen's influential political families elaborated on this urban–rural distinction in voting patterns:

> Tribesmen come to the cities, and while their villages are voting [for the ruling party], it's due to tribal politicking and tribal pressure. Their shaykhs have gone with the [ruling party] and are pressuring their villagers to vote that way as well. But in the cities these same tribesmen don't face those pressures to nearly the same degree, so they can vote their conscience.[111]

Fewer work and social opportunities in the rural areas compared to the cities, along with greater reliance on families for insurance and basic material welfare, combine to exert greater pressure on voters in the villages where families can bring greater penalties to bear on members who defy family decisions. The credibility of these threats, in turn, helps families make more credible commitments to their patrons.

Clientelistic politics takes on additional prominence in the villages, in part, because programmatically oriented parties and civil society organizations typically lack the resources to project into the rural areas. Hence, the Yemeni

---

[108] Interview, senior official in the Lebanese Association for Democratic Elections, Beirut, July 2008.
[109] Qat chew roundtable, election monitors, Sanaa, January 2006.
[110] Qat chew roundtable, official in democracy promotion NGO, Sanaa, January 2006.
[111] Qat chew roundtable, senior member of a politically influential family, Sanaa, May 2006.

notable just cited also observed that, "the cities are a true reflection of political currents in the country ... since in the cities it's actually party politics, while in the countryside it's tribal politics." Concurring, a Yemeni shaykh complained that the countryside had been "abandoned by the parties and the NGOs." Although "we've got thousands of NGOs," he continued, there are "only maybe 20 effective ones, and not really any in the tribal regions."[112] Hence, organizations offering alternatives to patronage-based parties cannot easily spread their messages in the rural areas where a supermajority of the population lives. Nor can independent civil society organizations afford to operate in the far-flung villages where they might otherwise hope to check the exploitation of voters.

Lebanon, despite its smaller size and better transport infrastructure, experiences a similar disparity between urban and rural areas. The director of a Lebanese civil society group tartly observed that most organizations do not work in the field "outside Beirut where it's not fashionable to have NGOs."[113] The election coordinator for one of the parties contrasted his campaign strategies between Lebanon's different regions. The Metn district, which borders the capital and counts as part of the greater Beirut metropolitan area, is "a very political district with lots of parties, [so the competition] is political" (where, by "political," he meant "program-oriented"). He contrasted the Metn with Kesrouan, the district just to the north of it, which he described as "traditional: it's about families" rather than parties and programs.[114] Hence, some areas, typically urban, do witness real competition based on programmatic politics, however hazily defined. Many other areas outside the main cities, meanwhile, still focus heavily on patronage politics.

In addition to advantages in transaction costs, rural voters may be more attractive clients than their urban counterparts because they make comparatively more modest demands for payoffs. Studies of clientelism and vote trafficking have long suggested that poor people make more attractive clients than their better-off peers because even relatively small material payoffs can be sufficiently important to them to sway their votes.[115] More evocatively, a member of Lebanon's electoral reform commission contrasted the voting behavior of poor and middle class Lebanese:

Poor people sell their votes. Slightly higher income groups – the lower middle class, although that makes it sound more scientific than it is – require different kinds of

---

[112] Interview, shaykhly director of a conflict-resolution NGO focused on resolving tribal revenge killings, Sanaa, June 2006.
[113] The director went on to describe some of her group's activities, including opening up an internet center in one of the towns in the northern district of Akkar. The town was, in turn, less than 50 miles from Tripoli, Lebanon's second largest city, but travel to Tripoli takes over 2 hours by car. Interview, Beirut, July 2008.
[114] Interview, election coordinator for one of the parties, Beirut, April 2009. Other observers made similar claims about tribal and family politics in, for example, the eastern Bekaa district.
[115] Blaydes (2011); Brusco et al. (2004); Hicken (2011); Stokes (2005, 2007); Stokes et al. (2013); Weitz-Shapiro (2014).

interventions, [like] getting a job. They won't sell their votes so readily ... Also, the middle class has a different discourse, and selling votes is shameful, [but] the poor can't afford that discourse.[116]

All else equal, then, poorer voters are more likely to be swayed by clientelistic appeals than their wealthier counterparts.

In most societies in the developing world, incomes tend to be significantly higher in cities; people in the rural areas tend to be poorer on average.[117] As such, rural voters may be easier to satisfy with cheaper rewards compared to their urban counterparts. Moreover, patrons can also leverage economies of scale in providing collective rewards such as infrastructure because they do not need to fear wasting resources on non-supporters.

Additionally, residents of villages in the rural hinterlands may be sufficiently satisfied by even modest infrastructural improvements, such as a new well dug for the village rather than a water pumping plant and distribution network for an entire city block. One of a number of political cartoons, for example, lampooned the provision of services to the rural areas by depicting a bemused citizen declaring that his village "has no [development] projects, electricity, water, or roads" – in response to which a sleazy-looking government official declares that "we'll declare it a nature preserve!"[118] The criticism, of course, is that government officials put almost nothing into the rural areas. My point here, however, is that villages start with minimal infrastructure, and that even minimal improvements off of this baseline can have large value for the citizens living there. Hence, payoffs to villages can serve as a rough collective analogue to the individual voter's "declining marginal utility of income" dynamic which makes poor people more attractive to patrons than their wealthier counterparts.

5.8 CONCLUSION

Why is clientelism pervasive in Lebanon and Yemen? How does it work in practice? This chapter has examined the linkage strategies used by elites and their constituents in Lebanon and Yemen. Based on information gathered from elite interviews and a smattering of public opinion data, the empirical evidence I have presented has corroborated some of the basic claims I made earlier in the book about the interaction of clientelistic and ethnic politics. Collectively,

---

[116] Interview, Boutros Commission member, Beirut, July 2008.
[117] Among my Yemeni survey respondents, the median urban family income was approximately $125–250 per month and $50–125 for their rural counterparts. Village dwellers also lacked access to electricity and piped water at far greater rates than people living in the cities. Questionnaire difficulties make it harder to demonstrate these differences in Lebanon due to higher-than-desirable non-response rates and what, after the fact, turned out to be less than ideal specification of income categories. The clearest differences in material well-being turned up in access to electricity: rural Lebanese lost access to electricity much more frequently than their urban counterparts.
[118] See caricature in *al-Nida*, 2005.

5.8 Conclusion

the evidence suggests that most people eschew programmatic linkages in favor of patron–client relationships. Parties provide platforms and programs because "everyone has to have one." Yet these platforms are commonly vague, couched in generalities, emphasize valence over positional issues, and often fail to distinguish one party from another. By and large, few people expect parties to implement their programs when in offices; outside of a few "true believers," voters typically discount programmatic promises or ignore them altogether.

Instead, politicians and their constituents typically connect through clientelism. Patrons and clients seek to conclude targeted, contingent rewards-for-support bargains, trading political support for material benefits, services, and favors. Politicians sometimes target rewards to individuals, as with jobs or scholarships, and other times offer targetable club goods such as schools or wells. Club goods, like the latter, prove particularly attractive to patrons when their supporters are concentrated residentially and vote in blocs.

Resources to cover these payoffs can come from a number of sources. Government funds are, of course, a central source – much to the chagrin of the technocrats fighting a never-ending battle to rationalize the state's expenditures. Patrons with access to the levers of government can hire people into the civil service, parcel out basic services, and offer other interventions such as "fixing" parking tickets, reducing legal penalties, and clearing bureaucratic regulations. Non-state resources, in turn, provide a complementary source of patronage for politicians to tap, and can allow patrons to operate even when they are out of power. Such sources commonly take the form of charitable organizations, business interests, or expatriate communities, but can also come from foreign governments seeking local allies.

Clientelistic exchanges, of course, have transaction costs, which patrons and clients try to minimize. In the absence of a viable third-party enforcer, politicians and their constituents use repeat interactions and reputation mechanisms to support clientelistic exchange. Patrons and clients can exploit the dense social networks within their ethnic communities to keep monitoring and policing costs down. Rather than rely on the wider networks found in Lebanon's sects and Yemen's major tribes, people instead conduct their clientelistic transactions within their extended family networks, which then scale up to sects and tribes. Family heads and tribal shaykhs frequently serve as go-betweens between patrons and members. Families, in turn, bargain their collective support in blocs while relying on dense internal networks to internalize the transaction costs. The ability of families to monitor themselves and pressure members to comply with collectively agreed bargains is, in turn, strongest in the rural areas, where members are especially dependent on family support for individual welfare and opportunities.

6

Captive Audiences and Public Services

6.1 INTRODUCTION

People throughout the world expect their governments to provide citizens with basic services and infrastructure such as schools, roads, electricity, and water. In many developing societies, however, this expectation is more aspirational than it is anticipated. Instead, demand for these services often outstrips supply – in some places by a little, and others by a lot. Simple, day-to-day activities that people in wealthy societies perform without thinking – flipping on a light switch, turning on a kitchen tap – cannot be taken for granted in much of the developing world.

Political cartoons, both in the independent and party newspapers, often illustrate this all-too-common frustration with a burning candle ("electricity in our country") – suggesting that the government is not serving *anyone* particularly well. They make no mention, of course, why the electricity services are so poor: perhaps it is due to bureaucratic incompetence, or a simple scarcity of resources. We might dig deeper, however, to see whether or not there is some variation in how those scarce resources get targeted: who makes out modestly better than their peers, and who can expect particularly poor service.

At the beginning of this book, I quoted several elites who complained about the neglect their communities faced from states run by members of their own communities. In Lebanon, a local notable in a Sunni city wanted to know why electricity and water services were so spotty, and why all clinics and schools previously promised to the city had not materialized. In Yemen, tribal shaykhs wanted to know why the state was not running roads out to tribal lands, building schools and clinics there, establishing irrigation projects, or even digging wells for clean drinking water. In both cases, key constituencies – those ostensibly helping to keep their elites in power – were seeing little in return for their political support.

Is there any substance to these complaints? One must be cautious about relying too heavily on elite quotations, of course: they may be inaccurate or self-serving. First, the complaints may reflect rhetoric rather than reality. Second, they may not be based on particularly well-informed reference points. Nearly everyone believes that the state ignores them and their communities, and to some degree they are right: the Lebanese and Yemeni governments serve no one particularly well. To assess neglect in relative terms, however, we need to move beyond the hardly disinterested say-so of elites and the anecdotal evidence offered by our non-random, day-to-day encounters with their constituents.

This chapter tests some of the book's core theoretical claims with survey data that provide a glimpse into the constituent's point of view. Communities that are dominated by a single leader lack internal competition to drive up demand for their support. As compared to elites in competitive communities, dominant leaders enjoy more discretionary control over which of their constituents get what – and how much. This chapter examines variation in the provision of basic public services, which have club goods properties; later chapters complement this analysis with an examination of private goods in the form of patronage employment. In particular, I examine access to two basic utilities, electricity and water, the spotty provision of which is an endemic source of discontent in both Lebanon and Yemen. Ultimately, the evidence supports the book's core contentions. Members of communities that are dominated by a single leader receive poorer utility coverage than do their peers in communities that enjoy greater competition. Further, the monopsony penalty is milder in the poorer and more homogeneous rural areas, where transaction costs are lower than in the urban areas. Together, these findings offer evidence in favor of the basic story that this book has tried to tell.

6.2 CHEAP VOTES AND POOR SERVICES

As Chapter 2 argues in detail, communal linkages facilitate clientelistic exchange by reducing transaction costs between members of the same community relative to the costs for members of different communities. These within-group advantages, in turn, buttress the strategic selection mechanism through which politicians and voters prefer to patronize and support, respectively, members of their own communal groups. In-group favoritism, however, implies that communal constituencies are protected vote markets because out-group candidates face barriers to entry insofar as it is difficult for them to make credible patronage promises. Meanwhile, descent-like membership rules severely curtail voters' exit options, so they cannot switch constituencies in pursuit of more lucrative payoffs. In the absence of within-community competition, voters have little choice but to take what they can get.

When insulated from electoral competition, politicians enjoy considerable discretion in how they reward supporters. In the absence of credible opponents to bid up the value of the vote, dominant leaders need only pay out their constituents' reservation prices – just enough to get them to turn out on election day. Moreover, they may not even need to patronize very many of their own supporters. Although high turnout might be crucial in diverse districts when competing against leaders from other communities, dominant leaders need only modest turnout in the districts their communities dominate demographically. Under such conditions, dominant leaders can target patronage to low-cost clients. Rewards are, consequently, cheaper and fewer under dominant leaders.

Politicians distribute rewards from a portfolio of different kinds of patronage which are not perfectly interchangeable. Privately consumed rewards, such as scholarships or government jobs, target individual recipients, while club goods such as schools or health clinics benefit only residents of a given locality. Private goods are, of course, precisely targetable and excludable; I take them up in subsequent chapters. Politicians may, however, be able to pay off their supporters more efficiently with club goods if the latter concentrate in localities to such a degree that the former can take advantage of economies of scale – rewarding people "wholesale" rather than "retail," as a number of Lebanese interviewees put it. The main disadvantage of club goods, of course, is that they cannot be targeted as precisely as individualized rewards. Consequently, they are blunter instruments for patrons to use because it is harder to enforce quids pro quo when engaging in "collective clientelism" (Hicken, 2011).

Politicians can, however, mitigate the bluntness of the club goods instrument by allocating collective benefits to localities that their supporters dominate demographically – hence sidestepping the dissipation of benefits on non-supporters. Doing so, in turn, helps them to conserve their stock of individually-targeted rewards, such as government jobs, for use on clients living in mixed localities, a point to which I return in the next chapter. Communal groups tend to cluster geographically, with large-scale groups concentrating in regions and smaller-scale constituent units such as clans and extended families clustering residentially in villages and neighborhoods. Politicians can, therefore, leverage constituents' physical and social proximity to allocate club goods to them while retaining the capacity, albeit limited, to enforce collective quids pro quo.

In practice, we might expect dominant leaders to privilege villages in the rural areas over their urban constituents when providing rewards in the form of club goods. Rural localities, which are frequently homogeneous – and certainly more homogeneous than most urban areas – combine several attractive characteristics for patronage-distributing politicians, but especially for dominant communal leaders. In stylized terms, social networks are denser in villages than in cities. Villagers are geographically proximate and, in many cases, also related to one another: extended families, clans, and other tribal sections often cluster residentially in hamlets and villages. Compared to their urban counterparts, villagers are less mobile, easier to track, and have far fewer alternative social networks from which to choose. Consequently, the networks they do have tend to be dense, and can facilitate monitoring and policing.

Kin units enjoy advantages over collectivities of unrelated individuals in coordinating on a single party or politician with whom to bargain for wholesale rewards, as described in previous chapters. Bloc voting at the village level, in turn, simplifies collective monitoring. When observing election returns at low levels of aggregation, dominant leaders need only look to see that turnout is sufficiently high, and that a sufficient proportion of the ballots cast support their tickets, to infer that their clients have collectively fulfilled their obligations. Such simplistic monitoring, of course, becomes untenable in more competitive situations. Problems of ecological inference become more challenging when localities split their votes between competing politicians; one can imagine, for example, the difficulty of inferring compliance from a 50–50 split. Ease of monitoring and improved expectations of compliance may, therefore, raise the expected value of the rural vote relative to its urban counterpart for dominant leaders, but may be less advantageous for politicians in competitive communities who may be less able to avoid ecological inference problems.

Finally, rural clients often have lower reservation prices compared to their urban counterparts. Poverty tends to be higher in rural areas than in urban ones, and the villages themselves often lack basic amenities or enjoy relatively crude ones. Consequently, modest services run out to a village may receive more plaudits than the same services offered to an urban area. Consequently, small, piecemeal expenditures yield relatively greater welfare gains in the rural areas than in the urban areas, even if the gains are not necessarily large in absolute terms. Hence, rural residents might be pleased with a new well or cistern for their village, whereas urban residents aspiring to 24-hour access to piped water would be decidedly unimpressed.

6.3 HYPOTHESES

Given the theoretical considerations developed in Chapter 2 and summarized earlier, as applied to the empirical settings in Lebanon and Yemen described in Chapters 3 and 4, we should expect the following two claims to hold:

Hypothesis 1 *Constituents in communities dominated by a single leader receive poorer public services than do constituents in internally-competitive communities.*

Hypothesis 2 *Dominant leaders concentrate club goods payoffs in rural areas, which mitigates the monopsony penalty for rural constituents relative to their urban counterparts.*

The first hypothesis reiterates that constituents captured by a vote monopsony receive less for their political loyalty than do constituents who have multiple patrons from whom to choose. Lacking both political competition to bid up the value of their votes and a credible exit option to exercise, constituents under dominant leaders have little choice but to tolerate poor services. In particular, such leaders can get away with supplying spotty services because they need meet only their constituents' reservation prices rather than the competitive market price. In line with the evidence from Chapters 3 and 4, we should observe Lebanese Sunnis and Yemeni Zaydis receiving poorer services than their co-nationals.

The second hypothesis complements and contextualizes the first. Dominant leaders enjoy discretionary market power, and so can be more selective of which clients they patronize. Consequently, they can target resources efficiently to low-cost voters – here, proxied by voters in rural areas. Compared to their urban counterparts, rural-dwellers are both easier to monitor and less demanding. Moreover, villages are usually homogeneous, so patrons can leverage economies of scale to target club goods to rural clients without dissipating the benefits on non-supporters. In practical terms, targeting rural voters should reduce the monopsony penalty they suffer relative to their urban counterparts.

6.4 DATA AND METHODS

I now briefly describe the data sources and research design with which I test the hypotheses described in the previous section. Here, I use my original mass attitude survey data from Lebanon and Yemen to examine access to basic services from the constituent's point of view. These data reveal considerable variation in the quality of services available to end consumers as measured by electricity and water coverage. Ultimately, the tests try to explain this variation according to respondents' community membership and residency in the countryside – tests which largely succeed.

I rely on survey data rather than cross-sectional government data for two main reasons. First, most elites I interviewed, including several who were employed in their respective countries' statistical bureaus, were highly skeptical of the extant government data.[1] They raised numerous concerns about conceptual and geographic coverage (they lacked information on much of the country), reporting and compilation (there were no data repositories), and especially accuracy (they cooked their books). Second, raw counts of facilities such as the number of schools or clinics per district would have hidden the wildly varying amenities I observed in the field. Having seen large numbers of dirt-floor clinics and roofless schools alongside many paved kilometers of the notorious "roads to nowhere," I chose the survey data as better reflecting the dynamics I hoped to investigate.

---

[1] Interviews, academics, technocrats, and foreign embassy staff, Sanaa, 2005–2006. Interviews, academics and technocrats, Beirut, June–July 2008.

6.4 Data and Methods

6.4.1 Outcomes: Electricity and Water Access

The basic outcomes I examine are constituent access to electricity and piped water in their homes. These two basic utilities have a direct impact on people's living standards, ranging from the ability to refrigerate food to running the air conditioning in the summer heat to getting a simple glass of drinking water from the kitchen tap. Residents of the developed world usually take their electricity and water supplies for granted. In contrast, utilities are often highly unreliable – or else reliably unreliable – throughout much of the developing world. Consumers cannot take a full day's supply for granted, where intermittant cuts and rolling blackouts are facts of life that necessitate backup plans for when services are interrupted.

More precisely, I ask survey respondents about interruptions to their utility supplies – more specifically, the average number of hours per day the electricity and water are off in their homes.[2] Hence, I measure these outcomes on a natural, 24 hour scale which offers comparable gradations of utility access. There are good reasons to prefer these measures to more common subjective assessments in which we ask respondents to rate the quality of various services and facilities in their neighborhoods. One of the main difficulties with subjective assessments is that the scales we offer respondents on which to rate their services can and do take on different meanings to different people.[3] For example, what constitutes a "good" school surely depends on the observer's point of reference – a one-room school house where previously there had been none may be "good" to a villager but "bad" to a city-dweller for whom it would appear primitive. In contrast, the natural scale precludes these differences in interpretation because the metric is the same for everyone: an hour off is an hour off for both the villager and the urbanite.

Table 6.1 summarizes the electricity and water supply as experienced by the Lebanese and Yemeni samples. It shows that the typical consumer in both countries suffers from significant interruptions to their utilities on a daily basis. For both conceptual and empirical reasons, I provide several ways to think about a "typical" respondent; as measures of central tendency, I report the mean, the square root of the mean, the mean of the square root, and the median outcome for both electricity and water outages. Average Lebanese consumers face about 8 hours of daily electricity blackouts and 5 hours without water.

---

[2] The question wording reads as, "On an average day, how many hours is the electricity (water) off in your home?"

[3] Compare the particularly stark vignette-based work in King et al. (2003), which demonstrated that naïve questions about subjective outcomes made Chinese respondents, living under an autocratic government, appear more politically efficacious than their Mexican counterparts, who had just evicted the PRI from its 70-year hold on power to complete the country's transition to democracy. Correcting for the different ways that people used the question scale returned the far more plausible result that Mexicans considered themselves more politically efficacious than Chinese.

TABLE 6.1: *Summary Statistics for Electricity and Water Access: Means and Medians (Standard Deviations, Interquartile Ranges)*

	Lebanon		Yemen	
	Electricity	Water	Electricity	Water
Mean	8.0 (5.4)	4.9 (4.9)	9.3 (10.1)	12.6 (10.5)
Square Root of Mean	2.8 (2.3)	2.2 (2.2)	3.1 (3.2)	3.6 (3.2)
Mean of Square Root	2.5 (1.2)	2.2 (2.2)	2.5 (1.7)	3.0 (1.9)
Median	8 (6, 12)	4 (3, 7)	3 (1, 24)	12 (10, 24)

Their typical Yemeni counterparts, in turn, go without electricity and water for roughly 9 and 13 hours per day.[4]

Hence, in absolute terms, neither government is performing admirably in supplying basic services to its citizens. Nonetheless, there is wide variation around these measures of central tendency. In Lebanon, the interquartile range shows that the middle 50 percent of the sample experiences 6–12 hours of electricity blackouts on any given day, along with no access to water for 3 to 7 hours. In Yemen, meanwhile, the interquartile range spans nearly the entire day for both electricity (3–24 hours) and water (2–24 hours). This high degree of variation in outcome suggests that, while aggregate service provision in either country is poor, the governments nonetheless serve some consumers better and others worse in relative terms.

What, then, explains this variation in coverage – why are some citizens relatively better or worse off than others? There are surely non-political reasons why utilities are more reliable in some places rather than others, such as physical topography or population density. Nonetheless, we might expect that direct political interventions also impact the quality of the services supplied as politicians seek to reward their constituents with club goods. Consequently, we can attempt to explain the observed variation in supply according to a key political variable: the competitiveness of the respondent's community.

6.4.2 Model Setup

Here, I model variation in respondents' access to electricity and water with ordinary least squares regression. The outcome variables are the ones described previously: the reported number of hours per day the water and electricity are off in survey respondents' homes. Larger numbers are, consequently, worse from

---

[4] Notice that the gap between the mean and median outcomes is greater in Yemen than it is in Lebanon. This difference reflects the reality that more Yemenis than Lebanese live in villages with no electricity or piped water whatsoever.

6.4 Data and Methods

the constituent's perspective and indicate poorer services. I model electricity and water loss with square-root transformations, which I use for two reasons. The first is a nod to pragmatism: doing so softens an empirical skew in the data. Second, the transformation captures the intuition that the initial hours of service interruption are substantively more meaningful than latter hours. For example, moving from 0 to 1 hours off constitutes a larger marginal drop in welfare than a move from 10 to 11 hours. Note, however, that alternate modeling strategies yield qualitatively similar results.[5]

Two key explanatory variables enable me to test the dynamics predicted in Hypotheses 1 and 2. First, *Dominated* distinguishes between membership in a community that is either dominated by a single leader or else internally competitive. As applied, Lebanese Sunnis and Yemeni Zaydis take the indicator, and their co-nationals do not. Second, *Rural* indicates which respondents live in the cities and which live in the rural areas, with the latter taking the indicator. Villages in both countries are predominantly homogeneous and, to the extent to which some are mixed, the measure's imperfection makes it harder rather than easier for me to detect the hypothesized dynamics.

In addition to the main predictor variables of interest, a set of basic controls rounds out the models to avoid confounding the expected relationships. As measures of socioeconomic status, I control for education and especially household income. One might reasonably expect wealthier individuals to have access to more reliable services, either because they demand them more or because they can afford to move to neighborhoods that enjoy better access. A second key control is residence in the capital, where the centers of government are physically located. We might anticipate that government offices require comparatively better services independently of citizen demand, but with the greater reliability spilling over to improve residential access as well.

Although the underlying modeling technique is linear regression, two necessary quirks complicate interpretation and presentation of the results. The first is the inclusion of an interaction term between community membership and urban/rural residence, which is the mathematical translation of the conditional relationship claimed by Hypothesis 2 (i.e., that the monopsony penalty is milder in the villages). The second complicating factor is the square-root transformation of the outcome variables. Although the estimated effects of monopsony and rural residence are linear in square-root hours off, a "square-root hour" is not an especially intuitive unit of time. Moreover, when converted back to raw

---

[5] Alternatives include least squares regression on the untransformed outcome variables, on the natural log of hours plus one (the latter to eliminate undefined values when the natural count is 0), as well as count and binomial modeling procedures. The latter are no less complicated to interpret substantively than the models I present in the main text, so they add little substantive value.

hours, the magnitude of the domination effect depends on the number of hours from which we start.[6]

The practical upshot of these two complications is that the usual method of reporting results for a linear model – a table of coefficient estimates – is unilluminating because it is impractical to extract the marginal effects from a glance at the coefficient of interest. Although I report the tables for completeness, I focus discussion on the graphical displays of the main results, plotted in Figures 6.1 and 6.2. The figures report the marginal effects of domination by a single leader in the urban and rural areas. I denote statistically detectable effects with a "*" or a "**" to indicate the conventional 90- and 95-percent confidence levels, respectively. Lines without stars, in turn, indicate that there is no detectable domination effect at conventional levels of statistical significance. With these clarifications in mind, let us now put my claims to the test and examine the results.

6.5 FINDINGS

Can we detect the political dynamics I have been describing? The first hypothesis claims that constituents in communities dominated by a single leader receive poorer public services than do their peers in communities that are internally competitive. If correct, it implies that Lebanese Sunnis and Yemeni Zaydis should lose water and electricity more often than their co-nationals in the other communities.

The second hypothesis contextualizes the first, and arguing that dominant leaders reallocate resources away from urban areas and toward rural constituents – and so the monopsony penalty should be milder for the latter than for their urban counterparts. To be clear, however, it does not suggest that life in the village is easy for residents – it is not. There are numerous, non-political factors that impede service delivery to villages, including longer distances, lower population density, and rougher terrain. Rather, it suggests only that dominant leaders follow a logic of political efficiency that partially offsets some of these basic constraints, even as politicians from internally competitive communities focus more heavily on urban constituents.

---

[6] Technical note: more precisely, for $\sqrt{y} = x\beta + z\gamma + \epsilon$, the marginal effect of covariate x on outcome variable $\sqrt{y}$ is $\partial \sqrt{y}/\partial x = \beta$. We are not interested in this quantity per se, but rather in the marginal effect of x on untransformed y itself. By the chain rule, $\partial y/\partial x = 2\beta\sqrt{y}$, which indicates that the magnitude of the effect of x depends on where on y one calculates the effect – that is, it is non-linear. Conveniently, the delta method reveals that we can rescale the measure of uncertainty by multiplying the standard error of $\partial \sqrt{y}/\partial x$ by $2\sqrt{y}$ to calculate the standard error of $\partial y/\partial x$. Note that the existence of a significant number of natural zeroes precludes me from utilizing a more convenient log-linear model given that $\ln(0)$ is undefined. The common workaround of $\ln(outcome + 1)$ does not make effects displays any less complicated because it no longer shares the convenient interpretation of 100β as the percentage change in y due to a unit change in x.

6.5 Findings

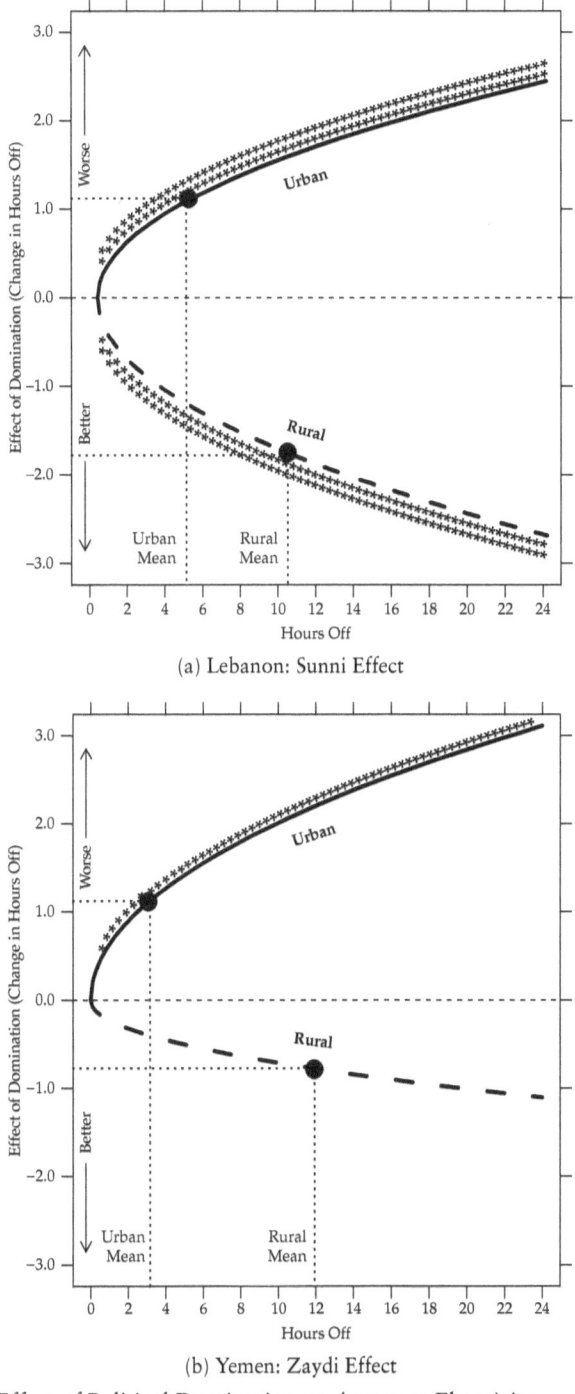

(a) Lebanon: Sunni Effect

(b) Yemen: Zaydi Effect

FIGURE 6.1: Effect of Political Domination on Access to Electricity

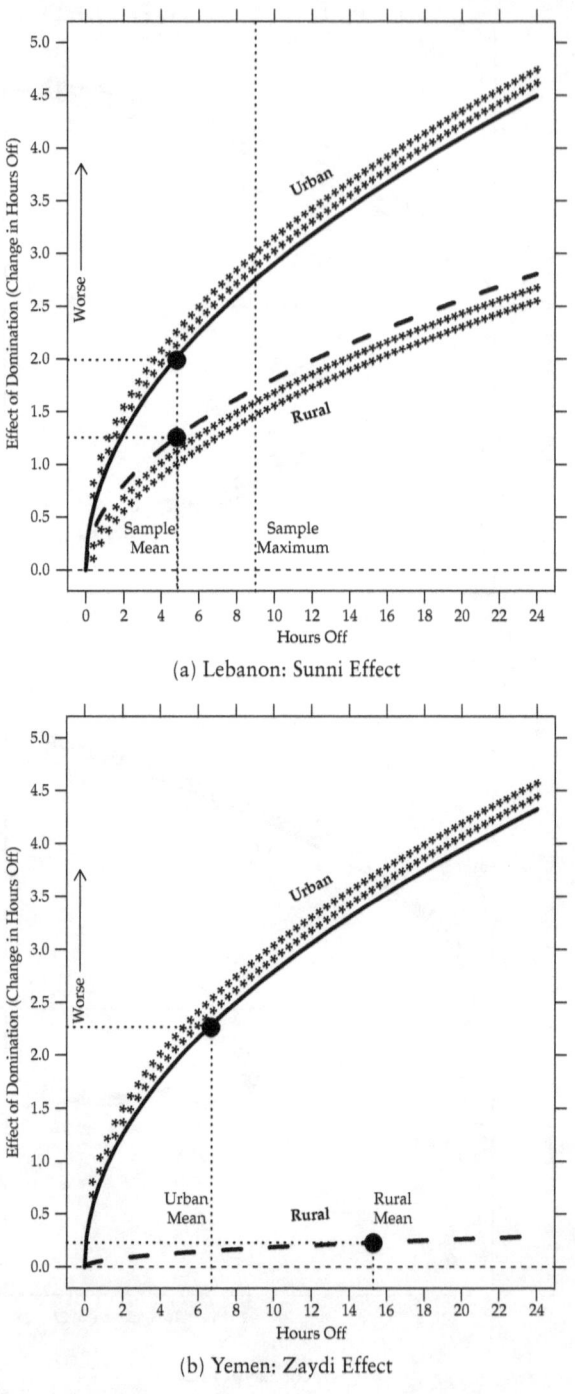

FIGURE 6.2: Effect of Political Domination on Access to Water

6.5 Findings

6.5.1 Electricity

I turn first to the findings about access to electricity (Table 6.2). Figure 6.1 plots the effect of political domination for urban and rural residents in the two countries – that is, the marginal impact of being Sunni in Lebanon (6.1a) or Zaydi in Yemen (6.1b) after controlling for other factors like socioeconomic status and location. In short, we do observe the theorized monopsony penalty in both countries. Moreover, as expected, the magnitude of that effect depends on whether constituents live in the cities or the countryside.

In both Lebanon and Yemen, there is a substantively strong and statistically detectable relationship between political dominance and electricity blackouts for urban constituents. Figure 6.1 depicts this effect with the line marked "Urban." In both cases, the line is above the 0 mark on the vertical axis, indicating the additional hours of service cuts attributable to the monopsony penalty. The stars decorating the lines, in turn, indicate that the effects are

TABLE 6.2: *Electricity Outages (Ordinary Least Squares on $\sqrt{hours/day}$)*

	Lebanon	Yemen	
(Intercept)	2.11**	2.58**	2.70**
	(0.11)	(0.17)	(0.18)
Income (NR)	0.26**	−0.54*	−0.22
	(0.12)	(0.31)	(0.31)
Income	0.19**	−0.16**	−0.09**
	(0.03)	(0.04)	(0.04)
Capital	−2.55**	−0.78**	−1.08**
	(0.08)	(0.13)	(0.14)
Education	−0.06**	−0.16**	−0.18**
	(0.03)	(0.04)	(0.04)
Rural	0.65**	1.20**	0.94**
	(0.06)	(0.11)	(0.13)
Dominated	0.25**	0.32*	0.15
	(0.07)	(0.18)	(0.18)
Dominated × Rural	−0.53**	−0.43*	−0.33
	(0.11)	(0.22)	(0.22)
South			−1.19**
			(0.22)
South × Rural			0.33
			(0.29)
R^2	0.71	0.25	0.28
N	963	1386	1386

**$p < 0.05$, *$p < 0.10$

distinguishable from 0 at conventional levels of statistical detectability – that is, we can be reasonably confident that we are detecting a systematic relationship rather than simply picking up chance variation.

More importantly, the relationship we have detected is not trivial in substantive terms. The typical city-dweller in either country – indicated on the figures at the "urban mean" – loses a little more than 1 additional hour of electricity per day, reaching as high as 2 hours in Lebanon and 3 in Yemen. An additional hour a day of blackouts is already a major inconvenience in absolute terms, but appears especially stark when we consider the relative difference in service supply for members of the two types of communities. In these terms, typical urban-dwelling Lebanese Sunnis spend about 22 percent more time in the dark than their counterparts in the other communities; the corresponding figure for Yemeni Zaydis is some 36 percent more.[7] Hence, consistent with Hypothesis 1, constituents in politically dominated communities receive poorer services compared to their peers in the politically competitive communities.

Although constituents in the cities suffer from a monopsony penalty in their access to a reliable electricity supply, these data tell a qualitatively different story out in the rural areas. In Yemen, the monopsony penalty evaporates in the rural areas. Although the effects marked "Rural" are below the 0 mark on the vertical axis, they are neither large in magnitude nor precisely estimated. As the lack of annotating stars indicates, we cannot reliably detect any relationship at conventional confidence levels, meaning we face the distinct possibility that the effect is, in fact, 0. Substantively, then, these data suggest that, in the rural areas, at least, there are no detectable differences between Zaydis and non-Zaydis. One should, of course, take note that the rural average is about 12 hours a day without electricity – so no one is being served very well.

In Lebanon, the urban/rural divergence is even more pronounced. In particular, rural Sunnis actually appear to suffer somewhat fewer electricity outages than their counterparts from the other communities – about an hour and a half less per day at the rural average of ten and a half hours. To provide some sense of proportion, however, Sunnis are, by far, the most urbanized of the Lebanese communities. Only about a quarter of the Sunni sample lives outside the cities, as compared to nearly two thirds of the non-Sunni sample. Hence, a small sub-sample of Sunnis receives a modest improvement against their rural peers, while the much larger urban sub-sample receives more blackouts instead.

---

[7] The urban mean in Lebanon is 5.13 hours off, and the predicted value of the monopsony penalty at that value is 1.13 additional hours. Hence, the relative difference – derived from the relative risk ratio – is 22 percent. The urban mean in Yemen, meanwhile, is 3.17 hours off, with a predicted monopsony penalty of 1.14 additional hours. For Yemen, the relative difference is 36 percent.

6.5.2 Water

I turn next to the findings about access to running water, which tell a story similar to the electricity findings (Table 6.3). Figure 6.2 provides an analog to Figure 6.1. It plots the effect of political domination conditional on urban/rural residence controlling for other factors – that is, the marginal impact of being a Lebanese Sunni (6.2a) or Yemeni Zaydi (6.2b). As before, the data from both countries reveal a detectable, substantively strong link between political dominance and water outages for urban constituents. The "Urban" effects in Figure 6.2 are both well above 0 on the vertical axis, indicating the additional amount of time that constituents go without water in their homes attributable to the monopsony penalty. The stars on the lines signal that these estimated effects are detectably different from 0 at conventional levels of statistical significance.

The effects are, moreover, substantively as well as statistically significant. The typical city-dweller – people at the "urban mean" of nearly 5 hours in Lebanon

TABLE 6.3: *Water Outages (Ordinary Least Squares on $\sqrt{hours/day}$)*

	Lebanon	Yemen	
(Intercept)	2.09**	3.40**	3.53**
	(0.06)	(0.18)	(0.19)
Income (NR)	0.02	−0.91**	−0.46
	(0.07)	(0.34)	(0.34)
Income	−0.01	−0.25**	−0.15**
	(0.02)	(0.04)	(0.04)
Capital	−0.54**	−0.71**	−1.12**
	(0.05)	(0.14)	(0.15)
Education	0.02	−0.09**	−0.12**
	(0.02)	(0.05)	(0.05)
Rural	0.03	1.05**	0.73**
	(0.03)	(0.12)	(0.14)
Dominated	0.46**	0.44**	0.21
	(0.05)	(0.20)	(0.20)
Dominated × Rural	−0.17**	−0.41*	−0.31
	(0.06)	(0.24)	(0.24)
South			−1.33**
			(0.21)
South × Rural			−0.10
			(0.30)
R^2	0.18	0.19	0.24
N	910	1417	1417

**$p < 0.05$, *$p < 0.10$

and 7 in Yemen – loses a little more than 2 additional hours of water per day, up to about 3 hours in Lebanon and 4 in Yemen at their sample maxima.[8] Although 2 hours is a lot of time in absolute terms, we can get another sense of proportion by translating that figure into relative terms. Hence, typical urban Sunnis in Lebanon spend 42 percent more time with no running water than do other Lebanese; the corresponding figure for Yemeni Zaydis is 34 percent more.[9] The water data thus provide another confirmation of Hypothesis 1: people in politically dominated constituencies receive poorer services – here, less access to running water – than do their peers in the more competitive communities.

Also as before, the water data tell a qualitatively different story about the cities and the villages. As with electricity, the monopsony penalty on running water disappears in the rural areas of Yemen. The estimated "Rural" effects are just barely above the 0 mark, and the lack of annotating stars indicates that we cannot, in fact, detect any difference from 0. In Lebanon, meanwhile, the monopsony penalty becomes milder out in the villages compared to the cities. The penalty still exists – the "Rural" effects are detectably above 0 – but they are also detectably smaller that the "Urban" effects. Indeed, the average villager loses an extra hour and a quarter of running water per day to the monopsony penalty, which, although clearly not desirable, is nonetheless better than the two hours lost by a comparable city-dweller. Hence, the water data provide evidence consistent with Hypothesis 2: the political domination effect is milder in the villages than in the cities.

6.5.3 Obverse Dynamics in the Yemeni South

I now present a final set of findings in keeping with the argument about the monopsony penalty: results from the Yemeni South. Recall from previous chapters that the Yemeni ruling party faces significant competition in the provinces of the former southern republic both from the main opposition parties as well as the former southern leadership in exile. Southern residents thus face tangible alternatives to the ruling party for their political loyalty, requiring the latter to expend extra effort to win over constituents and demonstrate to them the benefits of Yemeni unification. Hence, in contrast to the monopsony penalty,

---

[8] In Lebanon, the urban and rural sample means are virtually indistinguishable, so I report the full sample mean instead to avoid visual clutter. While the sample maximum for Yemen is a full 24 hours without running water, it is 9 hours in Lebanon. I plot the trend out to 24 hours for visual consistency with the other figures. We must, of course, be cautious about extrapolating too far beyond the sample maximum.

[9] The urban mean in Lebanon is 4.84 hours off, and the predicted value of the monopsony penalty at that value is 2.02 additional hours. Hence, the relative difference – derived from the relative risk ratio – is 42 percent. The urban mean in Yemen, meanwhile, is 6.70 hours off, with a predicted monopsony penalty of 2.28 additional hours. For Yemen, the relative difference is 34 percent.

6.5 Findings

we should expect to see a southern bonus. All else equal, residents of the south should receive better services compared to their counterparts in the northern provinces in the form of fewer electricity and water outages.

The Yemeni data conform to this expectation (last columns of Tables 6.2 and 6.3). Figure 6.3 plots the South effect, which amounts to the difference in service provision between southerners and northerners after taking the other modeled influences, including the effect of political dominance, into consideration. The key takeaway is this: despite the heated rhetoric about northern exploitation of the south, southerners are better off than northerners when it comes to service provision. To wit, there is a substantively strong and statistically significant South effect for both the supply of electricity (6.3a) and water (6.3b). In all cases, the estimated effect is well and detectably below 0, which means that southerners lose electricity and water less often than their northern counterparts.

The findings also indicate tha the magnitude of the South effect does not differ detectably between urban and rural residents. For water, the estimated "Urban" and "Rural" effects virtually overlap. And although visual inspection of Figure 6.3a hints at a gap between urban and rural residents in access to electricity, there is, in fact, no statistically detectable difference between the two.[10] The differences that do exist simply reflect the unremarkable differences between city and village in general, rather than the fact that they are located in the south.

In addition to their statistical significance, the South effect is sizeable in substantive terms. The average southern city-dweller and villager lose electricity about three and a half and four hours less often per day than do their northern counterparts, as well as about five and six hours of water. These are substantial improvements in basic service provisions in both relative and absolute terms. Moreover, they imply that the ruling party, faced with credible competition for the loyalties of southern constituents, has responded with improved material conditions in an attempt to convince southerners that unified Yemen is responsive to their needs. Further, these results also indicate that the ruling party, lacking the luxury to pick and choose where to distribute payoffs afforded by the lack of competition, has not attempted to target rural southerners at the expense of their urban counterparts. In summary, then, the findings from the Yemeni South confirm the main claim about monopsony penalties by demonstrating the obverse: competition bonuses for constituents with real political choice.

---

[10] These results also provide an inadvertent indication that Aden city is not driving the South effect. In brief, we might be concerned that the former capital city, which we would otherwise expect to have better infrastructure because it was the seat of the southern government, could artificially inflate the quality of services as compared to elsewhere in the country. These findings pick up no such Aden skew, as the effect in the rural South (over 40 percent of the southern sample) is indistinguishable from the effect among city-dwellers.

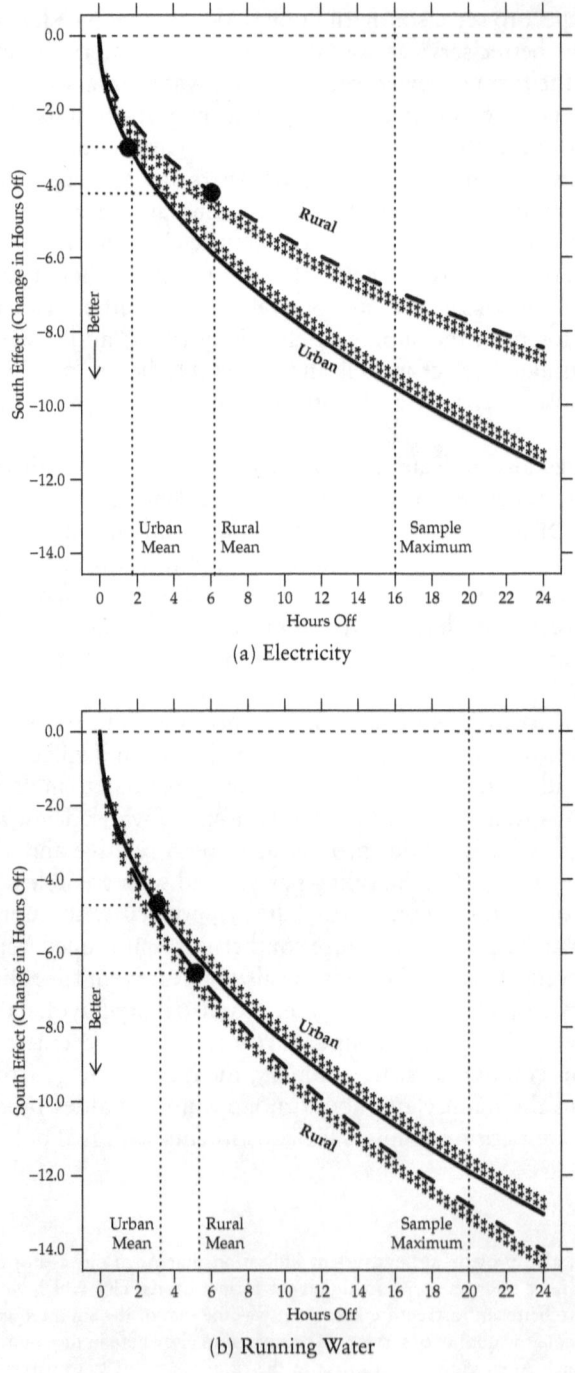

FIGURE 6.3: Southern Effect on Access to Services in Yemen

6.6 CONCLUSION

This chapter has examined one of the main claims of the ethnic monopsony argument by looking for evidence that constituents in politically dominated communities receive more meager payoffs for their political support than do their counterparts in communities that are internally competitive. Using original survey data from Lebanon and Yemen to examine evidence at the level of the individual constituent, this chapter has tested, and ultimately found support for, two empirical implications of this theory.

Empirically, this chapter employs comparable survey data from Lebanon and Yemen to test propositions about the effects of political dominance on service provision. To operationalize the outcome of interest, I use the frequency with which the electricity and water goes out in respondents' homes. These basic services, easily taken for granted in wealthy societies where a 24-hour supply of both is the norm rather than the exception, are anything but mundane in developing world societies where constant, uninterrupted access is decidedly the exception rather than the rule. Variation in the supply of these services, to the degree that community membership help to explain it, can thus tell us something about how politicians use public resources to reward their constituents.

The water and electricity data tell essentially the same story in Lebanon and Yemen, with minor variations on the main theme. Even after controlling for potentially confounding factors such as household wealth and residence in the capital, I find a substantively significant monopsony penalty in the supply of services to households in politically dominated communities. In absolute terms, I estimate that the average Lebanese Sunni and Yemeni Zaydi in the cities loses electricity and water one to two more hours per day more than their co-nationals in other communities. In relative terms, these figures equate to a 20–40 percent increase in the amount of time they go without these basic services. Taken together, these data lend support for Hypothesis 1.

Meanwhile, the effect of political dominance becomes milder in the rural areas – consistent with Hypothesis 2. In Yemen, the monopsony penalty evaporates in the villages, meaning that we can no longer detect a difference in the supply of services between Zaydi and non-Zaydi constituents on the basis of their community membership. In Lebanon, meanwhile, the relatively small number of rural Sunnis pay a milder monopsony penalty than their urban counterparts when it comes to water, which actually reverses to a small bonus when it comes to electricity supply. Despite these variations, the same theme is constant throughout: the monopsony effect on basic services is less deleterious to constituents in the rural areas.

The final piece of evidence I present in this chapter comes from the Yemeni South. It provides backhanded evidence in favor of both hypotheses by demonstrating the obverse: keen competition for constituents driving up the value of their votes and driving down their service outages. Even after controlling for other potentially confounding factors as well as the effect of political dominance, Southern residents, on average, lose electricity and water three to seven hours less per day than do their northern counterparts. Further, we cannot find any detectable difference between the cities and the villages in the magnitude of the South bonus, implying that the ruling party is attempting to win over as many constituents as possible. The contrast between southerners, who have plausible alternatives for their political loyalties, and Zaydis, who lack credible alternatives, is particularly stark, and as one empirical manifestation shows up in the provision of basic services.

The evidence in this chapter tells a story at odds with the conventional wisdom that envisions constituents in politically unified communities, particularly ruling groups, as having privileged access to government resources. Instead, the story is one of captive audiences, cheap votes, and efficient clientelism. There is, however, much more to say about the efficiency component of the argument. In particular, dominant leaders enjoy at least some flexibility in picking and choosing which constituents they reward, which in turn means that they can deploy their resources in pursuit of political efficiency: ensuring that rewards target supporters without being dissipated on non-supporters. But if such leaders have the incentive and capacity to discriminate between their nominal clients, we can envision them deploying different types of rewards – collectively versus individually targeted – to different constituents based on the diversity of their surroundings. I take up this inquiry in the next chapter.

7

Intermingled Vote Markets

7.1 INTRODUCTION

Politicians that dominate their communal groups enjoy the market power to provide their clients with cheap rewards, at least theoretically. Empirically, Chapter 6 suggests that such politicians do, indeed, exploit their market power – their constituents have spottier access to electricity and water services than do members of more competitive communities. The undersupply of desirable and productive public services is not, of course, the whole story. This chapter provides evidence that dominant leaders also aim for efficiency in how they allocate different *types* of payoffs to their clients – who gets club goods like electricity, and who gets privately consumable rewards like jobs.

Building off of the previous chapter, I note that patrons distribute rewards from a diversified portfolio of inducements, including club goods like public works projects and private goods like government jobs or scholarships. Politicians need to allocate these different types of rewards as efficiently as feasible. Ideally, they can distribute club goods to localities in which their clients predominate in order to leverage economies of scale, and reserve privately consumable payoffs for more diverse areas to take advantage of the precision with which they can hand out such rewards. As previously argued, dominant leaders are better positioned to pick and choose between their clients than are politicians in competitive communities. Yet as they lose their market power in a district – as it becomes more diverse – competition within (or against) other communities drives up the value of the vote among the former's constituents.

I test these claims using the Lebanese survey data because I can pair it with additional information on district and neighborhood diversity unavailable in the Yemen data. To examine the allocation of club goods at the district level, I again draw on the electricity and water consumption data analyzed in Chapter 6, but supplement these indicators with subjective assessments of infrastructure quality. Consistent with my argument, I find that dominant leaders undersupply their clients with club goods in homogeneous districts, but that their clients receive better services as districts become more diverse: competition seeps in and makes their votes more valuable. As indicators of privately consumed rewards, I examine perceived and actual distribution of government jobs. Again consistent with my claims, I find that constituents in dominated communities living in homogeneous neighborhoods fill far fewer government jobs than their peers, but those living in mixed neighborhoods get jobs at the same rate as everyone else. Put together, these results extend Chapter 6's findings and provide additional confirmation of the basic story this book has tried to tell.

7.2 DIVERSITY AND PATRONAGE TARGETING

One of the most common findings in empirical work on the political economy of ethnicity is that social diversity correlates with economic underdevelopment. In light of the rapidly accumulating evidence, Banerjee et al. (2005, 639) have gone so far as to describe the connection between diversity and underdevelopment as "one of the most powerful hypotheses in political economy" – although other scholars have criticized the enterprise on conceptual and measurement grounds.[1]

As described in Chapter 2, three of the most commonly cited families of mechanisms to account for the connection between ethnic diversity and underdevelopment are those invoking tastes, information technology, and strategic selection (Habyarimana et al., 2009). Tastes-based accounts posit that different groups have different preferences over the types of public goods and how to share out the burden of providing them. The latter two mechanisms, in turn, are largely complementary. Together, they posit that people are better able to monitor each other's contributions to a public good when they are in the same social networks. Diverse areas consequently suffer from shortfalls of information and monitoring capacity in the aggregate, and people tend to select their interaction partners strategically from within their own communities given the denser networks and better monitoring capacity.

The latter two mechanisms also underpin clientelistic transactions within communal groups by helping patrons and clients make credible commitments to each other when exchanging rewards for political support. In the abstract, the rewards that politicians offer take the form of a transfer of utility, which provides a convenient catch-all for the diverse goods and services that patrons deliver in applied settings. In their actual exchanges, of course, politicians do not distribute "utility," but rather rewards from which their constituents derive

---

[1] Compare Arcand et al. (2000); Bates (2008); Laitin and Posner (2001); Montalvo and Reynal-Querol (2005); Posner (2004).

utility. Patrons choose from a pool of different inducements when deciding which particular type of payoff to give to which particular client. Broadly, we can categorize the contents of this diversified portfolio based on how precisely the rewards can be targeted to their intended recipients.

Some payoffs are blunt instruments in that they are difficult to target with precision. Such rewards include many collectively consumed club goods such as a school or clinic for a village, from which it is infeasible to exclude non-supporters. Other rewards are much more precisely targetable – and, therefore, excludable – because their benefits are privately consumed. Such payoffs include public sector employment, government licenses and permits, "fixed" parking tickets, and the like. Assuming that a politician can distinguish supporters from non-supporters, there is no leakage of patronage benefits because only individual supporters receive these kinds of rewards.

We might, of course, expect politicians to dispense rewards of different types strategically – particularly in terms of who and how many people benefit from them. Allocating benefits from a diversified portfolio means trading off the economies of scale inherent to club goods against their non-excludability. Framed in this way, the patron's efficiency problem becomes one of deciding where to deploy club goods and to whom to offer privately consumed goods.

All else equal, we should expect patrons to condition their allocations on the diversity of the clientele that would benefit from the rewards. Consequently, we can expect patrons – and particularly those that dominate their communities – to concentrate club goods in places where their clients also concentrate to avoid dissipating resources on non-supporters. This argument provides a different interpretation for the consistent empirical correlation of diversity and the underprovision of infrastructure and public services. Rather than a dynamic in which different groups fail to agree on the type of good to supply or how to pay for it, this alternative posits that patrons simply allocate club goods to areas where they can maximize the number of supporters rewarded and minimize the dissipation of resources on non-supporters.

There is also a complementary aspect of the allocation logic to consider: what to do with privately consumed rewards. Although private goods do not offer economies of scale, politicians can target payoffs such as jobs or permits much more precisely than they can target club goods because the benefits accrue to individual clients rather than to collectivities. Hence, given the option, patrons should deploy club goods in homogeneous areas and save their limited cache of privately consumed rewards for places where club goods are wasteful: in diverse areas where they need precision targeting.

The ease and effectiveness with which politicians can allocate their portfolios in this way, however, may depend on how subject to competitive pressures they are. Leaders that dominate their communal groups enjoy considerably more discretion than do politicians from competitive communities – particularly in districts where their constituents are demographically dominant. As districts become more diverse, however, dominant leaders progressively lose their discretionary power because they control a shrinking segment of the vote market rather than the market as a whole. Consequently, the election's outcome depends increasingly on voters outside of that leader's own bailiwick.

Leaders that dominate their own communal groups may then pursue two different strategies to win elections in diverse districts. First, they can ally with politicians from other communities. Second, dominant leaders may try to boost within-community turnout by mobilizing more members. In the absence of competition, such leaders need pay out only reservation prices to induce a modest number of voters to show up to the polls. In more competitive districts, dominant leaders can tap the reserve pool of constituents to get more votes, but must also raise the value of the payoff to convince community members with higher reservation prices to turn out as well. In either case, constituents in dominated communities benefit from living in mixed areas. When they do, they receive more lucrative rewards for their votes because the electorate is diverse enough that other communities' competitiveness spills over and makes their own votes more relevant than they otherwise would be.

7.3 HYPOTHESES

The theoretical considerations I laid out earlier extend the concepts I discussed in Chapter 6. In particular, they introduce ideas about how diversity in the vote market influences how patrons choose to allocate payoffs from their portfolio of rewards. This theoretical discussion about diversity yields two distinct sets of implications. The first set makes predictions about how large-scale diversity influences the allocation of club goods to constituents:

Hypothesis 3 *Government services and infrastructure should be poorer in diverse districts.*

Hypothesis 4 *District diversity should mitigate the monopsony penalty.*

Hypothesis 3 begins in a familiar place by claiming that diversity reduces the quality of large-scale club goods such as infrastructure. This assertion follows the common empirical pattern identified by dozens of prior studies on the impact of diversity on development. In these studies, diversity produces an undersupply of public goods. Here, however, I lean on the logic to explain the supply of large-scale club goods such as infrastructure, which have public goods properties for members of the club – that is, people living in the area where the roads are paved or the electricity grid installed. In the main, there is little reason to expect that the established pattern of "more diversity, poorer services" should not repeat itself in Lebanon.

Hypothesis 4, meanwhile, suggests that diversity in the main is distinct from diversity in the breach. Ordinarily, we might expect people to prefer to live in homogeneous districts – if for no other reason than that infrastructure and government services tend to be of higher quality there. Yet homogeneous districts

7.4 Data and Methods

may, in reality, be problematic for members of politically dominated communities because such districts lack competitive pressure to induce leaders to provide better services. For such communities, diversity may provide a means to change their leaders' electoral incentives by introducing competition where it would otherwise not exist.

If diversity influences how patrons allocate club goods from their portfolios of rewards, we might also expect it to influence to whom they distribute alternate, more privately targetable rewards as well. The second set of hypotheses addresses how diversity considerations influence the allocation of private goods to constituents:

Hypothesis 5 *Constituents in politically dominated communities should hold fewer government jobs than their peers in other communities.*

Hypothesis 6 *Government employees from politically dominated communities should concentrate in mixed neighborhoods.*

These hypotheses suggest that we should be able to observe the monopsony penalty affecting not only government services, but also the allocation of privately-consumed payoffs such as government jobs. Hence, Hypothesis 5 predicts that, all else equal, Sunnis should be less likely to hold public sector employment than their counterparts in the other sectarian communities. We should, however, expect to observe heterogeneity within the Sunni community, with jobs concentrated among some. In particular, we might expect dominant leaders to condition their job offers on diversity at a very low level of aggregation such as neighborhood. Hence, Hypothesis 6 posits that government employment among Sunnis should concentrate in mixed neighborhoods. In this arrangement, club goods do not get dissipated on non-supporters in mixed neighborhoods, while jobs do not get wasted on constituents in Sunni-dominant areas who can be rewarded with club goods.

7.4 DATA AND METHODS

As in Chapter 6, I rely on survey data to test the propositions about payoffs in mixed and homogeneous areas. Here, however, I make use of the Lebanon data only because they contain information about district and neighborhood diversity that is unavailable in the Yemeni data. Neighborhood-level measures come from the survey itself, whereas the district-level counterparts come from voter roll information that I integrate with the survey data.

7.4.1 Outcomes: Infrastructure and Public Sector Jobs

The first set of outcomes I examine are familiar from Chapter 6: electricity and water consumption. As infrastructure programs of non-trivial size, these two outcomes cannot feasibly be targeted to individual supporters and withheld from non-supporters. Consequently, we can consider these two services to be club goods provided to residents of different localities. I also introduce a new club goods-oriented outcome variable to complement the electricity and water measures. For the new measure, I use respondents' subjective assessments of the quality of a variety of types of infrastructure in their area, including schools, health clinics, roads, landlines, and mobile phone networks. For simplicity, I create an additive index of these five different assessments and normalize it to a mean of 0 and standard deviation units. Insofar as the electricity and water measures count the number of hours *without* access – that is, larger values are bad from a constituent's perspective – I scale the index such that positive numbers indicate dissatisfaction with local infrastructure in order to remain consistent on the use of signs.[2]

In addition to club goods, however, politicians can also distribute private goods to clients on a more precisely targetable basis. Consequently, I complement the infrastructure payoffs, enjoyed by collectivities, with patronage jobs in the public sector, enjoyed by individual clients and their families. Paralleling the objective/subjective distinction I make on the club goods between electricity and water consumption versus the index of infrastructure assessments, I make use of two private rewards indicators here. The first indicator is an objective one: whether or not respondents or their spouses hold jobs in the public sector. In the sample, 11 ± 2 percent of respondents hold such jobs. Despite occasional efforts to begin civil service reform in Lebanon, the public sector is permeated with patronage hires (cf. Bashir, 1994, 2006). Patronage and merit are not, of course, mutually exclusive. Nonetheless, even if connections are not strictly necessary for employment, they remain strong determinants of success in getting hired and promoted.

Perceptions, in turn, generally emphasize the belief that connections condition access to public sector jobs and to promotion. Hence, the second indicator complements the first by measuring people's subjective assessments of the criteria used in allocating government jobs.[3] In particular, I asked respondents whether they thought hiring decisions were based primarily on merit, or primarily on political connections. The sample leaned heavily to "strongly about connections" (79 percent), so for the data analysis I perform in the following sections, I dichotomize their responses accordingly.[4] In principle, we can imagine that people in job-scarce environments are more likely to presume that connections are required to get government jobs.

---

[2] The constituent index items appear to be measuring the same underlying concept: Cronbach's $\alpha = 0.86$, well above the conventional cutoff of 0.70 as well as the more stringent 0.80. I rescale the index to give it a mean of 0 and a standard deviation of 1. The scale itself is therefore "unitless," and standard deviations become the unit of difference.
[3] This indicator plays a central role in Chapter 8, where I discuss it in more detail.
[4] That is, I dichotomize the measure such that people citing "strongly about connections" receive the indicator, and their peers, who acknowledge at least some role for merit, do not.

7.4.2 Model Setup

The argument about the allocation of club goods like infrastructure implies that we need to measure the concentration of constituents in sufficiently large geographic areas. Here, I use a measure of diversity within each of Lebanon's 30 administrative districts (*caza*s).[5] For each such district, I construct a Herfindahl index in which the groups are Shiites, Sunnis, Christians, and Druze; this measure is the analogue to the frequently used cross-national fractionalization indices.[6] The index ranges, in principle, from 0 to 1, and denotes the probability that any two randomly drawn people from the district will be from different sects.[7] The raw data for the index comes from the 2005 voter rolls, which lists voters by their sectarian affiliation, as released by the ministry of the interior and published by the Lebanese daily *al-Safir*.[8]

As a summary measure, Figure 7.1 plots the distribution of respondents experiencing different levels of district diversity within the sample.[9] The average Lebanese lives in a diverse district. The sample mean is 0.40 (with a median of 0.45), with the substantive interpretation that two randomly selected residents of the district have a 40-percent chance of being from different sects. There is, however, considerable variation across districts. The standard deviation is 0.23, and the interquartile range indicates that half the sample lives in districts ranging between diversity scores of 0.19 and 0.63. The sample minimum and maximum are 0.04 and 0.68, respectively. When plotting results, I generally extend them out to the scale's logical extreme, but readers should be cautious that doing so extrapolates into extreme forms of diversity that may or may not behave like the less extreme forms for which we have data.

The argument about the allocation of privately consumable rewards, meanwhile, implies that we need to measure constituent concentration at much lower

---

[5] The borders of Lebanese electoral districts vary from election to election, but almost always use the administrative districts as their bases. Electoral districts sometimes combine administrative districts, but rarely split them.

[6] Fractionalization indices are not without controversy among scholars of ethnic politics. One critique holds that such measures often fail to capture politically relevant cleavages when applied blindly to pre-existing demographic data. For Lebanon, however, I have constructed the index to reflect the salient cleavages. Another critique holds that polarization rather than fractionalization is more appropriate conceptually for many of the substantive outcomes we seek to explain. For patronage distribution purposes, however, constituency size and intermingling is more relevant conceptually than is polarization, and hence the fractionalization measure is appropriate here. For debate about fractionalization and polarization measures, see Alesina et al. (2003); Arcand et al. (2000); Esteban and Ray (1994); Fearon (2003); Laitin and Posner (2001); Montalvo and Reynal-Querol (2005); Posner (2004); Weidmann et al. (2010); Wucherpfennig et al. (2011).

[7] More precisely, $Diversity = 1 - \sum_i^n \pi_i^2$, where $i \in \{Shia, Sunni, Christian, Druze\}$ and thus, $n = 4$.

[8] Data published in the following issues: 26, 29, and 30 April, 10 and 12 May, 2005.

[9] Figure 7.1 is a kernel density plot (bandwidth = 0.05) – roughly speaking, a continuous analogue to the more common histogram.

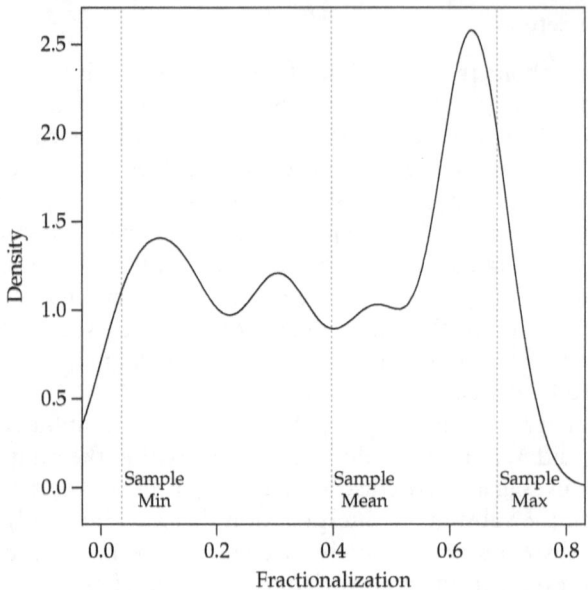

FIGURE 7.1: Distribution of Respondents at Different Levels of District Diversity

levels of aggregation. Here, I use a survey-based measure of the diversity of respondents' neighborhoods as the most disaggregated collectivity on which it is feasible to collect data.[10] The question reads: "do people from other religions or other sects within your religion live in your neighborhood?" Neighborhoods count as mixed when respondents indicate that members of other communities besides their own (Shia, Sunni, Christian, Druze) live there. By this measure, 43 percent of the aggregate sample lives in mixed neighborhoods, although the proportion is greater among Sunnis at 64 percent. This binary measure is, admittedly, somewhat crude. It does not indicate how mixed the neighborhoods are on a continuum, and it relies on respondents' familiarity with their area as well as their conceptions of what constitutes the extent of the neighborhood. Nonetheless, it still provides a reasonable first attempt to measure the underlying concept and can be improved upon in subsequent research.

The model setup for the club goods – electricity and water consumption, the infrastructure index – follows the same basic layout as in Chapter 6. In particular, I use the basic specification as before with the same set of control variables to guard against confounding relationships. I then progressively add in the district diversity measure, first additively and then interactively to capture the hypothesized conditional relationship between political dominance

---

[10] One might ask urban respondents about the diversity of their apartment buildings, for example, but it would be difficult to compare apartment-dwellers to single-family homes in either urban or rural areas.

7.5 Findings

and diversity. I use the square-root transformation for electricity and water outcomes; the infrastructure index, meanwhile, takes on its untransformed values due to its construction.

To examine access to the privately consumed rewards – public sector jobs, perceived job criteria – I begin the analysis with procedures that have fewer moving parts. I start with simple differences-in-proportions tests to establish the connection between monopsony and neighborhood diversity. I subsequently confirm the dynamics that fall out of these procedures with multivariate analysis (probit models) that use the same set of basic control variables to guard against confounds.

7.5 FINDINGS

Can we detect any of the patronage dynamics that I have been describing in this chapter? I have argued that politicians have diversified portfolios of rewards to allocate and try to deploy them efficiently. Broadly, we should expect patrons to use different rewards in different circumstances by deploying club goods in areas where their constituents concentrate and privately consumed rewards in intermingled vote markets. We should also be able to observe the effects of political dominance described throughout the book, with constituents in dominated communities receiving more meager payoffs than their peers, until such time as competition from other communities compels their leaders to provide better rewards.

7.5.1 Services and Infrastructure

The first set of tests I conduct examines the impact of district-level diversity on respondents' experiences in accessing electricity and running water, and in their subjective assessments of their local infrastructure. The basic model from Chapter 6 serves as the baseline model. As before, I present a table of coefficient estimates for completeness (Table 7.1), but present the main findings graphically and verbally for ease of interpretation.

For the first step, I include the diversity measure additively in the model specifications to provide a baseline point of comparison. As Table 7.1 reveals, the coefficient estimate for *Diverse* is positive and detectably different from 0 on all three measures, indicating that people's experiences with these outcomes become worse as diversity increases. By way of illustration, consider the deterioration of these services when comparing a fairly homogeneous district a standard deviation below the mean in diversity (0.17) to a more heterogeneous one a standard deviation above the mean (0.62). At the sample mean for electricity outages (8 hours), constituents in the more diverse district lose about 3 more hours of power than their peers in the more homogeneous district – a relative difference of 31 percent. Analogously for water (5 hours mean outage), the loss

TABLE 7.1: *Diversity, Services, and Infrastructure*

	Electricity		Water		Index	
	Model 1	Model 2	Model 3	Model 4	Model 5	Model 6
(Intercept)	1.71**	1.61**	2.01**	1.91**	−1.21**	−1.33**
	(0.11)	(0.11)	(0.07)	(0.06)	(0.15)	(0.15)
Income (NR)	0.32**	0.33**	0.03	0.02	0.48**	0.49**
	(0.11)	(0.11)	(0.07)	(0.07)	(0.16)	(0.16)
Income	0.22**	0.23**	−0.01	0.01	0.27**	0.28**
	(0.03)	(0.03)	(0.02)	(0.02)	(0.04)	(0.04)
Capital	−2.88**	−2.61**	−0.62**	−0.29**	−1.03**	−0.75**
	(0.08)	(0.09)	(0.05)	(0.06)	(0.11)	(0.13)
Education	−0.06**	−0.06**	0.02	0.02	−0.08**	−0.08**
	(0.03)	(0.03)	(0.02)	(0.02)	(0.04)	(0.04)
Rural	0.53**	0.54**	0.00	0.00	0.48**	0.49**
	(0.05)	(0.05)	(0.03)	(0.03)	(0.07)	(0.07)
Dominated	0.19**	0.81**	0.44**	1.10**	0.07	0.81**
	(0.07)	(0.14)	(0.04)	(0.08)	(0.10)	(0.20)
Diverse	1.12**	1.26**	0.25**	0.40**	1.18**	1.36**
	(0.10)	(0.10)	(0.06)	(0.06)	(0.14)	(0.15)
Dominated × Rural	−0.41**	−0.47**	−0.15**	−0.18**	0.06	−0.03
	(0.10)	(0.10)	(0.06)	(0.06)	(0.14)	(0.14)
Dominated × Diverse		−1.52**		−1.68**		−1.76**
		(0.29)		(0.18)		(0.41)
R^2	0.74	0.75	0.19	0.26	0.28	0.30
N	963	963	910	910	895	895

**$p < 0.05$, *$p < 0.10$

is about half an hour – about 10 percent in relative terms.[11] On the scaled infrastructure index, this move from low to high district diversity corresponds with half a standard deviation's drop in satisfaction. Put together, these findings confirm what many other studies have found: diversity appears to hamper the provision of infrastructure and government services.

The aggregate effect just described, however, represents a weighted average of the effect felt by Sunnis and non-Sunnis – people in politically dominated communities and the effect felt by their counterparts in the more competitive

---

[11] Recall that I have modeled electricity and water consumption on a square-root scale. To transform the marginal effect back to the natural, 24-hour scale, we must recalculate the effect as $2b\sqrt{y}$. Hence, y enters the calculation, which is why I scale the effect according to the sample means in the main text. For electricity with a sample mean $y = 8$ hours and an estimated coefficient $b = 1.12$, the absolute difference between the high (0.62) and low (0.17) diversity districts is $(high - low) \cdot 2b\sqrt{y} = 2.9$ hours. The relative difference, derived from the risk ratio and calculated at the sample mean, is 31 percent. For water (sample mean $y = 5$, estimated coefficient $b = 0.25$), the absolute difference is 0.51 hours, and the relative difference is 10 percent.

7.5 Findings

communities, respectively. Consequently, it does not tell us if these two types of constituents experience diversity in qualitatively similar or dissimilar ways. Hypothesis 4, however, suggests that the diversity effect should be conditional on the competitive environment within the communities. I capture this hypothesized conditional relationship by adding an interaction term between diversity and monopsony to the model. I report the political dominance effect as district diversity varies in Figure 7.2.[12]

Two of the the outcome indicators, electricity and water consumption, take a square-root transformation as in Chapter 6. For simplicity, Figures 7.2a and 7.2b plot the effect of political dominance, and its confidence intervals, on the square root of these outcomes as district diversity varies along the horizontal axis. The vertical axis on the left reports these effects on the square-root scale, while the vertical axis on the right translates these effects to outcomes on the natural, 24-hour scale taken at the sample mean values for electricity and water outages (8 and 5 hours, respectively). The final outcome, the index of subjective infrastructure assessments, is already on its "natural" (not square-root) scale, so I dispense with the rightmost vertical axis in Figure 7.2c; here, the outcome units are standard deviations. In each case, I plot the effect for the theoretical range of district diversity (0–1) for completeness, but, in practice, the sample maximum is 0.68, so we do not observe the more extreme values.

As Figure 7.2 reveals, all three outcomes follow the same pattern: a penalty for political dominance in homogeneous districts that grows milder with more diversity. In each case, the effect is above the 0 line at low levels of district diversity. This effect indicates that people in politically dominated communities, as compared to their more competitive counterparts, suffer a greater number of disruptions to their electricity and water supplies as well as express more dissatisfaction with the infrastructure in their area. Substantively, the penalty in the sample's most homogeneous areas (0.04) costs constituents nearly 3 hours of electricity and over 4 hours of water when translated back from the square-root scale to the natural, 24-hour scale. Analogously, it raises constituent dissatisfaction with their infrastructure by an estimated three quarters of a standard deviation on the infrastructure index.

As districts become more diverse, however, constituents experience a milder political dominance effect, as evident in the downward slope of the lines in Figure 7.2. By the time we reach the sample mean for district diversity (0.40), these data suggest that people in dominated communities lose electricity no more often than their peers, and are no more or less dissatisfied with their infrastructure. They still suffer more interruptions to their water supplies – about an hour and a half more per day – but this figure is down from the 4 hours in the most homogeneous areas. Intriguingly, there is some evidence that constituents in dominated communities may receive better services than their

---

[12] Note that the effects plotted in Figure 7.2 come from the interactive model reported in Table 7.1.

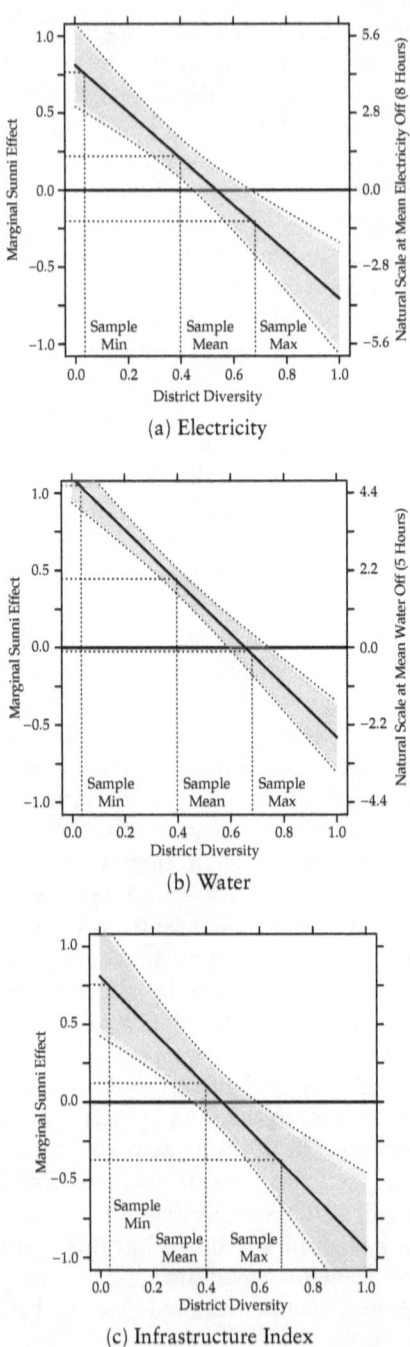

FIGURE 7.2: Political Dominance Decreases Electricity, Water, and Infrastructure Quality in Homogeneous Areas

7.5 Findings

peers in the most diverse areas. At the sample maximum for district diversity (0.68), they lose around 2 hours of electricity and half an hour of water *less* than their counterparts, and are a little more than a third of a standard deviation more satisfied with their infrastructure.

Overall, then, we observe two key dynamics in the provision of club goods such as infrastructure. First, constituents living in more diverse areas receive poorer services than those living in more homogeneous areas. Given the wealth of prior studies that find the same dynamic in other settings, this outcome is not surprising. The second finding, however, pulls apart this aggregate effect to compare the experiences of people in competitive and uncompetitive communities. When we do so, we observe a monopsony penalty where we should expect to see it: in homogeneous districts where dominant leaders enjoy their greatest discretion in who to target with rewards, and with how much. The penalty declines in magnitude, however, as districts become more diverse, and, consequently, more competitive, which bids up the value of what would otherwise be cheap votes.

7.5.2 Public Sector Employment

The results detailed previously suggest that dominant leaders consider efficiency motives when distributing rewards with club goods properties such as electricity, water, infrastructure. If, however, the efficient targeting story is correct, we should also expect a complementary logic to hold for the distribution of privately consumed rewards such as government jobs. Given that they are individually targetable, we might expect patrons to allocate them based on information as precise as the demographic composition of the neighborhood in which a client lives.

How well does this logic map onto Lebanon's different competitive environments? Consider Table 7.2, which tabulates Sunnis and non-Sunnis (the monopsony condition) against people who do and do not hold down jobs in the public sector. Only about 9 percent of Sunnis (27 of 316) have government jobs as compared to about 12 percent of non-Sunnis (81 of 679), for a modest difference of 3 percentage points. Overall, however, the relationship between political dominance and public hiring decisions in the aggregate population appears to be tentative ($\chi^2_1 = 2.22, p = .14$).

Table 7.2 conflates two different kinds of constituents, however: those that live in mixed neighborhoods, and those who live is homogeneous neighborhoods. Figure 7.3, meanwhile, compares these two types among Sunnis and non-Sunnis – that is in constituencies that are less and more competitive. The entries report, in proportion terms, the number of constituents holding government jobs conditional on being in or out of the monopsony condition and living in a mixed or homogeneous neighborhood. In other words: what do Sunnis get in the two types of neighborhoods? And how do they compare to non-Sunnis?

TABLE 7.2: *Political Dominance and Public Sector Jobs*

		Dominated		Public Base Rate
		No	Yes	
Public	No	60 (n = 598)	29 (n = 289)	89 (n = 887)
	Yes	8 (n = 81)	3 (n = 27)	11 (n = 108)
Dominated Base Rate		68 (n = 679)	32 (n = 316)	100 (n = 995)

TABLE 7.3: *Mixed Neighborhoods and Government Employment*

	Government Job	Merit in Hiring
(Intercept)	−1.67**	−0.29
	(0.30)	(0.25)
Income (NR)	−0.01	−0.83**
	(0.34)	(0.28)
Income	0.10	−0.12*
	(0.08)	(0.07)
Capital	−0.21	0.60**
	(0.21)	(0.18)
Education	0.07	−0.12*
	(0.08)	(0.06)
Rural	−0.01	0.23**
	(0.13)	(0.11)
Dominated	−1.01**	−0.70**
	(0.39)	(0.19)
Mixed	0.27*	0.00
	(0.14)	(0.12)
Dominated × Mixed	1.09**	0.41
	(0.43)	(0.25)
Log Likelihood	−313.42	−468.90
N	948	940

$^{**}p < 0.05, ^{*}p < 0.10$

Table 7.3 summarizes multivariate probit models of job holding and assessments of merit in hiring decisions. The main focus is the conditional relationship between Sunnis and neighborhood composition, while controlling for socioeconomic and locational indicators (simple trivariate relationships yield the same

7.5 Findings

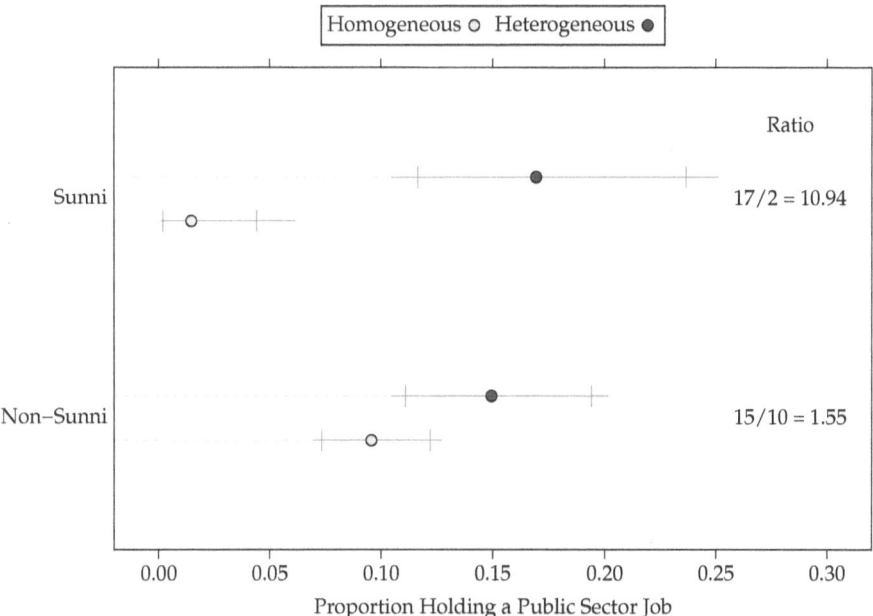

FIGURE 7.3: Political Dominance, Mixed Neighborhoods, and Public Sector Jobs

qualitative results). Given the probit link and the interaction term, I plot the main findings graphically for ease of interpretation.

The results reported in Figure 7.3 yield evidence consistent with Hypotheses 5 and 6. As the data show, Sunnis fill far fewer government jobs than do their peers – at least among those living in homogeneous neighborhoods. Under these conditions, some 10 percent of non-Sunnis are employed in government service, but only about 2 percent of Sunnis are similarly employed. This five-fold difference is easily detectable at the 95-percent confidence level. Sunnis in mixed neighborhoods are, in contrast, more than ten times as likely as their co-sectarians in homogeneous neighborhoods to hold government jobs, yet do not differ detectably from their non-Sunni peers in such neighborhoods.

The rows of Figure 7.3, in turn, speak more directly to Hypothesis 6. The bottom row shows that, for non-Sunnis, the switch from homogeneous to heterogeneous neighborhoods increases the number of constituents with government jobs from an estimated 10–15 percent. This difference, however, is tentative at best ($p = 0.13$). The top row, in contrast, shows that the neighborhood effect among Sunnis is dramatic. Here, the switch from homogeneous to mixed increases the proportion of government job holders from 2 to 17 percent – a 11-fold jump that is easily detectable at the 95-percent confidence level. In short, Sunnis from Sunni neighborhoods are virtually absent from the government payroll, but close the gap with their peers in the other communities in mixed neighborhoods.

An alternative way to consider the same underlying phenomenon is to examine not who actually holds government jobs, but rather what people believe to be the main criteria by which such jobs get assigned. The former measures actual allocations, while the latter measures perceptions about allocations. We might imagine that constituents vary in their beliefs about how much weight gets put on merit and ability versus political connections. As described earlier, with the measure I use here, people lean heavily toward the "connections" end of the scale. Consequently, I dichotomize their responses between those who believe connections are the paramount consideration in getting a government job, and those who believe that merit factors into the hiring decision at least somewhat.[13]

Analogous to Table 7.2, Table 7.4 presents a 2-by-2 comparison between Sunnis and non-Sunnis (the monopsony condition) and those who do and do not think merit plays some role in hiring decisions. About 18 percent of Sunnis (56 of 313) believe that merit factors in at least somewhat in securing a government job, while the other 82 percent believe that the paramount consideration is political connections. For non-Sunnis, the analogous figures are 23 percent (153 of 672) and 77 percent, for a between-communities difference of 5 percentage points. In the aggregate population, then, the relationship between political dominance and perceptions of public hiring decisions, as with the relationship with actual hiring decisions, is evident, but tentative ($\chi^2_1 = 2.75, p = 0.10$).

Table 7.4, as before, conflates the two different sub-constituency types: those living in mixed neighborhoods and those living in homogeneous neighborhoods. The key comparison to make, then, is between these sub-constituencies within both the less and the more competitive communities. I summarize these comparisons in Figure 7.4 which reports, in percentage terms, the quantity of people who believe merit plays at least some role in the hiring decision for government employment (again based on multivariate models reported in Table 7.3).

Analogous to the findings from Figure 7.3, Figure 7.4's results yield evidence consistent with Hypotheses 5 and 6. Sunnis living in homogeneous neighborhoods are far less likely than their similarly situated non-Sunni peers to believe that government jobs are distributed according to merit. Only about 10 percent of such Sunnis believe that merit plays any role in the hiring decision – 90

---

[13] The question wording is: "What is the most important thing to get a good *government* job, as opposed to a job in the private sector?" Respondents indicate which of two statements they agree with more, and whether they agree strongly or just somewhat. The first statement is: "Personal connections and *wasta* are the most important factors in getting a *government* job." The second statement reads: "The most important factors in getting a *government* job are merit and ability." Some 79 percent of the sample agreed strongly with the "connections" statement; given the skew in the data, I dichotomize responses as "strongly connections" versus all other responses, which indicate some merit considerations.

7.5 Findings

TABLE 7.4: *Political Dominance and Perceptions of Merit in Government Hiring*

		Dominated		Merit Base Rate
		No	Yes	
Merit	No	53 ($n = 519$)	26 ($n = 257$)	79 ($n = 776$)
	2*Yes	16 ($n = 153$)	6 ($n = 56$)	21 ($n = 209$)
Dominated Base Rate		68 ($n = 672$)	32 ($n = 313$)	100 ($n = 985$)

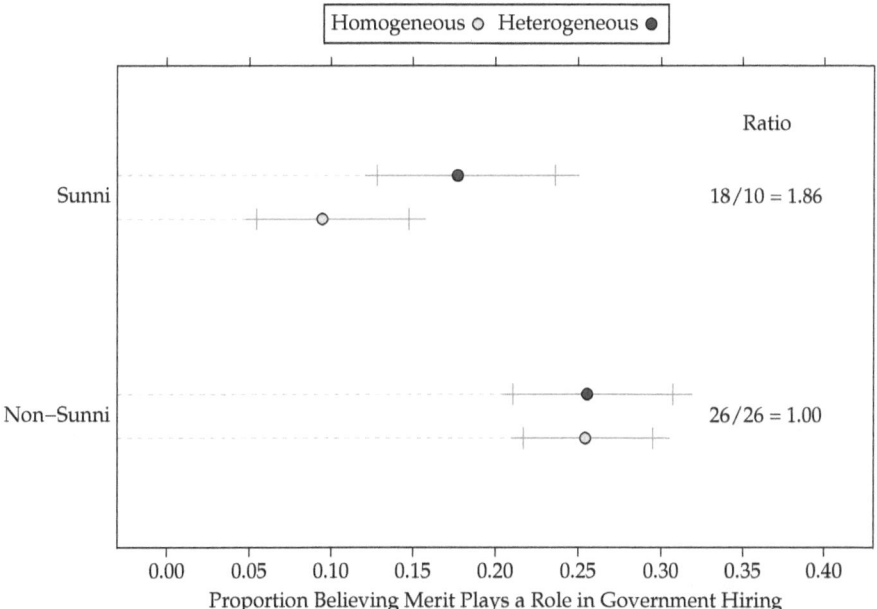

FIGURE 7.4: Political Dominance, Mixed Neighborhoods, and Perceptions of Merit in Government Hiring

percent believe connections are paramount – as compared to 26 percent of their non-Sunni counterparts. This 2.5-fold drop is statistically detectable at the 95-percent confidence level. Meanwhile, the bottom row reveals that non-Sunni perceptions do not vary by neighborhood type. About 26 percent of those in mixed and those in homogeneous neighborhoods believe that merit plays at least some role in government hiring decisions. Finally, and consistent with actual job allocations, Sunnis in homogeneous neighborhoods are far and away more likely to presume that connections are paramount in landing on the public payroll – whether compared to non-Sunnis, or to Sunnis in the mixed neighborhoods.

Overall, then, we observe two key dynamics in the data that are consistent with the argument about the targeting of different types of patronage rewards. First, we see a monopsony penalty for Sunnis living in homogeneous neighborhoods: they get fewer public sector jobs than their comparable peers in other communities. Second, the sectarian make-up of the neighborhood strongly conditions Sunnis' access to such jobs. Sunnis living in mixed neighborhoods get far more government jobs than do their co-sectarians in the homogeneous neighborhoods – comparable in number to jobs that go to members of other sectarian communities. These twin dynamics are consistent with the claims that monopsonists can diversify their patronage payoffs: targeting private payoffs (jobs) to clients living in mixed areas where club goods would be wasted on non-supporters.

7.6 CONCLUSION

This chapter built off of Chapter 6's empirical comparison of access to basic public services in competitive and uncompetitive communities. Here, I pursued implications about how patrons might choose to allocate the different kinds of patronage rewards they have available conditional on the diversity of the local vote market. In particular, it examined when, and to whom, leaders might provide club goods or private goods.

All else equal, we might expect patrons to deploy collectively consumed club goods such as public services and infrastructure in areas where their supporters concentrate in order to leverage economies of scale without dissipating resources on non-supporters. Unsurprisingly, and consistent with a large body of academic research, the evidence presented in this chapter suggests that residents of homogeneous areas enjoy, on average, more reliable services and better infrastructure than their peers in more heterogeneous areas.

More interestingly, we might also expect the effect of homogeneity to differ for members of competitive and uncompetitive communities. When the latter predominate in a district, there is little electoral pressure for their leaders to provide high quality services. As districts become increasingly mixed, however, competition from, and within, other communities compels leaders to offer better rewards for political support. Consistent with this expectation, the monopsony penalty that Sunnis suffer in homogeneous districts wanes and disappears in more heterogeneous districts.

The second set of implications addresses privately consumed payoffs such as permits, licenses, and jobs, the benefits of which are captured entirely by individual clients. We might imagine that patrons switch over from club goods to private payoffs when operating in intermingled vote markets where club goods payoffs would waste patronage resources on non-supporters. Although

7.6 Conclusion

dominant leaders might offer poorer private goods payoffs in general, they may also reserve the payoffs they do make for clients in mixed areas. Consistent with these expectations, the data show that Sunnis in homogeneous neighborhoods are much less likely than non-Sunnis to hold government jobs and more likely to presume that getting such jobs requires connections. Sunnis in mixed neighborhoods, in contrast, look essentially the same as their non-Sunni peers.

Taken together, then, the findings presented in this chapter provide evidence consistent with the book's theory of ethnic monopsonies. The data tell a story not of communal favoritism in a simple sense. Instead, they reveal a richer dynamic in which patrons attempt to allocate their diverse patronage portfolios efficiently. Politicians that dominate their communities politically need not, of course, provide rich rewards to their supporters. Dominant political leaders can, moreover, target the types of payoffs they provide accordingly, allocating modest club goods like infrastructure to areas where their constituents concentrate and privately consumed payoffs like jobs where their supporters intermingle with members of other communities.

8

Perverse Competition and Personalized Patronage

8.1 INTRODUCTION: WHO COMPETES FOR WHOM?

So far, this book has argued that people in politically dominated communities tend to receive poor rewards for their political support. Previous chapters examined some of the distributional consequences of political domination in terms of the provision of infrastructure, public services, and government jobs. Although constituents in such communities might grumble in private, their public statements often tell a different story: that of enduring fidelity to their patron. Party flags and laudatory political posters abound, while boisterous rallies chant embarrassingly obsequious slogans about the virtues of their leaders. Some, for example, urge "loyalty to Shaykh Saad al-Hariri" in Lebanon, while others beseech Ali Abdallah Salih to "finish the task" by standing for president of Yemen yet again. Why, though, would people who receive poor services in the aggregate make such public declarations of support?

This chapter explores a different set of empirical implications about ethnic monopsonies: who competes for whom. In politically dominated communities, patrons do not need the active support of all – or even most – of their nominal clientele to win elections. Politicians in such communities enjoy the luxury to pick and choose which members receive rewards; clients, in turn, must find ways to get picked over their peers. Rather than patrons competing for votes, clients compete for patronage – a reversal of the dynamics we expect to see in elections. One commonly overlooked tool for people to attract patronage, however, is to engage in public sycophancy: to send costly signals to patrons about their levels of commitment.

To examine the dynamics of public sycophancy, I return to the survey data from Lebanon and Yemen. I complement these attitudinal data, however, with a novel behavioral measure: whether or not respondents publicly display images and iconography such as party flags or posters outside their homes.

Consistent with my argument, members of the political dominated communities – Lebanese Sunnis and Yemeni Zaydis – are significantly more likely than their co-nationals to offer up "public displays of affection" for their leaders. Moreover, the survey data indicate that they do so for instrumental reasons. In particular, the data reveal a systematic connection between public displays of political images and patronage-seeking behavior – a link that is absent among people in the competitive communities. Put together, these findings lend credence to the claim that dominated communities engage in "perverse competition" in which voters compete with one another to attract patronage from their leaders.[1]

The rest of the chapter proceeds as follows. First, it theorizes on the politics of sycophancy, portraying it not as an irrational demand of megalomaniacal leaders, but as reasoned behavior on the part of clients that transmits information to patrons. I then describe the data in more detail, especially the novel iconography measures that serve as behavioral indicators. I next analyze these data and find that respondents in politically dominated communities are both more likely than their peers to display political iconography and do so in a patronage-seeking way. I conclude with implications of these findings for the broader story of perverse competition.

8.2 THE POLITICS OF SYCOPHANCY

When Syrian President Hafez al-Assad died in June 2000, Damascus exploded in a cacophony of shouts, honks, and tears as thousands of bereaved people, who could find no words to describe their sorrow, mourned their beloved leader. Weeping Syrian citizens poured into the streets on the day of the funeral to express not only their grief at the elder Assad's passing, but also to express their undying loyalty to Bashar al-Assad, his son and successor, chanting "With our souls, with our blood, we will protect you, oh Bashar." Or, at least, this description was the official Syrian take on the funeral scene. Although consistent with the many spectacles of Syrian public life under Assad, it is also consistent with a decidedly less flattering Ethiopian proverb: "When the great lord passes the wise peasant bows deeply and silently farts."[2]

Crocodile tears at Assad's death suggest that public statements of political support may not be entirely what they seem. Public sycophancy is hardly a new phenomenon, however. Assad himself purportedly drew inspiration from the cult of personality cultivated by North Korea's Kim dynasty, whose members

---

[1] "Perverse competition" is another facet of the "perverse accountability" of machine politics that Stokes (2005) describes.

[2] Whether the great lord "passes by" or "passes away," the notion is the same. The official Syrian take comes from www.presidentassad.net/Al_ASSAD_ANALYSES_NEWS/HAFEZ_ASSAD_FUNERAL.htm, accessed 25 February 2010. On spectacles in Syria, the seminal work is Wedeen (1999). The Ethiopian proverb comes from the epigraph in Scott (1990).

have been venerated as the "Great Leader," the "Dear Leader," and, more recently, the "Great Successor" and "Outstanding Leader."³ Among many other facets of his cult of personality, the president of Turkmenistan erected a rotating, 230-foot golden statue of himself.⁴ The notoriously corrupt president of Zaire, Joseph-Desiré Mobutu, took on such honorary titles as "the Guide," "the Father of the Nation," "the Helmsman," and "the Messiah."⁵ The list could easily go on.

Why would anyone go to this much trouble, expense, and patent absurdity? Common answers generally invoke some sort of deluded megalomania on the part of leaders and fearful compliance on the part of followers. In effect, such explanations assume that the leaders in question are idiots who believe their own nonsense parroted back at them, and citizens are helpless victims of circumstance with no independent agency of their own. Neither assumption, however, is particularly plausible. Instead, I will suggest that the *act* of public sycophancy – rather than its *content* – does indeed provide leaders with information about levels of commitment among their nominal supporters.

8.2.1 Political Dominance and Surplus Clients

In advanced democracies, candidates and parties court voters with mixtures of programmatic policies and pork payoffs. In weakly institutionalized democracies, aspiring officeholders use clientelistic linkages and patronage politics. In either case, however, we typically envision a *race* rather than a *coronation*: politicians compete with one another for the votes that win elections, the outcomes of which are unknown in advance. We have well-rehearsed normative reasons to prefer this dynamic: candidates strive to meet the policy demands of their constituents, are regularly subject to accountability mechanisms before their principals, and electoral competition bids up the value of the vote.

This idealized vision of democratic elections begins to blur, however, as the races become less and less competitive and the outcomes become more and more inevitable. We can begin to observe changes in dynamics between politicians and voters when we consider the races for "safe seats" in otherwise

---

³ The latter two appelations apply to Kim Jong Un, who took power after his father's death in 2011, and will almost certainly be supplemented by more titles. Not to be outdone, internet pranksters have also dubbed the new leader "Lil' Kim" after the American rapper. For a sampling of some 300-odd new slogans adopted by the country, see "Decoding North Korea's fish and mushroom slogans," *BBC News Magazine Monitor*, 12 February 2015.

⁴ The president in question was Separmurat Niyazov, who claimed the title of "Turkmenbashi," variously translated as "father of the Turkmens" or "leader of the Turkmens." After removing the statue following Niyazov's death, his successor re-erected it in a slightly more discrete place in the capital's suburbs. See Eurasianet.org, "Turkmenistan: Golden Turkmenbashi Statue is Back," 11 November 2011 (www.eurasianet.org/node/64458, accessed 20 September 2012).

⁵ See Hochschild (1998, 303). After taking the presidency, Mobutu eventually changed his name to "Mobutu Sese Seko," which translates loosely to "he who goes from conquest to conquest." His new name in full was much longer and much more grandiloquent.

8.2 The Politics of Sycophancy

solidly democratic polities, where turnover in unlikely, albeit still imaginable. Elections under dominant party regimes or electoral autocracies look even less like the democratic electoral ideal, even though the electoral ritual occurs with great frequency and regularity. In the limit, of course, we see very little overlap – beyond the physical act of voters dropping ballots into a box – between competitive, democratic elections and the orchestrated, "99-percent elections" that yield single-candidate coronations.

As elections become less competitive, they perform different functions than deciding who holds office, as described in Chapter 2. In particular, they provide mechanisms to gather information on popular support, regularize payoffs to clients, and deter splits in the ruling coalition.[6] To the degree that politicians dominate their own communities and face no credible electoral threat to retaining office, they do not need active support from most of their nominal constituents and can pick and choose among them. Insulated from competitive pressures, dominant leaders can create and manage scarcities of patronage, rationing out a limited supply of rewards and compelling constituents to compete for it. Hence, decreased competitiveness changes the relationship between politicians and voters in a subtle but crucial way: it reverses who competes for whom. Instead of politicians vying for votes, voters vie for patronage.

8.2.2 Surplus Clients and Perverse Competition

Inducing competition between clients helps politicians allocate patronage resources efficiently. All else equal, patrons prefer to target committed clients over uncommitted ones. Although each voter has exactly one vote, committed clients are more likely than their uncommitted peers to fulfill their obligations to the patron on election day. In expectations, then, a committed vote is worth more to the patron than an uncommitted one.

Implicitly, there is a conflict of interest between the two client types. The uncommitted prefer to maintain an undifferentiated clientele pool because it raises the chances that they can pass as committed and secure a share of the patronage for themselves. The committed, in contrast, prefer that patrons can discriminate between types – that is discriminate in their favor – because it eliminates competitors from the pool of patronage-seekers and reduces the number of people among whom the payoffs must be shared. Patrons and their committed clients consequently share an interest in the efficient deployment of patronage resources at the expense of nominal but uncommitted constituents. Hence, the committed are complicit in fostering competition among voters.

Patrons, however, confront the non-trivial problem of *how* to distinguish one type of client from the other. Transactions in the vote market occur in an environment of imperfect, asymmetric information. In particular, clients know their own levels of commitment, but patrons do not. But to distribute rewards

---

[6] Compare the arguments in Blaydes (2011); Gandhi and Lust-Okar (2009); Magaloni (2006).

efficiently, patrons must be able to infer what they cannot observe directly. Both committed and uncommitted clients want patronage, however, so as far as patrons are concerned, mere declarations of loyalty are uninformative cheap talk. Instead, patrons need a mechanism to induce clients to reveal their types in a credible fashion.

In compelling them to compete, patrons induce their clients to engage in costly behavior that sends informative signals about their levels of commitment.[7] To reach an outcome in which patrons can distinguish between committed and uncommitted clients, the committed must say or do things that the uncommitted find too costly to justify in light of the expected payoff. Observers can then infer client type from observed behavior because that behavior is an informative signal: committed types send it and the uncommitted do not. Consequently, patrons can condition their patronage payouts on what they observe because it reveals clients' latent types.

What options do clients have to demonstrate their commitment? The most immediately obvious route is to become an activist and perform services for the patron. These activities can include standard electioneering work such as distributing campaign literature, organizing rallies, canvassing door to door, and transporting voters to the polls. Activism is not, however, the only or even the most widely used strategy to attract patronage. Most clients are not themselves activists, but are, instead, the bulk of voters being mobilized. As such, only a small proportion of a patron's supporters actually use activism as a patronage-seeking strategy. Those that do, however, are conceptually distinct from other clients insofar as they perform the functions of party operatives and vote brokers. Rather than simply rewarding them for their votes, patrons compensate activists for their services in mobilizing others' votes.

The vast bulk of the electorate, then, is politically passive compared to the small group of activists. Relative inactivity does not, however, imply that these voters do not seek out patronage payoffs. To attract this patronage, however, they need some means of credibly signaling their commitment in ways observable to both patrons and their brokers. One effective but largely overlooked tool for doing so is public sycophancy.

8.2.3 Signaling with Sycophancy

Sycophancy has largely been ignored or treated as a quaint, if perverse, curiosity. With a few notable expections, most observers have tended to dismiss personality cults and propaganda machines as manifestations of megalomania on the part of totalitarian leaders and fear-induced, begrudging compliance on

---

[7] On signaling models, Spence (1973, 1974a,b) is the seminal contributor. See also a review in Riley (2001) that discusses some distinctions between signaling and screening dynamics, as well as the technical overview in Banks (1991) which reviews a variety of applications to political science topics.

8.2 The Politics of Sycophancy

the part of subjects living in the shadow of pervasive state terrorism. One journalistic account, for example, described the trappings of the cult of personality surrounding the Moroccan king in terms of the millions of official portraits on display, choirs singing songs of praise on television, and messages of fidelity that poured into the palace (Hughes, 2001, 117 *et passim*). In trying to make sense of what it all meant, the longtime country correspondent explained that:

> Rightly or wrongly, it was generally assumed that King Hassan was too intelligent to let the incubated adulation warp his mind. But he allowed it to go on, and on, and on, plumbing the depths of tedium. One can therefore assume he reveled in applause or fawning compliments from cringing sycophants ... One used to wonder when it would all end.

This explanation offers two opposing takes, mere sentences apart, on the public adulation: the king was too intelligent to believe the sycophancy, and yet he reveled in it. Are there alternative ways to explain why the king – by all accounts, an astute politician – would go to this much trouble, what he hoped to learn from public obsequiousness, and why his subjects might go along with it?

The few scholars to study the curiosity of sycophancy seriously have conceptualized public obsequiousness as a charade performed by the dissimulating weak before the strong (Scott, 1990); a necessary evil in which mass subjects engage in order to be left in peace by their rulers (Havel, 1978); or else a tool by which governments demonstrate their power by forcing people to engage in the ridiculous, preoccupying and tiring out their subjects in the process (Wedeen, 1999). These works are considerable advances over knee-jerk citations of megalomania or fearful compliance. Nonetheless, their explanations rest heavily on demonstrations of power for its own sake, and grant little active agency to the subjects in their choice of how obsequious to be. Here, I build on these prior insights by adding in an instrumental motive for patrons to encourage, and clients to engage in, sycophancy: it communicates information and helps patrons sort more from less committed clients.

In her seminal work on the cult of personality around the Syrian president, Wedeen details how the government encourages – and sometimes compels – ordinary Syrians to engage in sycophancy. These activities include investing in useless knowledge about the regime and its patron saints, reciting patently absurd slogans and formulae endorsed by the government, displaying obsequious political iconography in public, and participating in rallies that have obviously been staged – all of which compel Syrians to "say the ridiculous and to avow the absurd."[8] Wedeen ultimately interprets these outcomes as self-aware manifestations of state power in which the regime figuratively, and

---

[8] The quote is Wedeen's (1999, 12). I refer to patron saints in deference to Syrian jokes (told quietly, of course) about the presidential family. Many posters depicted images of former president Hafiz al-Assad and his sons, Basil and Bashar. Basil, who died in a car crash, was the original heir apparent, while Bashar eventually succeeded to the presidency after Hafiz's death. Accordingly, people referred to the three on the posters as "the father, the son, and the holy ghost."

sometimes literally, bends Syrians' bodies and minds to its will in order to demonstrate its power.

Fear and the implicit threat of compulsion always lurk in the background in Syria and similar societies. Regular people may participate in the charade simply to be left alone by officials, as when Havel's (1978) Eastern Bloc greengrocer displays Marxist propaganda "simply because it has been done that way for years, because everyone does it, and because that is the way it has to be." Failure to comply may elicit a range of punishments, from public beratement for small transgressions, denial of state benefits or loss of livelihood for larger ones, and imprisonment or disappearance for open defiance.

While fear of punishment may backstop people's sycophantic acts, so too does the potential for reward – and it is the latter that I wish to highlight here. For, by saying and doing the ridiculous more convincingly and fluently than their neighbors, clients can demonstrate their commitment to the existing order and claim patronage benefits for that support. They can do so because sycophancy is a costly act. In particular, engaging in it imposes opportunity, psychological, and social costs on clients which are easier for committed supporters to bear than for the uncommitted.

8.2.4 Signaling Costs and Sycophancy

Public sycophancy imposes at least two kinds of opportunity costs. First, it is a form of rent-seeking, and, as such, devoting time and resources to it means foregoing productive activity. Attaining fluency in regime mythology and sloganeering – and finding occasions to demonstrate that fluency – then amount to opportunity costs paid by committed clients to distinguish themselves from their less committed and less fluent peers. Compared to their disoriented counterparts that have been bussed in to swell the ranks of a demonstration, committed clients know how to behave at rallies, and, by dint of repetition, which empty slogans to shout. They go to the trouble of learning the most up-to-date iterations of regime formulae, as well as how to interject the formulae naturally in daily conversation, in interactions with bureaucrats and the police, and even in proposals for government contracts. Whether or not they believe what they are saying is a secondary issue as far as opportunity costs are concerned. Paying the costs to acquire fluency signals compliance with the rewards-for-support bargain rather than belief in the contents of the slogans.

Second, the public aspect of sycophancy creates another form of opportunity cost: not only does the targeted patron observe the signal, but, so too does the opposition. Sycophantic clients might expect poor treatment in the event of an opposition victory – at a minimum, the withdrawal of whatever patronage benefits they might enjoy – so public declarations of loyalty not only signal support, but also align client interests with the perpetuation of the existing leadership. In the event of an opposition victory, such clients might claim that

8.2 The Politics of Sycophancy

they had engaged in public sycophancy under duress, but non-sycophants – those who "signaled by omission" – could claim, more credibly, to oppose the old leadership as a matter of principle rather than as an opportunistic act.

Sycophancy also imposes psychological costs by forcing clients to lie, or at least exaggerate, with cultivated sincerity. Some people will pay heavy psychological costs for lying to others and themselves, whereas others will pay minimal costs because they accept that this is just the way one does business – they are more willing to be clients. In the limiting cases like Syria or North Korea in which the slogans are patently absurd, stating them aloud is an exercise in public dissimulation: few, if any, believe what they are saying, and few believe that anyone else believes them. Here, the psychological cost comes in the form of the self-control required to feign sincerity – to engage in what Wedeen aptly describes as the politics of "as if." In less extreme cases, however, some people may regard the sloganeering as merely poetic license rather than outright fabrications. In these circumstances, committed supporters are more likely to consider the slogans as tolerable exaggerations while the uncommitted find them to be embarrassing falsehoods. Hence, we can expect the marginal psychological cost for little white lies to be less than for outrageous ones, so the uncommitted should balk where the committed are willing to vocalize.

Lastly, sycophancy imposes social costs because it is a public act performed by clients before an audience of their peers. Clients consequently risk losing the respect of members of their social networks and damaging their chances for future interactions when they publicly debase themselves. In a famous open letter to the Moroccan king, for example, one of the monarch's critics asked:

> Has it ever occurred to you that every man has his dignity, and that he whom you oblige to prostrate himself before you, in front of everyone and on television, curses you in his heart because of your contempt for human dignity? You must be mad if you think that those who are at your service adore you, and prostrate themselves out of respect for your person and the kingdom.[9]

Presumably, similar ideas had, indeed, occurred to the king, who was, as described earlier, a leader "too intelligent to let the incubated adulation warp his mind." The point of the debasement, then, is not the content of the message per se, but rather to impose a dignity cost that only some people are willing to bear.

Ultimately, then, sycophancy, at least as practiced by voters, is not simply the act of fearful people flattering gullible despots, but rather a tool to reveal information when engaged in rent-seeking. Stokes (2005) examined the perverse accountability of machine politics; here, I have suggested that there is

---

[9] The quote comes from an open letter addressed to the king by Abdessalem Yassine, the founding leader of the Moroccan Islamist organization Justice and Charity (*Al Adl Wal Ihsane*). The open letter earned the author a three-year stay in a mental health asylum for criticizing the monarchy. Quoted in Hughes (2001, 298).

also perverse competition in communities dominated by a single leader. Rather than politicians competing with one another for votes, voters must compete with one another for patronage. In order to demonstrate their commitment and make themselves more viable recipients of largesse, clients can engage in public sycophancy in order to send costly signals of support. Doing so enables patrons to distinguish between their more and less committed supporters, and to target patronage rewards accordingly.

8.3 HYPOTHESES

Two propositions follow from the previous discussion of sycophantic signaling costs. People in Lebanon and Yemen frequently make public displays of their partisan loyalties, as described in the next section. We should, however, be able to explain variation in both the displays and the motivations behind them:

Hypothesis 7 *Members of politically dominated communities should display more political iconography than their counterparts in the more competitive communities.*

Hypothesis 8 *People in politically dominated communities should display political iconography more instrumentally than their counterparts in the more competitive communities.*

Both hypotheses draw out implications of one of the book's core theoretical predictions about constituent competition over patronage. Hypothesis 7 reiterates the basic claim that constituents of politically dominated communities are more likely to compete for patronage than their peers in other communities – here, by publicly displaying political iconography in order to demonstrate their commitment to their patrons. Dominant leaders, sheltered from credible electoral competition, do not need votes from all of their nominal clients. Although such patrons enjoy considerable leeway in choosing which clients to target with patronage payoffs, they need their constituents to reveal private information about commitment levels in order to distribute rewards efficiently. Constituents, in turn, try to earn a share of the largesse by signaling their reliability as clients with public displays of political iconography. In practice, then, we should observe Lebanese Sunnis and Yemeni Zaydis putting on more public displays of loyalty than their peers in the more internally competitive communities.

Hypothesis 8 draws out a further implication about the motivations for publicly displaying iconography. We might expect people to display political imagery for a variety of reasons, only one of which is competition for patronage. We might, for example, anticipate that at least some people engage in political expression or otherwise participate in public discourse to urge fellow voters to support a particular party without thought of personal reward (e.g., Corstange, 2012a). Hence, more iconography in dominated communities could simply indicate more political expression there rather than competition between constituents – the raw figures cannot discriminate between the two stories. The theory I posit, however, implies that such constituents respond disproportionately to instrumental motivations: they aim to claim some of the patronage largesse. As such, Hypothesis 8 anticipates that their decisions to post or not should follow from their perceptions of the utility of patron–client relationships to get them desirable payoffs. In practical terms, then, we should observe Lebanese Sunnis and Yemeni Zaydis basing their behavior on the importance they attribute to political connections to get patronage benefits.

8.4 DATA AND METHODS

As in Chapter 6, I use the survey data from Lebanon and Yemen to examine competition for patronage from the constituent's point of view. These data reveal that Lebanese and Yemeni respondents vary considerably in how likely they are to engage in public sycophancy. Ultimately, I try to explain the variation we observe according to the internal political competitiveness of respondents' communities and their assessments of the importance of having government connections to get desirable resources. Operationalizing and measuring sycophancy are not straightforward tasks for which we have clear empirical precedents, much less established best practices. As detailed here, I use a behavioral measure: the public display of political iconography outside respondents' homes.

8.4.1 Outcomes: Public Display of Political Iconography

The outcomes I examine are respondents' public displays of political posters, party flags and symbols, and other such paraphernalia outside their homes. Hariri-related items go virtually unchallenged in the Sunni areas of Lebanon while pictures of President Salih predominate in Yemen. As one travels around the different quarters of the main cities or among the mountain villages, one is subject to an array of colorful political posters, party flags, and militia symbols. Figures 8.1 and 8.2 reproduce examples of such items, which range, aesthetically, from muted and tasteful to the profoundly gaudy. From Saida, Rafik al-Hariri's birthplace, one poster urges residents to be loyal to the "son of the city" in the wake of his assassination (Figure 8.1a). In Beirut, meanwhile, another poster declares "loyalty to Shaykh Saad al-Hariri" and reminds people of his efforts to rebuild and develop the country (Figure 8.1b).[10]

---

[10] This image depicts the elder Hariri is soft focus, his son and political heir, Saad, and Fouad Siniora, a longtime Hariri loyalist that Saad had selected to be prime minister. The topmost text declares that "hand in hand we'll finish the task of developing Lebanon." The word used also has the connotation of "rebuilding," which refers to Rafik al-Hariri's central role in reconstruction in the aftermath of the civil war, and the Siniora government's attempts to rebuild after the 2006 Israel–Hizballah war. On this particular poster, see also Corstange (2012a).

(a) "Loyalty to Saida and her Son" (Saida, spring 2005)

(b) "Hand in Hand We'll Finish the Task of Developing Lebanon – Loyalty to Shaykh Saad al-Hariri" (Beirut, summer 2008)

FIGURE 8.1: Lebanon: Hariri Political Imagery

8.4 Data and Methods

From Sanaa, an image shows the Yemeni president against a background of cheering supporters and urges Salih to "finish the task" and run for yet another presidential term (Figure 8.2a).[11] Another poster (not shown) depicts Salih as a central figure in the millenia-long struggle for Yemeni unity, "our glory, our strength, the will of our people, the path of our ancestors, the future of our children" – placing Salih's name prominently in a list of "unifying leaders throughout history with their names in letters of gold." Yet another image shows a home in a mountain village in Mahwit province on which the owner had painted the ruling party's rearing horse logo (Figure 8.2b).

The crucial aspect of these images is that they are *publicly* observable – being displayed outside people's homes rather than hidden from public view inside them. According to the signaling dynamics I posited earlier, patrons rely on manifest observables to infer clients' latent levels of commitment for the purpose of distributing rewards. Patrons cannot, of course, see attitudes, and cannot condition payoffs on something that they cannot observe. As such, we need an indicator of the manifest signal itself, rather than the latent commitment it purports to denote, to assess my claims about signaling. Consequently, standard survey questions designed to assess party identification, placement on salient ideological dimensions, feeling thermometers, and so forth are inappropriate measures of the outcome of interest. Such attitudinal measures are unobservable to the politicians who are the signal's recipients – we can use them profitably to *explain* the outcome of interest, but not to *indicate* it.

I collected these data unobtrusively by instructing survey interviewers to note and describe any political imagery "such as political party flags, campaign posters, or militia symbols" displayed outside the respondents' homes. Consequently, for each respondent, I have details on whether or not they displayed political iconography publicly, which I subsequently post-coded into relevant categories.[12] The Lebanese parliamentary system implies that each party could, in principle, dispense patronage, so the relevant indicators are simply images relating to the parties and their leaders. Moreover, the Lebanese parties cater almost entirely to single-sect constituencies, so there is not a single party or leader that is equally relevant to patronage-seeking Lebanese regardless of their

---

[11] Salih had claimed in 2005 that he would not nominate himself again to stand for the presidency in the 2006 elections – which, unsurprisingly, turned into a farce when his supporters began to organize campaigns and rallies to convince him to change his mind. This poster claims to originate with a somewhat dubious organization calling itself the "Private Sector Committee to Nominate Ali Abdallah Salih to the Presidency." Other efforts were more comical still, as when another organization threatened to sue Salih in court if he did not run again.

[12] The surveys went into the field in both venues a few months after their most recent elections – parliamentary in Lebanon and presidential in Yemen – which raises the possibility that some people may have removed election-related iconography prior to the interviewers arriving. Were this dynamic to be true, it would make it harder rather than easier to detect the relationships I hypothesize. At least some of those who normally display iconography instrumentally would appear to be displaying nothing at all, yielding false negatives that add noise to the indicator and attenuating the observed relationships toward 0.

(a) "Finish the Task, 2006–2013" – Private Sector Committee to Nominate Ali Abdallah Salih to the Presidency (Sanaa, summer 2006)

(b) Ruling Party Logo Painted on the Side of a House (Mahwit, winter 2005)

FIGURE 8.2: Yemen: Salih Political Imagery

8.4 Data and Methods

TABLE 8.1: *Political Domination and the Display of Political Imagery*

(a) Lebanon: Sunnis Politically Dominated ($\chi^2 = 27.6, p < 0.01$)

		Dominated		Symbols Base Rate
		No	Yes	
Symbols	No	52 ($n = 516$)	19 ($n = 188$)	71 ($n = 704$)
	Yes	16 ($n = 133$)	13 ($n = 128$)	29 ($n = 291$)
Dominated Base Rate		68 ($n = 679$)	32 ($n = 316$)	100 ($n = 995$)

(b) Yemen: Zaydis Politically Dominated ($\chi^2 = 19.7, p < 0.01$)

		Dominated		Symbols Base Rate
		No	Yes	
Symbols	No	70 ($n = 987$)	14 ($n = 203$)	84 ($n = 1190$)
	Yes	11 ($n = 159$)	5 ($n = 68$)	16 ($n = 227$)
Dominated Base Rate		81 ($n = 1146$)	19 ($n = 271$)	100 ($n = 1417$)

sects. Yemen, meanwhile, uses a presidential system, and the election immediately preceding the data collection was presidential rather than legislative. The president's patronage network, moreover, transcends that of his own party, which is one of a number of conduits he uses to dispense payoffs.[13] Hence, in Yemen, the relevant indicators are pictures and posters of the president himself.

Table 8.1 tabulates the iconography indicator according to whether or not respondents were members of politically dominated communities (Sunnis in Lebanon, Zaydis in Yemen). The "Symbols Base Rate" columns show that sizeable proportions of both samples publicly display some form of political iconography – 29 and 16 percent, respectively. For our purposes, this variation is extremely useful: rather than near-universal or rare events, we see significant minorities of both populations putting up posters, flags, and other such symbols.

---

[13] On Salih's use of multiple channels to dispense patronage, see Alley (2010a); Phillips (2008, 2011).

The empirical question is: what explains this observed variation? Table 8.1 reveals that there does appear to be a detectable relationship between political dominance and iconography ($p < 0.01$ in both countries based on χ^2 tests). Yet we might also anticipate people in both more and less competitive communities to display these items for a number of reasons, not least of which is political expression. Nonetheless, if my claims about the incentives to engage in sycophancy are correct, constituents, particularly in the dominated communities, should be responding to instrumental motivations as well.

8.4.2 Explanatory Variables

Two key explanatory concepts help me to test the dynamics posited in Hypotheses 7 and 8. First, and most directly, I use the *Dominated* indicator to capture constituent membership in either communities under a dominant leader or those that are more competitive internally. As Hypothesis 7 predicts, members of the former face stronger incentives to engage in public sycophancy than do members of the latter, and should, therefore, be more likely to display political iconography. In application, Lebanese Sunnis and Yemeni Zaydis take the indicator, while their respective peers in the other communities do not.

Hypothesis 8, meanwhile, predicts that politically dominated constituents should be more instrumental in their decisions to display political iconography than their counterparts in the competitive communities. I measure this instrumental motivation with a survey question that asks respondents whether merit or connections is more important to get a government job, as described in Chapter 7. I later extend this concept to compare answers to the government jobs assessment to an analogous question on jobs in the private sector; I describe the rationale for doing so in detail when I introduce these tests.[14] Government employment has long been a mainstay of patronage politics and clientelism, evident in the emphasis placed upon it both in scholarly studies and by practitioners both operating or fighting the political machines.[15]

---

[14] Respondents answer a question about the criteria for obtaining a government job, and then answer a question about the criteria for obtaining a job in the private sector. The prompt for the first question reads, "What is the most important thing to get a good *government* job, as opposed to a job in the private sector?" Respondents indicate which of the following two statements they agree with more, and whether they agree strongly or just somewhat. The first statement reads, "personal connections and *wasta* are the most important factors in getting a *government* job." The second statement reads, "the most important factors in getting a *government* job are merit and ability." The next question follows up by asking respondents, "how about the *private sector*?" They receive the same instructions, and choose between the same two statements, except that the phrase "a job *in business or the private sector*" replaces "a *government* job."

[15] See, for example, Chubb (1982); Despres (2005); Kurtzman (1935); Riordon (1905); Robinson and Verdier (2013); Stokes (2005); Werner (1928). The importance of political connections can be seen throughout much of the developing world where clientelism is the norm; in the Arab world, we see it in the much-remarked emphasis on *wasta* Jamal (2007); Lust (2009); Lust-Okar (2009a,b), literally "intermediary" or "intercession."

8.4 Data and Methods

There are two important points to note about this indicator of instrumental motivation. First, government jobs are privately consumed rewards targeted at individual clients rather than club goods targeted at collectivities. As such, they match up conceptually with clients' individualized efforts to attract patronage via iconography displayed outside their own homes – privately consumed payoffs in exchange for privately paid costs. Second, government jobs represent rewards that are, at least potentially in the eyes of clients, explicitly connected to politics and distributed in exchange for political loyalty.

Figure 8.3 provides a scatterplot to visualize the relationship between government jobs (horizontal axis), private sector jobs (vertical axis), and the decision to display images of leaders publicly or not (dark and light circles, respectively). First, the figure reveals considerable variation in the degree to which respondents cited "connections" versus "merit" for private sector jobs; the median Lebanese respondent selected "somewhat connections," while the median Yemeni cited "somewhat merit."[16] Second, it also reveals a skew toward the connections end of the scale for government jobs, particularly in Lebanon. Consequently, I dichotomize the government jobs responses into "strongly connections" versus responses that indicate some degree of merit in the hiring decision. On this measure, 79 percent of Lebanese and 55 percent of Yemeni respondents take the "connections" indicator.[17]

Third, Figure 8.3 also suggests that people's views on government jobs and private sectors jobs are linked. Although the figure reveals considerable variation in pairs of responses, people tend to give similar ratings on the scales for the two types of jobs – either on the "merit" end for both or, more commonly, on the "connections" end for both. Responses correlate positively in both Lebanon ($r = 0.28$) and Yemen ($r = 0.51$); given this positive correlation, anomolous answers fall into the top-left and bottom-right quadrants of the grid.

Unsurprisingly, the top-left quadrant – merit in government but connections in private – is sparsely populated in both countries. More comprehensibly, and much more interesting for my story, is the shaded, bottom-right quadrant: people who cite merit in private but connections in government. As compared to their peers who simply cite "connections" for *everything* – respondents in the

---

[16] The interquartile range spans the entire scale in both countries. In Lebanon, the median Sunni selected "somewhat merit" while the median non-Sunni cited "somewhat connections." In Yemen, the median Zaydi selected "strongly merit," while the median non-Zaydi cited "neither."

[17] Note that the greater concentration of Lebanese responses on "strongly connections" compared to Yemeni responses should not be taken as a priori evidence that connections are more important in Lebanon than they are in Yemen. We must be cautious because we can neither confirm nor disconfirm with these data that Lebanese and Yemeni respondents are using the same mental scales when offering their responses.

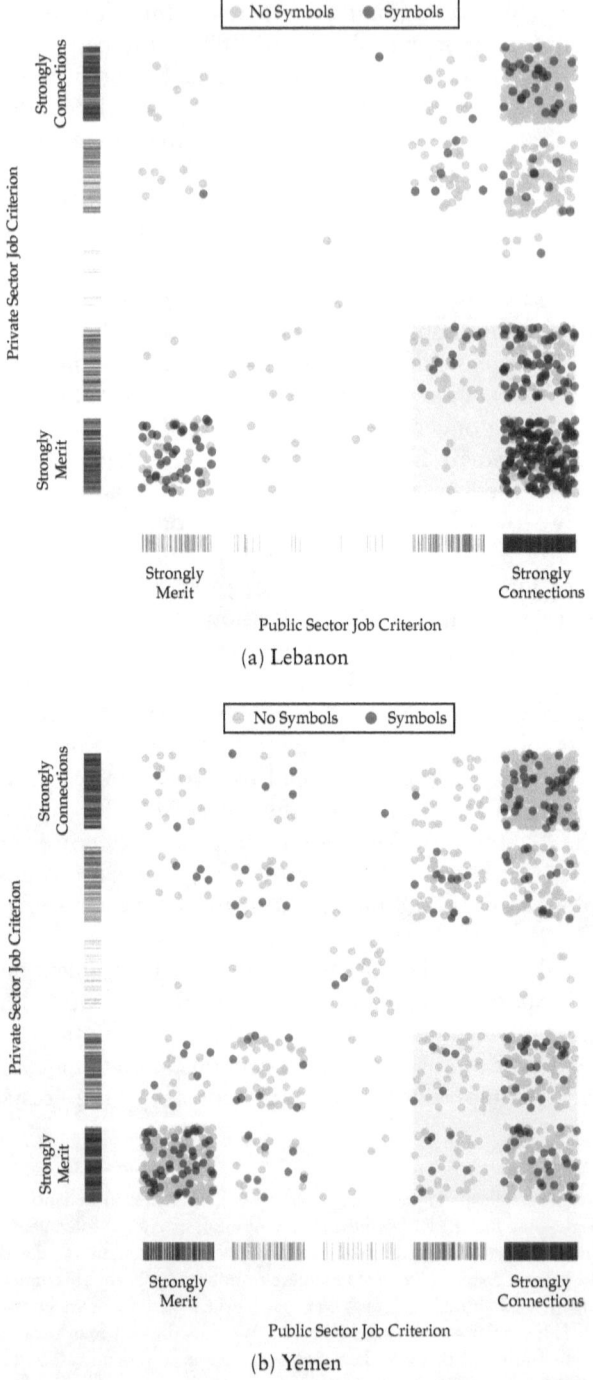

FIGURE 8.3: Public and Private Sector Jobs and Political Iconography

top-right – these respondents are the ones who see the greatest gap between job criteria in the public and private sectors.[18] Moreover, we might expect precisely the individuals who acknowledge this difference to be most likely to cultivate their political connections.

8.4.3 Model Setup

To test Hypothesis 7 on broad group differences, I begin simply by calculating, from Table 8.1, the probabilities of displaying iconography within the different communities and the relative differences between them. I then move on to a multivariate setting to test Hypothesis 8 on the underlying motivations for posting the images. I begin by modeling the probability of displaying political iconography according to respondents' community, their public sector jobs assessments, and a set of basic control variables to guard against confounding relationships. Subsequently, I "scale" people's motivations by considering their views on connections in the private sector alongside their views on connections in government – again, with the expectation that people who see the greatest gap in the criteria will be most likely to cultivate their patrons with political activity.

Because the outcome variable is binary – iconography displayed or not – I estimate generalized linear models with a probit link. Because the models are non-linear and also include interaction terms, however, I translate the otherwise difficult to interpret coefficient estimates into graphical plots. I use the observed-value approach when calculating the predicted probabilities and differences (Hanmer and Kalkan, 2012). The figures are dotplots that report 95-percent confidence intervals as bars on either end of the point estimate (i.e., the dot), with the 90-percent counterpart indicated by the hashes.

8.5 FINDINGS

Ultimately, these data support both Hypotheses 7 and 8. First, members of less competitive communities are more likely to display political iconography publicly than are their counterparts in the more competitive communities. Second, they do so for instrumental reasons: to acquire politically allocated rewards for which they believe they need connections. Third, people in competitive communities do not evince the same rent-seeking behavior: their decisions to display political iconography appear to be unconnected to efforts to secure patronage.

---

[18] In Lebanon, 51 percent of respondents noticed this gap, citing "strongly connections" for government jobs and something else for private sector jobs (Sunnis and non-Sunnis: 70 and 43 percent, respectively). In Yemen, the corresponding figures were 28 percent overall, 21 percent among Zaydis, and 30 percent among non-Zaydis.

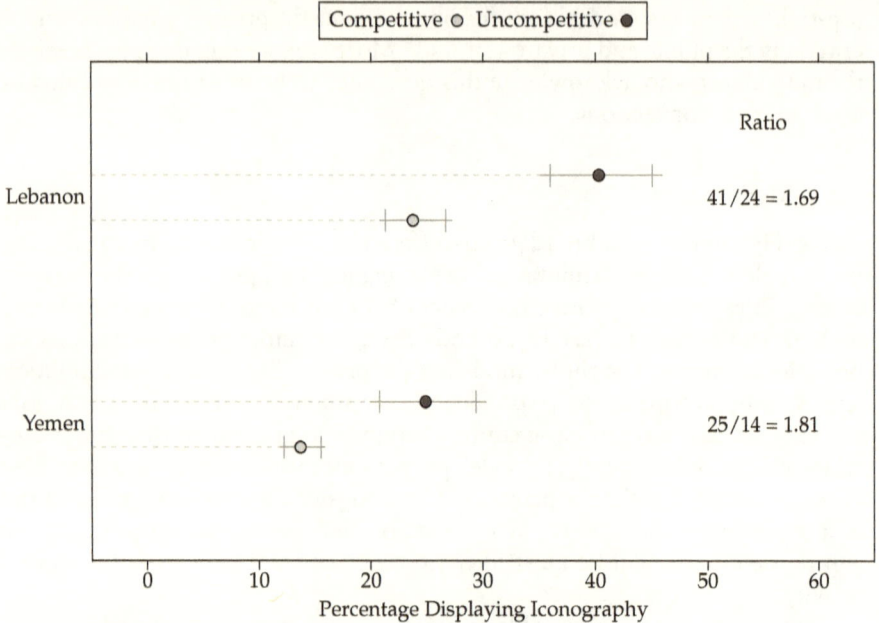

FIGURE 8.4: Dominated Constituents Display More Iconography

8.5.1 Public Displays of Iconography

Hypothesis 7 lays out the basic claim that constituents in politically dominated communities are more likely to display political iconography than are their counterparts in the more competitive communities. A simple test of this proposition looks for aggregate differences between the two broad constituency types. In application, we can do so by rearranging the information in Table 8.1. We first compare the probabilities of posting iconography within each community, and then calculate the magnitude of the difference between them.[19]

While Table 8.1 reveals that some 29 percent of the Lebanese and 16 percent of Yemenis displayed some form of iconography, these aggregate figures obscure important differences between the constituency types, as shown in Figure 8.4. The latter plots the percentage of iconography posters by community competitiveness, along with 90- and 95-percent confidence intervals. In Lebanon,

---

[19] More precisely, we calculate the conditional probabilities $p = \Pr(Symbols = Yes \mid Dominated = Yes)$ and $q = \Pr(Symbols = Yes \mid Dominated = No)$ from Table 8.1. The difference in means $(p - q)$ gives us the absolute difference between the two communities. The ratio of means (p/q) gives us the risk ratio, which we can adapt to give the relative difference between the communities. We can calculate the approximate confidence intervals of the latter using either the delta method (as I do here) or bootstrapping.

8.5 Findings

41 percent of Sunni respondents posted an item compared to 24 percent of respondents in the more competitive communities. Analogously, 25 percent of Yemeni Zaydis displayed some form of iconography compared to 14 percent of their peers. In both Lebanon and Yemen, then, the politically dominated constituencies are more publicly demonstrative of their loyalties. In relative terms, Lebanese Sunnis are roughly 70 percent more likely than other Lebanese to display political iconography, while Yemeni Zaydis are 80 percent more likely than their co-nationals.[20]

The findings reported in Figure 8.4 come from simple, bivariate relationships between community membership and iconographic displays. These findings are, in turn, robust to the inclusion of a basic set of controls in a multivariate setting as estimated via probit regression (see Table 8.2, first column). The between-community differences are smaller in magnitude in the presence of the controls. Lebanese Sunnis are an estimated 6 percentage points more likely than their co-nationals to display images, while Yemeni Zaydis are 9 percentage points more likely – 22 and 62 percent more likely in relative terms, respectively. Nonetheless, the direction and statistical detectability of the effects remain. Hence, the constituent-level survey data yield strong support for Hypothesis 7.

8.5.2 Connections and Iconography

As I suggested previously, however, the aggregate figures do not – and cannot – tell the whole story. We can think of other reasons why people might plausibly choose to display political iconography besides patronage-seeking. Not least among these alternatives is iconography for expressive purposes: to take part in their country's public discourse. Under this alternative, people post the images and symbols to register their approval of a party or platform, or to persuade their peers about the merits of their choice. Here, competing for patronage may not enter the iconographic rationale at all – it is expression rather than sycophancy (cf. Corstange, 2012a).

Moreover, were it the case that constituents in politically dominated communities were simply more expressive than their counterparts in the competitive communities, then the findings reported earlier would not be evidence in favor of the "competing for patronage" claim. The idea that members of the former community should be more expressive than the latter would, of course, be difficult to sustain on its face. As discussed previously, there is not much to express in clientelistic settings given the non-credibility (or absence) of policy

---

[20] From Table 8.1a, we see that 128 of 316 Lebanese Sunnis (41 percent) versus 163 of 679 non-Sunnis (24 percent) posted some form of iconography for an absolute difference of 16 percentage points and a risk ratio of $41/24 \approx 1.70$. Analogously in Table 8.1b, we see that 68 of 271 Yemeni Zaydis (25 percent) and 159 of 1146 non-Zaydis (14 percent) displayed the imagery for an absolute difference of 11 percentage points and a risk ratio of $25/14 \approx 1.80$ (the ratios reported in Figure 8.4 are calculated before rounding the proportions).

TABLE 8.2: *Explaining Political Iconography Display (Probit Regression)*

(a) Lebanon: Sunnis Politically Dominated

	Model 1	Model 2	Model 3
(Intercept)	−0.29 (0.22)	0.11 (0.25)	0.13 (0.26)
Income (NR)	0.55** (0.24)	0.55** (0.26)	0.51* (0.27)
Income	−0.22** (0.06)	−0.11 (0.07)	−0.11 (0.07)
Capital	0.39** (0.14)	0.30* (0.16)	0.31* (0.16)
Education	0.12** (0.06)	0.02 (0.07)	0.01 (0.07)
Rural	−0.23** (0.10)	−0.14 (0.11)	−0.15 (0.11)
Dominated	0.19* (0.11)	−0.42 (0.28)	−1.25** (0.48)
Private		−0.35** (0.03)	−0.34** (0.10)
Public		0.15 (0.14)	0.13 (0.18)
Dominated × Public		0.68** (0.29)	1.66** (0.50)
Dominated × Private			0.41** (0.21)
Public × Private			0.00 (0.11)
Dominated × Public × Pirvate			−0.52** (0.22)
Log Likelihood	−534.73	−444.95	−440.86
N	992	979	979

(b) Yemen: Zaydis Politically Dominated

	Model 1	Model 2	Model 3
(Intercept)	−1.57** (0.17)	−1.41** (0.19)	−1.44** (0.20)
Income (NR)	0.60** (0.28)	0.56** (0.28)	0.56** (0.28)
Income	0.03 (0.04)	0.02 (0.04)	0.02 (0.04)
Capital	0.51** (0.12)	0.50** (0.13)	0.49** (0.13)
Education	0.02 (0.04)	0.01 (0.04)	0.02 (0.04)
Rural	0.37** (0.11)	0.38** (0.11)	0.39** (0.11)
Dominated	0.34** (0.10)	0.11 (0.13)	0.03 (0.16)
Private		−0.03 (0.03)	−0.01 (0.05)
Public		−0.14 (0.10)	−0.05 (0.14)
Dominated × Public		0.47** (0.20)	0.64** (0.28)
Dominated × Private			0.12 (0.10)
Public × Private			−0.05 (0.06)
Dominated × Public × Pirvate			−0.16 (0.13)
Log Likelihood	−600.87	−596.97	−594.87
N	1417	1417	1417

** $p < 0.05$, * $p < 0.10$

8.5 Findings

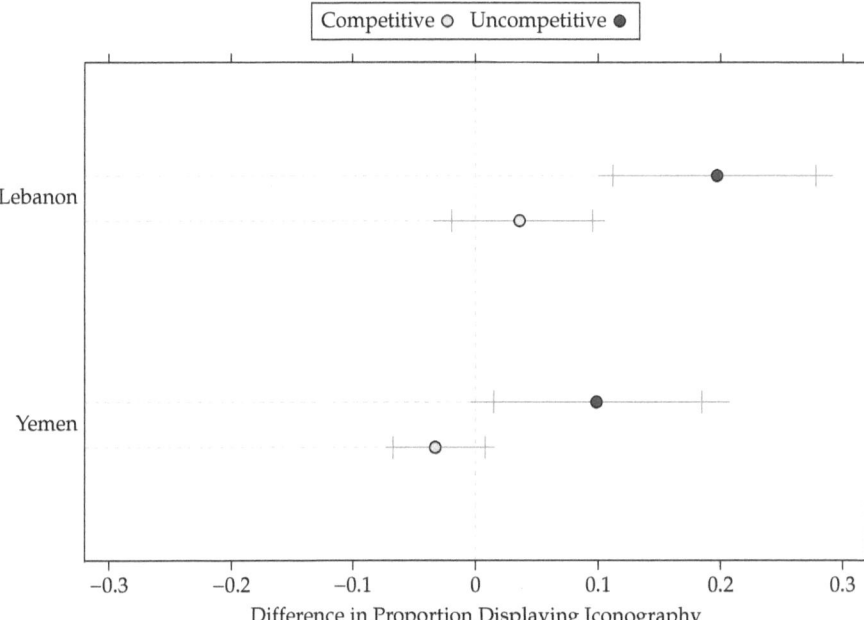

FIGURE 8.5: Effect of Connections on Iconography Display

platforms distinguishing the parties. Moreover, there is even less to express in politically dominated communities because there is no real choice to be made. Nonetheless, if my story is correct, then Hypothesis 8 should also find support in the data: constituents subject to a dominant leader should be instrumental in their iconographic displays.

A straightforward test of this proposition compares respondents across community types conditional on the importance they place on connections to get a public sector job. The second column of Table 8.2 reports the estimated results of a multivariate probit model, while Figure 8.5 summarizes the take-away points graphically. The key dynamic to observe is that the connections effect is qualitatively different for more and less competitive constituencies. People in the dominated communities – Lebanese Sunnis and Yemeni Zaydis – post significantly more political imagery when they believe connections are paramount compared to when they believe that merit plays some role in public sector hiring. In contrast, the iconographic behavior of their counterparts in the more competitive communities appears unrelated to their beliefs about the importance of connections – the estimated effect is small in size and not detectably different from 0 at conventional levels of statistical significance.

How much more likely are people in the dominated communities to display iconography based on their beliefs about connections? As Figure 8.5

demonstrates, the connections effect adds 10 percentage points to a baseline of about 18 points in Yemen, for a relative increase of 57 percent. In Lebanon, it adds 20 percentage points to a baseline of about 15 points, for a relative increase of 136 percent. In substantive terms, then, these beliefs have significant effects on people's behavior, making them far more likely to display political imagery in public.

Hence, we see very different iconographic dynamics in the two constituency types in a way that is consistent with Hypothesis 8. Clients subject to a dominant leader behave instrumentally when choosing whether or not to display political imagery: doing so much more frequently when they consider connections to be important. In contrast, iconographic display in the more competitive communities does not appear to follow a patronage logic as its defining feature – such constituents do not appear to be competing with each other. This latter non-dynamic is, in turn, consistent with the interpretation that their iconographic displays are more about political expression and less about patronage-seeking.

8.5.3 Emphasizing *Political* Connections

Hence, the evidence cited here suggests that perceptions about the importance of government connections drives clients in politically dominated communities to display political iconography publicly. This finding, however, begs a follow-up question: government connections as opposed to what? Patronage appointments are classic clientelistic rewards, and if political connections are useful anywhere, we would expect to see it in public sector hiring decisions. We also imagine government employment to be much more prone to patronage hiring than is the case for employment in the private sector, where we expect market forces to push employers to hire on merit. Implicitly, then, we counterpose connections-based hiring in the public sector with merit-based hiring in the private sector. Separating out the two sectors is important given the common tendency for people to cite connections in casual conversation as a general indictment of "the way things work here," yet to acknowledge when pressed that connections are more important in some circumstances than others.

Our interest, of course, remains focused on the public sector connections indicator. The complementary private sector indicator, meanwhile, helps us to put some perspective on people's perceptions. In particular, the latter indicator provides a means to distinguish between people who cite connections for *everything*, and those who perceive a difference in employment criteria for the public and private sectors. People who cite connections for both sectors essentially see no difference in the criteria used to allocate jobs in and out of government. In contrast, people who distinguish between connections in the public sector and merit in the private sector perceive, at least potentially, an instrumental reason to engage in activity that is explicitly political.

8.5 Findings

If these expectations are correct, we should expect the public sector connections effect studied previously to vary in strength with perceptions about private sector connections. In particular, we should expect to see the largest effect when there is the largest gap between the assessments: connections-based hiring in government, but merit-based hiring in the private sector. As the gap recedes and people perceive connections operating beyond the political sphere, the effect should diminish as people perceive little utility in cultivating *political* connections specifically. The private sector indicator, in essence, scales the relevance of the public sector indicator. These anticipated dynamics do, however, make it impractical to examine the data with the simple procedures I used earlier. I now turn to multivariate analysis that models the binary iconography choice (via probit regression) according to the public and private sector indicators along with the same basic set of control variables used previously (income, education, urban/rural, and residence in the capital).

To capture the conceptual intuition behind the scaling claims – that the connections effect should be most pronounced when the public–private gap is largest – I reestimate the model with an interaction term between the two connections indicators, with results in the third column of Table 8.2. Figure 8.6, in turn, reports the key elements of this latter model (note the scale differences on the vertical axis). In particular, it plots the difference between people citing "connections" versus some form of merit in *government* hiring decisions as their views about *private sector* hiring decisions vary (along the horizontal axis). Points located above zero indicate the predicted difference – that people who believe connections are paramount to getting a government job are more likely to display political iconography.

Consistent with prior results, we only observe a connections effect among Lebanese Sunnis and Yemeni Zaydis in both countries – *some* of these points are detectably above zero in the graph. As expected, the connections effect for respondents in dominated communities is strongest precisely where the gap in perceived job criteria is the widest – "strongly connections" for government jobs, but "strongly merit" for the private sector. In Yemen, the probability of posting iconography doubles (from an estimated 0.18–0.36), while in Lebanon, the increase is more than five-fold (from an estimated 0.12–0.65). The effect then trails off and disappears as public and private sector criteria converge on connections. Meanwhile, we cannot detect any effect anywhere among constituents in the more competitive communities. In practice, there is no empirical link between these constituents' decisions to display political iconography and their views on what it takes to get a government job – posting appears to be neither patronage-seeking nor sycophantic activity.

Put together, then, this evidence suggests that a predictable subset of the electorate in either country posts political images in order to attract patronage. People in politically dominated communities, and particularly those who recognize the importance of having connections for achieving public sector (as opposed to private sector) employment, display posters for instrumental

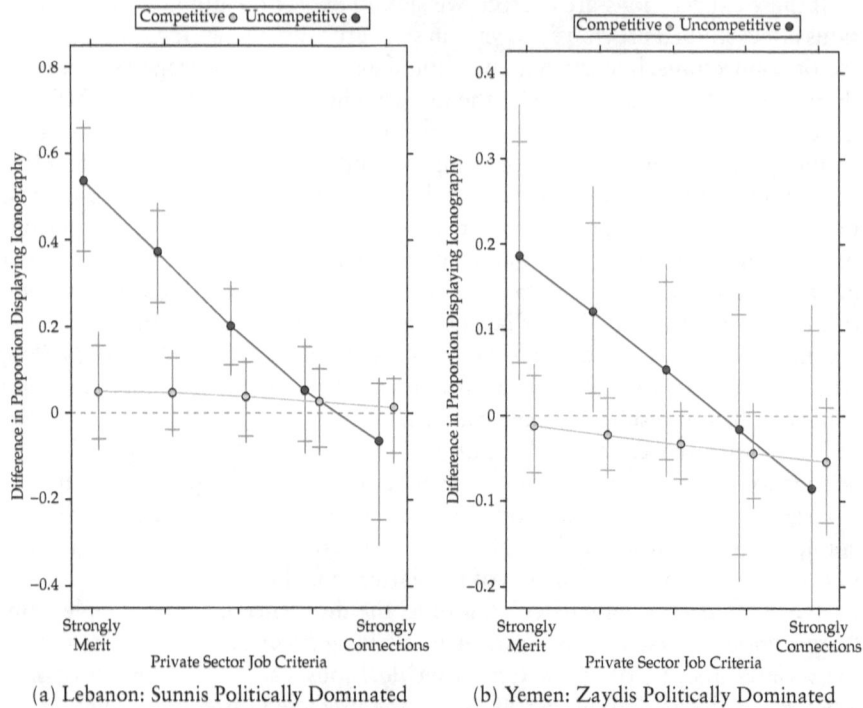

FIGURE 8.6: Effect of Importance of Government Connections on the Increase in Iconographic Postings by Community Type

reasons, at least in part. Their counterparts in competitive communities do not appear to link their posters to their views on the importance of connections. Hence, the most plausible alternative explanation for their behavior is that they engage in political expression (Corstange, 2012a). Not only do they have credible options from which to choose, but expression is a luxury they are better able to afford when leaders compete for their votes.

8.6 CONCLUSION

This chapter started off with a curious empirical puzzle: why and when do we see people resorting to public sycophancy? Why would political leaders demand it of their populations, and what do they get out of it? Common explanations include megalomania and simple delusion on the part of the dictators who cultivate cults of personality, along with fear-tinged acquiescence on the part of the people who behave obsequiously in public. In contrast, the alternative explanation I provide in this chapter does not rest on irrationality, the deluded

8.6 Conclusion

idiocy of leaders, or the helpless lack of agency on the part of regular people. Instead, the *act* of sycophancy, rather than its *content*, transmits a costly signal of political support from clients to patrons, providing the latter with useful information when determining how to allocate patronage rewards.

This chapter's examination of public sycophancy, in turn, builds off of the book's arguments about the perverse competitive dynamics that exist in politically dominated communities. Sheltered from competitive pressures, hegemonic leaders face few electoral threats to their positions and enjoy the discretion to pick and choose their clients. Hence, while politicians in internally competitive communities compete for their constituents' votes, clients under a dominant leader compete with one another for patronage. Among the various ways they can do so, public sycophancy provides a tool to signal their commitment and demonstrate that they – rather than others in their communities – deserve access to their patron's largesse. The *content* of sycophantic appeals is, of course, absurd and unbelievable, but engaging in the public *act* provides a costly, observable signal of support that leaders can use to target their rewards to supporters.

Empirically, this chapter combined survey data from Lebanon and Yemen with a novel behavioral measure: whether or not respondents displayed political iconography – political posters, party flags, and the like – in public outside their homes. It provided a progressively refined analysis of why different people might go to the trouble of displaying political images. In the raw data, people in the politically dominated communities – Lebanese Sunnis and Yemeni Zaydis – posted more images than their co-nationals, a dynamic consistent with the greater competition within their communities to win patronage from elites. Subsequently, the chapter showed that there was an instrumental motivation behind the displays in these communities: people who saw connections as paramount to getting government jobs were systematically more likely to display posters and flags than were those who believed that merit played some role in the hiring process. In contrast, this instrumental motivation was absent in the display decisions of people in internally competitive constituencies. This lack of relationship does not imply that the latter people were uninterested in patronage, but rather that public sycophancy does not appear to be a mechanism they use to attract it in a systematic fashion. Overall, then, this chapter provides evidence consistent with the book's larger theory of ethnic monopsonies by tracing the qualitative differences in electoral behavior in more and less competitive communities.

9

Conclusion

9.1 INTRODUCTION

This book has investigated the links between ethnic and communal constituencies and clientelism in the developing world. In doing so, it has addressed several interrelated questions. Why do politicians and voters connect to each other via patron–client relationships rather than programmatic linkages? How does coethnicity facilitate these clientelistic relationships? What do regular people get out of supporting their co-ethnic elites? Why do some voters receive far more meager rewards than common narratives about "ethnic favoritism" seem to imply?

To explain some of this variation in outcomes, I have offered a theory of ethnic vote monopsonies, in which only one political leader or organization can credibly serve its co-ethnics. Ethnic networks lower transaction costs between patrons and clients, but also segment the vote market into ethnic constituencies. Some of these segments are internally competitive, while others have fallen under the political domination of a single leader. Sheltered from competition for their community members' votes, these hegemonic leaders can act as discriminating monopsonists, picking and choosing which clients to patronize and how much to give them.

I examined a number of empirical implications of this theory in Lebanon and Yemen, two diverse societies in the Arab world where sectarian, tribal, and regional distinctions impact the day-to-day distribution of material resources. Many of Lebanon's sectarian communities are internally competitive to at least some degree, yet a dominant leader emerged in the country's Sunni community. In Yemen, meanwhile, the president and his ruling party have – or at least had, prior to the Arab Spring – developed an effective monopsony over the country's Zaydi tribesmen, while still competing for votes in the Sunni communities. Consistent with expectations, I provide evidence that members of both dominated communities – Sunnis in Lebanon, Zaydis in Yemen – tend to receive poorer services and less lucrative rewards than their counterparts in the communities that benefit from competition for their support.

9.2 REVIEWING THE SCOPE OF THE ARGUMENT

The empirics for this book center on Lebanon and Yemen: two diverse and unstable societies in the Arab world with dubious electoral institutions. Can we apply the central elements of the book's story beyond these two countries in particular, or the Arab world more generally? What are the scope conditions – to what kinds of societies do vote monopsonies apply? Although the core arguments clearly apply best to diverse societies within which we might expect to find ethnic constituencies, many elements of the theory extend more generally to the patronage-based democracies and electoral autocracies of the developing world.

Patronage politics and discretionary targeting are core elements of the book's story. Politicians offer mediated access to material resources and the state: the discretion to offer or withdraw assistance, and the ability to make such offers contingent on political support, is what makes them clientelistic. As such, this component of the argument applies to many areas of the developing world, irrespective of ethnic demographics, where clientelism is a central feature of political life.[1] The most obvious applied settings for these linkages are countries that Chandra (2004, 6) describes as "patronage democracies" – states where elected officials enjoy wide discretion in the distribution of government jobs and public services and the selective implementation of laws. Yet we might expect to see qualitatively similar dynamics in electoral autocracies as well, where the electoral pretext of lawmaking is thinner still and where people self-consciously elect "service deputies" on the basis of their ability to channel resources to supporters.[2]

The book, of course, pitches a story about *ethnic* monopsonies. In so doing, it focuses on how shared social networks facilitate transactions by reducing monitoring and policing costs, while ascriptive membership rules restrict people's ability to join or leave specific constituencies. Put differently, the story is not about the content of ethnicity per se, nor does it invoke inherent affinities between members of the same communities. Rather, it emphasizes the structural factors of such constituencies that facilitate exchange. As such, it opens up the possibility that key elements of this theory of vote monopsonies extend beyond ethnic groups to other constituencies that share analogous structural features, or can otherwise mimic them.

---

[1] See Hicken (2011); Kitschelt (2000); Kitschelt and Kselman (2013); Kitschelt and Wilkinson (2007b); Stokes et al. (2013).
[2] See, for example, Blaydes (2011); Corstange (2012b); Jamal (2007); Lust (2009).

The book focuses on ethnic networks as a form of information technology that enables patrons and clients to monitor each other. Collecting information and keeping track of voters was, however, precisely one of the functions performed by the leviathan-like machines at the turn of the twentieth century, and which contemporary machines perform in various places in the developing world.[3] My point is not that it is impossible to develop such organizations without ethnic networks, but rather that such networks provide an efficient tool for patrons and clients to employ. Given these advantages, it is perhaps unsurprisingly that many of the great urban machines built up what amounted to federations of ethnic constituencies rather than an undifferentiated mass of clients.

The other core element of the theory of vote monopsonies is the idea of impermeable boundaries: that people cannot switch constituencies at will in pursuit of a better deal for their votes. A common simplification is that ethnic groups, given their descent-based membership rules, have perfectly impermeable boundaries. Such an ideal type is useful conceptually, even though it is untrue in practice. In applied terms, switching groups is costly – often very costly – rather than impossible, and costs of entry and exit are, themselves, subject to manipulation as people find reasons to police social boundaries.

That being said, ethnic boundaries are not the only ones that can be costly to cross. Rather than restrictions on social mobility, there may, instead, be much more prosaic constraints on simple, physical mobility between geographically bound constituencies. Voter registration laws, for example, may tie people to particular districts, while the practical costs of moving home may loom large for voters – particularly poor ones – who are dissatisfied with their representatives. Hence, as I argued in the book, one of several reasons that rural voters are desirable clients is that they are less mobile than their urban counterparts. Consequently, the vote monopsony argument can help us think about rural voting behavior in the developing world – particularly in countries where ruling parties dominate the countryside but face stiff opposition in the cities. It also provides a friendly amendment to Bates's observation that post-independence African states focused their attention on placating urban constituents rather than implementing policies favorable to the rural areas, where the majority of their populations resided: competition for the former compelled governments to attend more to urban voters and less to their rural counterparts (1981; 2008).

Part of Bates's story focused on the potential for unrest in the urban areas. Political instability also plays a role in this book's theory of vote monopsonies, particularly with respect to their establishment. Competition for office takes on characteristics of a tournament: we commonly assume that politicians are office-seekers, but we also realize that the number of offices is

---

[3] Compare Auyero (2001); Calvo and Murillo (2013); Erie (1992); Golway (2014); Magaloni (2006); Stokes et al. (2013).

far smaller than the number of aspirants – so we should not expect to run out of ambitious politicians. Under ordinary circumstances, then, it would be difficult to imagine such politicians consenting to perpetual exclusion from office, or entrepreneurial entrants not trying to capitalize on unmet demands from dissatisfied constituents. Violence and other forms of political instability can, however, disrupt this default pattern of competitiveness.

In the absence of a neutral state capable of policing party behavior, small-scale violence and intimidation could, of course, deter candidate entry and voter participation – in which case unfair competition stifles the vote market by adding costs that the less committed may be unwilling to bear. Larger-scale violence in the form of revolutions, coups, or civil wars, although rare events, may enable one faction to eliminate its rivals by force. If so, subsequent elections take place in a qualitatively different vote market, and presumably a less competitive one than might have otherwise prevailed. Hence, violence and instability can contribute to the restriction of competition and, potentially, the emergence of vote monopsonies.

9.3 RAMIFICATIONS

The theory of ethnic monopsonies that I have presented in this book contributes to several lines of research. In particular, it offers a revision to how we think about clientelism and ethnic politics, and suggests how to synthesize these two concepts in future work. Clientelistic linkages between politicians and voters are common in much of the developing world, and many of its societies are multiethnic or otherwise diverse. Consequently, how we understand the connections between these two concepts has implications for how we understand political development more broadly – particularly with respect to democracy and elections. The book's arguments draw attention to the possibility of electoral market failures, which have normative ramifications for democratic representation and accountability.

9.3.1 Ethnic Politics

Studies of ethnic politics often invoke debate over the paradigmatic *-isms* in the academic literature – primordialism, constructivism, instrumentalism, and various others (e.g., Varshney, 2007). I have largely eschewed this debate insofar as it is tangential to the book's substantive focus. However, the patronage politics I examine rest on an instrumental logic, and I emphasize that people do attempt to leverage their ethnic identities to their own advantage. They can, of course, act instrumentally in pursuit of *non*-material payoffs, but my focus on development outcomes has meant that I have emphasized material benefits in this book.[4] Competition for material payoffs is obviously not the whole story, but it is an important part.

The claim that people use ethnicity instrumentally is neither new nor particularly controversial, but the mechanisms by which they deploy their identities remain unsettled. The theory I have presented highlights the importance of transaction costs in clientelistic exchange, and argues that ethnic networks provide a tool to reduce these costs between patrons and clients. In so doing, it builds off of prior work that examine information technology and strategic selection dynamics in explaining ethnic favoritism (e.g., Habyarimana et al., 2007a, 2009). This transactions-based mechanism, in turn, complements alternative explanations for people's reliance on ethnicity.

In particular, one alternate but common claim is that ethnic affinity explains people's preferences for interacting with co-ethnics. One important limitation of such claims is that they are circular and explain ethnocentric outcomes on the basis of ethnocentric preferences – that is, they label what they purport to explain. However, to the degree that such a thing as ethnic affinity exists, it complements the transactions-based mechanism by further reducing the costs of transacting. In the abstract, networks based on other social categories besides ethnicity could help us account for lower transaction costs. To the degree that we wish to bring affinity into our story, however, we would expect networks with an affinal component to be especially cost-effective for members.

Affinity may also, however, trigger considerations of group fate and vulnerability among members of a group. We might, therefore, expect vulnerability to motivate members to demand that the group close ranks against non-members. If so, we might also expect people to be more willing to trade off personalized rewards for collectively consumed payoffs such as group status or physical security. Moreover, we might imagine vulnerability to coincide with greater efforts to police group boundaries – presuming that the group can overcome the free-rider problem associated with policing. Greater zeal for enforcing group boundaries could, in turn, further reduce the costs of transacting on the ethnic network even as it increases the costs of transacting *across* networks. As the cost differential between transactions on and across networks increases, people face increasingly strong incentives to stay on their own networks and avoid interactions across ethnic groups.

Consequently, strategic elites have self-interested reasons to police boundaries. By keeping within-network transactions cheap, policing enables both patrons and clients to conclude credible rewards-for-support bargains. Elites can, in turn, protect their vote markets by keeping the transaction cost differentials high. Moreover, by encouraging people to think in terms of group vulnerability, elites can even get their constituents to pay part of the cost of

---

[4] On non-material "identity goods" and trade-offs with material payoffs, see, for example, Chandra (2004); Corstange (2013); Varshney (2003).

9.3 Ramifications

boundary maintenance. Scholars have often observed that ethnic entrepreneurs "play the ethnic card" or otherwise attempt to sow conflict between members of different ethnic groups.[5] This argument spells out one plausible rationale for doing so: to protect their vote markets and lower the cost of votes within them.

Transaction costs and the challenge of credible exchange between patrons and clients also provide incentives for elite collusion. To the degree that they recognize the difficulties of making cross-ethnic appeals, politicians face incentives to focus on their own communities when pursuing short-term electoral interests. However, they also face incentives to keep payoffs low, which they can achieve by minimizing transaction costs and, ideally, by dominating their own vote markets. Consequently, elites face incentives to collude with each other to divvy up markets with power-sharing institutions, favorable electoral laws, and the like. Well-intentioned leaders may adopt some of these tools as a way to mitigate conflict between communities. However, "conflict reduction mechanisms" may, intentionally or incidentally, produce ethnic vote markets dominated by just a few elites.[6]

9.3.2 Clientelism

In addition to its contributions to the study of ethnic politics, this book has offered new ideas on clientelism as well. Current work on clientelism and vote trafficking emphasize the contingency of patron–client exchanges and the importance of monitoring in those interactions. This book expands on the contingent nature of clientelistic relationships and develops ideas about monitoring on and across networks. In particular, it emphasizes that both patrons *and* clients must make credible commitments to each other, and shows how ethnic networks can increase certainty and lower transaction costs sufficiently to undergird clientelistic exchange. As a central contribution, the book develops the idea that the competitiveness of the environment within which these transactions occur influences the quantity of exchanges that take place, which clients can hope to receive rewards, and the lucrativeness of the payoffs.

In the abstract, clientelistic exchange should be rife with opportunism as patrons and clients face temptations to renege on their promises to each other. Consequently, monitoring becomes a crucial component of clientelistic relationships because it enables the parties to the exchange make credible commitments to each other. Although we customarily conceive of patrons monitoring their clients – the former build the machines to do so, after all – we should

---

[5] Compare Eifert et al. (2010); Ferree (2006, 2011); Mendelberg (2001).
[6] Compare the debates over electoral systems in multiethnic societies in Andeweg (2000); Birnir (2007); Horowitz (1985, 1991); Lijphart (1977); Reilly (2006).

also recognize that clients monitor their patrons as well. Information flows on networks help patrons keep track of their clients' behaviors, as well as the latter's idiosyncratic needs for purposes of targeting. Clients, in turn, can use the collective experiences of fellow network members to assess the reliability of particular patrons – an important point for clients expecting payoffs at some point in the indefinite future rather than in a simple spot exchange.

Information flows on networks, then, increase certainty and lower transaction costs for clientelistic exchange. Moreover, the more that information concentrates within networks and does not cross between them, the larger is the differential in transaction costs for exchanges on versus across networks. Ethnic networks therefore make useful tools for patrons and clients insofar as they are information-rich environments. They are also self-limiting, however, to the degree that information on the network does not flow between groups. Under these conditions, the differential transaction costs makes it prohibitively expensive to make credible commitments and transact across ethnic lines – yielding the often-observed dynamic of "ethnic favoritism."

A subcomponent of the contemporary literature on clientelism has focused on the "core versus swing" debate: do parties target their core supporters for rewards, or do they chase after swing voters? There are plausible reasons why parties might choose to target one set of voters or the other – or both – and empirical research has found support for both propositions in differing settings. Rather than focus on the false dichotomy of core supporters and swing voters, this book has suggested examining a continuum of support and the networks on which patrons and clients conduct their exchanges. Transaction costs imply that parties must attend – at least in part – to which people they can reach in a cost-effective manner. Voters may be viable targets for clientelistic exchanges if they are embedded in a network, regardless of whether they are strong supporters or indifferents.[7]

Moreover, the frequent use of ethnic networks to undergird clientelistic constituencies also implies that the concepts of core and swing must be updated, or at least adapted, in diverse societies. To the degree that ethnic constituencies really do have completely impermeable boundaries, then an electorate organized along ethnic lines should have no swing voters at all – *if* we also assume ethnic groups to be unified, corporate entities. By acknowledging the possibility of internal competition within ethnic communities, however, we can return to a variation on the "core versus swing" theme. In the abstract, everyone within a constituency with impermeable boundaries counts as a core supporter for coethnic elites – unless there are multiple, competing factions. In the latter case, we can conceive of the "swing of the core" in which some members of the group may credibly promise their support to one or another

---

[7] For recent contributions on the core–swing debate, compare Gans-Morse et al. (2014); Stokes et al. (2013). On partisan networks and access to patronage, see Calvo and Murillo (2013).

9.3 Ramifications

coethnic, even though they may be unable to conduct exchanges with elites across ethnic lines. The difficulty of making credible promises may constrain and channel competition, but it need not eliminate it.

Another stylized fact to emerge in the study of clientelism is the presumption that patrons focus heavily on poor voters who, for a variety of reasons, have lower asking prices for their political support. Empirical evidence on the "poor voter" proposition, however, has been mixed: although some parties do seem to pursue poor people, clientelistic transactions appear to reach well into the middle- and upper-income ranges as well. To the degree that ethnic groups comprise "societies in miniature" with a full complement of occupations, levels of education, placements at different stages in the lifecycle, and so on, we should expect that ethnic networks, in the broad sense, to encompass rich, poor, and middle-income voters alike. As I suggested earlier in the book, patrons and parties have portfolios of patronage resources to dispense. To the degree that they have the capacity to target these payoffs, we would expect them to allocate different components of their portfolios to different kinds of constituents. As such, we would expect them to accommodate rich and poor voters with different rewards, and perhaps to demand various kinds of support from different constituencies in exchange.

Finally, this book has emphasized the importance of examining different competitive environments to understand clientelism. Implicitly or explicitly, scholars often make the "single machine assumption," in which a single patron or party has the capacity and credibility to conduct materially based exchanges with voters. As this book has pointed out, such an assumption is not always appropriate – and, more importantly, it assumes away some of the most interesting dynamics about patronage politics. By explicitly comparing different types of competitive environments, we can examine how machines operate when insulated from competitive pressures, and how they operate when forced to compete directly with one another for people's votes. As the book has demonstrated, the presence or absence of competitive pressures has important substantive ramifications for what regular people get in exchange for their political support.

9.3.3 Democracy

Put together, the connected concepts of ethnic politics and clientelism have important ramifications for the study of democracy in the developing world. Empirically, part of this book examined the distribution of basic government services to regular people and found that services varied in quality and extent depending on the degree of political competition. There are theoretical reasons to care about this variation: under what conditions do politicians attend to the needs of their constituents, and under what conditions do they disregard those needs? There are also substantive reasons we care, however: all told, we would prefer to see more children in school, better-staffed health clinics, and a wider supply of clean drinking water in the societies of the developing world, and the provision of these services depends on improving governance. More broadly, though, the normative implications of the story I have told about ethnic politics and clientelism also touch on more abstract problems of representation and accountability.

Issues of representation become more complex in diverse societies. When constituencies track ethnic lines, many people automatically assume that politicians represent their own ethnic community by virtue of shared ethnicity. Coethnicity may be sufficient to achieve *descriptive* representation, but it does not guarantee *substantive* representation. Indeed, as this book has suggested, ethnicity can limit representation of people's interests by compelling voters to make do with co-ethnic elites – even when the latter perform poorly. Restricting voters to co-ethnic politicians becomes especially problematic when a single politician comes to dominate the community and eliminates even this constrained choice for community members.

Clientelism, in turn, poses another barrier to representation. Put strongly, clientelistic linkages between patrons and clients define transactions between them rather than the representation of the latter by the former. When voters trade their support for patronage payoffs, they surrender the expectation that elites should represent their interests outside the scope of the exchange. In the simple, idealized version of programmatic competition – the "responsible partisan model" – voters sanction parties that renege on their campaign promises by voting them out of office in the next election. Under clientelistic exchange, however, voters base their sanctioning decisions on promises made to individuals, and, sometimes, to small collectivities, for patronage payoffs. Although relatively easy to verify, many voters lack the leverage to discipline their patrons. In the absence of a coordinating mechanism for clients, individual voters have minimal capacity to sanction underperforming patrons beyond shifting their votes to a competitor.

As this book has argued, however, ethnic groups have additional accountability problems with which to contend: voters may lose their ability to sanction with the ballot in the absence of within-group competition for their votes. Basing political constituencies on social categories with high barriers to entry and exit limits the amount of punishment voters can mete out to politicians. Voters may, in principle, be able to switch their support from an underperforming patron or party to a competitor within their own community – if a credible one exists. In dominated communities, voters have few options to sanction their leaders beyond staying home on election day.

Accountability is not just a problem about elites, however. Instead, it can extend, perversely, to voters as well. Accountability is asymmetric under programmatic competition: voters assess elites and hold the latter accountable when they fail to fulfill their promises, but voters are under no obligation to promise anything to elites and face no penalties if they change their minds. The core of clientelism, however, is *contingent* exchange, and voters that fail to fulfill their obligations to patrons are subject to sanctions and the withdrawal of benefits. Ethnic networks, in turn, help patrons monitor their clients and, consequently, hold them accountable for their behavior. Put together, patrons have strong motives and a strong tool to enforce the contingent bargains they strike with voters.

More troubling than perverse accountability may be the dynamics of perverse *competition* that we observe in dominated constituencies. As the book has argued, dominant politicians that are sheltered from electoral competition do not need the active support of much of their nominal clientele, and enjoy discretion in who to patronize and how much to offer. Under these conditions, voters not only lack a credible sanctioning tool, but they also end up competing against one another for a share of the largesse being dispensed. Put together, vote market failure can produce normatively undesirable outcomes: voters competing for patronage rather than politicians competing for votes.

9.3.4 Durability

How durable are vote monopsonies? The "politics as usual" of day-to-day clientelism seems to favor their perpetuation, but questions about durability are not idle curiosities. Despite the Arab world's reputation as a bastion for durable authoritarianism, the Arab Spring revolts brought down several long-serving autocrats and injected considerable instability into countries that did not experience a change of leaders.

Yemen
After surviving more than three decades of coup attempts, tribal conflicts, various insurrections, and a civil war, Ali Abdallah Salih became the third Arab president, after his counterparts in Tunisia and Egypt, to lose office to the Arab Spring – although it took a year of protests, the defection of many of his allies, a near-miss assassination attempt, and an internationally mediated agreement before he finally ceded power to his vice president. By the late-2000s, the Yemeni government faced a number of challenges, including the on-again, off-again Houthi insurgency in the far north, an increasingly assertive southern movement, and a projected fiscal crisis as the country's oil reserves began to dwindle.[8] As in many other electoral autocracies, however, the regime's opponents remained divided. Although opposition party elites in the capital had coalesced into an alliance of sorts, it remained vulnerable to defections and splits, enjoyed only spotty cooperation in the provinces, and engaged in little to no coordination with other opponents such as the northern insurgents or the southern movement. A priori, then, it was unclear that the

---

[8] See Alley (2010b); Colton (2010); Day (2012); Longley and al Iryani (2008); Phillips (2008, 2011); Salmoni et al. (2010); Wedeen et al. (2009).

various elements of the opposition could mount a sustained, credible challenge to the ruling regime.

Consciously modeled after the revolutions in Tunisia and Egypt, however, the Arab Spring protests that began in early-2011 provided a focal point around which Salih's disparate opponents could coordinate their efforts. After sustained, large-scale demonstrations and a wave of elite defections failed to dislodge the president, he suffered grievous wounds in an assassination attempt and left the country for medical treatment in Saudi Arabia – only to return three months later. After painstaking negotiations, Salih signed, in late-2011 and after repeated false starts, a Gulf-brokered accord that transferred power to his vice president, Abdurabbuh Mansour Hadi, in exchange for immunity from prosecution for himself and his relatives. In early 2012, Hadi, the sole nominee, won the presidential election and began a transition period which included unity governments, national dialogue conferences, and attempts to phase the former president's loyalists out of government and the military.[9]

By most accounts, Salih began to subvert the transitional government almost immediately. Unlike Tunisia's and Egypt's ousted leaders – in exile and prison, respectively – Salih simply stayed put in Sanaa, untouched and apparently untouchable, where he continued to lead the GPC and its parliamentary supermajority. Amidst frequent rumors of coup plots, the former president tapped some of the billions of dollars expropriated during his rule to shore up his support, allied with his former opponents in the Houthi movement, and worked with supporters in the military and the tribes to undermine pro-government forces seeking to halt Houthi advances from their northern base. Salih loyalists in the military stood down while the Houthis, effectively unopposed, occupied the capital in late-2014. The latter subsequently overthrew the government in early-2015, at which point Hadi fled to Aden and then to Saudi Arabia as Houthi militiamen and army units loyal to Salih pushed southwards.[10]

The details of Yemen's ongoing crisis are beyond the scope of this book, of course, but we can still consider some of its ramifications for the durability of monopsonies and of authoritarian regimes. Yemenis and outside observers had

---

[9] See Lynch (2011, 2012) for a summary of early events.
[10] See Charles Schmitz, "Yemen's Ansar Allah: Causes and effects of its pursuit of power," *Middle East Institute*, 14 February 2015 (www.mei.edu/content/at/yemens-ansar-allah-causes-and-effects-its-pursuit-power); "Houthi armed groups challenge Yemen power structure," *Al-Monitor*, 30 April 2014; "Houthi victory is defeat for Yemen's Islah," *Al-Monitor*, 29 September 2014; "Eyeing return, Yemen's ousted Saleh aids Houthis," *Al Arabiya*, 23 October 2014; "Yemen ex-leader's party to protest over U.N. sanctions move," *Naharnet*, 6 November 2014; "Ex-Yemen President Saleh sanctioned by United States," *BBC News*, 10 November 2014; "Shiite militia tightens grip on Yemen after 'coup,'" *Naharnet*, 7 February 2015; "Yemen ex-leader Saleh 'amassed up to $60 bn' – UN probe," *BBC News*, 25 February 2015; "Yemen's Houthi rebels get boost from country's ousted dictator," *Washington Post*, 31 March 2015; "Yemen's ousted President Saleh helps propel Houthi rebel advance," *Wall Street Journal*, 10 April 2015.

long discussed the possibility of regime collapse or state failure – but as the years ticked by, Salih remained in place through the adept use of day-to-day, clientelistic rewards and punishments. Ultimately, Salih lost power not through elections, but through the spread of a region-wide revolution – and, amazingly, retains enough influence that he may be able to restore either himself or his son to the presidency. Irrespective of a possible counter-revolution, the system of daily rule that Salih built over three decades in power was indeed durable – just not impervious to the Arab Spring's truly exceptional events.

Lebanon

In Lebanon, meanwhile, the Arab Spring registered not as a revolution against a sitting regime or the country's system of government, but rather indirectly via the impact of the Syrian civil war on Lebanese domestic politics. Lebanon had lurched through a quick succession of crises after the 2005 "independence intifada" and elections, including the 2006 Israel–Hizballah war, a long-running opposition sit-in that paralyzed state institutions, and Hizballah's 2008 armed take-over of the capital. After international mediation ended the immediate crisis, the country held its closely contested 2009 elections, which, as in 2005, returned a slim March 14 majority. Hariri himself was named prime minister and spent nearly half a year cobbling together a fractious unity government, which survived for a year before its March 8 members brought it down just days before the Tunisian president fled his country in January 2011.

From its inception, Hariri's cabinet was extremely fragile – unsurprising given its polarized members and the coalition arithmetic that enabled the March 8 parties to topple it at their discretion.[11] Given Lebanon's patchwork diversity, its governments depend on support across the sectarian spectrum; Hariri's cabinet collapsed not because he lost support within his own Sunni constituency, but because parties representing other sects withdrew theirs.[12] Syria and Hizballah subsequently put enormous pressure on Hariri's Druze ally to abandon him in

---

[11] The details are more complicated than the main text suggests, but the results are the same. Former March 14 stalwart Walid Jumblatt left the coalition shortly after the election, but was represented in the government under March 14's share of the seats. March 14 took only half the seats in the cabinet; making simple decisions thus required them to achieve consent from at least one minister aligned with either March 8 or with the president, who also had a small share in the cabinet. March 8 received exactly one-third of the seats, which required them, in principle, to convince one other minister to resign if they wished to topple the government. The president, however, appointed one minister who was expected to vote with March 14, and one who was expected to vote with March 8. In effect, March 8 had secured the capacity to bring down the government.

[12] The precipitating event was Hariri's refusal to withdraw support for the internationally-sponsored Special Tribunal for Lebanon (STL), created by the United Nations Security Council in 2007 to investigate the 2005 assassination of Rafik al-Hariri and others and to try its accused perpetrators. Hizballah denounced the STL as a western conspiracy to disarm the party, and brought down Hariri's government once it became clear that prosecutors would indict Hizballah party members in the assassination.

parliament, which enabled the March 8 parties to form an alternative government by peeling away a small number of Sunni MPs from Hariri's coalition – after which Hariri went into both opposition and quasi-exile abroad due to fears of assassination emmanating from Syria and, possibly, Hizballah.[13]

Hariri's dominance of the Sunni community had never been absolute; in reality, he co-opted many local elites rather than replace them outright, which exposed him to the risk of defection for the right price. The politicians that switched sides did so for instrumental reasons – they harbored ambitions to the premiership, but the only realistic way to obtain it was through the support of parties from *outside* the Sunni community. The new, March 8-dominated government proved to be not much more stable than its predecessor; it collapsed after two years and paved the way for Hariri's return and the formation of another unity government headed by a Hariri ally. In light of the political gridlock and worsening security environment due to spillover from the Syrian civil war, that government twice postponed the parliamentary elections to 2017.

As with Yemen, the details of Lebanon's ongoing political crisis are beyond the scope of this book, but we can still consider some of its ramifications for the durability of monopsonies. Fundamentally, Hariri lost the premiership not because he lost control over his own vote market, but because of between-community politicking at the elite level: the premiership in Lebanon is not solely a Sunni decision to make. Each non-Hariri government in the post-civil war period has lasted only a short time, however, and no other Sunni organization has the capacity to compete with the Hariri machine on the national level. Rather than another party, the biggest potential threats to Hariri's dominance are radical groups spilling over from the Syrian civil war, whose methods are unlikely to include anything as genteel as simple electioneering. Hence, although subject to between-sect rivalries and outflanking threats from militants, Hariri remains the only electoral game in town for Sunni voters.

Durable Monopsonies?

What can these ongoing events in Lebanon and Yemen tell us about the durability of vote monopsonies? It is tempting, of course, to declare them fragile – both leaders lost office. At the same time, neither suffered electoral

---

[13] Jumblatt had, in fact, lobbied against the collapse of Hariri's unity government, and his ministers refused to resign. His subsequent decision to support a rival premier split his own parliamentary bloc and left the parliament exactly divided – at which point March 8 offered the premiership and senior ministries to a few Sunni MPs from Tripoli to switch sides. See "Hezbollah putting more pressure on Jumblatt to switch, report," *Ya Libnan*, 17 January 2011; "Lebanon Druze leader Walid Jumblatt sides with Hezbollah in crisis," *Los Angeles Times*, 22 January 2011; "'National Struggle Front' new name for Jumblat's Democratic Gathering," *Naharnet*, 24 January 2011. Karlin, Mara E., "The Druze factor," *Foreign Affairs*, 16 February 2011, (www.foreignaffairs.com/articles/67454/mara-e-karlin/the-druze-factor); "Safadi's choice not to run sends mixed message to rival coalitions," *Daily Star*, 6 October 2012.

9.3 Ramifications

defeat: one lost the premiership in an ongoing conflict with parties outside his own community, and the other lost the presidency to a once-in-a-generation, region-wide revolution. Moreover, neither have disappeared as political forces. Hariri returned to Lebanon, and his party returned to the cabinet, while Salih stayed in Yemen, untouched and, seemingly, untouchable, to influence Yemeni politics from behind the scenes. The events of the last few years have demonstrated not that monopsonies are fragile, but rather that they are not invincible.

One might make similar observations about the so-called "durable authoritarian" regimes of the Middle East. Scholars had long argued that the Arab world's ruling regimes were deeply entrenched and unlikely to change in more than cosmetic ways, but were then subject to sustained criticism for "missing" the Arab Spring. Yet counterclaims of "authoritarian fragility" – often made in the immediate aftermath of the uprisings, and sometimes in the middle of them – not only conflated explanation with prediction, but also did not age well in light of the "modest harvest" a few years after the Tunisian and Egyptian revolutions.[14] Again, that several regimes fell to popular uprisings does not demonstrate that they were fragile so much as it demonstrates that they were not invincible. Understandably, people noticed the revolutions that toppled dictators in 2011. Yet many failed to notice the revolutions that did *not* happen in 2010, or 2009, or 2008, or in the years that stretch back into decades of authoritarian government.

Although the Arab world's autocratic regimes have used their security services to stifle dissent, they have also used clientelistic linkages to manufacture support – or at least acquiescence – as well. Most of these regimes tolerated some form of organized opposition, but kept it fragmented, on the ideological margins, and starved of resources to hamper its ability to appeal to large swaths of the population. Presidents and ruling party legislators made it their business to cultivate constituencies with patronage payoffs.[15] By constraining competition, regime leaders could enjoy many of the advantages of monopsony in order to keep their costs down and discretion high.

Like the vote monopsonies I described in Lebanon and Yemen but on a larger scale, the autocratic regimes of the Arab world have been durable entities – in the context of the day-to-day, clientelistic politics that they employed for decades. Their durability, in turn, rested in part on their ability to keep constituents satisfied with their payoffs, or at least insufficiently dissatisfied to do something about it. By keeping people demobilized and divided, the regimes kept opponents from coordinating to challenge incumbents. We may, therefore,

---

[14] On durable authoritarianism, see, among others, Bellin (2004); Blaydes (2011); Brownlee (2007); Jamal (2007); Lust-Okar (2004, 2005); Schlumberger (2007). On explaining versus forecasting revolutions, see Keddie (1995); Kuran (1991, 1995). On missing the Arab Spring and its modest harvest, see Brownlee et al. (2013); Gause (2011).

[15] Compare Blaydes (2011); Lust-Okar (2004, 2005, 2009a,b).

look upon the momentous events of the Arab Spring precisely as what they are: momentous events that provided regular people with a revolutionary moment to turn "now out of never" (Kuran, 1991).

9.4 FUTURE RESEARCH

Future research on ethnic monopsonies can entertain a number of possibilities. An obvious next step includes expanding the sample of countries, but, in the process of doing so, selecting for meaningful variation on key, system-level characteristics that could influence the structure of the vote market. Such factors would almost certainly include formal electoral rules, the political salience of ethnic identities and the prior history of conflict between groups, and the demographic composition of society – not simply diversity or fractionalization, but also the number and size of groups that politicians seek to mobilize. Plausibly, these and other factors affect the extent to which particular groups can become meaningful constituencies, as well as the degree to which their elites can eliminate internal rivals and foreclose the attractiveness or viability of multiethnic – or non-ethnic – coalitions.[16]

In addition to the development of ethnic constituencies, future research can also build on the growing literature that examines transitions from clientelistic to programmatic politics. Much of this literature acknowledges that politicians tend to rely less on clientelism as their countries develop – but, as the authors would, no doubt, caution, "go get richer" is an aspiration rather than a theory. Various, discrete steps to limit parties' abilities to use clientelistic linkages, or to make such linkages unattractive compared to programs, might include reforms to the civil service, campaign finance, and media access. They may also include institutional changes such as decentralization, term limits, technical reform of electoral registration and balloting, and broader electoral system reform in favor of larger, more diverse districts – making it costlier to win via retail politics and relatively more attractive to try public goods provisioning instead. Citing reforms is, of course, much easier than implementing them, particularly insofar as the parties that win from the existing system may, understandably, be unenthusiastic about changing rules from which they benefit. Successful reform may, therefore, benefit from studies on democratization and the transition from authoritarian rule, which study how ruling elites may be persuaded – or else compelled – to open up their vote markets to freer, fuller, more programmatic competition.[17]

---

[16] Baldwin (2013); Birnir (2007); Chandra et al. (2001); Geertz (1963); Horowitz (1985, 1991); Lijphart (1977, 1994); Posner (2005); Reilly (2006).

[17] Brancati (2006); Chandra (2004); Corstange (2012b); De La O (2013); Hicken (2011); Keefer (2007); Keefer and Vlaicu (2008); Kitschelt and Kselman (2013); Kitschelt and Wilkinson (2007b); Stokes et al. (2013); Weitz-Shapiro (2012, 2014).

Bibliography

Abd al-Khaliq, J. (2006). *The 2005 Independence Elections*. Beirut: Annahar Press. Arabic.
Abu Ghanim, F. A. A. (1985). *The Tribal Structure in Yemen Between Continuity and Change*. Damascus: Arab Writer Press. Arabic.
Abu Ghanim, F. A. A. (1990). *Tribe and State in Yemen*. Cairo: Lighthouse Press. Arabic.
Abu Talib, H. (1994). *Yemeni Unity*. Beirut: Centre for Arab Unity Studies. Arabic.
Afandi, M. A. (Ed.) (2003). *Yemeni Strategic Report 2003*. Sanaa: Yemeni Center for Strategic Studies. Arabic.
Ajami, F. (1986). *The Vanished Imam: Musa al Sadr and the Shia of Lebanon*. Ithaca: Cornell University Press.
Akarli, E. D. (1993). *The Long Peace: Ottoman Lebanon, 1861–1920*. Berkeley: University of California Press.
al Zubayri, M. M. (2004). *The Imamate and its Danger for Yemeni Unity*. Sanaa: Ministry of Culture and Tourism. Arabic.
Aldrich, J. H. (1995). *Why Parties?* Chicago: University of Chicago Press.
Alesina, A., R. Baqir, and W. Easterly (1999). Public goods and ethnic divisions. *Quarterly Journal of Economics* 114(4), 1243–1284.
Alesina, A., R. Baqir, and W. Easterly (2000). Redistributive public employment. *Journal of Urban Economics* 48(2), 219–241.
Alesina, A., A. Devleeschauwer, W. Easterly, S. Kurlat, and R. Wacziarg (2003). Fractionalization. *Journal of Economic Growth* 8, 155–194.
Alesina, A. and E. La Ferrara (2005). Ethnic diversity and economic performance. *Journal of Economic Literature* 43(3), 762–800.
Alesina, A. and S. E. Spear (1988). An overlapping generations model of electoral competition. *Journal of Public Economics* 37(3), 359–379.
Alley, A. L. (2010a). The rules of the game: Unpacking patronage politics in Yemen. *Middle East Journal* 64(3), 385–409.
Alley, A. L. (2010b). Yemen's multiple crises. *Journal of Democracy* 21(4), 72–86.
Anderson, B. (1991). *Imagined Communities* (Revised ed.). London: Verso.

Andeweg, R. (2000). Consociational democracy. *Annual Review of Political Science* 3, 509–536.

Annett, A. (2001). Social fractionalization, political instability, and the size of government. *IMF Staff Papers* 48(3), 561–592.

Arcand, J.-L., P. Guillaumont, and S. G. Jeanneney (2000). How to make a tragedy: On the alleged effect of ethnicity on growth. *Journal of International Development* 12, 925–938.

Asal, V., M. Brown, and A. Dalton (2012). Why split? Organizational splits among ethnopolitical organizations in the Middle East. *Journal of Conflict Resolution* 56(1), 94–117.

Auyero, J. (1999). "From the client's point(s) of view": How poor people perceive and evaluate political clientelism. *Theory and Society* 28(2), 297–334.

Auyero, J. (2001). *Poor People's Politics: Peronist Survival Networks and the Legacy of Evita*. Durham, NC: Duke University Press.

Axelrod, R. (1984). *The Evolution of Cooperation*. New York: Basic Books.

Axelrod, R., R. Riolo, and M. Cohen (2002). Beyond geography: Cooperation with persistent links in the absence of clustered neighborhoods. *Personality and Social Psychology Review* 6(4), 341–346.

Baldwin, K. (2010). *Big Men and Ballots: The Effects of Traditional Leaders on Elections and Distributive Politics in Zambia*. PhD thesis, Columbia University, New York.

Baldwin, K. (2013). Why vote with the chief? Political connections and public goods provision in Zambia. *American Journal of Political Science* 57(4), 794–809.

Baldwin, K. (2014). When politicians cede control of resources: Lands, chiefs, and coalition-building in Africa. *Comparative Politics* 46(3), 253–271.

Baldwin, K. and J. D. Huber (2010). Economic versus cultural differences: Forms of ethnic diversity and public goods provision. *American Political Science Review* 104(4), 644–662.

Banerjee, A., L. Iyer, and R. Somanathan (2005). History, social divisions, and public goods in rural India. *Journal of the European Economic Association* 3(2–3), 639–647.

Banks, J. S. (1991). *Signaling Games in Political Science*. New York: Harwood Academic Publishers.

Bashir, I. (1994). *Development in Lebanon*. Beirut: Learning for the Millions Press. Arabic.

Bashir, I. (2006). *Sectarianism in Lebanon Until When?* Beirut: University Institute for Studies. Arabic.

Bates, R. H. (1974). Ethnic competition and modernization in contemporary Africa. *Comparative Political Studies* 6(4), 457–484.

Bates, R. H. (1981). *Markets and States in Tropical Africa*. Berkeley: University of California Press.

Bates, R. H. (1983a). *Essays on the Political Economy of Rural Africa*. New York: Cambridge University Press.

Bates, R. H. (1983b). Modernization, ethnic competition, and the rationality of politics in contemporary Africa. In D. Rothchild and V. Olorunsola (Eds.), *State Versus Ethnic Claims: African Policy Dilemmas*, pp. 152–171. Boulder, CO: Westview Press.

Bates, R. H. (1990). Capital, kinship, and conflict: The structuring influence of capital in kinship societies. *Canadian Journal of African Studies* 24(2), 151–164.

Bates, R. H. (2001). *Prosperity & Violence*. New York: W.W. Norton & Company.
Bates, R. H. (2008). *When Things Fell Apart*. New York: Cambridge University Press.
Baylouny, A. M. (2006). Creating kin: New family associations as welfare providers in liberalizing Jordan. *International Journal of Middle East Studies* 38(3), 349–368.
Baylouny, A. M. (2010). *Privatizing Welfare in the Middle East: Kin Mutual Aid Associations in Jordan and Lebanon*. Bloomington, IN: Indiana University Press.
Bellin, E. (2004). The robustness of authoritarianism in the Middle East. *Comparative Politics* 36(2), 139–157.
Benstead, L. J. (2008). *Does Casework Build Support for a Strong Parliament? Legislative Representation and Public Opinion in Morocco and Algeria*. PhD thesis, University of Michigan, Ann Arbor, MI.
Binder, L. (Ed.) (1999). *Ethnic Conflict and International Politics in the Middle East*. Gainesville: University Press of Florida.
Birnir, J. K. (2007). *Ethnicity and Electoral Politics*. New York: Cambridge University Press.
Blanford, N. (2006). *Killing Mr Lebanon*. New York: I.B. Tauris.
Blaydes, L. (2011). *Elections and Distributive Politics in Mubarak's Egypt*. New York: Cambridge University Press.
Boix, C. and S. C. Stokes (Eds.) (2007). *The Oxford Handbook of Comparative Politics*. New York: Oxford University Press.
Bonnefoy, L. (2011). *Salafism in Yemen*. New York: Columbia University Press.
Bowles, S. and H. Gintis (2004). Persistent parochialism: Trust and exclusion in ethnic networks. *Journal of Economic Behavior & Organization* 55(1), 1–23.
Brancati, D. (2006). Decentralization: Fueling the fire or dampening the flames of ethnic conflict and secessionism? *International Organization* 60(3), 651–685.
Brancati, D. (2009). *Peace by Design: Managing Intrastate Conflict Through Decentralization*. New York: Oxford University Press.
Bratton, M. (2008). Vote buying and violence in Nigerian election campaigns. *Electoral Studies* 27(4), 621–632.
Bratton, M., R. Bhavnani, and T.-H. Chen (2012). Voting intentions in Africa: Ethnic, economic, or partisan? *Commonwealth and Comparative Studies* 50(1), 27–52.
Brewer, M. B. and R. J. Brown (1998). Intergroup relations. In D. T. Gilbert, S. T. Fiske, and G. Lindzey (Eds.), *Handbook of Social Psychology* (Fourth ed.), Volume 2, pp. 554–594. Boston: McGraw-Hill.
Browers, M. (2007). Origins and architects of Yemen's Joint Meeting Parties. *International Journal of Middle East Studies* 39(4), 565–586.
Browers, M. (2009). *Political Ideology in the Arab World: Accommodation and Transformation*. New York: Cambridge University Press.
Brownlee, J. (2007). *Authoritarianism in an Age of Democratization*. New York: Cambridge University Press.
Brownlee, J., T. Masoud, and A. Reynolds (2013). Why the modest harvest? *Journal of Democracy* 24(4), 29–44.
Brusco, V., M. Nazareno, and S. C. Stokes (2004). Vote buying in Argentina. *Latin American Research Review* 39(2), 66–88.
Buchman, D. (1997). The underground friends of god and their adversaries: A case study and survey of Sufism in contemporary Yemen. *Bulletin of the American Institute for Yemeni Studies* (39), 21–24.

Burrowes, R. D. (1987). *The Yemen Arab Republic: The Politics of Development, 1962–1986*. Boulder, CO: Westview Press.

Burrowes, R. D. (1991). Prelude to unification: The Yemen Arab Republic, 1962–1990. *International Journal of Middle East Studies* 23(4), 483–506.

Burrowes, R. D. and C. M. Kasper (2007). The Salih regime and the need for a credible opposition. *Middle East Journal* 61(2), 263–280.

Calvo, E. and M. V. Murillo (2004). Who delivers? Partisan clients in the Argentine electoral market. *American Journal of Political Science* 48(4), 742–757.

Calvo, E. and M. V. Murillo (2013). When parties meet voters: Assessing political linkages through partisan networks and distributive expectations in Argentina and Chile. *Comparative Political Studies* 46(7), 851–882.

Cammett, M. (2011). Partisan activism and access to welfare in Lebanon. *Studies in Comparative International Development* 46(1), 70–97.

Cammett, M. (2014). *Compassionate Communalism: Welfare and Sectarianism in Lebanon*. Ithaca, NY: Cornell University Press.

Cammett, M. and S. Issar (2010). Bricks and mortar clientelism: Sectarianism and the logics of welfare allocation in Lebanon. *World Politics* 62(3), 381–421.

Carapico, S. (1993a). Campaign politics and coalition building: The 1993 parliamentary elections. *Yemen Update* 33(Summer/Fall), 37–39.

Carapico, S. (1993b). The economic dimension of Yemeni unity. *Middle East Report* (184), 9–14.

Carapico, S. (1993c). Elections and mass politics in Yemen. *Middle East Report* (185), 2–6.

Carapico, S. (1998). *Civil Society in Yemen*. New York: Cambridge University Press.

Caton, S. C. (1987). Power, persuasion, and language: A critique of the segmentary model in the Middle East. *International Journal of Middle East Studies* 19(1), 77–101.

Caton, S. C. (1990). *Peaks of Yemen I Summon: Poetry as Cultural Practice in a North Yemeni Tribe*. Berkeley: University of California Press.

Chalabi, T. (2006). *The Shi'is of Jabal 'Amil and the New Lebanon*. New York: Palgrave MacMillan.

Chandra, K. (2004). *Why Ethnic Parties Succeed*. Cambridge: Cambridge University Press.

Chandra, K. (2006). What is ethnic identity and does it matter? *Annual Review of Political Science* 9, 397–424.

Chandra, K., A. Lijphart, D. Laitin, D. Posner, S. Wilkinson, S. Van Evera, and I. Lustick (2001). Symposium: Cumulative findings in the study of ethnic politics. *APSA-CP: Newsletter of the Organized Section in Comparative Politics of the American Political Science Association* 12(1), 7–25.

Charbel, G. (2008). *The Palace Curse: Interviews with Elias Hrawi, Nabih Berri, Rafic Hariri, Michel Aoun*. Beirut: Riad El-Rayyes Books. Arabic.

Chhibber, P. and I. Nooruddin (2004). Do party systems count? The number of parties and government performance in the Indian states. *Comparative Political Studies* 37(2), 152–187.

Christia, F. (2008). Following the money: Muslim versus Muslim in Bosnia's civil war. *Comparative Politics* 40(4), 461–480.

Christia, F. (2012). *Alliance Formation in Civil Wars*. New York: Cambridge University Press.

Bibliography

Chubb, J. (1982). *Patronage, Power, and Poverty in Southern Italy*. New York: Cambridge University Press.

Chwe, M. S.-Y. (2001). *Rational Ritual: Culture, Coordination, and Common Knowledge*. Princeton, NJ: Princeton University Press.

Clark, J. A. (2004). *Islam, Charity, and Activism: Middle-Class Networks and Social Welfare in Egypt, Jordan, and Yemen*. Bloomington, IN: Indiana University Press.

Cohen, M., R. Riolo, and R. Axelrod (2001). The role of social structure in the maintenance of cooperative regimes. *Rationality and Society* 13(1), 5–32.

Collier, P. (1999). The political economy of ethnicity. See Pleskovic and Stiglitz (1999), pp. 387–411.

Collier, P. and A. Hoeffler (1998). On economic causes of civil war. *Oxford Economic Papers* 50(4), 563–573.

Collins, K. (2006). *Clan Politics and Regime Transition in Central Asia*. New York: Cambridge University Press.

Colton, N. A. (2010). Yemen: A collapsed economy. *Middle East Journal* 64(3), 410–426.

Corstange, D. (2007). Yemen (1962–1970). In K. DeRouen and U. Heo (Eds.), *Civil Wars of the World*, Volume 2, pp. 809–827. Santa Barbara: ABC-CLIO.

Corstange, D. (2010). The parliamentary election in Lebanon, June 2009. *Electoral Studies* 29(2), 285–289.

Corstange, D. (2012a). Religion, pluralism, and iconography in the public sphere: Theory and evidence from Lebanon. *World Politics* 64(1), 116–160.

Corstange, D. (2012b). Vote trafficking in Lebanon. *International Journal of Middle East Studies* 44(3), 483–505.

Corstange, D. (2013). Ethnicity on the sleeve and class in the heart. *British Journal of Political Science* 43(4), 889–914.

Corstange, D. and N. Marinov (2012). Taking sides in other people's elections: The polarizing effect of foreign intervention. *American Journal of Political Science* 56(3), 655–670.

Coulson, N. J. (1978 [1964]). *A History of Islamic Law*. Edinburgh: Edinburgh University Press.

Cox, G. W. (1997). *Making Votes Count*. Cambridge: Cambridge University Press.

Cox, G. W. (2010). Swing voters, core voters, and distributive politics. In I. Shapiro, S. C. Stokes, E. J. Wood, and A. S. Kirshner (Eds.), *Political Representation*, pp. 342–357. New York: Cambridge University Press.

Cox, G. W. and J. M. Kousser (1981). Turnout and rural corruption: New York as a test case. *American Journal of Political Science* 25(4), 646–663.

Cox, G. W. and M. D. McCubbins (1986). Electoral politics as a redistributive game. *Journal of Politics* 48(2), 370–389.

Cremer, J. (1986). Cooperation in ongoing organizations. *Quarterly Journal of Economics* 101(1), 33–50.

Cunningham, D. E. (2006). Veto players and civil war duration. *American Journal of Political Science* 50(4), 875–892.

Cunningham, K. G. (2011). Divide and conquer or divide and concede: How do states respond to internally divided separatists? *American Political Science Review* 105(2), 275–297.

Cunningham, K. G., K. M. Bakke, and L. J. M. Seymour (2012). Shirts today, skins tomorrow: Dual contests and the effects of fragmentation in self-determination disputes. *Journal of Conflict Resolution* 56(1), 67–93.

Cunningham, K. G. and N. B. Weidmann (2010). Shared space: Ethnic groups, state accommodation, and localized conflict. *International Studies Quarterly* 54(4), 1035–1054.

Cutler, F. (2002). The simplest shortcut of all: Sociodemographic characteristics and electoral choice. *Journal of Politics* 64(2), 466–490.

Daghir, V. (1995). *Sectarianism and Human Rights*. Cairo: Cairo Center for Human Rights Studies. Arabic.

Dal Bó, E. (2007). Bribing voters. *American Journal of Political Science* 51(4), 789–803.

Davis, E. (2008). A sectarian Middle East? *International Journal of Middle East Studies* 40(4), 555–558.

Day, S. (2008). Updating Yemeni national unity: Could lingering regional divisions bring down the regime? *Middle East Journal* 62(3), 417–436.

Day, S. (2010). The political challenge of Yemen's Southern Movement. Middle East Program 108, Carnegie Endowment for International Peace, Washington, DC.

Day, S. (2012). *Regionalism and Rebellion in Yemen*. New York: Cambridge University Press.

De La O, A. L. (2013). Do conditional cash transfers affect electoral behavior? Evidence from a randomized experiment in Mexico. *American Journal of Political Science* 57(1), 1–14.

Deeb, L. (2006). *An Enchanted Modern: Gender and Public Piety in Shi'i Lebanon*. Princeton, NJ: Princeton University Press.

Dekel, E., M. O. Jackson, and A. Wolinsky (2008). Vote buying: General elections. *Journal of Political Economy* 116(2), 351–380.

Despres, L. M. (2005). *Challenging the Daley Machine: A Chicago Alderman's Memoir*. Evanston: Northwestern University Press.

Deutsch, K. (1961). Social mobilization and political participation. *American Political Science Review* 55, 493–514.

Dhahir, N. (2008). *On Parties and the State in Lebanon*. Beirut: Annahar Press. Arabic.

Dixit, A. (2004). *Lawlessness and Economics, Alternative Modes of Governance*. New York: Oxford University Press.

Dixit, A. and J. Londregan (1996). The determinants of success of special interests in redistributive politics. *Journal of Politics* 58(4), 1132–1155.

Downs, A. (1957). *An Economic Theory of Democracy*. New York: Harper & Row.

Dresch, P. (1988). Segmentation: Its roots in Arabia and its flowering elsewhere. *Cultural Anthropology* 3(1), 50–67.

Dresch, P. K. (1986). The significance of the course events take in segmentary systems. *American Ethnologist* 13(2), 309–324.

Dresch, P. K. (1993 [1989]). *Tribes, Government, and History in Yemen*. Oxford: Clarendon Press.

Dresch, P. K. (1995). The tribal factor in the Yemeni crisis. In J. S. Al-Suwaidi (Ed.), *The Yemeni War of 1994: Causes and Consequences*, pp. 33–55. Abu Dhabi: The Emirates Center for Strategic Studies and Research.

Dresch, P. K. (2000). *A History of Modern Yemen*. New York: Cambridge University Press.

Dresch, P. K. and B. Haykel (1995). Stereotypes and political styles: Islamists and tribesfolk in Yemen. *International Journal of Middle East Studies* 27(4), 405–431.

Dunbar, C. (1992). The unification of Yemen: Process, politics, and prospects. *Middle East Journal* 46(3), 456–476.

Easterly, W. and R. Levine (1997). Africa's growth tragedy: Policies and ethnic divisions. *Quarterly Journal of Economics* 112(4), 1203–1250.

Egel, D. (2013). Tribal heterogeneity and the allocation of publicly provided goods: Evidence from Yemen. *Journal of Development Economics* 101, 228–232.

Eifert, B., E. Miguel, and D. N. Posner (2010). Political competition and ethnic identification in Africa. *American Journal of Political Science* 54(2), 494–510.

el Khazen, F. (2000). *The Postwar Lebanese Elections of 1992, 1996, and 2000: Democracy Without Choice*. Beirut: Annahar Press. Arabic.

el Khazen, F. (2002). *Political Parties in Lebanon: The Limits of Democracy in Party Experience*. Beirut: The Lebanese Center for Policy Studies. Arabic.

el Khazen, F. (2003). Political parties in postwar Lebanon: Parties in search of partisans. *Middle East Journal* 57(4), 605–624.

Entelis, J. P. (1974). *Pluralism and Party Transformation in Lebanon: Al-Kata'ib, 1936–1970*. Leiden: Brill.

Erie, S. P. (1992). *Rainbow's End*. Berkeley: University of California Press.

Esteban, J.-M. and D. Ray (1994). On the measurement of polarization. *Econometrica* 62(4), 819–851.

Fadlallah, H. (1997). *The Political and Reformist Thought of Imam Musa al-Sadr*. Beirut: Dar al-Hadi. Arabic.

Fadlallah, M. H. (2001). *Princes and Tribes: Lebanese Facts and Secrets*. Beirut: Riad El-Rayyes Books. Compilation: Najib Nour al-Din. Arabic.

Fafchamps, M. (1992). Solidarity networks in preindustrial societies: Rational peasants with a moral economy. *Economic Development and Cultural Change* 41(1), 147–174.

Farah, M. H. (2002). *Landmarks in the Terms of the Presidents of the Republic in Yemen 1962–1999*. Sanaa: SABA Center for Research and Information. Arabic.

Farah, M. H. (2005). *Yemen's Multiparty Parliamentary and Presidential Elections 1993–2003*. Sanaa: Obadi Center. Arabic.

Farshakh, G. (2006). *Fadl Shalaq: My Experience With Hariri*. Beirut: Arab Scientific Publishers. Arabic.

Fearon, J. D. (1998). Commitment problems and the spread of ethnic conflict. In D. A. Lake and D. Rothchild (Eds.), *The International Spread of Ethnic Conflict*, pp. 107–126. Princeton, NJ: Princeton University Press.

Fearon, J. D. (1999, June 16). Why ethnic politics and "pork" tend to go together. Presented at a MacArthur Foundation-sponsored conference on Ethnic Politics and Democratic Stability held at Wilder House, University of Chicago, May 21–23.

Fearon, J. D. (2003). Ethnic and cultural diversity by country. *Journal of Economic Growth* 8, 195–222.

Fearon, J. D. and D. D. Laitin (1996). Explaining interethnic cooperation. *American Political Science Review* 90(4), 715–735.

Fearon, J. D. and D. D. Laitin (2000). Violence and the social construction of ethnic identity. *International Organization* 54(4), 845–877.

Fearon, J. D. and D. D. Laitin (2003). Ethnicity, insurgency, and civil war. *American Political Science Review* 97(1), 75–90.

Ferree, K. (2006). Explaining South Africa's racial census. *Journal of Politics* 68(4), 803–815.

Ferree, K. (2011). *Framing the Race in South Africa*. New York: Cambridge University Press.

Finan, F. S. and L. Schechter (2012). Vote-buying and reciprocity. *Econometrica* 80(2), 863–881.

Firro, K. M. (2003). *Inventing Lebanon: Nationalism and the State Under the Mandate*. New York: I.B. Tauris.

Fleck, R. K. (1999). The value of the vote: A model and test of the effects of turnout on distributive policy. *Economic Inquiry* 37(4), 609–623.

Fleck, R. K. (2001). Inter-party competition, intra-party competition, and distributive policy: A model and test using New Deal data. *Public Choice* 108(1/2), 77–100.

Gandhi, J. and E. Lust-Okar (2009). Elections under authoritarianism. *Annual Review of Political Science* 12, 403–422.

Gans-Morse, J., S. Mazzuca, and S. Nichter (2014). Varieties of clientelism: Machine politics during elections. *American Journal of Political Science* 58(2), 415–432.

Gause, F. G. (2011). Why Middle East studies missed the Arab Spring. *Foreign Affairs* 90(4), 81–90.

Gavin, R. (1975). *Aden Under British Rule, 1839–1967*. New York: Barnes & Noble Books.

Geertz, C. (1963). The integrative revolution. In C. Geertz (Ed.), *Old Societies and New States*, pp. 269–299. New York: The Free Press.

Gellner, E. (1983). *Nations and Nationalism*. Ithaca: Cornell University Press.

Gellner, E. and H. Munson, Jr. (1995). Segmentation: Reality or myth? *The Journal of the Royal Anthropological Institute* 1(4), 821–832.

Gerber, A. S., G. A. Huber, D. Doherty, C. M. Dowling, and S. J. Hill (2013). Do perceptions of ballot secrecy influence turnout? Results from a field experiment. *American Journal of Political Science* 57(3), 537–551.

Gharib, H. K. (2001). *Toward an Intellectual–Political History of the Shia of Lebanon*, Volume 2. Beirut: Literary Treasures Press. Arabic.

Glosemeyer, I. (2004). Local conflict, global spin: An uprising in the Yemeni highlands. *Middle East Report* (232), 44–46.

Golway, T. (2014). *Machine Made: Tammany Hall and the Creation of Modern American Politics*. New York: W.W. Norton & Company.

Gosnell, H. F. (1927). *Getting Out the Vote: An Experiment in the Stimulation of Voting*. Chicago: University of Chicago Press.

Gosnell, H. F. (1937). *Machine Politics: Chicago Model*. Chicago: University of Chicago Press.

Green, D. P. and R. Seher (2003). What roles does prejudice play in ethnic conflict? *Annual Review of Political Science* 6, 509–531.

Greene, K. F. (2007). *Why Dominant Parties Lose: Mexico's Democratization in Comparative Perspective*. New York: Cambridge University Press.
Greif, A. (1994). Cultural beliefs and the organization of society: A historical and theoretical reflection on collectivist and individualist societies. *Journal of Political Economy* 102(5), 912–950.
Greif, A. (2006). *Institutions and the Path to the Modern Economy*. New York: Cambridge University Press.
Grzymala-Busse, A. (2007). *Rebuilding Leviathan: Party Competition and State Exploitation in Post-Communist Democracies*. New York: Cambridge University Press.
Habyarimana, J., M. Humphreys, D. N. Posner, and J. M. Weinstein (2007a, August). Placing and passing: Evidence from Uganda on ethnic identification and ethnic deception. Working Paper.
Habyarimana, J., M. Humphreys, D. N. Posner, and J. M. Weinstein (2007b). Why does ethnic diversity undermine public goods provision? *American Political Science Review* 101(4), 709–725.
Habyarimana, J., M. Humphreys, D. N. Posner, and J. M. Weinstein (2009). *Coethnicity: Diversity and the Dilemmas of Collective Action*. New York: Russell Sage Foundation.
Halliday, F. (1974). *Arabia Without Sultans*. New York: Vintage Books.
Hamilton, R. A. B. (1942). The social organization of the tribes of the Aden Protectorate. *Journal of the Royal Central Asian Society* 29(3/4), 238–248.
Hammond, R. A. and R. Axelrod (2006). The evolution of ethnocentrism. *Journal of Conflict Resolution* 50(6), 926–936.
Hanmer, M. J. and H. O. Kalkan (2012). Behind the curve: Clarifying the best approach to calculating predicted probabilities and marginal effects from limited dependent variable models. *American Journal of Political Science* 57(1), 263–277.
Hardin, R. (1982). *Collective Action*. Baltimore: The Johns Hopkins University Press.
Hardin, R. (1995). *One for All: The Logic of Group Conflict*. Princeton, NJ: Princeton University Press.
Harik, J. P. (2004). *Hezbollah: The Changing Face of Terrorism*. New York: I.B. Tauris.
Hashishu, N. (1998). *Parties in Lebanon*. Beirut: Center for Strategic Studies, Research, and Documentation. Arabic.
Havel, V. (1985 [1978]). The power of the powerless. In J. Keane (Ed.), *The Power of the Powerless: Citizens Against the State in Central-Eastern Europe*, pp. 23–96. Armonk, NY: M.E. Sharpe.
Haykel, B. (1995). A Zaydi revival? *Yemen Update* 36, 20–21.
Haykel, B. (1999). Rebellion, migration or consultative democracy? The Zaydis and their detractors in Yemen. See Leveau et al. (1999), pp. 193–201.
Haykel, B. (2003). *Revival and Reform in Islam: The Legacy of Muhammad al-Shawkani*. New York: Cambridge University Press.
Hess, Jr., C. G. and H. L. Bodman, Jr. (1954). Confessionalism and feudality in Lebanese politics. *Middle East Journal* 8(1), 10–26.
Hewstone, M., M. Rubin, and H. Willis (2002). Intergroup bias. *Annual Review of Psychology* 53, 575–604.
Hicken, A. D. (2011). Clientelism. *Annual Review of Political Science* 14, 289–310.

Hilton, J. L. and W. von Hippel (1996). Stereotypes. *Annual Review of Psychology* 47, 237–271.
Hobsbawm, E. J. (1992 [1990]). *Nations and Nationalism Since 1780* (Second ed.). New York: Cambridge University Press.
Hochschild, A. (1998). *King Leopold's Ghost*. New York: Houghton Mifflin.
Hoff, K. and A. Sen (2006). The kin system as a poverty trap? In S. Bowles, S. N. Durlauf, and K. Hoff (Eds.), *Poverty Traps*, pp. 95–115. New York: Russell Sage Foundation.
Horowitz, D. L. (1985). *Ethnic Groups in Conflict*. Berkeley: University of California Press.
Horowitz, D. L. (1991). *A Democratic South Africa? Constitutional Engineering in a Divided Society*. Berkeley: University of California Press.
Horowitz, D. L. (1999). Structure and strategy in ethnic conflict: A few steps toward synthesis. See Pleskovic and Stiglitz (1999), pp. 345–385.
Hottinger, A. (1966). Zu'ama' in historical perspective. In L. Binder (Ed.), *Politics in Lebanon*, pp. 85–105. New York: John Wiley & Sons.
Huddy, L. (2001). From social to political identity: A critical examination of social identity theory. *Political Psychology* 22(1), 127–156.
Huddy, L. (2003). Group identity and political cohesion. In D. O. Sears, L. Huddy, and R. Jervis (Eds.), *Oxford Handbook of Political Psychology*, pp. 511–558. New York: Oxford University Press.
Hudson, M. C. (1968). *The Precarious Republic: Political Modernization in Lebanon*. New York: Random House.
Hughes, S. O. (2001). *Morocco Under King Hassan*. Reading, UK: Ithaca Press.
Humphrey, M. (1989). *Islam, Sect and State: The Lebanese Case*. Number 11 in Papers on Lebanon. Oxford: Centre for Lebanese Studies.
Huntington, S. P. and J. M. Nelson (1976). *No Easy Choice: Political Participation in Developing Countries*. Cambridge: Harvard University Press.
Hyde, S. D. and N. Marinov (2012). Which elections can be lost? *Political Analysis* 20(2), 191–210.
Ichino, N. and N. L. Nathan (2013). Crossing the line: Local ethnic geography and voting in Ghana. *American Political Science Review* 107(2), 344–361.
International Crisis Group (2008). The new Lebanese equation: The Christians' central role. Middle East Report 78, International Crisis Group, Brussels.
International Crisis Group (2009). Yemen: Defusing the Saada time bomb. Middle East Report 86, International Crisis Group, Brussels.
International Crisis Group (2010). Lebanon's politics: The Sunni community and Hariri's Future Current. Middle East Report 96, International Crisis Group, Brussels.
International Crisis Group (2012). Yemen: Enduring conflicts, threatened transition. Middle East Report 125, International Crisis Group, Brussels.
Jabar, F. A. and H. Dawod (Eds.) (2003). *Tribes and Power: Nationalism and Ethnicity in the Middle East*. London: Saqi Books.
Jamal, A. A. (2007). *Barriers to Democracy: The Other Side of Social Capital in Palestine and the Arab World*. Princeton, NJ: Princeton University Press.
Johnson, M. (1986). *Class & Client in Beirut: The Sunni Muslim Community and the Lebanese State 1840–1985*. London: Ithaca Press.
Joseph, S. (2008). Sectarianism as imagined sociological concept and as imagined social formation. *International Journal of Middle East Studies* 40(4), 553–554.

Kasara, K. (2007). Tax me if you can: Ethnic geography, democracy, and the taxation of agriculture in Africa. *American Political Science Review* 101(1), 159–172.
Kasfir, N. (1976). *The Shrinking Political Arena*. Berkeley: University of California Press.
Keddie, N. (Ed.) (1995). *Debating Revolutions*. New York: New York University Press.
Keefer, P. (2005, June). Democratization and clientelism: Why are young democracies badly governed? World Bank Policy Research Working Paper No. 3594.
Keefer, P. (2007). Clientelism, credibility, and the policy choices of young democracies. *American Journal of Political Science* 51(4), 804–821.
Keefer, P. (2010). The ethnicity distraction? Political credibility and partisan preferences in Africa. Web commentary, Carnegie Endowment for International Peace, Washington, DC.
Keefer, P. and S. Knack (2002). Polarization, politics and property rights: Links between inequality and growth. *Public Choice* 111, 127–154.
Keefer, P. and R. Vlaicu (2008). Democracy, credibility, and clientelism. *Journal of Law, Economics, & Organization* 24(2), 371–406.
Kerr, M. H. (1971). *The Arab Cold War: Gamal 'abd al-Nasir and His Rivals, 1958–1970* (Third ed.). New York: Oxford.
Kertzer, D. I. and D. Arel (2002). Censuses, identity formation, and the struggle for political power. In D. I. Kertzer and D. Arel (Eds.), *Census and Identity*, pp. 1–42. New York: Cambridge University Press.
Khashan, H. (1992). *Inside the Lebanese Confessional Mind*. New York: University Press of America.
Khoury, P. and J. Kostiner (Eds.) (1990). *Tribes and State Formation in the Middle East*. Berkeley: University of California Press.
King, G., C. Murray, J. Salomon, and A. Tandon (2003). Enhancing the validity and cross-cultural comparability of measurement in survey research. *American Political Science Review* 97(4), 567–583.
Kitschelt, H. (2000). Linkages between citizens and politicians in democratic polities. *Comparative Political Studies* 33(6–7), 845–879.
Kitschelt, H. (2010, May). Democratic accountability relations: Exploring global patterns. Unpublished Manuscript, Duke University.
Kitschelt, H. and D. M. Kselman (2013). Economic development, democratic experience, and political parties' linkage strategies. *Comparative Political Studies* 46(12), 1453–1484.
Kitschelt, H. and S. I. Wilkinson (2007a). Citizen-politician linkages. See Kitschelt and Wilkinson (2007b), pp. 1–49.
Kitschelt, H. and S. I. Wilkinson (Eds.) (2007b). *Patrons, Clients, and Policies*. New York: Cambridge University Press.
Knack, S. and P. Keefer (1995). Institutions and economic performance: Cross-country tests using alternate institutional measures. *Economics and Politics* 7(3), 207–227.
Knysh, A. (2000). *Islamic Mysticism*. Boston: Brill.
Knysh, A. (2001). The *Tariqa* on a landcruiser: The resurgence of Sufism in Yemen. *Middle East Journal* 55(3), 399–414.
Kreps, D., P. Milgrom, J. Roberts, and R. Wilson (1982). Rational cooperation in the finitely repeated prisoners' dilemma. *Journal of Economic Theory* 27(2), 245–252.
Kuper, A. (1982). Lineage theory: A critical retrospect. *Annual Review of Anthropology* 11, 71–95.

Kuran, T. (1991). Now out of never: The element of surprise in the East European revolution of 1989. *World Politics* 44(1), 7–48.
Kuran, T. (1995). *Private Truths, Public Lies.* Cambridge: Harvard University Press.
Kurtzman, D. H. (1935). *Methods of Controlling Votes in Philadelphia.* PhD thesis, University of Pennsylvania, Philadelphia.
Laitin, D. D. and D. N. Posner (2001). The implications of constructivism for constructing ethnic fractionalization indices. *APSA-CP: Newsletter of the Organized Section in Comparative Politics of the American Political Science Association* 12(1), 13–17.
Landa, J. T. (1994). *Trust, Ethnicity, and Identity.* Ann Arbor, MI: University of Michigan Press.
Landau, J. M. (1961). Elections in Lebanon. *Western Political Quarterly* 14(1), 120–147.
Lasswell, H. D. (1958 [1935]). *Politics: Who Gets What, When, How.* New York: Meridian Books.
Laurent, A. (1991). A war between brothers: The army–Lebanese Forces showdown in East Beirut. *Beirut Review* 1(1), 88–101.
Lawson, C. and K. F. Greene (2014). Making clientelism work: How norms of reciprocity increase voter compliance. *Comparative Politics* 47(1), 61–85.
Lemarchand, R. (1972). Political clientelism and ethnicity in tropical Africa: Competing solidarities in nation-building. *American Political Science Review* 66(1), 68–90.
Lemarchand, R. and K. Legg (1972). Political clientelism and development: A preliminary analysis. *Comparative Politics* 4(2), 149–178.
Leveau, R., F. Mermier, and U. Steinbach (Eds.) (1999). *Le Yémen Contemporain.* Paris: Editions Karthala.
Lijphart, A. (1969). Consociational democracy. *World Politics* 21(2), 207–225.
Lijphart, A. (1977). *Democracy in Plural Societies.* New Haven, CT: Yale University Press.
Lijphart, A. (1981). Consociational theory: Problems and prospects, a reply. *Comparative Politics* 13(3), 355–360.
Lijphart, A. (1994). *Electoral Systems and Party Systems.* Oxford: Oxford University Press.
Lijphart, A. (2001). Constructivism and consociational theory. *APSA-CP: Newsletter of the Organized Section in Comparative Politics of the American Political Science Association* 12(1), 11–13.
Lindbeck, A. and J. W. Weibull (1987). Balanced-budget redistribution as the outcome of political competition. *Public Choice* 52(3), 273–297.
Lindholm, C. (1986). Kinship structure and political authority: The Middle East and Central Asia. *Comparative Studies in Society and History* 28(2), 334–355.
Lipset, S. M. and S. Rokkan (1967). Cleavage structures, party systems, and voter alignments. In S. M. Lipset and S. Rokkan (Eds.), *Party Systems and Voter Alignments: Cross-National Perspectives*, pp. 1–64. New York: Free Press.
Longley, A. and A. G. al Iryani (2008). Fighting brushfires with batons: An analysis of the political crisis in South Yemen. Policy Brief 7, Middle East Institute, Washington, DC.
Luqman, H. A. (1986). *The History of the Yemeni Tribes*, Volume 1: Southern Yemen. Sanaa: Dar al-Kalima. Arabic.
Lust, E. (2009). Democratization by elections? Competitive clientelism in the Middle East. *Journal of Democracy* 20(3), 122–135.

Lust-Okar, E. (2004). Divided they rule: The management and manipulation of political opposition. *Comparative Politics* 36(2), 159–179.
Lust-Okar, E. (2005). *Structuring Conflict in the Arab World*. New York: Cambridge University Press.
Lust-Okar, E. (2009a). Competitive clientelism: Rethinking elections in the MENA and the prospects for democracy. In A. J. Langlois and K. E. Soltan (Eds.), *Global Democracy and Its Difficulties*, pp. 130–145. New York: Routledge.
Lust-Okar, E. (2009b). Legislative elections in hegemonic authoritarian regimes. In S. I. Lindberg (Ed.), *Democratization by Elections*, pp. 226–245. Baltimore, MD: The Johns Hopkins University Press.
Lynch, M. (2011). Yemen: The final days of Ali Abdullah Saleh? POMEPS Briefings 3, Project on Middle East Political Science, Washington, DC.
Lynch, M. (2012). *The Arab Uprising*. New York: Public Affairs.
Madini, T. (1999). *Amal and Hizballah*. Damascus: al-Ahali. Arabic.
Magaloni, B. (2006). *Voting for Autocracy: Hegemonic Party Survival and its Demise in Mexico*. New York: Cambridge University Press.
Magaloni, B. and R. Kricheli (2010). Political order and one-party rule. *Annual Review of Political Science* 13, 123–143.
Mainwaring, S. E. (2003). Party objectives in authoritarian regimes with elections or fragile democracies: A dual game. In S. E. Mainwaring and T. R. Scully (Eds.), *Christian Democracy in Latin America: Electoral Competition and Regime Conflicts*, pp. 3–29. Stanford: Stanford University Press.
Makdisi, U. (2000). *The Culture of Sectarianism*. Berkeley: University of California Press.
Makdisi, U. (2008). Moving beyond Orientalist fantasy, sectarian polemic, and nationalist denial. *International Journal of Middle East Studies* 40(4), 559–560.
Makhlafi, A. (2004). The events in Saada. In M. A. Afandi (Ed.), *Yemeni Strategic Report 2004*, pp. 132–173. Sanaa: Yemeni Center for Strategic Studies. Arabic.
Maktabi, R. (1999). The Lebanese census of 1932 revisited. Who are the Lebanese? *British Journal of Middle Eastern Studies* 26(2), 219–241.
Malhah, J. (2003). *The Governments of Lebanon*. Beirut: Librairie du Liban. Arabic.
Mansour, B. A. (1999). *The Ruling Political Elite in Yemen, 1978–1990*. Cairo: Madbuli Bookstore. Arabic.
Mansour, B. A. (2004). *Political Parties and Democratic Transformation*. Cairo: Madbuli Bookstore. Arabic.
Maqalih, M. M. (1998). The Yemeni Congregation for Reform from group to party. *Contemporary Affairs* 8(Fall), 41–61. Arabic.
Mauro, P. (1995). Corruption and growth. *Quarterly Journal of Economics* 110(3), 681–712.
Mauro, P. (1998). Corruption and the composition of government expenditure. *Journal of Public Economies* 69(2), 263–279.
McCaffery, P. (1993). *When Bosses Ruled Philadelphia*. University Park, PA: Pennsylvania State University Press.
Melson, R. and H. Wolpe (1970). Modernization and the politics of communalism: A theoretical perspective. *American Political Science Review* 64(4), 1112–1130.
Mendelberg, T. (2001). *The Race Card*. Princeton, NJ: Princeton University Press.

Miguel, E. (2004). Tribe or nation? Nation building and public goods in Kenya versus Tanzania. *World Politics* 56(3), 327–362.

Miguel, E. and M. K. Gugerty (2005). Ethnic diversity, social sanctions, and public goods in Kenya. *Journal of Public Economics* 89(11–12), 2325–2368.

Momen, M. (1985). *An Introduction to Shi'i Islam*. New Haven, CT: Yale University Press.

Monroe, K. R., J. Hankin, and R. B. Van Vechten (2000). The psychological foundations of identity politics. *Annual Review of Political Science* 3, 419–447.

Montalvo, J. G. and M. Reynal-Querol (2005). Ethnic diversity and economic development. *Journal of Development Economics* 76(2), 293–323.

Muhammad, A. S. (1998). The General People's Congress: Challenges in shifting the congress to parties and power from the rulers to the people. *Contemporary Affairs* 8(Fall), 23–39. Arabic.

Mutawakkil, M. A. (2004). *Political Development*. Sanaa?: n.p. Arabic.

Nichter, S. (2008). Vote buying or turnout buying? Machine politics and the secret ballot. *American Political Science Review* 102(1), 19–31.

Norton, A. R. (1987). *Amal and the Shi'a: Struggle for the Soul of Lebanon*. Austin: University of Texas Press.

Norton, A. R. (1999). *Hizballah of Lebanon: Extremist Ideals vs. Mundane Politics*. Muslim Politics Project. New York: Council on Foreign Relations.

O'Ballance, E. (1971). *The War in the Yemen*. London: Faber and Faber.

Olson, M. (1965). *The Logic of Collective Action*. Cambridge: Harvard University Press.

Ordeshook, P. and O. Shvetsova (1994). Ethnic heterogeneity, district magnitude, and the number of parties. *American Journal of Political Science* 38(1), 100–123.

Ostrom, E. (1990). *Governing the Commons*. New York: Cambridge University Press.

Patel, D. S. (2007). *Islam, Information, and Social Order: The Strategic Role of Information in Muslim Societies*. PhD thesis, Stanford University, Stanford, CA.

Pearlman, W. and K. G. Cunningham (2012). Nonstate actors, fragmentation, and conflict processes. *Journal of Conflict Resolution* 56(1), 3–15.

Peteet, J. (2008). Imagining the "New Middle East". *International Journal of Middle East Studies* 40(4), 550–552.

Phillips, S. (2008). *Yemen's Democracy Experiment in Regional Perspective*. New York: Palgrave Macmillan.

Phillips, S. (2011). *Yemen and the Politics of Permanent Crisis*. New York: Routledge.

Platteau, J.-P. (1991). Traditional systems of social security and hunger insurance. In E. Ahmad, J. Drèze, J. Hills, and A. Sen (Eds.), *Social Security in Developing Countries*, pp. 112–170. New York: Clarendon Press.

Pleskovic, B. and J. Stiglitz (Eds.) (1999). *Annual World Bank Conference on Development Economics 1998*. Washington, DC: World Bank.

Posner, D. N. (2004). Measuring ethnic fractionalization in Africa. *American Journal of Political Science* 48(4), 849–863.

Posner, D. N. (2005). *Institutions and Ethnic Politics in Africa*. New York: Cambridge University Press.

Powell, J. D. (1970). Peasant society and clientelist politics. *American Political Science Review* 64(2), 411–425.

Putnam, R. (1993). *Making Democracy Work*. Princeton, NJ: Princeton University Press.

Rabushka, A. and K. A. Shepsle (1972). *Politics in Plural Societies*. Columbus, OH: Merrill.

Rauch, J. E. (2001). Business and social networks in international trade. *Journal of Economic Literature* 39(4), 1177–1203.

Reilly, B. (2006). *Democracy and Diversity: Political Engineering in the Asia–Pacific*. New York: Oxford University Press.

Remmer, K. L. (2007). The political economy of patronage: Expenditure patterns in the Argentine provinces 1983–2003. *Journal of Politics* 69(2), 363–377.

Republic of Yemen (2004). *The 2003 Parliamentary Elections*. Sanaa: Republic of Yemen, Supreme Commission for Elections and Referendum. Arabic.

Richards, A. and J. Waterbury (1996). *A Political Economy of the Middle East* (Second ed.). Boulder, CO: Westview Press.

Rida, M. J. (1992). *The Struggle Between State and Tribe in the Arab Gulf*. Beirut: Centre for Arab Unity Studies. Arabic.

Riley, J. G. (2001). Silver signals: Twenty-five years of screening and signaling. *Journal of Economic Literature* 39(2), 432–478.

Riordon, W. L. (Ed.) (1963 [1905]). *Plunkitt of Tammany Hall*. New York: E. P. Dutton.

Robinson, J. A. and T. Verdier (2013). The political economy of clientelism. *Scandinavian Journal of Economics* 115(2), 260–291.

Roccas, S. and M. B. Brewer (2002). Social identity complexity. *Personality and Social Psychology Review* 6(2), 88–106.

Rose-Ackerman, S. (1999). *Corruption and Government*. New York: Cambridge University Press.

Rubinstein, A. (1982). Perfect equilibrium in a bargaining model. *Econometrica* 50(1), 97–109.

Saad-Ghorayeb, A. (2002). *Hizbu'llah: Politics and Religion*. London: Pluto Press.

Sadr, M. (2000a). *Press Interviews*, Volume 1. Beirut: Imam Sadr Center for Research and Studies. Arabic.

Sadr, M. (2000b). *Press Interviews*, Volume 2. Beirut: Imam Sadr Center for Research and Studies. Arabic.

Said, A. Q. (1995). *The Muslim Brotherhood and the Fundamentalist Movement in Yemen*. Cairo: Madbuli Bookstore. Arabic.

Salem, P. (1991). Two years of living dangerously: General Awn and the precarious rise of Lebanon's 'Second Republic'. *Beirut Review* 1(1), 62–87.

Salem, P. (2008, May). Hizbollah attempts a coup d'état. Web commentary, Carnegie Endowment for International Peace, Beirut.

Salibi, K. (1988). *A House of Many Mansions: The History of Lebanon Reconsidered*. Berkeley: University of California Press.

Salmoni, B., B. Loidolt, and M. Wells (2010). *Regime and Periphery in Northern Yemen*. Washington, DC: RAND Corporation.

Salti, N. and J. Chaaban (2010). The role of sectarianism in the allocation of public expenditure in postwar Lebanon. *International Journal of Middle East Studies* 42(4), 637–655.

Sarraf, A. (1992). *South Yemen From Colonialism to Unity*. London: Riad El-Rayyes Books. Arabic.

Schaffer, F. C. (Ed.) (2007a). *Elections For Sale: The Causes and Consequences of Vote Buying*. Boulder, CO: Lynne Rienner.

Schaffer, F. C. (2007b). Why study vote buying? See Schaffer (2007a), pp. 1–16.

Schedler, A. (2002). Elections without democracy: The menu of manipulation. *Journal of Democracy* 13(2), 36–50.

Scheiner, E. (2006). *Democracy Without Competition in Japan: Opposition Failure in a One-Party Dominant State*. New York: Cambridge University Press.

Scheiner, E. (2007). Clientelism in Japan: The importance and limits of institutional explanations. See Kitschelt and Wilkinson (2007b), pp. 276–297.

Schlumberger, O. (Ed.) (2007). *Debating Arab Authoritarianism: Dynamics and Durability in Nondemocratic Regimes*. Stanford, CA: Stanford University Press.

Schneider, M. (2015). *Whither the Quid Pro Quo? Essays on Party–Voter Linkages and Distributive Politics in Rural India*. PhD thesis, Columbia University, New York.

Schwedler, J. (2004). The Islah Party in Yemen: Political opportunities and coalition building in a transitional polity. In Q. Wiktorowicz (Ed.), *Islamic Activism*, pp. 205–228. Bloomington, IN: Indiana University Press.

Schwedler, J. (2006). *Faith in Moderation: Islamist Parties in Jordan and Yemen*. New York: Cambridge University Press.

Scott, J. C. (1969). Corruption, machine politics, and political change. *American Political Science Review* 63(4), 1142–1158.

Scott, J. C. (1972). Patron–client politics and political change in Southeast Asia. *American Political Science Review* 66(1), 91–113.

Scott, J. C. (1976). *The Moral Economy of the Peasant*. New Haven, CT: Yale University Press.

Scott, J. C. (1990). *Domination and the Arts of Resistance*. New Haven, CT: Yale University Press.

Selten, R. (1978). The chain store paradox. *Theory and Decision* 9, 127–159.

Serjeant, R. B. (1982). The interplay between tribal affinities and religious (Zaydi) authority in the Yemen. *Al-Abhath* 30, 11–50.

Shams al-Din, M. M. (2002). *Bequests*. Beirut: Annahar Press. Arabic.

Shanahan, R. (2005). *The Shi'a of Lebanon: Clans, Parties, and Clerics*. New York: I. B. Tauris.

Sharjabi, Q. N. (1986). *Traditional Social Categories in Yemeni Society*. Sanaa: Modern Press. Arabic.

Sharjabi, Q. N. (1990). *The Village and the State in Yemeni Society*. Beirut: Solidarity Press. Arabic.

Shils, E. (1957). Primordial, personal, sacred and civil ties. *British Journal of Sociology* 8(2), 130–145.

Smith, M. G. (1956). On segmentary lineage systems. *The Journal of the Royal Anthropological Institute of Great Britain and Ireland* 86(2), 39–80.

Smyth, P. (2011). The 'independent Shi'a' of Lebanon: What Wikileaks tells us about American efforts to find an alternative to Hizballah. *Middle East Review of International Affairs* 15(4), 11–25.

Snider, L. W. (1984). The Lebanese Forces: Their origins and role in Lebanon's politics. *Middle East Journal* 38(1), 1–33.

Spence, A. M. (1973). Job market signaling. *Quarterly Journal of Economics* 87(3), 355–374.

Spence, A. M. (1974a). Competitive and optimal responses to signals: An analysis of efficiency and distribution. *Journal of Economic Theory* 7(3), 296–332.

Spence, A. M. (1974b). *Market Signaling*. Cambridge: Harvard University Press.

Staniland, P. (2012). Between a rock and a hard place: Insurgent fratricide, ethnic defection, and the rise of pro-state paramilitaries. *Journal of Conflict Resolution* 56(1), 16–40.
Steiner, J. (1981). The consociational theory and beyond. *Comparative Politics* 13(3), 339–354.
Stokes, S. C. (1999). Political parties and democracy. *Annual Review of Political Science* 2, 243–267.
Stokes, S. C. (2005). Perverse accountability: A formal model of machine politics with evidence from Argentina. *American Political Science Review* 99(3), 315–325.
Stokes, S. C. (2007). Political clientelism. See Boix and Stokes (2007), pp. 604–627.
Stokes, S. C. (2009). Pork, by any other name ... building a conceptual scheme of distributive politics. Paper presented at the 2009 Annual Meeting of the American Political Science Association.
Stokes, S. C., T. Dunning, M. Nazareno, and V. Brusco (2013). *Brokers, Voters, and Clientelism*. New York: Cambridge University Press.
Sulayman, A. (1998). *The Second Republic Between Text and Practice*. Beirut: n.p. Arabic.
Szwarcberg, M. (2012). Uncertainty, political clientelism, and voter turnout in Latin America: Why parties conduct rallies in Argentina. *Comparative Politics* 45(1), 88–106.
Szwarcberg, M. (2014). Political parties and rallies in Latin America. *Party Politics* 20(3), 456–466.
Tajfel, H. (1982). Social psychology of intergroup relations. *Annual Review of Psychology* 33, 1–39.
Tannouri, M. (1998). Sectarianism in Lebanese society. *University Papers* 17/18, 419–450. Arabic.
Traboulsi, F. (2007). *A History of Modern Lebanon*. London: Pluto Press.
Trockel, W. (1986). The chain-store paradox revisited. *Theory and Decision* 21, 163–179.
Van Cott, D. L. (2007a). *From Movements to Parties in Latin America: The Evolution of Ethnic Politics*. New York: Cambridge University Press.
Van Cott, D. L. (2007b). Latin America's indigenous peoples. *Journal of Democracy* 18(4), 127–142.
van de Walle, N. (2007). Meet the new boss, same as the old boss? The evolution of political clientelism in Africa. See Kitschelt and Wilkinson (2007b), pp. 50–67.
van den Berghe, P. (1978). Race and ethnicity: A sociobiological perspective. *Ethnic and Racial Studies* 1(4), 401–411.
Varshney, A. (2002). *Ethnic Conflict and Civic Life: Hindus and Muslims in India*. New Haven, CT: Yale University Press.
Varshney, A. (2003). Nationalism, ethnic conflict, and rationality. *Perspectives on Politics* 1(1), 85–99.
Varshney, A. (2007). Ethnicity and ethnic conflict. See Boix and Stokes (2007), pp. 274–294.
vom Bruck, G. (1999). Being a Zaydi in the absence of an Imam: Doctrinal revisions, religious instruction, and the (re-)invention of ritual. See Leveau et al. (1999), pp. 169–192.

vom Bruck, G. (2010). Regimes of piety revisited: Zaydi political moralities in republican Yemen. *Die Welt des Islams* 50(2), 185–223.
Wang, C.-S. and C. Kurzman (2007a). Dilemmas of electoral clientelism: Taiwan, 1993. *International Journal of Political Science* 28(2), 225–245.
Wang, C.-S. and C. Kurzman (2007b). The logistics: How to buy votes. See Schaffer (2007a), pp. 61–78.
Wantchekon, L. (2003). Clientelism and voting behavior: Evidence from a field experiment in Benin. *World Politics* 55(3), 399–422.
Wedeen, L. (1999). *Ambiguities of Domination: Politics, Rhetoric, and Symbols in Contemporary Syria*. Chicago: University of Chicago Press.
Wedeen, L. (2008). *Peripheral Visions: Publics, Power, and Performance in Yemen*. Chicago: University of Chicago Press.
Wedeen, L., A. L. Alley, A. G. al Iryani, S. Carapico, S. Day, and S. Phillips (2009). Discerning Yemen's political future. Viewpoints 11, Middle East Institute, Washington, DC.
Weidmann, N. B., J. K. Rød, and L.-E. Cederman (2010). Representing ethnic groups in space. *Journal of Peace Research* 47(4), 491–499.
Weingrod, A. (1968). Patrons, patronage, and political parties. *Comparative Studies in Society and History* 10(4), 377–400.
Weir, S. (1997). A clash of fundamentalisms: Wahhabism in Yemen. *Middle East Report* (204), 22–23, 26.
Weitz-Shapiro, R. (2012). What wins votes: Why some politicians opt out of clientelism. *American Journal of Political Science* 56(3), 568–583.
Weitz-Shapiro, R. (2014). *Curbing Clientelism in Argentina*. New York: Cambridge University Press.
Wenner, M. (1967). *Modern Yemen 1918–1966*. Baltimore: The Johns Hopkins University Press.
Werner, M. R. (1928). *Tammany Hall*. Garden City, NY: Doubleday, Doran & Co.
Wiktorowicz, Q. (2000). The Salafi movement in Jordan. *International Journal of Middle East Studies* 32, 219–240.
Wilkinson, S. I. (2006). *Votes and Violence: Electoral Competition and Ethnic Riots in India*. New York: Cambridge University Press.
Williamson, O. E. (1985). *The Economic Institutions of Capitalism*. New York: Free Press.
Wucherpfennig, J., N. B. Weidmann, L. Girardin, L.-E. Cederman, and A. Wimmer (2011). Politically relevant ethnic groups across space and time. *Conflict Management and Peace Science* 28(5), 423–437.
Yadav, S. P. (2013). *Islamists and the State: Legitimacy and Institutions in Yemen and Lebanon*. New York: I.B. Tauris.
Yahya, N. A. (Ed.) (2004). *The Views of Shaykh Abdallah bin Hussein al-Ahmar*. Sanaa: Horizons Press. Arabic.
Young, M. (2010). *The Ghosts of Martyrs Square*. New York: Simon & Schuster.
Zabarah, M. A. (1982). *Yemen: Traditionalism vs. Modernity*. New York: Praeger.
Zahiri, M. M. (1996). *The Political Role of the Tribes in Yemen, 1962–1990*. Cairo: Madbuli Bookstore. Arabic.
Zahiri, M. M. (2004). *Society and the State in Yemen*. Cairo: Madbuli Bookstore. Arabic.

Index

al-Ahmar, Abdallah (Paramount Shaykh of Hashid Confederation), 3, 98, 105, 114–116
Amal Movement, 45, 54, 57, 58, 60–61, 66–67, 70–77, 80, 88, 136
Aoun, Michel (Free Patriotic Movement leader), 45, 52, 58–66, 88, 136
Arab Spring, 103
Arab Spring, 90, 91, 105, 118, 229–231, 233–234

Baath Party, 93, 106, 110, 112, 123
Bakil tribal confederation, 41, 101, 106, 113, 140
Berri, Nabih (Amal leader), 70, 73, 75–77

Chamoun, Dory (National Liberal Party leader), 59, 64, 88
Christians, 55
  and civil war, 45, 56, 58–59
  and French Mandate, 54, 57, 58
  and parties, 18, 52–54, 57, 60–67, 79, 87–89, 135
  and services, 64–65
  and Syrian repression, 59
civil war, 44–45
  Lebanese, 17, 18, 45, 55–56, 58–59, 62, 63, 67, 69–71, 77–81, 89, 203
  Yemeni (1962–1970), 45, 92
  Yemeni (1986), 104
  Yemeni (1994), 18, 45, 90–91, 95, 103, 127
clientelism
  and authoritarianism, 233–234
  and brokers, 33–34, 79, 120, 141–144
  and competition, 43, 47–50, 227
  and core versus swing voters, 8, 14, 226–227
  and democracy, 29, 196, 227–228
  and development, 234
  and ethnicity, 1, 8–10, 27–28, 35–36, 42–43, 50, 137, 157, 226, 228–229
  and monitoring, 11, 31–33, 42, 141, 150, 225–226
  and poor voters, 48, 153–154, 227
  and programmatic politics, 7–8, 27, 29, 50, 119–121, 124, 126, 134–135, 137, 154–155, 215
  and rural areas, 150–154
  and targeting, 21–22
  and transaction costs, 12–13, 29–30, 33, 39–40, 225
  collective, 158, 177
  definition, 5, 10, 28–29, 221
cloning (of political parties), 109–111

Daley Machine (Chicago), 34, 151
Druze, 60, 135, 232
  and civil war, 56, 58, 80
  and parties, 57

Eddé, Carlos (National Bloc leader), 59, 63
Egypt, 17, 92, 127, 229, 230, 233
Eido, Walid (Future Movement MP), 52
ethnicity
  and between-group competition, 7, 25, 44, 46

ethnicity (cont.)
  and clientelism, 1, 8–9, 13–15, 25–28, 39–40, 42–43, 47, 50, 220, 223, 226–229
  and development, 4–6, 176
  and fractionalization indices, 181
  and networks, 6–7, 9, 12–13, 35–36, 38–42, 50, 155, 221–222, 224, 226
  and outbidding, 45
  and services, 16, 25, 193
  and within-group competition, 1–2, 10, 14–15, 25–26, 43–44, 46, 49–51, 193–194, 219–220, 228
  definition, 4–5, 18

families, 40–41, 151, 158
  and clientelism, 141–143
  and collective voting, 138, 142–143, 149–150, 152, 155
  and ethnicity, 12–13, 40, 137
  and services, 138, 140–141, 158
  and tribes, 106, 139–140, 158
fractionalization index, 181
Frangieh, Suleiman (Marada Movement leader), 59, 88
Free Patriotic Movement, 52, 59–62, 64, 66, 67, 87–88
Future Movement, 52–54, 66, 81, 83–85, 88–89, 132, 136

Geagea, Samir (Lebanese Forces leader), 58–59, 62–64, 67, 88, 136
al-Gemayel, Amin (Kataeb Party leader), 52–53, 58, 59, 64, 67, 88, 136, 149
General People's Congress (GPC), 90, 93–95, 100, 102–104, 106–113, 115–118, 124, 126, 127, 133, 139, 146, 152, 170–171, 230

al-Haqq Party, 106–109, 111–112
al-Hariri, Rafik, 2, 54, 56, 59, 60, 77, 80–83, 86, 89, 203, 231
al-Hariri, Saad (Future Movement leader), 54, 60, 65, 66, 77, 81, 83–86, 89, 132, 135, 136, 194, 203, 231–233
Hashid tribal confederation, 41, 92, 101, 106, 140
Hizballah, 45, 54, 57, 60–63, 66–67, 71–77, 84, 88, 124, 133, 135, 141, 144, 231–232
  Iranian funding, 75–76, 136
  Israel–Hizballah War (2006), 203, 231
Hobeika, Eli (Wa'ad Party leader), 58, 59

al-Hoss, Salim, 59, 70, 82
Houthi Movement, 21, 105, 106, 111–112, 229–230

institutions, 49, 17–49, 57–58, 77, 82, 234
  and electoral law, 54–55, 82, 125, 135–136, 151, 222, 225
  and power sharing, 5, 57, 17–57, 78, 89, 95
Iran, 61–62, 70–71
  Hizballah funding, 75–76, 136
Islah Party, 94–95, 100, 102, 103, 106–109, 111–117, 122–124, 126, 127, 134–135, 139
Israel, 56, 70, 71, 75, 80
  Israel–Hizballah War (2006), 203, 231

Joint Meeting Parties (JMP), 90, 107–110, 121–122, 124, 126, 170–171, 229
Jumblatt, Walid (Progressive Socialist Party leader), 60, 65, 77, 88, 135, 136, 231–232

Karami, Omar (Sunni politician), 2, 78, 82–84, 89
Kataeb Party (Phalanges libanaises), 58–59, 62, 64, 67, 88, 136, 138

Lahoud, Emile, 82
Lebanese Forces, 45, 58–59, 61–62, 64, 67, 87–88, 136
Lebanese National Pact, 55, 58, 78

March 14 Coalition, 56–57, 59–61, 63–67, 72–75, 77, 87–88, 123–124, 135, 231
March 8 Coalition, 56–57, 60–61, 66, 72, 74, 75, 77, 85, 87–88, 123–124, 231–232
Mathhaj tribal confederation, 101
Mikati, Najib (Sunni politician), 77, 83, 85–86, 89
monopsony, 18–19, 47, 54, 71–72, 82–83, 88–89
  and clientelism, 16, 22–23, 49, 194–195, 197, 219
  and ethnicity, 1–2, 10, 14–16, 43, 50–51, 220–221, 228
  and services, 2–3, 15, 21–22, 26, 48, 157–160, 167–170, 173, 175–176, 178–179, 185–187, 190, 192–193, 221
  and sycophancy, 194–195, 201–203, 208, 212–213, 215–216, 219
  and targeting, 15–16, 21–22, 48, 160, 175, 177–178, 187, 192–193

Index

maintenance, 45–47, 49–50, 225, 232–233
origins, 43–45
al-Mourabitoun, 79–80, 82
Muslim Brotherhood, 83, 93–94, 100, 106–109, 124

Nasirist Party, 93, 100, 112, 117, 123

Palestine Liberation Organization (PLO), 55–56, 58, 79–80
patronage democracy, 17, 221

Qornet Shehwan Gathering, 59, 60, 63

regionalism, 2
  and ethnicity, 18
  and services, 101–104, 119–120, 171, 173–174
  Yemeni, 90–104, 119, 170–171, 173–174, 229
Republican Organization (Philadelphia), 34, 144, 151

Saad, Osama (Sunni politician), 84
al-Sadr, Musa (Shia religious figure), 69–70
Safadi, Muhammad (Sunni politician), 77, 83, 85–86, 89
Salafis, 84, 90, 93, 94, 98–100, 105, 107–109, 111–113, 127
Salam, Tammam, 85
Salih, Ali Abdallah, 98, 103, 109, 112, 115, 116, 140, 194, 203–205, 207, 229–231
Saudi Arabia, 92
  Lebanon funding, 81, 84, 136
  Yemen funding, 108, 135
sects, 2, 55, 90–92, 95–99, 119, 220
  and ethnicity, 4–5, 18
  and extended families, 138–139, 150, 155
  and militias, 56, 79–81
  and parties, 62, 66, 71–72, 81–82, 89, 96, 207
  and power sharing, 18, 54–57, 61, 78, 89, 95, 149, 231–232
  and sectarian rhetoric, 55, 74, 83–84, 89, 107–109, 126
  and services, 89, 105, 119–120
service deputies, 132, 137, 221
Shafais, 92, 119
  and doctrine, 92–94, 98–100
  and regionalism, 96–99, 117
  and tribalism, 96, 101

Shia, 76–77
  and civil war, 45, 70–71
  and doctrine, 70
  and parties, 18, 54, 66–67, 71–77, 88–89
  and services, 68, 69, 75–76, 136
  and Zaydism, 3, 19, 91
  pre-civil war, 67–69
Special Tribunal for Lebanon (STL), 231
Sunnis, 78
  and civil war, 56, 79–81, 89
  and doctrine, 112
  and French Mandate, 54
  and Hariri, 66, 80–83, 88–89, 232
  and Islah Party, 116–117
  and parties, 18, 19, 22, 23, 52–54, 57, 66, 77–80, 83–85, 88–89, 100, 105, 112–113, 117, 195, 202, 207, 213, 232
  and regionalism, 100
  and Salafis, 90, 100
  and services, 2–3, 21–22, 81, 84–85, 156, 160, 164, 168–170, 173, 179, 187, 189–193, 203, 209, 211, 215, 217, 221
  and Shafais, 92, 100
  and tribalism, 101, 113
  Yemeni, 90, 91, 99–100, 104
Syria, 18, 56, 59, 62, 64, 67, 71–72, 80–83, 135, 195, 199–201, 232
  civil war, 231, 232
Syrian Accountability Act, 61

Taif Accord, 56, 59, 62
Tammany Hall (New York), 34, 125, 131, 143, 144, 151
Tashnaq Party, 88
tribes, 2, 21, 40–41, 45, 90–92, 95–99, 102, 105–106, 119, 130, 131, 139, 152–153, 158, 220
  and ethnicity, 5, 18
  and extended families, 40, 106, 139–140, 153, 155
  and General People's Congress (GPC), 19, 94, 101, 106, 109, 113–114, 117–118
  and Islah Party, 94, 101, 106, 114–116
  and services, 3, 101, 103–105, 114, 117, 156
  and Yemeni Socialist Party (YSP), 93, 101, 106
shaykhs, 91, 95, 105, 113–114, 118, 125, 141–142
Tunisia, 229, 230, 233

UN Security Council Resolution 1559, 61
Union of Popular Forces Party (UPF), 106, 109–112

Yemeni Socialist Party (YSP), 93–95, 100–104, 107, 112, 115–117, 123, 126, 127

Zaydis, 21, 92, 105–106, 119
   and doctrine, 3, 92, 93, 98–99, 108, 112
   and General People's Congress (GPC), 19, 90–91, 105, 109, 118
   and Islah Party, 94, 116
   and parties, 22, 23, 105–106, 109–113, 195, 202, 207, 213
   and regionalism, 96–99, 102, 104
   and services, 3, 21, 22, 95, 160, 164, 168–170, 173, 174, 203, 209, 211, 215, 217, 221
   and tribalism, 96, 101, 106, 113, 118
   and Zaydi revivalism, 98, 108, 111–112
al-Zindani, Abd al-Majid (Salafi religious figure), 100, 108, 109, 127

Other Books in the Series (*Continued from page ii*)

Carles Boix, *Democracy and Redistribution*
Carles Boix, *Political Order and Inequality: Their Foundations and Their Consequences for Human Welfare*
Carles Boix, *Political Parties, Growth, and Equality: Conservative and Social Democratic Economic Strategies in the World Economy*
Catherine Boone, *Merchant Capital and the Roots of State Power in Senegal, 1930-1985*
Catherine Boone, *Political Topographies of the African State: Territorial Authority and Institutional Change*
Catherine Boone, *Property and Political Order in Africa: Land Rights and the Structure of Politics*
Michael Bratton, Robert Mattes, and E. Gyimah-Boadi, *Public Opinion, Democracy, and Market Reform in Africa*
Michael Bratton and Nicolas van de Walle, *Democratic Experiments in Africa: Regime Transitions in Comparative Perspective*
Valerie Bunce, *Leaving Socialism and Leaving the State: The End of Yugoslavia, the Soviet Union, and Czechoslovakia*
Daniele Caramani, *The Nationalization of Politics: The Formation of National Electorates and Party Systems in Europe*
John M. Carey, *Legislative Voting and Accountability*
Kanchan Chandra, *Why Ethnic Parties Succeed: Patronage and Ethnic Headcounts in India*
Eric C. C. Chang, Mark Andreas Kayser, Drew A. Linzer, and Ronald Rogowski, *Electoral Systems and the Balance of Consumer-Producer Power*
José Antonio Cheibub, *Presidentialism, Parliamentarism, and Democracy*
Ruth Berins Collier, *Paths toward Democracy: The Working Class and Elites in Western Europe and South America*
Pepper D. Culpepper, *Quiet Politics and Business Power: Corporate Control in Europe and Japan*
Rafaela M. Dancygier, *Immigration and Conflict in Europe*
Christian Davenport, *State Repression and the Domestic Democratic Peace*
Donatella della Porta, *Social Movements, Political Violence, and the State*
Alberto Diaz-Cayeros, *Federalism, Fiscal Authority, and Centralization in Latin America*
Jesse Driscoll, *Warlords and Coalition Politics in Post-Soviet States*
Thad Dunning, *Crude Democracy: Natural Resource Wealth and Political Regimes*
Gerald Easter, *Reconstructing the State: Personal Networks and Elite Identity*
Margarita Estevez-Abe, *Welfare and Capitalism in Postwar Japan: Party, Bureaucracy, and Business*
Henry Farrell, *The Political Economy of Trust: Institutions, Interests, and Inter-Firm Cooperation in Italy and Germany*
Karen E. Ferree, *Framing the Race in South Africa: The Political Origins of Racial Census Elections*
M. Steven Fish, *Democracy Derailed in Russia: The Failure of Open Politics*
Robert F. Franzese, *Macroeconomic Policies of Developed Democracies*
Roberto Franzosi, *The Puzzle of Strikes: Class and State Strategies in Postwar Italy*
Timothy Frye, *Building States and Markets After Communism: The Perils of Polarized Democracy*

Geoffrey Garrett, *Partisan Politics in the Global Economy*
Scott Gehlbach, *Representation through Taxation: Revenue, Politics, and Development in Postcommunist States*
Edward L. Gibson, *Boundary Control: Subnational Authoritarianism in Federal Democracies*
Jane R. Gingrich, *Making Markets in the Welfare State: The Politics of Varying Market Reforms*
Miriam Golden, *Heroic Defeats: The Politics of Job Loss*
Jeff Goodwin, *No Other Way Out: States and Revolutionary Movements*
Merilee Serrill Grindle, *Changing the State*
Anna Grzymala-Busse, *Rebuilding Leviathan: Party Competition and State Exploitation in Post-Communist Democracies*
Anna Grzymala-Busse, *Redeeming the Communist Past: The Regeneration of Communist Parties in East Central Europe*
Frances Hagopian, *Traditional Politics and Regime Change in Brazil*
Henry E. Hale, *The Foundations of Ethnic Politics: Separatism of States and Nations in Eurasia and the World*
Mark Hallerberg, Rolf Ranier Strauch, Jürgen von Hagen, *Fiscal Governance in Europe*
Stephen E. Hanson, *Post-Imperial Democracies: Ideology and Party Formation in Third Republic France, Weimar Germany, and Post-Soviet Russia*
Silja Häusermann, *The Politics of Welfare State Reform in Continental Europe: Modernization in Hard Times*
Michael Hechter, *Alien Rule*
Gretchen Helmke, *Courts Under Constraints: Judges, Generals, and Presidents in Argentina*
Yoshiko Herrera, *Imagined Economies: The Sources of Russian Regionalism*
J. Rogers Hollingsworth and Robert Boyer, eds., *Contemporary Capitalism: The Embeddedness of Institutions*
John D. Huber and Charles R. Shipan, *Deliberate Discretion? The Institutional Foundations of Bureaucratic Autonomy*
Ellen Immergut, *Health Politics: Interests and Institutions in Western Europe*
Torben Iversen, *Capitalism, Democracy, and Welfare*
Torben Iversen, *Contested Economic Institutions*
Torben Iversen, Jonas Pontusson, and David Soskice, eds., *Unions, Employers, and Central Banks: Macroeconomic Coordination and Institutional Change in Social Market Economies*
Thomas Janoski and Alexander M. Hicks, eds., *The Comparative Political Economy of the Welfare State*
Joseph Jupille, *Procedural Politics: Issues, Influence, and Institutional Choice in the European Union*
Stathis Kalyvas, *The Logic of Violence in Civil War*
David C. Kang, *Crony Capitalism: Corruption and Capitalism in South Korea and the Philippines*
Stephen B. Kaplan, *Globalization and Austerity Politics in Latin America*
Junko Kato, *Regressive Taxation and the Welfare State*
Orit Kedar, *Voting for Policy, Not Parties: How Voters Compensate for Power Sharing*
Robert O. Keohane and Helen B. Milner, eds., *Internationalization and Domestic Politics*

Herbert Kitschelt, *The Transformation of European Social Democracy*
Herbert Kitschelt, Kirk A. Hawkins, Juan Pablo Luna, Guillermo Rosas, and Elizabeth J. Zechmeister, *Latin American Party Systems*
Herbert Kitschelt, Peter Lange, Gary Marks, and John D. Stephens, eds., *Continuity and Change in Contemporary Capitalism*
Herbert Kitschelt, Zdenka Mansfeldova, Radek Markowski, and Gabor Toka, *Post-Communist Party Systems*
David Knoke, Franz Urban Pappi, Jeffrey Broadbent, and Yutaka Tsujinaka, eds., *Comparing Policy Networks*
Allan Kornberg and Harold D. Clarke, *Citizens and Community: Political Support in a Representative Democracy*
Amie Kreppel, *The European Parliament and the Supranational Party System*
David D. Laitin, *Language Repertoires and State Construction in Africa*
Fabrice E. Lehoucq and Ivan Molina, *Stuffing the Ballot Box: Fraud, Electoral Reform, and Democratization in Costa Rica*
Mark Irving Lichbach and Alan S. Zuckerman, eds., *Comparative Politics: Rationality, Culture, and Structure*, 2nd edition
Evan Lieberman, *Race and Regionalism in the Politics of Taxation in Brazil and South Africa*
Richard M. Locke, *Promoting Labor Standards in a Global Economy: The Promise and Limits of Private Power*
Pauline Jones Luong, *Institutional Change and Political Continuity in Post-Soviet Central Asia*
Pauline Jones Luong and Erika Weinthal, *Oil Is Not a Curse: Ownership Structure and Institutions in Soviet Successor States*
Julia Lynch, *Age in the Welfare State: The Origins of Social Spending on Pensioners, Workers, and Children*
Doug McAdam, John McCarthy, and Mayer Zald, eds., *ComparativePerspectives on Social Movements*
Lauren M. MacLean, *Informal Institutions and Citizenship in Rural Africa: Risk and Reciprocity in Ghana and Côte d'Ivoire*
Beatriz Magaloni, *Voting for Autocracy: Hegemonic Party Survival and its Demise in Mexico*
James Mahoney, *Colonialism and Postcolonial Development: Spanish America in Comparative Perspective*
James Mahoney and Dietrich Rueschemeyer, eds., *Comparative Historical Analysis in the Social Sciences*
Scott Mainwaring and Matthew Soberg Shugart, eds., *Presidentialism and Democracy in Latin America*
Isabela Mares, *From Open Secrets to Secret Voting: Democratic Electoral Reforms and Voter Autonomy*
Isabela Mares, *The Politics of Social Risk: Business and Welfare State Development*
Isabela Mares, *Taxation, Wage Bargaining, and Unemployment*
Cathie Jo Martin and Duane Swank, *The Political Construction of Business Interests: Coordination, Growth, and Equality*
Anthony W. Marx, *Making Race, Making Nations: A Comparison of South Africa, the United States, and Brazil*

Bonnie M. Meguid, *Party Competition between Unequals: Strategies and Electoral Fortunes in Western Europe*
Joel S. Migdal, *State in Society: Studying How States and Societies Constitute One Another*
Joel S. Migdal, Atul Kohli, and Vivienne Shue, eds., *State Power and Social Forces: Domination and Transformation in the Third World*
Scott Morgenstern and Benito Nacif, eds., *Legislative Politics in Latin America*
Kevin M. Morrison, *Nontaxation and Representation: The Fiscal Foundations of Political Stability*
Layna Mosley, *Global Capital and National Governments*
Layna Mosley, *Labor Rights and Multinational Production*
Wolfgang C. Müller and Kaare Strøm, *Policy, Office, or Votes?*
Maria Victoria Murillo, *Political Competition, Partisanship, and Policy Making in Latin American Public Utilities*
Maria Victoria Murillo, *Labor Unions, Partisan Coalitions, and Market Reforms in Latin America*
Monika Nalepa, *Skeletons in the Closet: Transitional Justice in Post-Communist Europe*
Ton Notermans, *Money, Markets, and the State: Social Democratic Economic Policies since 1918*
Eleonora Pasotti, *Political Branding in Cities: The Decline of Machine Politics in Bogotá, Naples, and Chicago*
Aníbal Pérez-Liñán, *Presidential Impeachment and the New Political Instability in Latin America*
Roger D. Petersen, *Understanding Ethnic Violence: Fear, Hatred, and Resentment in Twentieth-Century Eastern Europe*
Roger D. Petersen, *Western Intervention in the Balkans: The Strategic Use of Emotion in Conflict*
Simona Piattoni, ed., *Clientelism, Interests, and Democratic Representation*
Paul Pierson, *Dismantling the Welfare State?: Reagan, Thatcher, and the Politics of Retrenchment*
Marino Regini, *Uncertain Boundaries: The Social and Political Construction of European Economies*
Kenneth M. Roberts, *Changing Course in Latin America: Party Systems in the Neoliberal Era*
Marc Howard Ross, *Cultural Contestation in Ethnic Conflict*
Ben Ross Schneider, *Hierarchical Capitalism in Latin America: Business, Labor, and the Challenges of Equitable Development*
Lyle Scruggs, *Sustaining Abundance: Environmental Performance in Industrial Democracies*
Jefferey M. Sellers, *Governing from Below: Urban Regions and the Global Economy*
Yossi Shain and Juan Linz, eds., *Interim Governments and Democratic Transitions*
Beverly Silver, *Forces of Labor: Workers' Movements and Globalization since 1870*
Prerna Singh, *How Solidarity Works for Welfare: Subnationalism and Social Development in India*
Theda Skocpol, *Social Revolutions in the Modern World*
Dan Slater, *Ordering Power: Contentious Politics and Authoritarian Leviathans in Southeast Asia*

Regina Smyth, *Candidate Strategies and Electoral Competition in the Russian Federation: Democracy Without Foundation*
Richard Snyder, *Politics after Neoliberalism: Reregulation in Mexico*
David Stark and László Bruszt, *Postsocialist Pathways: Transforming Politics and Property in East Central Europe*
Sven Steinmo, *The Evolution of Modern States: Sweden, Japan, and the United States*
Sven Steinmo, Kathleen Thelen, and Frank Longstreth, eds., *Structuring Politics: Historical Institutionalism in Comparative Analysis*
Susan C. Stokes, *Mandates and Democracy: Neoliberalism by Surprise in Latin America*
Susan C. Stokes, ed., *Public Support for Market Reforms in New Democracies*
Susan C. Stokes, Thad Hall, Marcelo Nazareno, and Valeria Brusco, *Brokers, Voters, and Clientelism: The Puzzle of Distributive Politics*
Duane Swank, *Global Capital, Political Institutions, and Policy Change in Developed Welfare States*
Sidney Tarrow, *Power in Movement: Social Movements and Contentious Politics, Revised and Updated 3rd Edition*
Tariq Thachil, *Elite Parties, Poor Voters: How Social Services Win Votes in India*
Kathleen Thelen, *How Institutions Evolve: The Political Economy of Skills in Germany, Britain, the United States, and Japan*
Kathleen Thelen, *Varieties of Liberalization and the New Politics of Social Solidarity*
Charles Tilly, *Trust and Rule*
Daniel Treisman, *The Architecture of Government: Rethinking Political Decentralization*
Guillermo Trejo, *Popular Movements in Autocracies: Religion, Repression, and Indigenous Collective Action in Mexico*
Lily Lee Tsai, *Accountability without Democracy: How Solidary Groups Provide Public Goods in Rural China*
Joshua Tucker, *Regional Economic Voting: Russia, Poland, Hungary, Slovakia and the Czech Republic, 1990-1999*
Ashutosh Varshney, *Democracy, Development, and the Countryside*
Jeremy M. Weinstein, *Inside Rebellion: The Politics of Insurgent Violence*
Stephen I. Wilkinson, *Votes and Violence: Electoral Competition and Ethnic Riots in India*
Jason Wittenberg, *Crucibles of Political Loyalty: Church Institutions and Electoral Continuity in Hungary*
Elisabeth J. Wood, *Forging Democracy from Below: Insurgent Transitions in South Africa and El Salvador*
Elisabeth J. Wood, *Insurgent Collective Action and Civil War in El Salvador*

For EU product safety concerns, contact us at Calle de José Abascal, 56–1°, 28003 Madrid, Spain or eugpsr@cambridge.org.

www.ingramcontent.com/pod-product-compliance
Lightning Source LLC
LaVergne TN
LVHW091534060526
838200LV00036B/602